# ANTARCTIC CONQUEST

# ANTARCTIC

The Bobbs-Merrill Company, Inc.
A subsidiary of Howard W. Sams & Co., Inc.
Publishers   Indianapolis   Kansas City   New York

# CONQUEST

## THE GREAT EXPLORERS IN THEIR OWN WORDS

by

Robert S. Ilverberg, ed.

elected and introduced by WALKER CHAPMAN [pseud]

*To Dudley Frasier*

# ACKNOWLEDGMENTS

For permission to use extracts from the books mentioned, I am grateful to the following:

The Hakluyt Society for *The Journals of Captain James Cook,* Volume II, edited by J. C. Beaglehole (copyright 1961 by The Hakluyt Society) and for *The Voyage of Captain Bellingshausen to the Antarctic Seas,* edited by Frank Debenham (copyright 1945 by The Hakluyt Society).

William Heinemann, Ltd., for *Heart of the Antarctic* by Sir Ernest Shackleton (copyright 1909 by William Heinemann, Ltd.) and for *Home of the Blizzard* by Sir Douglas Mawson (copyright 1915 by William Heinemann, Ltd.).

Dodd, Mead & Company, Inc., for *Scott's Last Expedition* by Rob-

# CONTENTS

FOREWORD                                                                                                                   xiii


I


TERRA AUSTRALIS INCOGNITA          1506-1777                    3
Ludovico di Varthema          5
Amerigo Vespucci          6
Francis Fletcher          8
Cornelius Wytfliet          10
Juan Luis Arias          11
Jacob le Maire          13
Anthony de la Roché          16
Lionel Wafer          18
George Shelvocke          19
Bouvet de Lozier          22
James Cook          26


II


THE WHALING AND SEALING ERA          1821-1839          41
Edward Bransfield          43
Nathaniel Palmer          47
Palmer's Voyage in Edmund Fanning's Account          48
Fabian Gottlieb von Bellingshausen          51
John Davis          61
Christopher Burdick          62
James Weddell          63
James Eights          74
John Biscoe          79
John Balleny          85
Charles Darwin          87

## III

TOWARD THE MAGNETIC POLE    1841-1874                91
Dumont d'Urville    93
Charles Wilkes    107
James Clark Ross    118
H. N. Moseley    129

## IV

THE HEROIC AGE    1896-1920                           137
H. J. Bull    138
The *Belgica* Expedition    142
Carstens Borchgrevink    149
Louis Bernacchi    157
Robert Falcon Scott—First Expedition    161
C. J. Skottsberg—Winter on Paulet Island    173
The Scotia Expedition    188
Ernest Shackleton    196
Robert Falcon Scott—Second Expedition    211
Apsley Cherry-Garrard    219
Roald Amundsen    236
Sir Douglas Mawson    253
Shackleton's Boat Journey    268

## V

THE AGE OF MECHANIZED EXPLORATION
1930–Present                                          285
Byrd's Flight to the South Pole    286
Byrd's Second Expedition    303
Byrd's Last Flight to the South Pole    315
The Norwegian-British-Swedish Expedition    317
Dr. Paul Siple    321
Fuchs: South Ice to the South Pole    331
The Antarctic Treaty    347

INDEX                                                 357

# LIST OF ILLUSTRATIONS

*Facing page 192*

Captain James Cook.

The *Resolution* and the *Adventure*. Cook's second expedition.

Captain Nathaniel Palmer.

Admiral Fabian Gottlieb von Bellingshausen.

Weddell's ships, the *Jane* and the *Beaufoy*.

Captain James Weddell.

Adélie penguins. Hallett Station, Antarctica.

Admiral Dumont d'Urville.

Lieutenant Charles Wilkes.

Wilkes' men ashore.

James Clark Ross.

Ross' ships anchored off Mt. Erebus, 1841.

Two U. S. Navy ships in McMurdo Sound, 1963.

Dr. Frederick Cook ashore during 1898 voyage of the *Belgica*.

Otto Nordenskjöld.

Men of the *Antarctica* chasing king penguins, 1901.

Robert Falcon Scott with the wallet that carried his journals.

Scott's ship, the *Discovery*.

Sir Ernest Shackleton.

Douglas Mawson.

Roald Amundsen.

Amundsen and his men at the South Pole, 1911.

Admiral Richard E. Byrd.

Adélie penguin.

Eights Station, Antarctica, 1963.

One-and-one-half-million-ton iceberg in
  McMurdo Sound, 1964.

Sir Vivian Fuchs.

USNS *Arneb* at Ross Ice Shelf, 1962.

Antarctic landscape, 1963.

USNS *John Towle* near McMurdo Station, 1963.

Weddell seal, McMurdo Sound, 1963.

# FOREWORD

At the bottom of the world sprawls a nearly unknown continent which, with its fringing shelves of ice, has an area twice that of the United States. Once, millions of years ago, it was a fertile land of pines and ferns, but today 22 quadrillion tons of ice cover it—90 per cent of all the ice in the world. In some places, the ice is 9,000 feet thick. Temperatures as low as —120°F. have been recorded there.

This frigid continent, Antarctica, has held the fancy of men for centuries. Medieval theorists debated the existence of a southern land; promoters of the Renaissance propagandized for its colonization, though they lacked proof of its existence; venturesome captains of the eighteenth century drew close to it, and saw that it was a land of ice, unfit for habitation. Still the explorers came, and their names now are legend: Cook and Palmer and Bellingshausen and Bransfield, Wilkes and Ross and D'Urville, Scott, Shackleton, Amundsen, Byrd—a long roster of heroism. One wonders why these men staked their lives against the fierce and inhospitable Antarctic wastes, and then one reads their accounts, and one understands.

In an earlier book, *The Loneliest Continent* (New York Graphic Society, 1964), I told the story of the conquest of the Antarctic. This present volume should be considered a supplement to that one, and that to this. Here are gathered the documentary sources from which I drew the material for *The Loneliest Continent*. That book tells the continuous story; I have cannibalized it to some extent for the prefaces used here, but have not attempted to relate a detailed account of the explorations a second time. Here, we have explorers' narratives, bound together by enough commentary to make them intelligible. In nearly all cases, I have used only primary sources—the first-person narratives of the explorers. The only exceptions stem from the absence of such sources (as in Palmer and La Roché), and there I have used the closest contemporary accounts.

Rather than provide a series of snippets, I have tried to use cohesive and continuous selections from each work. Such few editorial interpolations as are employed are marked by [brackets]. I have resisted the temptation to festoon the book with footnotes, and in fact have deleted many footnotes supplied by the explorers themselves where I felt they were no longer relevant, or not meaningful in context. Where I have made cuts within a section, they are indicated by three dots. . . .

Although it was not feasible to include an excerpt from every narrative of Antarctic adventure, the book does present at least some material from each of the major expeditions through 1958. The period after 1958 has been scanted for many reasons, the chief one being that, while rich in accomplishment, it is poor in drama. Furthermore, the sheer profusion of Antarctic expeditions today makes a just selection impossible. The conquest of Antarctica is by no means ended, but I think it is fair to say that an epoch-marking milestone was reached with the Fuchs-Hillary trans-Antarctic crossing of 1957-58, and that the inclusion of more recent material can well wait for a later anthologist, a generation or two hence.

I had assistance from many people in the preparation of this book.

## FOREWORD

I am particularly grateful to Dudley Frasier for his encouragement and advice, and to my wife for the heroic part she played in helping me ready the book for publication. Thanks are due, also, to the librarians of Columbia University and the American Geographical Society, and to the staff of the Rare Books Room at the New York Public Library's Forty-second Street branch. And, of course, I feel a special debt to the copyright holders whose co-operation made the compilation of this anthology possible.

—WALKER CHAPMAN

# PART I

## TERRA AUSTRALIS INCOGNITA 1506-1777

□   The ancient Greeks, nothing if not logical, began the great quest. They argued some twenty-four hundred years ago that the known continents of the north must necessarily be balanced by other land to the south. The northern part of the world lay under the constellation Arctos, the Bear, and hence was called the Arktikos. The unknown land in the south, then, must be the Antarktikos, the total opposite.

The Egyptian geographer Claudius Ptolemy gave the theory his blessing about A.D. 150, when he wrote—in Greek—of a vast southern continent, an enormous land mass joining Africa and Asia beyond the torrid zone. This Terra Australis Incognita, the "unknown southern land," was, Ptolemy suggested, fertile and populous, *but cut off from the northern countries by a zone of fire. The idea was an exciting one; despite later opposition from Christian fathers, who found the thought of Terra Australis Incognita uncomfortably heretical, the fascinating possibility endured.*

*No one ventured far from home in the first thousand years of the Christian era. Men speculated about remote regions, but they did not search for them. They wrote of an "ocean unknown to the sons of Adam," and labeled their maps with comments such as "Frigida" and "Perusta"—frozen and burned. Imaginative men invented inhabitants for the southern continent, creatures with sixteen fingers, and others "whose heads do grow beneath their shoulders."*

*Eventually men began to travel again. Late in the thirteenth century, Marco Polo journeyed eastward to the court of Kublai Khan in fabled Cathay, and from there struck southward toward the regions now called Cambodia and Indonesia. He wrote of a kingdom abounding in gold, spices, and elephants, lying somewhere to the south. He probably meant Cambodia, but there were those who took him to mean Terra Australis Incognita. Thus Marco fueled the flame of curiosity, and led later men to continue the quest.*

*Another early traveler, not nearly so well known as he should be, was Ludovico di Varthema, a Bolognese, who left Italy about 1502 and traveled to Egypt, joined an Islamic garrison, and took part in the pilgrimage to Mecca; after a variety of exploits and imprisonments he toured Arabia and India and Persia, returning to India in an unsuccessful attempt to reach Samarkand, and thence through the Malay Peninsula and the islands of Indonesia. His wanderings brought him in time to Africa, and finally to Lisbon about 1509. The following year his account of his travels, the* Itinerary, *was published at Rome, and was eagerly read throughout Europe.*

*While en route from Borneo to Java in 1506, Varthema acquired this nugget of information about the unknown southern land, and embedded it in his book to tantalize generations of explorers. The translation is by John Winter Jones, done for The Hakluyt Society in 1863.* ◻

4

# LUDOVICO DI VARTHEMA

When the chartered vessel was supplied with provisions, we took our way towards the beautiful island called Giava [Java], at which we arrived in five days, sailing towards the south. The captain of the said ship carried the compass with the magnet after our manner, and had a chart which was all marked with lines, perpendicular and across. My companion asked the Christians: "Now that we have lost the north star, how does he steer us? Is there any other north star than this by which we steer?" The Christians asked the captain of the ship this same thing, and he showed us four or five stars, among which there was one which he said was *contrario della* (opposite to) our north star, and that he sailed by the north because the magnet was adjusted and subjected to our north. He also told us that on the other side of the said island, towards the south, there are some other races, who navigate by the said four or five stars opposite to ours; and, moreover, they gave us to understand that beyond the said island the day does not last more than four hours, and that there it was colder than in any other part of the world. Hearing this we were much pleased and satisfied.

□   *While Varthema detected rumors of a land south of Asia, Amerigo Vespucci was heading southward along the eastern coast of newly discovered South America. This Florentine merchant and adventurer, whose claims have been much disputed, made his first voyage to the New World in 1497, his second in 1499, according to his own often-contradictory writings. A third voyage supposedly took place in 1501; Vespucci told of it in a letter to Lorenzo Piero Francesco de Medici, the head of the firm that employed him. He declares that on this voyage his vessel reached as far as 52° S. lati-*

5

*tude, though he also talks of a night fifteen hours long on April 7,*
*which could not be experienced at that time of the year except at*
*latitude 72° S. That would be on the Antarctic Continent itself, and*
*Vespucci certainly was not there; the land he describes is probably*
*Patagonia, though some think he reached South Georgia or one of*
*the other subantarctic islands, and others that he did not get nearly*
*so far south as he claims. The translation, by Clements R. Markham,*
*is from The Hakluyt Society's 1894 edition of Vespucci's letters.* □

# AMERIGO VESPUCCI

Having held a consultation, it was decided that the course should
be taken which seemed good to me; and the command of the fleet
was entrusted to me. I gave orders that the fleet should be supplied
with wood and water for six months, such being the decision of the
officers of the ships. Having made our departure from this land, we
began our navigation with a southerly course on the 15th of February [1502], when already the sun moved towards the equinoctial,
and turned towards our Hemisphere of the North. We sailed so far
on this course that we found ourselves where the South Pole had a
height above our horizon of 52° and we could no longer see the stars
of *Ursa Minor* or of *Ursa Major*. We were then 500 leagues to the
south of the port whence we had departed, and this was on the 3rd
of April. On this day such a tempest arose on the sea that all our
sails were blown away, and we ran under bare poles, with a heavy
southerly gale and a tremendous sea; the air being very tempestuous.
The gale was such that all the people in the fleet were much alarmed.
The nights were very long, for the night we had on the 7th of April
lasted fifteen hours, the sun being at the end of Aries, and in that
region it was winter, as your Magnificence will be well aware. Sailing in this storm, on the 7th of April we came in sight of new land,
along which we ran for nearly 20 leagues, and found it all a rocky
coast, without any port or inhabitants. I believe this was because
the cold was so great that no one in the fleet could endure it. Finding
ourselves in such peril, and in such a storm that we could scarcely
see one ship from another, owing to the greatness of the waves and

6

the blinding mist, it was agreed with the principal captain that a signal should be made to the ships that they should make for land, and then shape a course for Portugal. This was very good counsel, for it is certain that if we had delayed another night all would have been lost; for, as we wore round on the next day, we were met by such a storm that we expected to be swamped. We had to undertake pilgrimages and perform other ceremonies, as is the custom of sailors at such times. We ran for five days, always coming towards the equinoctial line, where the air and sea became more temperate. It pleased God to deliver us from such peril. Our course was now between the north and north-east, for our intention was to reach the coast of Ethiopia, our distance from it being 300 leagues, in the Gulf of the Atlantic Sea. By the grace of God, on the 10th day of May, we came in sight of land, where we were able to refresh ourselves, the land being called *La Serra Liona*. We were there fifteen days, and thence shaped a course to the islands of the *Azores,* which are distant nearly 750 leagues from that *Serra*. We reached the islands in the end of July, where we remained fifteen days taking some recreation. Thence we departed for Lisbon, distant 300 leagues to the west, and arrived at that port of Lisbon on the 7th of September 1502, may God be thanked for our salvation, with only two ships. We burnt the other at *Serra Liona,* because she was no longer seaworthy. We were employed on this voyage nearly fifteen months; and for eleven days we navigated without seeing the North Star, nor the Great or Little Bears, which they call *el corno,* and we were guided by the stars of the other Pole. This is what I saw on this voyage.

□ *In a third part of the world—Africa—some of the questions about Terra Australis Incognita were being answered. Portuguese sailors sent by Prince Henry the Navigator were progressing down Africa's western coast; they had crossed the equator by the middle of the fifteenth century, and in 1488 Bartholomew Diaz attained the southern tip of Africa, driven by storms until he came to land's*

7

*end. Mutiny forced him back, but not before he had shown that open sea, and not a wealthy southern continent, lay south of Africa.*

*A second Portuguese captain, whom we know by his Spanish name of Magellan, amputated another lobe of Ptolemy's Terra Australis Incognita in 1520. Following the coastline of South America, Magellan found a broad channel leading westward at about 52° S.—and his figure is more accurate than that of Vespucci, who probably came no farther south than 32°. Magellan's fleet passed through the strait; to their left, which is to say the south, they could see land, perhaps the northern reaches of Terra Australis Incognita. The voyage showed that South America was not joined to the southern continent, but it helped to strengthen the belief that land of some sort did lie at the bottom of the world, south of what became known as Magellan's Strait.*

*Sir Francis Drake, Queen Elizabeth's own buccaneer, carried the exploration a step further in 1578. Commissioned to halt the spread of Spanish influence in the New World, Drake set out to locate and enter the Strait of Magellan, passing into the Pacific and exploring the western coastline of South America to open friendly relations with the natives. Drake's ship entered the Strait on August 17, 1578; after emerging, eighteen days later, the English fleet was hit by a storm and carried far to the south, into open sea. Francis Fletcher, Drake's chaplain, set down his observations in a journal published fifty years later as* The World Encompassed by Sir Francis Drake *(London, Nicholas Bourne, 1628).* □

# FRANCIS FLETCHER

. . . at length wee fell with the uttermost part of land towards the South Pole, and had certainly discovered how farre the same doth reach Southward from the coast of America aforenamed. The uttermost cape or Headland of all these Ilands, stands neere in 56 deg., without which there is no maine nor Iland to be seen to the Southwards, but that the Atlanticke Ocean and the South Sea, meete in a most large and free scope.

□   *The place where the oceans meet now is known as Drake Passage. Fletcher's "uttermost cape or Headland" is probably Cape Horn at the very tip of South America. Beyond the open sea to the south lay land, but no one had knowledge of it, and Drake's voyage seemed to render Terra Australis Incognita less probable.*

*The same voyage had another notable incident, somewhat earlier, during the passage through the Strait: the first meeting between Englishmen and penguins, again recorded by Fletcher.*   □

The 24 of *August* [1578], being Bartholomew day, we fell with three Ilands, bearing triangle-wise one from another; one of them was very faire and large and of a fruitfull soile, upon which, being next unto us and the weather very calme, our Generall with his gentlemen and certaine of his mariners, then landed, taking possession thereof in her Majesties name, and to her use, and called the same *Elizabeth* Iland.

The other two, though they were not so large nor so faire to the eye, yet were they to us exceeding usefull, for in them wee found great store of strange birds, which could not flie at all, nor yet runne so fast as that they could escape us with their lives; in body they are less than a goose, and bigger than a mallard, short and thicke sett together, having no feathers, but insteed thereof a certaine hard and matted downe; their beakes are not much unlike the bills of crowes, they lodge and breed upon the land, where making earthes, as the conies doe, in the ground, they lay their egges and bring up their young; their feeding and provision to live on is in the sea, where they swimm in such sort, as nature may seeme to have granted them no small prerogative in swiftnesse, both to prey upon others, and themselves to escape from any others that seeke to cease upon them; and such was the infinite resort of these birds to these Ilands, that in the space of 1 day we killed no lesse than 3000, and if the increase be according to the number, it is not to be thought that the world hath brought forth a greater blessing, in one kinde of creature in so small a circuit, so necessarily and plentifully serving the use of man; they are a very good and wholesome victuall. Our Generall named these Ilands, the one *Bartholomew*, according to the day, the other Saint *Georges,* in honour of England, according to the ancient custom there observed.

□ *The Portuguese voyages, and that of Drake, seemed to show only empty sea south of Africa and South America, but the dream of Terra Australis persisted. Explorations in the South Pacific led men to adopt Varthema's old story of a rich and substantial land beyond Java. In the first half of the sixteenth century, the great island of New Guinea was discovered, and was thought to be either the northernmost projection of Terra Australis, or else separated from it only by a narrow strait. Thus the geographer Cornelius Wytfliet, publishing an augmented edition of Ptolemy at Louvain in 1598, gave this information concerning Terra Australis:* □

# CORNELIUS WYTFLIET

The terra Australis is therefore the southernmost of all other lands, directly beneath the antarctic circle; extending beyond the tropic of Capricon to the West, it ends almost at the equator itself, and separated by a narrow strait lies on the East opposite to New Guinea, only known so far by a few shores because after one voyage and another that route has been given up and unless sailors are forced and driven by stress of winds it is seldom visited. The terra Australis begins at two or three degrees below the equator and it is said by some to be of such magnitude that if at any time it is fully discovered they think it will be the fifth part of the world. Adjoining Guinea on the right are the numerous and vast Solomon Islands which lately became famous by the voyage of Alvarus Mendanius.

◻ *The Portuguese seaman Pedro Fernandez de Quiros sailed for New Guinea in 1605. Bad weather took him off course, and he arrived at the island group now called the New Hebrides. Quiros dubbed it Australia del Espiritu Santo, and assumed that he had found the southern continent, declaring as he took possession, "O land so long sought for, believed in by so many, so earnestly longed for by me!" Meanwhile his second-in-command, Luis Vaez de Torres, reached New Guinea, sailed completely around it, and discovered the strait that bears his name. Torres showed what Wytfliet had guessed: that New Guinea was separate from any southern continent. He saw, also, indications of land to the south of New Guinea. A vast continent did indeed lie there—Australia. It was a southern continent, but not the southern continent.*

*The voyages of Quiros and Torres spurred European hopes of discovering a new part of the globe even richer than the Americas. Quiros agitated for further voyages of discovery, as did many others. Typical of the memorials addressed to the Spanish monarch, Philip III, was this one by Juan Luis Arias, a scholarly priest with an interest in furthering Spanish glory by conquest of the South Polar regions. Arias' memorial was written between 1606 and 1621; the translation is by R. H. Major in Early Voyages to Terra Australis, published by The Hakluyt Society in 1859. Its full title is "A Memorial Addressed to His Catholic Majesty, Philip the Third, King of Spain, by Dr. Juan Luis Arias, Respecting the Exploration, Colonization, and Conversion of the Southern Land."* ◻

# JUAN LUIS ARIAS

Some have asked, as already pointed out, whether the southern hemisphere be not all water, forming, as it were, a great part of the ocean, so as to leave but little of the surface of the earth in it uncovered. The reply to this is, that, according to what we are taught by sacred writ and by philosophical reasoning, there is proportionably as great a surface of land uncovered in the southern hemisphere as in the northern. For the fiat of the Creator, that the waters should be collected into certain hollows of the earth, in order that there should remain uncovered the portion that was necessary for the production of vegetation, as where He says in Genesis the 1st: "Let the waters under the heaven be gathered together into one place, and let the dry land appear," supposes this water to have been created an entire orb, which covered and surrounded the whole of the earth, in the same manner as we reckon the positions of the elements; the land the lowest, in the middle of which is the centre of the whole elementary and celestial machine, then the water, and after that the air and igneous substance or the fire, which reaches its culmination or convex part in the concave of the celestial firmament. Then if, when God commanded that the waters should be gathered together, it was to be understood solely with reference to the northern hemisphere, the water in the southern hemisphere would remain as it was, surrounding and covering all, and the whole sphere of water could not be contained beneath one spherical surface equidistant to the centre of gravity, which always seeks to be united with the centre of the whole machine. And thus all the water of the southern hemisphere would be more remote from the said centre than that of the other hemisphere, without being contained in any sinus, and thus would be much higher, and naturally could not contain itself without flowing towards the other hemisphere, until it placed itself in equilibrium with the said centre of gravity; as is plainly gathered from the demonstration of Archimedes, in his work "De Insidentibus Aquae," and is manifestly seen in the ebb and flow of the ocean; in which it is observed, that when the water rises above the surface of equidistance from its centre of gravity, it immediately outflows its ordinary limits until it finds its level with that surface; so that the gathering together of the waters was proportional in the two halves of the sphere of earth and water, gathering itself into certain hollows of the earth, which also have their means of correspondence between the two hemispheres. For as the quiet and equilibrium of the parts of the earth and water with respect to the centre of gravity consist in the equal tendencies of the opposite parts towards the same centre, it follows that the sinuses or receptacles of water in the one half are nearly proportioned in their position and other respects to those of the other. From all which it follows, that in the southern hemisphere there is an uncovered surface of land correspondent, or nearly so, to that which has been discovered in the northern hemisphere.

◻ *As the Spanish ruler pondered these learned theories, Dutch navigators began to explore the southern hemisphere. Among the first were Willem Schouten and Jacob le Maire, two men of the town of Hoorn, who were sent out by local merchants in 1615 to find a profitable southern sea route to the Indies. Instead of reaching the Pacific via the Strait of Magellan, they went farther south, discovering a second strait, the Strait le Maire, separating the land Magellan called Tierra del Fuego from an easterly island they dubbed Staten Land. Rounding the southernmost tip of South America, they named it Cape Hoorn for their native city; today it is Cape Horn. Jacob le Maire's narrative,* Australische Navigatien, *was first published at Amsterdam in 1618 under Schouten's name, and appeared in seven editions that year; in 1619 it reappeared at Leyden credited to le Maire, and was reprinted many times. The present translation, by J. A. J. de Villiers, was published by The Hakluyt Society in 1906 under the title* The East and West Indian Mirror. ◻

# JACOB LE MAIRE

Early on the morning of the 24th [of January, 1616] we sighted land to starboard, lying not more than a good mile away; we found the bottom in 40 fathoms and had a westerly wind. The land ran east by south with very high mountains, which were all white with snow. We continued to sail along the land, and about noon we came to the end of it and saw more land east of the last, also very high and dangerous looking. These countries lay in our opinion about 8 miles from each other, and there appeared to be a good channel between them both; this we opined the more firmly because we observed that a strong current to the south ran in between these two countries. At noon our latitude was 54° 46'; in the afternoon we got a northerly wind. We made for this channel, but towards the evening the wind fell, and we drifted on all night with a strong current and little wind. We saw immense numbers of penguins here, also whales by thousands, so that we were compelled to be constantly on our guard, loofing up and with a drag-sail set, in order to avoid the whales and not run into them.

On the morning of the 25th we were close to the more easterly land, which was very high and perilous, extending on the north side to the east-south-east, as far as we could see. We gave this the name of Staten-landt, but the land to the west of us we called Mauritius de Nassauw. We are of opinion that good roadsteads and sand-bays would be found on both sides, for there was on both sides fine sandy beach and gently rising sand bottom. Fish, penguins and seals are there in great abundance, also birds and water in sufficiency, but we could see no trees. We had a northerly wind to carry us into the channel, sailing sou'-sou'-west, with good progress. At noon our latitude was 55° 36', when we set our course south-west, with a fresh breeze and rain, with excellent progress. We saw the land south of the channel stretching away from the most westerly end of Mauritius de Nassauw land to the west-sou'-west and south-west, as far as our eyes could carry: all very high and perilous land. In the evening the wind veered to the south-west, and we then ran southward that night with a heavy roll from the south-west and very blue water, from which we opined and were certain that we had open and deep water on the weatherside, not doubting that it was the great South Sea, whereat we were very glad, holding that a way had been discovered by us which had until then been unknown to man, as we afterwards found to be the truth. We saw here enormously large gannets or sea-gulls, bigger in body than swans; their wings when extended were each more than a fathom long. These birds, unaccustomed to the sight of human beings, came and sat on board our ship and allowed themselves to be seized by the men and killed.

At noon, on the 26th, our latitude was 37°, with a flying storm from the west and south-west that lasted the whole of twenty-four hours, and a very rough, blue sea. We kept her head to the south with a try-sail, and saw more high land in the north-west; at night we turned her to the north-west, still with a try-sail.

At noon, on the 27th, our latitude was 56° 51′; the weather was cold, with hailstorms and rain. The wind was west and west-sou'-west; we first ran to the south, afterwards turning to the north under try-sails.

On the morning of the 28th, we hoisted our top-sails again, and had a heavy roll from the west. The wind was at first westerly, afterwards north-easterly, we sailing first to the south, then west by south, afterwards west and west by south. At noon our latitude was 56° 48′.

At daybreak, on the morning of the 29th, we had a south-west wind and proceeded in a south-westerly direction.

After breakfast, we saw two islands ahead of us, to the west-sou'-west, but we were unable to sail to the windward of them, so that we circumnavigated them on the north. They were barren grey rocks, with a few smaller ones lying around them, and situated in 57° of latitude south of the equator. We gave them the name of the Islands of Barnevelt.

We continued to sail to the west-nor'-west; towards the evening we again saw land to the north-west and nor'-nor'-west of us. This was the land south of the Strait of Magellaen, which stretches away to the south. It consisted entirely of high mountains covered with snow, and ends in a sharp corner, which we called the Cape of Hoorn, and which lies in latitude 57° 48′.

□  *The Dutch were busy in southern waters now that Schouten and le Maire had shown the way. In 1642, Abel Tasman reached the land Torres had seen south of New Guinea, sailed around it, and proved that it was a vast island, the continent of Australia. Terra Australis Incognita thus retreated still farther toward the South Pole. A year later, one Hendrik Brouwer revisited Cape Horn and was carried around Staten Land, showing that it, too, was an island. Other mer-*

15

*chants, both Dutch and English, followed. One whose voyage was particularly memorable was an Englishman named Anthony de la Roché, who made a trading journey to the Pacific in 1674 and 1675. On the return trip to Europe in April, 1675, the vessel carrying la Roché was unable to enter the Strait of Magellan or the Strait le Maire; buffeted by storms, the ship reached a hitherto unknown snow-covered island far to the east. This was probably the island known as South Georgia, at about 55° S., and la Roché became the first actually to set foot on land in the outskirts of the Antarctic regions.*

*Unfortunately his own account of the voyage has disappeared; all that survives is a secondhand report by a Spanish captain, Francisco de Seixas y Lovera, published at Madrid in 1690. The translation used is by Alexander Dalrymple, from* A Collection of Voyages Chiefly in the Southern Atlantick Ocean *(London, printed for the author, 1775).*  □

# ANTHONY DE LA ROCHÉ

. . . having left Teneriff 5th July [1674], they passed the Strait Le Maire, 18th Sept^r. and thence directly to the Coast of Peru, where having sold a small part of their Cargo, they returned to careen their two Vessels and refresh their People on the Coast of the Island Chiloe, where having taken on board all kinds of Provisions for the Passage to Europe, and being solicitous to pass by the said Strait Le Maire in April 1675, they could not, the Winds and Currents having carried them so far to the Eastward; and being unable to return towards the Land of the Strait of Magellan, nor to make Staten Land to sail into the N°. Sea by Brower's Strait, and seeing that it was far advanced in April and beginning of Winter in that Climate, it would be much if they escaped with Life, particularly as they had no Knowledge or Intimation of the Land which they *now began to see toward the East* which making and using all endeavors to get near it, they found a Bay, in which they anchored close to a Point or Cape which stretches out to the SE with 28. 30. and 40. fath. Sand and Rock, in

16

which situation they had sight of some Snow Mountains near the Coast, with much bad Weather; they continued there 14 days, at the end of which time having the Weather cleared up, they found that they were at the end of that Land, near which they anchored, and looking to the SE and South, they saw another High Land covered with snow, leaving which, and the Wind setting in gently at SW and sailed out in sight of the said coast of the Island which they left to the Westward, seeing the said Southern land in the said Quarters, it appearing that from one to the other was about 10 lea$^s$. little more or less, and that there was a great Current to the NE, to which Point sailing, and steering ENE they found themselves in the N$^o$. Sea, in 3 Glasses disemboguing thro' the said passage, which they say is very short; for the land which appears to form the said New Island is small; which leaving and sailing one whole day to the NW, the Wind set in so strong and stormy at S. that they sailed other 3 days to N. till they were in 46° where appearing to be now secure they say, that coming in quest of the Bahia de Todo Sanctos, they found in 45° S. a very large pleasant Island with a good Port toward the E. side in which they found Water, Wood and Fish, but saw no People, notwithstanding they staid there 6 days, at the end of which they passed to the Bay of All Saints in Brazil, and from thence to the City of Rochelle in France, where they arrived 29th Sept. 1675.

□   *Not all who roved those seas were merchants. Some were pirates, such as Ambrose Cowley, Bartholomew Sharpe, and Edward Davis, who reported being carried into latitudes above 60°S., seeing floating ice and no sign of land. Typical of these adventurers was Lionel Wafer, surgeon and buccaneer, whose piratical career ended in 1688 with his imprisonment at Jamestown, Virginia. Late in 1687, Wafer found himself south of Cape Horn on his way to the West Indies from the Pacific, and set down one of the earliest descriptions of icebergs. Wafer's book,* A New Voyage & Description of the Isthmus of America, *was published at London in 1699, and reprinted many times, most recently by The Hakluyt Society in 1934.* ▫

# LIONEL WAFER

We were now standing out to Sea again, to double *Terra del Fuego.* We were in a terrible Storm for about three Weeks before we came off Cape *Horn.* We did not see Cape *Horn,* being a great way to the South of it, and in the Lat. of 62 Deg. 45 Min. S. nor did we well know what Course to steer, having but very indifferent Seamen aboard. It was now about the heighth of Summer here; for I remember that upon *Christmas* day, 1687, we were just clear of the Storm, and in the Latitude we mention'd, off Cape *Horn.* Running hence to the Northward again, being now got out of the South Sea, we met several Islands of Ice; which at first seemed to be real Land. Some of them seemed a League or two in length, and some not above half a Mile. The biggest seemed, as we sail'd by them, which we did before the Wind for several Days, to be about 4 or 500 Foot high. We sounded near them, but found no Ground; so that it may reasonably be concluded they were afloat; and perhaps reach'd as deep into the water, as their heighth was above it. We saw no such Islands of Ice as I went into the South Sea with Mr. *Dampier;* neither did I ever hear that Captain *Sharp* met with any in his return out of that Sea. These Islands appear'd to us so plain at Night, that we could easily see how to steer clear of them. But there were some which lay under Water, which we could not possibly shun, but sometimes they would shake our Ship: yet they never did us much Dammage. From these Hills of Ice came very cold Blasts of Wind; insomuch that our Men, newly coming out of a hot Country, could hardly endure the Deck.

In all our Passage round *Terra del Fuego* the Weather was so stormy, for 3 Weeks that we lay to the Southward of Cape *Horn,* and the Sun and Stars so obscur'd, that we could take no Observation of our Lat. yet, by our Reckoning, we were in very near 63 Deg. S. Lat. which is the farthest to the South that any *European,* probably, ever yet was, and perhaps any Man.

◻   *Another privateer, but this one officially sponsored, was George Shelvocke of Shropshire, who entered the English navy about 1690, when he was fifteen. The perennial hostility between England and Spain was alive again in 1718, when Shelvocke was commissioned to enter the Pacific and harry Spanish shipping. Shelvocke departed from England in February, 1719, and took the route through the Strait le Maire. What might otherwise have been a routine passage was marked by one significant episode, the shooting of a certain large bird that followed the ship for several days. When in 1797 Coleridge was planning "The Ancient Mariner," he had been reading the account of Shelvocke's voyage, and at the suggestion of his friend Wordsworth made the shooting of an albatross in high southern latitudes the central action of the poem. Coleridge gave verse to the voyage into the icy southern seas; Shelvocke's prose account is its direct inspiration. His book,* A Voyage Round the World, *was published at London in 1726, and was reprinted by Cassell and Company, Ltd., in 1928 as a volume of The Seafarer's Library.*   ◻

# GEORGE SHELVOCKE

Before we came on the coast of Tierra del Fuego, we had not been sensible of any helps or hindrance, by any currents, from the time that we had got to the Southward of the River of Plate; but this afternoon we were hurried with incredible rapidity into the Straits, and just as we had gained somewhat more than the mid-passage the tide slacked. We then sounded, and had but twenty-seven fathom, a rocky bottom. At the same time I took an opportunity to make what observations I could of the place. We had a clear view of Staten Land, which yields a most uncomfortable landscape of a surprising height, covered with snow to the very wash of the sea, and bears more of a likeness of a huge white cloud than of firm land. These Straits seem to answer very well to Monsieur Frezier's map of them, being about seven leagues through, six leagues wide, and lie almost North and South. But the northern tide rushing upon us with an equal violence with what had brought us in, it prevented my making any further remarks, and afforded matter of astonishment to us all to see how fast we were driven out again, notwithstanding we had a fresh, fair gale at North West, and when at the same time we went six knots by the log, by which I cannot judge this tide can run less than ten knots in an hour. In short, we were quite carried out of these Straits again in about an hour's time. Upon the shifting of this tide to windward there arose such a short sea which at the same time was so lofty, that we alternately dipped our bowsprit end and poop lant-horns into the water. Our ship laboured in the most violent manner, and became insensible of the guidance of her helm; but at midnight the tide shifted, and we put through the Straits, steering South with a brisk gale at North West, without seeing the land, distinctly, and in the morning had a very good offing to the Southward.

After we had got well to sea we unstocked our anchors, and brought them aft, and got in our spritsail yard to ease our bows, and make every thing as snug as possible. We had found it very cold before we came this length, but now we began to feel the extremity of it. The bleak westerly winds of themselves would have been suf-ficiently piercing, but they were always attended either with snow or sleet, which continually beating on our sails and rigging had cased the masts and every rope with ice, and had, in a manner, rendered our sails almost useless to us. So much were we accustomed to the most severe storms that we used to think it tolerable weather if we could but bear a reefed mainsail; for it was common with us to be two or three days together lying to under bare poles, exposed all the while to the assaults of prodigious seas, much larger than any I ever saw. Now we began to be thoroughly sensible of our awning, and, indeed, we could scarce have lived without it. The winds reigning thus tempestuously, without intermission, in the western board, we were driven into the latitude of 61 deg. 30 min. of South latitude. Add to this our misfortune of having continual misty weather, which laid us under hourly apprehensions of falling foul of islands of ice: but, thank God, we escaped that danger, though we had many alarms by fog banks, and other false appearances. Notwithstanding we had the days very long, yet it was very seldom we could get a sight of the sun; so that we had but one observation of the variation in all this passage, which was in the latitude of 60 deg. 37 min. South, 5 deg. 00 min. to the Westward of the Straits of Le Mair, where we found it 22 deg. 6 min. North East.

Thursday, October 1 [1719]. At seven in the evening, as we were furling the mainsail, one William Camell cried out that his hands were so benumbed that he could not hold himself; but before those who were next to him could come to his assistance he fell down and was drowned.

The cold is certainly more insupportable in these than in the same latitudes to the Northward; for though we were pretty much advanced in the summer season and had the days very long, we were nevertheless subject to continual squalls of sleet, snow and rain, and the heavens were perpetually hidden from us by gloomy, dismal clouds. In short, one would think it impossible that anything living could subsist in so rigid a climate, and indeed we all observed that we had not had the sight of one fish of any kind since we were come to the Southward of the Straits of Le Mair; nor one sea-bird excepting a disconsolate black albatross, who accompanied us for several days, hovering about us as if he had lost himself, till Hatley (my second captain) observing, in one of his melancholy fits, that this bird was always hovering near us, imagined, from his colour, that it might be some ill omen. That which, I suppose, induced him the more to encourage his superstition, was the continued series of contrary tempestuous winds, which had oppressed us ever since we had got into this sea. But be that as it would, he, after some fruitless attempts, at length shot the albatross, not doubting (perhaps) that we should have a fair wind after that. I must own, that this navigation is truly melancholy, and was the more so to us, who were by ourselves without a companion, which would have somewhat diverted our thoughts from the reflection of being in such a remote part of the world and, as it were, separated from the rest of mankind to struggle with the dangers of a stormy climate, far distant from any port to have recourse to, in case of the loss of masts, or any other accident; nor any chance of receiving assistance from any other ship. These considerations were enough to deject our spirits, when we were sensible of the hourly danger we were in of losing our masts, by the incessant continuance of such stormy weather as we

21

underwent; but the hopes of enjoying a long repose in the Pacific Sea, on the coast of Peru, lightened our cares and gave us some small relief.

◻   *The French entered the Antarctic quest late. In 1503, a French merchant named Binot Paulmier de Gonneville, following Vasco da Gama's pioneering route around Africa, was blown off course and discovered a large island he called Southern India. (It probably was Madagascar.) Not until 1737 did another French expedition enter southern seas. A young captain named Bouvet de Lozier talked the French East India Company into equipping two ships, the* Aigle *and the* Marie, *for a voyage in search of Gonneville's Southern India. The hope was to find a fertile southern continent and claim it for France.*

*Bouvet's hopes were not realized. He found no huge tropical land, only a desolate sea dotted with icebergs, and a lonely, miserable island that now is known by his name. (The position he gives for it uses an obsolete system of reckoning longitude; Bouvet Island is actually at 54°15′ S. and 5° E., an isolated spot of land roughly southwest of the Cape of Good Hope.) Bouvet's journal, published at Paris after his return, was translated into English in Volume III of* Terra Australis Cognita: or, Voyages to the Terra Australis, or Southern Hemisphere, during the Sixteenth, Seventeenth, and Eighteenth Centuries, *edited by John Callander (Edinburgh, A. Donaldson, 1768).*   ◻

# BOUVET DE LOZIER

We left *Port L'Orient* July 19, 1738, and shaped our course for the island St. Catharine. Hence we failed again in our search of unknown lands, which, by our instructions, we were to look for about 44 degrees south-latitude, longitude 355 degrees. November 26, in latitude 35 degrees, longitude 344, we began to meet with fogs, which continued close with us, and wet our cloaths like rain, and was often so thick, that even when the two ships were so near that we would cheer our consorts crew working, yet we could not see them. We always fired guns during the day, and had our lanthorns lighted at night, not withstanding all which we had much difficulty to keep together. In the first week of December, from 39, to 44 degrees latitude, we found the herb called by our sailors *Goulmon*, which either grows at the bottom of the sea hereabouts, or else is torn by the waves from the rocks. This sea weed we saw for many days together. Tho' it was now summer, yet the weather was cold, with frequent showers of hail, and claps of thunder. The birds now began to show themselves in much greater numbers than formerly. Some of these resembled land fowl, which made us think we were near some coast, but we found no ground with 180 fathoms of line.

December 10, we found ourselves at the intersection of the 44th parallel with the first meridian, where the charts commonly place the *Terra del Visto*, or the *Cape* of the *Southern Continent*. Still, however, we saw no land; whether it was that the fogs hindered us from seeing it, or that in reality there is no land thereabouts, except some small island, or perhaps islands of ice, which had been taken, at a distance, for a coast. On the 15th of December we first saw ice in a latitude corresponding to that of *Paris*. I was much pleased on seeing this ice, as I took it for a certain sign of land being near us. I had observed that the height of these icy isles generally corresponded with that of the lands near where they were formed, and these high lands are generally safe to approach. We saw some of these islands of ice so high, that we could observe them eight leagues off, and when the fogs cleared up, they presented us with several amusing figures, resembling fortresses, houses, ships, etc.

In these unknown seas, the risques we run were very great, for the ice is much more dangerous than the shore, as each piece of it is a floating rock, against which, were we driven, there could be no hope of saving our lives. The smaller pieces of ice are even more dangerous than the larger, because they swim just level with the surface of the water, and when the sea runs high, it becomes very difficult to distinguish them. These dangers began to discourage the

23

crews, so that, in order to animate them, I read those articles of our instructions in which rewards were promised in case the discovery was perfected.

We now made sail to the southward, but were quickly so hemmed with ice, that we were forced to stand east in order to find some passage. The sea here was very deep, and we saw great numbers of divers, penguins and sea wolves. The needle gave different variations on different compasses, declining 24 minutes east on one, while on another it would vary 50 minutes west, with the same irregularity of motion that has been observed on approaching the ice in *Hudson*'s bay and *Davis*'s straits.

January 1, 1739, I discovered land. It was exceedingly high, covered with snow, and almost hid in fogs. From the festival celebrated on this day, I called it *Cape Circumcision*; and the pilot of the *Eagle*, who first saw this land, had a reward of twenty piastres. It lies in 54 degrees south latitude, and about 27 degrees, or 28 degrees longitude, stretching from north-west to south-east. Its coasts are very high and rugged, and so pestered with ice, as to be quite inaccessible. We found it surrounded with little isles of pure, hard ice, standing up two or three hundred feet perpendicular and from one to two or three leagues in circumference. Here the needle varied 6 degrees, 50 minutes west. On the 6th of January we were suddenly surrounded by a prodigious flight of fowls, of the size of a pigeon, and quite white. We kept standing along this course during 12 days, without daring to go near the shore, or even to send our boats ashore on account of the fogs, the ice, and the contrary winds. Hence we stood eastward, under 57 degrees latitude, till January 25, in which time we ran 425 leagues, always along the ice, and seeing great numbers of whales, sea wolves, and other large fishes. Despairing at length to find an inlet hereabouts, we quitted the *Austral* land, which seemed inaccessible, and stood to the north-east, in hopes of finding the coast that *Gonneville* landed on, and which his account affirms to lye in the latitude corresponding to that of *France*. Next we shaped a north course to longitude 52 degrees, and saw great quantities of the sea-weed we mentioned before, quite to latitude 43 degrees. Here the two vessels separated, the *Eagle* standing for the island *Bourbon*, while I returned to *France* with the *Mary*, by way of the *Cape of Good Hope*. I landed the 24th of June, 1739, having not lost a man during the fatiguing voyage, except one, who fell over board near the isle of *Fernand Noronha.*

◻ *An era of doubt ended when James Cook demolished the myth of a fertile southern continent late in the eighteenth century. Cook, a Yorkshireman born in 1728, learned the seafaring trade aboard coal-hauling brigs and merchant vessels, and enrolled in the Royal Navy in 1755 as an able seaman, perhaps the most able able seaman ever to sign on. His superb abilities as a navigator and leader of men quickly became apparent, and he rose to the rank of master, or chief navigator. While serving in Canada during the Seven Years' War, Cook studied mathematics, astronomy, and marine surveying, and after the war he was placed in command of a surveying vessel, spending five years charting the western and southern coasts of Newfoundland.*

*In 1768, he was selected by the Royal Society to lead a scientific expedition into the South Pacific. Its ostensible purpose was to make astronomical observations of Venus, but it also was sent to search for Terra Australis, still Incognita. The motivating force was fiery, dogmatic Alexander Dalrymple, astronomer, geographer, and Fellow of the Royal Society, who firmly believed that the long-sought prize still existed somewhere in the Pacific. Dalrymple hoped to command the expedition himself, but as a civilian he was refused, and he never forgave Cook for assuming the place he coveted.*

*On this expedition, Cook rounded Cape Horn, explored New Zealand, Australia, and the islands of the South Pacific, and returned home in three years without having seen any Terra Australis. "As to a southern continent," he wrote, "I do not believe any such thing exists, unless in a high latitude." Dalrymple continued to press his belief, supposing that "the number of inhabitants in the southern continent is probably more than 50 millions." His tireless propagandizing led to a second expedition specifically instructed to search for the southern continent. Cook, again, was placed in charge. He had two ships, the* Resolution *and the* Adventure, *and carried a comple-*

ment of astronomers, naturalists, and other scientists. (Dalrymple remained home once more.)

The expedition sailed on July 13, 1772. After a futile search for Bouvet Island, Cook headed south, and on January 17, 1773, became the first captain to cross the Antarctic Circle and enter the true polar region. The first of the excerpts below describes this historic crossing. Blocked by ice, Cook retreated, sailed eastward above the Antarctic Circle for two months, and spent the rest of 1773 in New Zealand and the South Pacific. By December, he was attempting another polar voyage; the first try had been south of Africa, this one southward from New Zealand. Again he crossed the Circle, as told below, seeing albatrosses and other birds; again ice halted his progress. It seemed to him that the field of ice must stretch southward to the pole, and that Dalrymple's theory of a warm, inhabited southern continent could only be a fantasy. A third crossing of the Circle in January, 1774, confirmed this opinion, and Cook returned to England in 1775 entertaining only the gloomiest thoughts about the southern continent. The following year he embarked on a third expedition, this time to explore the western coast of North America and the islands of the North Pacific, and in 1779 he was slain by the natives of Hawaii.

Cook's journal of his second voyage was published in England in 1777 as A Voyage towards the South Pole, and Round the World. This book has been reprinted many times. However, Cook's roughhewn text was edited and substantially rewritten by a professional literary man, Dr. John Douglas. The Hakluyt Society has begun to reprint the original texts of Cook's manuscript journals, under the editorship of J. C. Beaglehole, and I have used Beaglehole's edition here. The extracts that follow are from The Journals of Captain James Cook, Volume II, edited by J. C. Beaglehole (The Hakluyt Society, Cambridge, 1961), and are reprinted by permission of The Hakluyt Society.  □

# JAMES COOK

SATURDAY 16th [of January, 1773]. Thermr'. 34 to 35. Winds East & EBS. Course S 2° W. Dist. Sailed 58 Miles. Lat. in South

64°31'. *Longde. in E. Greenwich Reck.g* 39°35' *Watch* 38°32'. *Long$^{de}$ made E. of C.G.H.* 21°12'. After Dinner having but little wind we brought to under an Island of Ice and sent a Boat to take up some loose pieces, while this was doing we shifted the two Topsails and Fore sail. At 5 o'clock the Breeze freshened at East attended with snow and we made Sail to the Northward, but finding that we were only returning to the North on the same track we had advanced to the South we at 8 Tacked and stood to the Southward close upon a Wind, which was at EBS, having alternatly snow showers and fair Weather and during the whole am saw but one Island of Ice.

SUNDAY 17*th. Thermr.* 34. *Winds EBS. Course South. Dist. Sailed* 125 *Miles. Lat. in South* 66°36½'. *Longde. in E. Greenwich Reck.g* 39°35'. *Long$^{de}$ made E. of C.G.H.* 21°12'. In the PM had fresh gales and Clowdy weather. At 6 o'Clock, being then in the Latitude of 64°56' s I found the Variation by Gregorys Compass to be 26°41' West, at this time the Motion of the Ship was so great that I could not observe with D$^r$ Knights Compass. In the AM had hazy weather with Snow Showers and saw but one Island of Ice in the Course of these 24 hours so that we begin to think that we have got into a clear Sea. At about a ¼ past 11 o'Clock we cross'd the Antarctic Circle for at Noon we were by observation four Miles and a half South of it and are undoubtedly the first and only Ship that ever cross'd that line. We now saw several Flocks of the Brown and White Pintadoes which we have named Antarctic Petrels because they seem to be natives of that Region; the White Petrels also appear in greater numbers than of late and some few Dark Grey Albatrosses, our constant companions the Blue Petrels have not forsaken us but the Common Pintadoes have quite disapeared as well as many other sorts which are Common in lower Latitudes.

MONDAY 18*th. Winds EBS. Course North. Distce. Sailed* 44 *Miles. Lat. in South* 65°52'. *Longde. in East Greenwich Reck.g* 39° 35'. *Longde. East Cape G. Hope* 21°12'. In the PM had a Fresh gale and fair Weather. At 4 o'Clock we discovered from the Mast head thirty eight Islands of Ice extending from the one Bow to the other, that is from the SE to West, and soon after we discovered Feild or Packed Ice in the same Direction and had so many loose pieces about the Ship that we were obliged to loof for one and bear up for another, the number increased so fast upon us that at ¾ past Six, being then in the Latitude of 67°15' s, the Ice was so thick and close that we could proceed no further but were fain to Tack and stand from it. From the mast head I could see nothing to the Southward but Ice, in the Whole extent from East to WSW without the least appearance of any partition, this immence Feild was composed of different kinds of Ice, such as high Hills or Islands, smaller pieces packed close together and what Greenland men properly call field Ice, a piece of this kind, of such extend that I could see no end to it, lay to the SE of us, it was 16 or 18 feet high at least and appeared of a pretty equal height. I did not think it was consistant with the safty of the Sloops or any ways prudent for me to persevere in going farther to the South as the summer was already half spent and it would have taken up some time to have got round this Ice, even supposing this to have been practicable, which however is doubtfull. The Winds Continued at East and EBS and increased to a strong gale attended with a large Sea, hazy weather Sleet and Snow and obliged us to close reef our Topsails. . . .

TUESDAY 21st [of December, 1773]. *Therm.r. Noon 33. Winds NE. Course S 41° E. Dist. Sailed 70 Miles. Lat. in South 66°50'. Longde. in West Reck.g. 66°50'. Long. made C. Pallisser 38°11'.* In the pm the wind increased to a strong gale attended with a thick fogg sleet and rain which constitutes the very worst of weather, our rigging was so loaded with ice that we had enough to do to get our Topsails down to double reef. At 7 o'Clock we came the second time under the Polar Circle and stood to the SE till 6 o'Clock in the am when being in Lat 67°5' South, Longitude 145°49' West, the fogg being exceeding thick we came close aboard a large Island of ice and being at the same time a good deal embarrass'd with loose ice we with some difficulty wore and stood to the NW untill Noon when the fogg being some what disipated we resumed our Course again to the SE. The ice islands we fell in with in the morning, for there were more than one, were very high and rugged terminating in many Peaks, whereas all those we have seen before were quite flat at top and not so high. A great Sea from the North. Grey Albatroses and a few Antarctick Petrels.

WEDNESDAY 22nd. *Therm.r. Noon 31 to 33. Winds Northerly. Course S 70°15' E. Dist. Sailed 109 Miles. Lat. in South 67°27'. Longde. in West Reck.g. 141°55'. Long. made C. Pallisser 42°39'.*

Fresh gales the most part of this day, at times very thick and hazey and other times tolerable clear. Saw not fewer than twenty ice islands, some grey Albatroses and a few Antarctick Petrels. In the PM a squall of wind took hold of the Mizen Top-sail and tore it all to pieces, and rendered it for ever useless.

THURSDAY 23rd. *Therm.r. Noon 33. Winds Northerly. Course N 80°15' E. Dist. Sailed 94 Miles. Lat. in South 67°12'. Longde. in West Reck.g. 138°00' Watch 137°41'. Long. made C. Pallisser 46°39'.* Moderate gales and Pirceing cold, very thick and hazey at times. At Noon Twenty three ice islands were seen from the Deck and twice that number from the mast head.

FRIDAY 24th. *Therm.r. Noon 32. Winds Northerly. Course S 40° W. Dist. Sailed 9 Miles. Lat. in South 67°19'. Longde. in West Reck.g. 138°15'. Long. made C. Pallisser 46°24'.* At 4 o'Clock in the PM as we were standing to the SE, fell in with such a vast quantity of field or loose ice as covered the whole Sea from South to East and was so thick and close as to obstruct our passage, the wind at this time being pretty moderate, brought to in the edge of this feild, hoisted out two boats and sent them to take some up, and in the mean time we slung several large pi[e]ces along side and hoisted them in with our tackles, by such time as the Boats had made two trips it was Eight o'Clock when we hoisted them in and made sail to the westward under double reef'd Top-sails and Courses, with the wind notherly a strong gale attended with a thick fog Sleet and Snow which froze to the Rigging as it fell and decorated the whole with icicles. Our ropes were like wires, Sails like board or plates of Metal and the Shivers froze fast in the blocks so that it required our utmost effort to get a Top-sail down and up; the cold so intense as hardly to be endured, the whole Sea in a manner covered with ice, a hard gale and a thick fog: under all these unfavourable circumstances it was natural for me to think of returning more to the North, seeing there was no probability of finding land here nor a possibility of get[ting] farther to the South and to have proceeded to the East in this Latitude would not have been prudent as well on account of the ice as the vast space of Sea we must have left to the north unexplored, a space of 24° of Latitude in which a large track of land might lie, this point could only be determined by makeing a stretch to the North. While we were takeing up the ice two of the Antarctick

Petrels so often mentioned were shott; we were right in our conjectures in supposeing them of the Petrel tribe; they are about the size of a large pigeon, the feathers of the head, back and part of the upper side of the wings are a lightish brown, the belly and under side of the wings white, the tail feathers which are 10 in number are white tiped with brown. At the same time we got another new Petrel smaller than the former, its plumage was dark grey. They were both casting their feathers and yet they were fuller of them than any birds we had seen, so much has nature taken care to cloath them sutable to the climate in which they live. At this time we saw two or three Chocolate coloured Albatrosses with yellowish Bills, these as well as the Petrels above mentioned are no were seen but among the ice. The bad weather continuing without the least variation for the better which made it necessary for us to proceed with great caution and to make short boards over that part of the Sea we had in some measure made our selves accquainted with the preceeding day, we were continually falling in with large ice islands which we had enough to do to keep clear of. . . .

SUNDAY 30th [of January, 1774]. *Winds ESE. Course S 20° E. Dist. Sailed 51 Miles. Lat. in South 70°48′. Longd. in W. Reck.g. 106°34′.* Continued to have a gentle gale at NE with Clear pleasant weather till towards the evening, when the Sky became Clowded and the air Cold atten[d]ed with a smart frost. In the Latitude of 70°23′ the Variation was 24°31′ East; some little time after saw a piece of Rock Weed covered with Barnacles which one of the brown Albatroses was picking off. At 10 o'Clock pass'd a very large Ice island which was not less than 3 miles in circuit, presently after came on a thick fog, this made it unsafe to stand on, especially as we had seen more Ice Islands ahead; we therefore tacked and made a trip to the North for about one hour and a half in which time the fog dissipated and we resumed our Cou[r]se to the SSE, in which rout we met with several large ice islands. A little after 4 AM we precieved the Clowds to the South near the horizon to be of an unusual Snow white brightness which denounced our approach to field ice, soon after it was seen from the Mast-head and at 8 o'Clock we were close to the edge of it which extended East and West in a streight line far beyond our sight; as appear'd by the brightness of the horizon; in the Situation we were now in just the Southern half of the horizon was enlightned by the Reflected rays of the Ice to a considerable height. The Clowds near the horizon were of a perfect Snow whiteness and were difficult to be distinguished from the Ice hills whose lofty summits reached the Clowds. The outer or No[r]thern edge of this immence Ice field was compose[d] of loose or broken ice so close packed together that nothing could enter it; about a Mile in began the firm ice, in one compact solid boddy and seemed to increase in height as you traced it to the South; In this field we counted Ninety Seven Ice Hills or Mountains, many of them vastly large. Such Ice Mountains as these are never seen in Greenland, so that we cannot draw a comparison between the Greenland Ice and this now before us: Was it not for the Greenland Ships fishing yearly among such Ice (the ice hills excepted) I should not have hisitated one moment in declaring it as my opinion that the Ice we now see extended in a solid body quite to the Pole, and that it is here, i.e. to the South of this parallel, where the many Ice Islands we find floating about in the Sea are first form'd, and afterwards broke off by gales of wind and other causes, be this as it may, we must allow that these numberless and large Ice Hills must add such weight to the Ice feilds, to which they are fixed, as must make a wide difference between the Navigating this Icy Sea and that of Greenland: I will not say it was impossible anywhere to get in among this Ice, but I will assert that the bare attempting of it would be a very dangerous enterprise and what I believe no man in my situation would have thought of. I whose ambition leads me not only farther than any other man has been before me, but as far as I think it possible for man to go, was not sorry at meeting with this interruption, as it in some measure relieved us from the dangers and hardships, inseparable with the Navigation of the Southern Polar regions. Sence therefore we could not proceed one Inch farther South, no other reason need be assigned for our Tacking and stretching back to the North, being at that time in the Latitude of 71°10' South, Longitude 106°54' W.[1] We had not be[en] long tacked before

[1] This was not merely Cook's farthest south, but the farthest south anyone has ever attained by sea in this longitude. It is probable that the "firm ice" Cook saw did at that time extend "in a solid body quite to the Pole." He was now only about 120 miles from the nearest land, which lay roughly to the southwest—the Walgreen coast of Marie Byrd Land, the line of which is still conjectural, discovered by Admiral Byrd from the air in 1929. [Beaglehole's note.]

we were involved in a very thick fog, so that we thought our selves very fortunate in having clear weather when we approach'd the ice. I must observe that we saw here very few Birds of any kind; some Penguins were heard but none seen, nor any other signs of land whatever.

SUNDAY 30*th*. At 4 oClock in the Morning we preceived the C[l]ouds over the horizon to the South to be of an unusual Snow white brightness which we knew denounced our approach to field Ice; soon after it was seen from the Top-mast head and at 8 oClock we were close to the edge of it, it extended east and west far beyond the reach of our sight. In the situation we were in just the Southern half of our horizon was illuminated by the rays of light which were reflected from the Ice to a considerable height. Ninety Seven Ice hills were distinctly seen within the feild, besides those on the outside and many of them were very large and looked like a ridge of Mountains rising one above another till they were lost in the clouds. The outer or Northern edge of this immense field, was composed of loose or broken ice close packed together, so that it was not possible for any thing to enter it, this was about a mile broad, within which was solid Ice in one continued compact body; it was rather low and flat (except the hills) but seemed to increase in hieght as you traced it to the South in which direction it extended beyound our sight. Such Mountains of Ice as these were, I believe, never seen in the Greenland Seas, at least not that I ever heard or read of, so that we cannot draw a comparison between the Ice here and there; it must be allowed that these prodigeous Ice Mou[n]tains must add such additional weight to the Ice fields which inclose them as must make a great difference between the Navigating this Icy sea and that of Greenland. I will not say it was impossible any where to get farther to the South, but the attempting it would have been a dangerous and rash enterprise and what I believe no man in my situation would have thought of. It was indeed my opinion as well as the opinion of most on board, that this Ice extended quite to the Pole or perhaps joins to some land, to which it had been fixed from the creation and that it [is] here, that is to the South of this Parallel, where all the Ice we find scatered up and down to the North are first form'd and afterwards broke off by gales of Wind or other cause and brought to the North by the Currents which we have always found to set in that direction in the high Latitudes.

32

As we drew near this Ice some Penguins were heard but none seen and but few other birds or any other thing that could induce us to think any land was near; indeed if there was any land behind this Ice it could afford no better retreat for birds or any other animals, than the Ice it self, with which it must have been wholy covered. I who had Ambition not only to go farther than any one had done before, but as far as it was possible for man to go, was not sorry at meeting with this interruption as it in some measure relieved us, at least shortned the dangers and hardships inseparable with the Navigation of the Southern Polar Rigions; Sence therefore, we could not proceed one Inch farther to the South, no other reason need be assigned for my Tacking and Standing back to the north, being at this time in the Latitude of 71°10′ S, Longitude 106°54′ W. It was happy for us that the Weather was Clear when we fell in with this Ice and that we discovered it so soon as we did for we had no sooner Tacked then we were involved in a thick fog. The Wind was at East and blew a fresh breeze, so that we were inabled to return back over that space we had already made our selves acquainted with. At Noon the Mercury in the Thermometer stood at 32½ and we found the air exceeding cold. . . .

SUNDAY 5th [of February, 1775]. This day we saw no Penguins, we also observed that the Sea was changed to its usual Colour, whereas all the time we were about the land or rather from our falling in with the Isle of Georgia, to this day it had been of a pale or Milkish colour, the same as Water tinged with milk: this Colour was not caused by the reflection of Clouds, &cᵃ as is sometimes the case, because it kept the same Colour after it was taken up out of the Sea, had we been all the time in Soundings I should have thought that had been the Cause of it, but as we were not I confess myself at a loss how to account for it: let what will have been the cause I no where ever saw Sea Water of so pale a Colour before. The Sea resuming its usual colour and the Penguins leaving us, as it were all at once, made us conjecture that we were leaving the land behind us and that we had already seen its northern extremity. At Noon we were in the Latitude of 57°8′ S, Longitude 23°34′ west, which was 3°00′ of Longitude to the East of Saunders isle; it was not possible for us to gain this westing without much time for in the after noon the Wind shifted to that direction; this however enabled us to stretch to the south and to get into the Latitude of the land, that if it took an East direction we might again fall in with it. In the Latitude of 57°15′ S, Longitude 23°00′ W the Variation was 5°18′ East.

MONDAY 6th. We continued to steer to the South and SE till noon at which time we were in the Latitude of 58°15′ S, Longitude 21°34′ West and seeing neither land nor signs of any, I concluded that what we had seen, which I named *Sandwich Land* was either a group of Islands or else a point of the Continent, for I firmly beleive that there is a tract of land near the Pole, which is the Source of most of the ice which is spread over this vast Southern Ocean: and I think it also probable that it extends farthest to the North opposite the Southern Atlantick and Indian Oceans, because ice has always been found farther to the north in these Oceans than any where else which, I think, could not be if there was no land to the South, I mean a land of some considerable extent; for if we suppose there is not, and that ice may be formed without, it will follow of Course that the cold ought to be every where nearly equal round the Pole, as far as 70° or 60° of Latitude, or so far as to be out of the influence of any of the known Continents, consequently we ought to see ice every where under the same Parallel or near it, but the Contrary has been found. It is but few ships which have met with ice going round Cape Horn and we saw but little below the sixtieth degree of Latitude in the *Southern Pacifick Ocean.* Whereas in this ocean between the Meridion of 40° West and 50° or 60° East we have found Ice as far north as 51°. Bouvet found some in 48° and others have seen it in a much lower Latitude. It is however true that the greatest part of this Southern Continent (supposeing there is one) must lay within the Polar Circile where the Sea is so pestered with ice, that the land is thereby inacessible. The risk one runs in exploreing a coast in these unknown and Icy Seas, is so very great, that I can be bold to say, that no man will ever venture farther than I have done and that the lands which may lie to the South will never be explored. Thick fogs, Snow storms, Intense Cold and every other thing that can render Navigation dangerous one has to encounter and these difficulties are greatly heightned by the enexpressable horrid aspect of the Country, a Country doomed by Nature never once to feel the warmth of the

Suns rays, but to lie for ever buried under everlasting snow and ice. The Ports which may be on the Coast are in a manner wholy filled up with frozen Snow of a vast thickness, but if any should so far be open as to admit a ship in, it is ever dangerous to go in, for she runs a risk of being fixed there for ever, or coming out in an ice island. The islands and floats of ice on the Coast, the great falls from the ice clifts in the Port, or a heavy snow storm attended with a sharp frost, would prove equally fatal. After such an explanation as this the reader must not expect to find me much farther to the South. It is however not for want of inclination but other reasons. It would have been rashness in me to have risked all which had been done in the Voyage, in finding out and exploaring a Coast which when done would have answerd no end whatever, or been of the least use either to Navigation or Geography or indeed any other Science; Bouvets Discovery was yet before us, the existence of which was to be cleared up and lastly we were now not in a condition to undertake great things, nor indeed was there time had we been ever so well provided. These reasons induced me to alter the Course to East, with a very strong gale at North attended with an exceeding heavy fall of Snow, the quantity which fell into our sails was so great that we were obliged every now and then to throw the Ship up in the Wind to shake it out of the Sails, otherways neither them nor the Ship could have supported the wieght. In the evening it ceased to snow, the weather cleared up, the Wind backed to the West and we spent the night makeing two short boards under close reefed Top-sails and fore-sail. . . .

I had now made the circuit of the Southern Ocean in a high Latitude and traversed it in such a manner as to leave not the least room for the Possibility of there being a continent, unless near the Pole and out of the reach of Navigation; by twice visiting the Pacific Tropical Sea, I had not only settled the situation of some old discoveries but made there many new ones and left, I conceive, very little more to be done even in that part. Thus I flater my self that the intention of the Voyage has in every respect been fully Answered, the Southern Hemisphere sufficiently explored and a final end put to the searching after a Southern Continent, which has at times ingrossed the attention of some of the Maritime Powers for near two Centuries past and the Geographers of all ages. That there may be a Continent or large tract of land near the Pole, I will not deny, on the contrary I am of opinion there is, and it is probable that we have seen a part of it. The excessive cold, the many islands and vast floats of ice all tend to prove that there must be land to the South and that this Southern land must lie or extend farthest to the North opposite the Southern Atlantick and Indian Oceans, I have already assigned some reasons, to which I may add the greater degree of cold which we have found in these Seas, than in the Southern Pacific Ocean under the same parallels of Latitude. In this last Ocean the Mercury in the Thermometer seldom fell so low as the freezing point, till we were in Sixty and upwards, whereas in the others it fell frequently as low in the Latitude of fifty four: this was certainly owing to there being a greater quantity of Ice and extending farther to the North in these two Seas than in the other, and if Ice is first formed at or near land, of which I have no doubt, it will follow that the land also extends farther North. The formation or Coagulation of Ice Islands has not, to my knowledge, been throughly investigated: Some have supposed them to be formed by the freezing of the Water at the Mouths of large Rivers or great Cataracts and so accumulate till they are broke of by their own weight. My observations will not allow me to acquiesce in this opinion because we never found any of the Ice which we took up incorporated with Earth or any of its produce which I think it must, had it been coagulated In land waters. It is also a doubt with me that there are any Rivers in these Countries, the interior parts being so much elevated as never to enjoy heat sufficient to melt the snow in any quantity. It is very certain that we saw not a River or stream of Water on all the coast of Georgia, or on any of the Southern lands; nor did we ever see a stream of Water run from any of the Ice Islands. How are we then to suppose that there are large rivers in these Countries, the Vallies are covered many fathoms deep with everlasting snow and at the sea they terminate in Ice clifts of vast heights. It is here where the Ice islands are formed, not from streames of Water, but from Consolidated snow which is allmost continually falling or drifting down from the Mountains, especially in Winter when the frost must be intence. During that Season, these Ice clifts must so accumulate as to fill up all the Bays be they ever so large, this is a fact which cannot be doubted as we have seen it so in summer; also during that season the Snow may fix and consolidate to ice to most of the other coasts and there also form Ice clifts. These clifts accumulate by continual falls of snow and what drifts from the Mountains till they are no longer able to support their own weight and then large pieces break off which we call Ice islands. Such as have a flat even Surface must be of the Ice formed in the bays and before the flat Vallies, the others which have a spired unequal surface must be formed on or under the side of a Coast, composed of spired Rocks and precepices, or some such uneven surface, for we cannot suppose that snow alone, as it falls, can form on a plain surface, such as the Sea, such a variety of high spired peaks and hills as we have seen on many of the Ice isles. It is certainly more reasonable to suppose that they are formed on a Coast whose Surface is something similar to theirs. I have observed that all the Ice islands of any extent, and before they begin to break to pieces, are terminated by perpendicular clifts or sides of clear ice or frozen snow, always on one or more sides, but most generally all round. Many, and those of the largest size, who had a hilly and spired surface, have shewed a perpendicular clift or side from the summit of the highest peak down to its base. This to me was a convincing proof that these, as well as the flat isles, must have broke off from a substance like themselves, that is from some large tract of ice. . . .

If this imperfect account of the formation of these extraordinary floating islands of ice, which is written wholly from my own observation, does not convey some useful hints to some abler pen, it will however convey some Idea of the Lands where they are formed, Lands doomed by nature to everlasting frigidness and never once to feel the warmth of the Suns rays, whose horrible and savage aspect I have no words to describe; such are the lands we have descovered, what may we expect those to be which lie more to the South, for we may reasonably suppose that we have seen the best as lying most to the North, whoever has resolution and perseverance to clear up this point by proceding farther than I have done, I shall not envy him the honour of the discovery but I will be bold to say that the world will not be benefited by it.

# PART II

**THE WHALING AND SEALING ERA 1821-1839**

◻ *Captain Cook saw no use for the Antarctic regions, but he was a better navigator than prophet. He had spied seals and whales on South Georgia and other islands in the icy sea off South America. Whale oil was a valuable fuel in that pre-petroleum age, while the pelts of seals were precious commodities that could be sold at high prices in the Orient.*

*Whalers and sealers from England and the newborn United States headed for the far south as the nineteenth century began. Since their ventures were commercial ones, they kept their logs secret, unlike explorers such as Cook, who published their journals for the information of all. The early years of the sealing industry in the Antarctic are thus cloaked in mystery. We know, though, that a New England* skipper named Edmund Fanning went south on a seal-hunting voyage in 1800, and that by 1815 many ships had plundered the subantarctic islands, such as the Falklands, off the coast of Argentina.

In the mists beyond the sealing islands lay Antarctica: an upthrust thumb, a peninsula jutting from the unknown continent. Islands clustered along the borders of this peninsula, steppingstones that could lead men to the continent itself. As the demand for new whaling and sealing grounds grew, the hunters risked moving ever southward in search of profit.

In February, 1819, a merchant captain named William Smith, voyaging from Montevideo to Valparaiso via Cape Horn, met with stormy weather, and veered southward in search of clearer sailing. He came upon an island at 62°40′ S., 60° W., and on a return voyage in October of the same year he claimed it for England, naming it New South Britain. The island—soon to be renamed New South Shetland—was one of a group, the South Shetland Islands.

Two months later, Smith reported his discovery to Captain Shireff of H.M.S. Andromache, in Valparaiso. Shireff chartered Smith's brig, the Williams, and placed the master of the Andromache, Edward Bransfield, in command, with instructions to explore the islands Smith had found. About Bransfield we know very little, except that he was probably the first man to set eye on any part of the Antarctic continent. He reached the South Shetlands on January 16, 1820, explored the group for a week, and sailed southwest on January 27. Three days later he sighted land to the south. Exactly what he saw has been the subject of hot geographical debate for decades, but the evidence indicates that he was glimpsing the northern tip of what is now called the Antarctic Peninsula, a part of Antarctica proper.

One brief eyewitness report of Bransfield's voyage was published in an English magazine, The Literary Gazette, for November 24, 1821. Its author, a midshipman named Thomas Bone, said that a chain of islands was sighted on January 30, 1820: "The whole of these formed a prospect the most gloomy that can be imagined, and the only cheer the sight afforded was in the idea that this might be the long-sought Southern Continent, as land was undoubtedly seen in latitude 64°, and trending to the eastward."

A more detailed account is that of a Dr. Young, an English naval surgeon who accompanied the Williams under Bransfield. His *narrative, published anonymously in* The Edinburgh Philosophical Journal *for April, 1821, has priority as the earliest description of Bransfield's voyage. Bransfield's name is misspelled "Barnsfield" throughout.*   □

# EDWARD BRANSFIELD

*Notice of the Voyage of Edward Barnsfield, Master of his Majesty's Ship Andromache, to New South Shetland.*

About a twelvemonth ago, an English merchant brig, in performing a voyage to this port, made what they supposed to be land, several degrees to the southward of Cape Horn, and in a situation in which it is positively asserted that no land *can* exist. From the difference in opinion of those on board the vessel, and, from some other circumstances, little credit was attached to it at that time; but the master being fully convinced that what had been seen was actually land, determined to put it beyond a doubt, should he come round again. He accordingly made the land again last October, and having sailed along it for some considerable distance, he returned about the beginning of December to this port, and laid before the Naval Commander in Chief here, such charts and views, as induced him to hire the same brig on account of Government, to complete the discovery. The command of the expedition was given to Mr Edward Barnsfield, master of H. M. S. Andromache, with three midshipmen from the same ship, to assist him in his nautical researches; and as it was deemed necessary to send a medical officer, I went as a volunteer on the occasion. We sailed from Valparaiso on the 20th of December 1819, but did not arrive on cruising ground till the 16th of January 1820, having been almost constantly harassed with baffling winds and calms till we arrived in a high southern latitude. On that day, however, we had the good fortune to discover the land to the south-eastward, extending on both bows as far as the eye could reach. At a distance, its limits could scarcely be distinguished from the light white clouds which floated on the tops of the mountains. Upon a nearer approach, however, every object became distinct. The whole line of coast appeared high, bold, and rugged; rising abruptly from the sea in perpendicular snowy cliffs, except here and there where the naked face of a barren black rock shewed itself amongst them. In the interior, the land, or rather the snow, sloped gradually and gently upwards into high hills, which appeared to be situated some miles from the sea. No attempt was made to land here, as the weather became rather threatening, and a dense fog came on, which soon shut every thing from our view at more than a hundred yards distance. A boat had been sent away in the mean time to try for anchorage; but they found the coast completely surrounded by dangerous sunken rocks, and the bottom so foul, and the water so deep, that it was not thought prudent to go nearer the shore in the brig, especially as it was exposed to almost every wind. The boat brought off some seals and penguins which had been shot among the rocks; but they reported them to be the only animated objects they had discovered. The latitude of this part of the coast was found to be 62°26′ S. and its longitude to be 60°54′ W. . . .

Three days after this, we discovered and anchored in an extensive bay, about two degrees farther to the eastward, where we were enabled to land, and examine the country. Words can scarcely be found to describe its barrenness and sterility. Only one small spot of land was discovered on which a landing could be effected upon the Main, every other part of the bay being bounded by the same inaccessible cliffs which we had met with before. We landed on a shingle beach, on which there was a heavy surf beating, and from which a small stream of fresh-water ran into the sea. Nothing was to be seen but the rugged surface of barren rocks, upon which myriads of sea-fowls had laid their eggs, and which they were then hatching. These birds were so little accustomed to the sight of any other animal, that, so far from being intimidated by our approach, they even disputed our landing, and we were obliged forcibly to open a passage for ourselves through them. They consisted principally of four species of the penguin; with albatrosses, gulls, pintadoes, shags, sea-swallows, and a bird about the size and shape of the common pigeon, and of a milk-white plumage, the only species we met with that was not web-footed. We also fell in with a number of the animals described in Lord Anson's voyage as the Sea-Lion, and said by him to be so plentiful at Juan Fernandez, many of which we killed. Seals were also pretty numerous; but though we walked some distance into the country, we could observe no trace either of inhabitants, or of any terrestrial animal. It would be impossible, indeed, for any but beasts of prey to subsist here, as we met with no sort of vegetation except here and there small patches of stunted grass growing upon the surface of the thick coat of dung which the sea-fowls left in the crevices of the rocks, and a species of moss, which occasionally we met with adhering to the rocks themselves. In short, we traced the land nine or ten degrees east and west, and about three degrees north and south, and found its general appearance always the same, high, mountainous, barren, and universally covered with snow, except where the rugged summits of a black rock appeared through it, resembling a small island in the midst of the ocean; but from the lateness of the season, and the almost constant fogs in which we were enveloped, we could not ascertain whether it formed part of a continent, or was only a group of islands. If it is insular, there must be *some* of an immense extent, as we found a gulf nearly 150 miles in depth, out of which we had some difficulty in finding our way back again.

The discovery of this land must be of great interest in a geographical point of view, and its importance to the commercial interests of our country, must be evident from the very great numbers of whales with which we were daily surrounded; and the multitudes of the finest fur-seals and sea-lions which we met both at sea and on every point of the coast, or adjacent rocky islands, on which we were able to land. The fur of the former is the finest and longest I have ever seen; and from their having now become scarce in every other part of these seas, and the great demand for them both in Europe and India, they will, I have no doubt, become, as soon as the discovery is made public, a favourite speculation amongst our merchants. The oil procured from the sea-lion is, I am told, nearly equal in value to that of the spermaceti whale. And the great number of whales we saw every where near the land, must also be an important thing to our merchants, as they have lately been said to be very scarce to the northward.

We left the coast on the 21st of March, and arrived at this place on the 14th of April, having touched at Juan Fernandez for refreshment.

H. M. S. SLANEY,
*Valparaiso, 26th May 1820.*

◻ *Since Bransfield's voyage is not documented with complete certainty, America's geographers have long put their own man forward as the discoverer of Antarctica. He is Nathaniel Palmer, born in Connecticut in 1799. Despite the fairly convincing evidence of Bransfield's charts, Palmer's partisans insist that he was the first to glimpse the Antarctic mainland.*

*Palmer was a protégé of Edmund Fanning, the veteran New England whaling and sealing captain. In 1819, Fanning took Palmer on as second mate of the brig* Hersilia, *part of an expedition setting out to look for new sealing islands. In February, 1820, Palmer reached the South Shetlands, discovered only the year before by William Smith and until then regarded by the English as their private hunting grounds. When Palmer returned to Connecticut later that year and told Fanning of the islands, a new expedition was outfitted at once, five ships in all, with Nat Palmer in command of the sloop* Hero. *He was not quite twenty-one.*

*The New Englanders sighted the South Shetlands on November 10, 1820. Captain Benjamin Pendleton, who commanded the entire party, ascended a high point on Deception Island, one of the Shetlands, and thought he saw land to the southward. He asked Palmer to investigate. On November 16, Palmer set out through an icy sea, and the following day approached the land. His entry in the log of the* Hero *for November 17 appears to show that he came within hailing distance of the Antarctic Peninsula—ten months after Bransfield, it would seem.*

*The log of the* Hero *is in the Library of Congress. Palmer's entry for November 17, 1820—the only formal statement he ever made about his glimpse of Antarctica—is as follows:* ◻

46

# NATHANIEL PALMER

These 24 hours commences with fresh Breeses from SWest and Pleasant    at 8 P.M. got over under the Land found the sea filled with imense Ice Bergs    at 12 hove Too under the Jib    Laid off & on until morning—at 4 A.M. made sail in shore and Discovered— a strait—Trending SSW & NNE—it was Literally filled with Ice and the shore inaccessible    we thought it not Prudent to Venture in ice    Bore away to the Northerd & saw 2 small islands and the shore every where Perpendicular we stood across toward friesland Course NNW—the Latitude of the mouth of the strait was 63–45 S    Ends with fine weather wind at SSW.

□   *Nat Palmer left no account at all of his second most celebrated Antarctic exploit. We must rely on secondhand information, and, as we shall see, not the most reliable secondhand information at that.*

*Our source is Edmund Fanning, who told the story in his book,* Voyages Round the World; with Selected Sketches of Voyages to the South Seas, North and South Pacific Oceans, China, etc., *Performed under the Command and Agency of the Author* (New York, Collins & Hannay, 1833). *Fanning supposedly heard the story from Palmer after the latter's return to Connecticut in 1822.*

*According to Fanning, Palmer was on his way back to the South Shetlands from his viewing of Antarctica in November, 1820, when he encountered a Russian exploring party under the command of Captain Fabian Gottlieb von Bellingshausen. Bellingshausen's own report on this meeting is considerably less dramatic than Fanning's, and places it two months later, in January, 1821. Fanning's book was reprinted in abridged form in 1924 under the title* Voyages & Discoveries in the South Seas, 1792-1832, *as Publication Number 6 of the Marine Research Society of Salem, Massachusetts.*   □

# PALMER'S VOYAGE IN EDMUND FANNING'S ACCOUNT

The next season after the *Hersilia's* return from the South Shetlands, a fleet of vessels, consisting of the brig *Frederick*, Captain Benjamin Pendleton, the senior commander, the brig *Hersilia*, Captain James P. Sheffield, schooners *Express*, Captain E. Williams, *Free Gift*, Captain F. Dunbar, and sloop *Hero*, Captain N. B. Palmer, was fitted out at Stonington, Connecticut, on a voyage to the South Shetlands. From Captain Pendleton's report, as rendered on their return, it appeared that while the fleet lay at anchor in Yankee Harbor, Deception Island, during the season of 1820 and 21, being on the lookout from an elevated station, on the mountain of the island during a very clear day he had discovered mountains (one a volcano in operation) in the south; this was what is now known by the name of Palmer's Land; from the statement it will be perceived how this name came deservedly to be given it, and by which it is now current in the modern charts. To examine this newly discovered land, Captain N. B. Palmer, in the sloop *Hero*, a vessel but little rising forty tons, was despatched; he found it to be an extensive mountainous country, more sterile and dismal if possible, and more heavily loaded with ice and snow, than the South Shetlands; there were sea leopards on its shore, but no fur seals; the main part of its coast was ice bound, although it was in the midsummer of this hemisphere, and a landing consequently difficult.

On the *Hero's* return passage to Yankee Harbor she got becalmed in a thick fog between the South Shetlands and the newly discovered continent, but nearest the former. When this began to clear away, Captain Palmer was surprised to find his little barque between a frigate and sloop of war, and instantly run up the United States' flag; the frigate and sloop of war then set the Russian colors. Soon after this a boat was seen pulling from the commodore's ship for the *Hero*, and when alongside, the lieutenant presented an invitation from his commodore for Captain Pendleton to go on board; this, of course, was accepted. These ships he then found were the two discovery ships sent out by the Emperor Alexander of Russia, on a voyage round the world. To the commodore's interrogatory if he had any knowledge of those islands then in sight, and what they were, Captain Pendleton replied, he was well acquainted with them, and that they were the South Shetlands, at the same time making a tender of his services to pilot the ships into a good harbor at Deception Island, the nearest by, where water and refreshments such as the island afforded could be obtained; he also informing the Russian officer that his vessel belonged to a fleet of five sail, out of Stonington, under command of Captain B. Pendleton, and then at anchor in Yankee Harbor, who, would most cheerfully render any assistance in his power. The commodore thanked him kindly, "but previous to our being enveloped in the fog," said he, "we had sight of those islands, and concluded we had made a discovery, but behold, when the fog lifts, to my great surprise, here is an American vessel apparently in as fine order as if it were but yesterday she had left the United States; not only this, but her master is ready to pilot my vessels into port; we must surrender the palm to you Americans," continued he, very flatteringly. His astonishment was yet more increased when Captain Palmer informed him of the existence of an immense extent of land to the south, whose mountains might be seen from the mast-head when the fog should clear away entirely. Captain Palmer, while on board the frigate, was entertained in the most friendly manner, and the commodore was so forcibly struck with the circumstances of the case, that he named the coast then to the south, Palmer's Land; by this name it is recorded on the recent Russian and English charts and maps which have been published since the return of these ships. . . .

The following season, in 1821 and 22, Captain Pendleton was again at Yankee Harbor, with the Stonington fleet; he then once more despatched Captain Palmer in the sloop *James Monroe*, an excellent vessel of upwards of 80 tons, well calculated for such duties, and by her great strength well able to venture in the midst of and wrestle with the ice. Captain Palmer reported on his return, that after proceeding to the southward, he met ice fast and firmly attached to the shore of Palmer's Land; he then traced the coast to the eastward, keeping as near the shore as the ice would suffer; at times he was able to come along shore, at other points he could not approach within from one to several miles, owing to the firm ices, although it was in December and January, the middle summer months in this hemisphere. In this way he coasted along this continent upwards of fifteen degrees, viz. from 64 and odd, down below the 49th of west longitude. The coast, as he proceeded to the eastward, became more clear of ice, so that he was able to trace the shore better; in 61 degrees 41 minutes south latitude, a strait was discovered which he named Washington Strait. This he entered, and about a league within came to a fine bay which he named Monroe Bay. At the head of this was a good harbor; here they anchored, calling it Palmer's Harbor.

The Captain landed on the beach [of an island] among a number of those beautiful amphibious animals, the spotted glossy-looking sea leopard, and that rich golden-colored noble bird, the king penguin. Making their way through these, the Captain and party traversed the coast and country for some distance around without discovering the least appearance of vegetation excepting the winter moss.

The sea leopards were the only animals found. There were, however, vast numbers of birds, several different species of the penguin, Port Egmont hens, white pigeons, a variety of gulls, and many kinds of oceanic birds. The valleys and gulleys were mainly filled with those never dissolved icebergs, their square and perpendicular fronts, several hundred feet in height, glistening most splendidly in a variety of colors as the sun shone upon them.

The mountains on the coast, as well as those to all appearance in the interior, were generally covered with snow, except when their black peaks were seen here and there peeping out.

□   *Fanning's romantic account of the Palmer-Bellingshausen meeting went unchallenged for many years, largely because Bellingshausen's own version, published in Russian in 1831, remained without an English translation until 1945. Fabian Gottlieb von Bellings-*

hausen, an aristocratic Russian naval officer forty-one years old, was selected by Czar Alexander I to lead a voyage of discovery to the Antarctic, "to help in extending the fields of knowledge" and to investigate "the possibilities of establishing future sea-communications or places for the repair of ships," in 1819. With two ships, the Vostok and the Mirnyi, Bellingshausen reached South Georgia in the final days of that year, and on January 27, 1820, crossed the Antarctic Circle—the first commander to do so since Cook. Bellingshausen repeated Cook's feat of circumnavigating Antarctica, though the girdle of ice surrounding the continent prevented him from getting close enough actually to see it. He crossed the Circle repeatedly, making important scientific observations and discovering new land off the Antarctic continent: a large island he called Peter I Island, and a mountainous place given the name of Alexander I Land, which later proved to be an island also. Bellingshausen had been in the Antarctic for nearly a year when he had his meeting with Nat Palmer early in 1821; he returned to Russia in July of that year, and lived until 1852.

Bellingshausen's narrative was published at St. Petersburg in 1831 as Two Voyages of exploration in the Antarctic Ocean and a circumnavigation of the world in the years 1819, 1820, 1821. A partial German translation by H. Gravelius was published at Leipzig in 1902. Professor Edward Bullough of Cambridge University prepared an English version in 1924, which was later examined and revised by other hands, and finally published by The Hakluyt Society in 1945 under the editorial supervision of Frank Debenham as The Voyage of Captain Bellingshausen to the Antarctic Seas, 1819-1821. The following excerpts from that translation are reprinted here by permission of The Hakluyt Society.   □

# FABIAN GOTTLIEB VON BELLINGSHAUSEN

Our voyage among the ice had now run into a second summer and we had again encountered everywhere icefields, high flat icebergs, and masses of ice of irregular formation, which fill the Antarctic

Ocean: I think therefore that it will not be superfluous if I here set down my opinions on the origin of this ice, on its formation into large fields (which we had had occasion to observe extend for 300 miles in some cases), on the formation of large flat icebergs, and finally on their transformation into irregular bergs, with sharp-pointed summits or of varying outward appearance.

On February 5th, 1820, when we were in Lat. 68° 58′ S., Long. 15° 52′ W., and 9° of frost, I hung out at an equal height from above the sea two tins side by side, filled the first with fresh and the second with salt water. At 8 o'clock the following morning, when we were out of the ice, the temperature was 27° F., and the water was found to be frozen in both tins. Taking care that the ice did not melt in the sun, we examined the water in both tins, and found that the ice from the fresh water was more compact and that the salt water ice, although it was of the same thickness, was more brittle and consisted of thin horizontal layers. The top layers had already fused with each other, but nearer the bottom they became more and more brittle, so that the very lowest layers were still separated. When we placed this brittle ice in a shady place with the layers standing on end, and when the salt water in it had drained off, we found on melting the ice that the water was almost sweet, and if I had had the patience to let all the salt water off no doubt the water from the melted ice would have been entirely fresh. As a better proof I can mention the fact that we constantly broke off ice formed by the frost from the spray and foam in the form of icicles or of a whole sheath from the stays about the head of the vessel, and the water from this ice proved to be quite fresh.

This experiment, contrary to the opinion of many writers, proves that ice is formed from salt water just as from fresh water, except that it requires a few more degrees of frost. . . .

When we were in high southern latitudes in the midst of ice we very often noticed small clear stretches quite ready to freeze with 7° to 8° of frost. On the surface of the sea the very thinnest skin of ice was heaped up in layers by the wind, each layer exerting pressure on the other, and the resulting parallel layers were half a foot to a foot in thickness. At the same time they were transformed by the frost into hard ice, which was broken up into pieces by wind and waves, and those pieces pressing one on another congealed and formed large ice blocks especially in the heavy winters. If we suppose that in the southern hemisphere, as in the northern, the hardest winter frosts occur rather when there is no wind, then the sea can very easily freeze even during slight frosts, especially in bays where hard stationary ice exists; and then the first swell will begin to break up this ice, beginning from the edges, after which the process continues. All these blocks of ice with which the Antarctic Ocean is crowded are carried by winds and currents, and are finally pressed into one large tract, when their reciprocal pressure forces them one on the top of the other, forming thick large masses. We happened to see such compressed or continuous ice formations stretching over 300 miles from west to east, and if the breadth from north to south corresponded to, or even exceeded, this distance, as is highly probable, there is no doubt that the ice in the centre is entirely firm, freezes together, is further added to by falling snow, hail and sleet, and is finally transformed into solid ice. In this way the ice sinks in the water as its thickness is increased on the top, and as it was found from experiments carried out by us that ice is formed also from below by the addition of thin layers, it is evident that ice blocks in the sea can increase in thickness from above and below, while maintaining themselves in equilibrium, that is seven-eighths remaining under water and an eighth part showing above the surface.

As the ice does not increase equally in all directions it cannot maintain its equilibrium in all cases and, in consequence, fractures occur in various places. This may also happen from a heavy fall of snow near one edge of the ice. Farther south the freezing of the ice from below must be greater than in the north. The ice breaks into large pieces from various causes and is then dispersed by storms or currents. Again, ice less submerged is exposed to stronger action from the winds than that with a greater submerged mass. These broken masses of ice, being separated from each other, form icebergs of various sizes. Icebergs with flat surfaces almost always have sheer edges. In time of frost they continue to grow by the addition of thin layers* under water and are added to by snow, which is afterwards transformed into ice by the first frost. We often observed that the

* At a depth of 230 fathoms experiments showed the water to be colder than on the surface of the sea, at that depth it was 2° and on the surface 1° below freezing. [Bellingshausen's note.]

surface of this flat ice became irregular in warm weather through the action of the water which flowed from it, but afterwards, when snow and frost set in, it resumed its regular formation. When sailing past ice we often observed this change taking place; on some icebergs new layers could be distinguished from the old by their whiteness.

At the end of the present summer [1821] we encountered more icebergs of irregular and misshaped formations. These irregular icebergs are formed from flat icebergs, probably in the following manner. All icebergs have flat surfaces to begin with. In the summer they suffer damage on the side exposed to greater heat; the opposite side, preserving its original consistency, outweighs the other, and then the ice begins to incline. We encountered many of these formations and we observed the inclination of a small iceberg when we knocked off a piece from one of its sides with a cannon ball. Thus, the more these icebergs lose their equilibrium, the greater is their inclination; finally, when they turn over with one edge upwards, they become either pointed in shape or assume some other quite irregular form. After such a capsize the ice, which was formerly submerged, stands up out of the water and is a beautiful green-blue in colour.

These pointed icebergs are higher than the flat-topped ones, and sometimes look like a Gothic building with towers, obelisks, or monuments on pedestals, etc. They are more subject to change and to disintegration into the small irregular blocks of ice which one encounters everywhere when navigating the higher southern latitudes.

The pieces of ice which remain whole throughout the summer and are detached from the edges of flat-topped blocks of ice are carried by the wind and stream, and may encounter a compact icefield, or may, in the aforesaid manner, unite, grow and divide and float about as huge separate icebergs similar to the others.[1]

Huge icebergs, which as the pole is approached rise in size into veritable mountains, I call "mother-icebergs". Assuming that if in the height of summer there is a temperature of 9° freezing, farther south the cold will certainly not decrease, I therefore conclude that

[1] The only serious fallacy in these hypotheses is in the confusion between sea ice, frozen on the sea, and icebergs which are either land ice or snow masses collected over a period of years. [Debenham's note.]

54

this ice must extend across the Pole and must be immovable and attached in places to shallows or to such islands as Peter I Island, which undoubtedly exist in the high southern latitudes and near the land, which we thought must exist in the neighbourhood of the longitude and latitude where we saw sea swallows. These birds, although their toes are joined by a thin membrane, belong to the coast and are not sea birds. It is worthy of note that all sea birds, particularly those living in high latitudes and feeding on the surface of the sea, have curved beaks, but terns, gulls and other shore birds have straight beaks. We also saw sea swallows about South Georgia and Peter I Island, but we never encountered them at any distance from land. . . .

13th [of January, 1821].  Towards noon the wind, which was blowing from the south-east, fell completely; the clouds all drifted towards the north, and the temperature was 2° above zero. We were then in Lat. 67° 36′ 09″ S., Long. 86° 8′ 15″ W., variation 33° 36′ E., and steered to the south-east. During the calm we lowered a rowing boat and Messrs Zavodovski, Lyeskov and Demidov shot several grey albatrosses and some of those birds which we had seen for the first time on the previous day, as well as several polar birds. From this time we travelled southwards with variable winds.

14th.  After midnight fine snow fell frequently; no ice was encountered anywhere. In the morning sufficient sea water was heated for the entire crew to wash themselves. They washed in this way every two weeks, cleanliness, especially in cold climates, being indispensable for the preservation of health. At noon we were in Lat. 68° 15′ 48″ S., Long. 85° 07′ 17″ W. From midday the wind shifted from south by east; we changed to a S.E. by ½ E. course close to the wind. Soon the sky became overcast and the wind began to freshen; we took in the top-gallant sail, and took a reef in the topsail. At 11 o'clock it rained. To-day the same birds and Egmont hens appeared, but the white albatrosses had entirely left us, and do not frequent these higher latitudes. On the other hand, grey ones always accompanied us. These birds were encountered all the way from the equator to high latitudes.

15th.  At noon we were in Lat. 68° 30′ 19″ S., Long. 80° 46′ 51″ W. We proceeded slowly towards the east and south with variable wind; in the evening hail fell. The birds which we had seen on the evening before flew round us in great numbers. In the stomachs of the albatrosses which were shot we found a quantity of feathers and egg-shells; probably these birds had recently been to some land unknown to us for food.

To-day we changed the iron knee in my cabin. We remade this out of strip-iron after the manner of a laminated spring, of three leaves, and fastened it under the beam. We were often uneasy about the weakness of the upper parts of the ship, despite the fact that we had reduced the masts and yards, lowered all the guns on the decks into the hold and orlop deck, and lashed the boats arranged athwartships near the mizzen mast to the taffrail.

16th. At midnight, with a light wind from the south-south-west, we travelled close-hauled on the starboard tack to the south-east. The sky was covered with clouds, and the temperature was 30° F. At 3.0 a.m. the wind freshened. At 8 o'clock we saw the ice blink from solid icefields to the south-east. Towards noon the weather cleared and we fixed our position as Lat. 69° 09′ 42″ S., Long. 77° 43′ 21″ W.; there was 1° of frost. At 2.0 p.m. from the look-out we saw continuous ice, in the middle of which several large icebergs were wedged. At 3 o'clock we observed an unusual change of colour on the surface of the sea. This phenomenon immediately caught our attention, as we had been so long accustomed to see the bluish colour of the sea and now it had suddenly grown darker. We hove to and cast the lead: we found no bottom at 170 fathoms and yet we began to think that land was near. Seeing the impossibility of going farther south, on account of the ice, we steered to the north-east along the icefield which formed projecting headlands. Here we met snow petrels, Egmont hens, and terns. These last I always looked upon as infallible indications of the nearness of land, because I believe them to be shore birds. In the evening we were in Lat. 69° 08′ S., Long. 76° 51′ 46″ W., variation 32° 3′ E. At 7.0 p.m. penguins were calling to each other round the ships, and we saw a seal lying on the ice, probably of the species we had previously encountered.

The southern portion of the sky was brightly lit, and all the remainder covered with clouds. We continued to skirt the low-lying field of ice.

17th. At midnight the temperature was 9° below freezing point; on the lower deck in the crew's quarters it was 54° F. and the temperature of the sea was 30° F. At 5.0 a.m. there was a slight wind from the east and the sun lit up the horizon, but the temperature was only 23° F.

At 11.0 a.m. we sighted land. One of its headlands stretched to the northward and ended in a high mountain which was separated by an isthmus from another mountain chain extending to the south-west. I advised Mr. Lazarev of this. It was the most beautiful day that could have been desired in high southern latitudes. From observations taken we fixed our position at Lat. 68° 29′ 02″ S., Long. 75° 40′ 21″ W. At this time the above-mentioned cape was 40 miles east-south-east from us, from which it follows that the position of the high mountain separated by the isthmus is in Lat. 68° 43′ 20″ S., Long. 73° 09′ 36″ W. A light east wind was blowing; we altered course to south-south-east, as this tack brought us closer up to the land. At 3:30 p.m. we passed quite close to drifting ice floes and had to turn away without being able to approach the shore. At that time ice floes closing up were visible from the look-out on all sides and prevented us from approaching the land within a closer distance than 40 miles. We considered ourselves very fortunate, because the clear weather and cloudless sky permitted us to see and survey the shore.

As we were proceeding to the higher southern latitudes in execution of the command of His Imperial Majesty the Emperor, I felt it my duty to call the land discovered by us "Alexander I Land", as it was due to him that this discovery was made. Monuments erected to great men are erased from the face of the earth by time the destroyer, but "Peter I Island" and "Alexander I Land" are indestructible monuments which will commemorate the name of our Emperors to the remotest posterity.

I call this discovery "land" because its southern extent disappeared beyond the range of our vision. The shore was covered with snow, but there was no snow on the slope of the mountain and on the steep cliffs. The slight change of colour of the surface of the sea suggested that the land is extensive or at any rate does not consist only of that part which we could see. . . .

24th [of January, 1821]. At 11.0 p.m. the wind blew from south-west by south, but the fog and damp continued until 2.0 a.m. on the following day. At this time I made night signals to the *Mirnyi* to come astern and alter course to south-east by east; the sky was covered with thin clouds and the stars glimmered through them, but very thick black clouds to the east hid the land we were looking for. We travelled with a light wind at a rate of 7 or 8 knots, with a strong swell from the west. We met numerous pintades, blue petrels, albatrosses, cormorants and terns.

At 7.0 a.m. there was a hail from the forecastle: "Land in sight above the clouds!" We were all greatly pleased, for we possessed two pieces of information about the existence of this land; one . . . from Baron de Teille von Seraskerken, and the other was given us by the Captain of an East Indian ship in Port Jackson. There was a difference of 1° of latitude in the positions given in the two accounts. I relied more on the first report. The weather seemed to us very warm; the thermometer showed 40° F. At 8.0 a.m. we set our course S. 17° E., with the intention of approaching the south side of New Shetland, in the event of the land sighted not proving to be a continent. In the mist we saw bearing N. 89° E. the northern cape of the western shore of South Shetland, on which rose a hill; the southwestern cape lay S. 37° E. from us. The latter runs into the sea in a sharp stone ridge, and rises out of the water, ending in two high cliffs like Peak Freezeland, which has a height above sea level of 751 feet. Between these two cliffs lie rocks on which the sea breaks. On the summit of one of the cliffs are two projections which stand out like an ass's ears. Owing to the thick mist we could not examine the north-west shore line but there was much less snow and ice on that side than on the shore which faces south.

At noon we doubled the high projecting cliffs forming the southwestern extremity of New Shetland. The weather cleared and we were able to fix our position, which proved to be Lat. 63° 09' 14" S., Long. 63° W.; variation 24° 24' E. The lead did not touch bottom at 115 fathoms. According to the above-mentioned observation, the position of the highest cliff to the west is Lat. 63° 06' S., Long. 63° 04' W.

From noon the *Vostok* sailed on the course N. 50½ ° E., parallel to the high steep shore which it seems hardly possible to scale from the south; the heights above the shore were lost in the clouds. After proceeding 13 miles at a distance of 2½ or 3 miles from the shore, we were becalmed. Here the lead did not touch bottom at 200 fathoms. This led us to put farther out to sea again to pick up the wind. The eastern cape, surrounded by a small field of low-lying ice, bore N. 10° 32′ E. distant 9½ miles; the length of the island is therefore 20½ miles and its width 8 miles; the centre of it being in Lat. 62° 58′ S., Long. 62° 49′ W. The rocky walls on this shore had a blackish appearance and the stratification appeared vertical. Otherwise the shore was covered with snow and ice wherever they could lie. The northern cape consisted of high mountains. I called this island "Borodino Island" in commemoration of the famous battle.

From the look-out we saw rocks ahead, and beyond them more land, separated from the eastern end of the high island lying to the westward by a strait 20 miles wide. There was a light wind, and, when we passed across the strait, there was a noticeable swell which caused the ships to roll. At 10.0 p.m. we passed the south side of the land visible ahead of us. It rises towards the centre and is surrounded on almost every side by rocks showing above the water. The length of this land is 9 miles and its breadth 5 miles, and its position is Lat. 62° 42′ S., Long. 61° 39′ W. I called this land "Little Yaroslavetz", in memory of the victory won near this town.

Before darkness came on we put about south-south-east from shore and shortened sail with the intention of keeping in the vicinity of this place till daybreak of the following day. Meanwhile the *Mirnyi* had time to come up with us. At night heavy dew fell; the temperature was about 34° F.

*25th.* At 2.0 a.m. I made night signals to turn, and we returned to the point where we had finished our survey of the shore the day before. We made more sail. At 3 o'clock we approached the shore and rounded the eastern cape of Little Yaroslavetz, from which a reef of rocks extends for 1½ miles. At this time we were at the entrance to a strait 3½ miles wide, running in the direction west-north-west. It was doubtful whether a ship could pass through this strait because of the quantity of submerged rocks and the breakers. In front of the low-lying shore we saw eight British and American sealing vessels at anchor near the north-east shore of this strait—the depth at the entrance to the strait was 23 fathoms, bottom thin mud. Proceeding farther along the southern shore to the east-south-east, I soon saw to starboard of our course a high island, with steep cliffs and its heights covered with clouds. I called this island after Major-General Baron de Teille in grateful recognition of the information he had given us. "Teille Island" is in Lat. 62° 58′ S., Long. 61° 55′ W.; it has a circumference of 20 miles and is separated from the high rocky headlands opposite by a strait 11 miles wide.

At 10 o'clock we entered the strait and encountered a small American sealing boat. I lay to, despatched a boat, and waited for the Captain of the American boat. The lead did not touch bottom at 115 fathoms. Soon after Mr Palmer arrived in our boat and informed us that he had been here for four months' sailing in partnership with three American ships. They were engaged in killing and skinning seals, whose numbers were perceptibly diminishing. There were as many as eighteen vessels about at various points, and not infrequently differences arose amongst the sealers, but so far it had not yet come to a fight. Mr. Palmer told me that the above-mentioned Captain Smith, the discoverer of New Shetland, was on the brig *Williams*, that he had succeeded in killing as many as 60,000 seals, whilst the whole fleet of sealers had killed 80,000. As other sealers also were competing in the destruction of the seals there could be no doubt that round the South Shetland Islands just as at South Georgia and Macquarie Islands the number of these sea animals will rapidly decrease. Sea elephants, of which there also had been many, had already moved from these shores farther out to sea. According to Mr Palmer the bay in which we saw the eight ships lying at anchor is protected from all winds and has a depth of 18 fathoms, thin mud. Owing to the peculiar nature of the bottom the vessels frequently got adrift even with two anchors out. Two British ships and one American one had dragged their anchors and been wrecked. Mr Zavodovski shot a tern with blackish feathers above the neck, light grey on the back. The beak and claws were of a bright red colour. Round about us birds were diving, penguins were calling, albatrosses, gulls, pintades, blue petrels and cormorants were flying about in all directions. Mr Palmer soon returned to his ship, and we proceeded along the shore.

◻ *In that busy season of 1820-21, Palmer and Bellingshausen were not the only captains operating in Antarctic waters. About thirty American sealers and some two dozen British ones were in the South Shetlands. More than one skipper went off on a brief exploring voyage, and one of them, John Davis of the New Haven sealer Huron, may have been the first to make a landfall on the Antarctic mainland. Davis' log, in the Yale University Library, is too vague to provide certain proof, but if he did reach continental Antarctica, he is the only man in history whose name can be recorded as the first to set foot on a continent. His entry for February 7, 1821, declares:* ◻

# JOHN DAVIS

Commences with open Cloudy Weather and Light winds a Standing for a Large Body of Land in that direction SE at 10 A.M. close in with it, out Boat and Sent her on Shore to look for Seal at 11 A.M. the Boat returned but found no signs of Seal at noon our Latitude was 64°-01' South. Stood up a Large Bay, the Land high and covered intirely with Snow the wind comming Round to the North'd & Eastward with Thick weather. Tacked ship and headed off Shore. at 4 P.M. fresh Gale and Thick weather with Snow. Reefed the main Sail and took the Bonnet off the fore sail. [The day] Ends with Strong Gales at ENE with Cloudy unpleasant weather attended with Snow and a heavy Sea. Concluded to make the Best of our way for the Ship. I think this Southern Land to be a Continent.

◻ *Another American sealer sailed south from the Shetlands a few days after John Davis, likewise saw land, and came to the same conclusion, that the land was continental. He was Christopher Burdick of the* Huntress, *whose log entry for February 12, 1821, is quoted here. Like the Davis log above, Burdick's was published in* The Voyage of the Huron and the Huntress, *by Edouard A. Stackpole (Hartford, Conn., Connecticut Printers, Inc., 1955).*  □

# CHRISTOPHER BURDICK

Begins with Light airs and variable with Calms pleasant weather at Meredian Lat by obs. 63. .17 S President Island Bearing North 3 Leagues mount Pisco SW b W dist 7 Leagues the Peak of Frezeland NE ½ W 11 Leagues Deception Island NE by N 8 Leagues and a small low Island SSW 6 Leagues to which I am bound and Land from South to ESE which I suppose to be a Continent. Later part fresh breze at North. At 6 P.M. came to anchor under low island among a parcel of rocks Sent the Boat on shore She returned with 22 Seal So end thes 24 hours.

□   *The activities of Palmer, Davis, Bransfield, and Burdick centered on the western side of what is now called the Antarctic Peninsula. A few years after their voyages, a Scot named James Weddell carried out an extraordinary journey to the east. Weddell, who had served in the Royal Navy during the War of 1812, had been released from service in 1816, and several years later he joined the ranks of the seal hunters. In 1820-21, Weddell scouted and charted the South Shetlands, returning to the sealing grounds in 1821-22 and again in 1822-23. In January, 1823, commanding the brig* Jane *with twenty-two men, Weddell sailed south in search of new sealing grounds, accompanied by a smaller ship, the* Beaufoy, *with fourteen men under Matthew Brisbane.*

*No land appeared, and Weddell and Brisbane boldly continued toward the Pole. They surpassed Cook's southerly record of 71° 10′ and eventually reached 74° 15′ S., closer to the Pole than anyone*

*would get for decades. Nor has anyone been able to duplicate
Weddell's feat precisely, since he traveled through an open sea that
in most other years has been covered with a solid shelf of ice. The
sea he entered, lying to the east of the Antarctic Peninsula, is known
today as the Weddell Sea. A species of seal that he discovered on his
1820-21 voyage also bears his name.*

*Weddell was a man of little education, but he valued knowledge
highly and took careful observations with the few scientific instruments aboard. Though the motive of his voyage was profit, that he
was more than simply a sealing skipper is clear from his own testimony. When he returned to England in May, 1824, he wrote an account of his trip entitled* A Voyage Towards the South Pole, Performed in the Years 1822-'24 *(London, Longman, Hurst, Rees,
Orme, Brown, and Green, 1825). It was well received and a second
edition was necessary. The passages that follow are from the first
edition of Weddell's book. Little is known of his life after his great
exploit in Antarctica; he died in 1834 at the age of forty-seven.* □

# JAMES WEDDELL

On 27th [of January, 1823] at noon we had reached the latitude of
64° 58′, our longitude by means of chronometers was 39° 40′ 30″.
The variation of the compass at 10 o'clock in the forenoon, by
azimuth, was 10° 37′ east. The temperature of air in the shade was
37°, that of water 34°; but in the rays of the sun, when clouded, the
thermometer rose to 48 degrees. The weather being here so much
more settled than in the lower latitudes of 60 and 61 degrees, could
we but find land with produce, I had little doubt, but that in three
or four weeks both vessels might have had their cargoes on board.
As, however, we were to the southward of South Shetland, I stood
back to the northward, considering it probable that land might be
found between the South Orkneys and Sandwich Land; and as the
summer season was now far advanced, it was advisable to examine
those lower latitudes while the nights were yet but short,—since
darkness added to fog makes navigation in an icy sea still more
dangerous.

We stood to the northward with the wind between S.E. and S.W., and on the 29th at noon our latitude at observation was 61° 18', and longitude by chronometers 40° 32' 15". The temperature of air was 34°, that of water 34°. Ice islands were our constant companions, and indeed they had become so familiar that they were little dreaded.

At 11 o'clock at night we passed within two ships' length of an object, which had the appearance of a rock. The lead was immediately thrown out, but finding no bottom, we continued lying to, till the chief mate ascertained it to be a dead whale very much swollen: such objects seen imperfectly in the night are often alarming.

We carried easy sail to the northward with the wind westerly, much fog and falls of snow. On the 1st of *February*, at noon, our latitude was 58° 50', longitude 38° 51'. As there was no sign of land in this situation, we stood to the south-east, making an angle with our course, coming northward, which would enable us to see land midway.

I had offered a gratuity of 10*l.* to the man who should first discover land. This proved the cause of many a sore disappointment; for many of the seamen, of lively and sanguine imaginations, were never at a loss for an island. In short, fog banks out of number were reported for land; and many, in fact, had so much that appearance, that nothing short of standing towards them till they vanished could satisfy us as to their real nature.

In the morning of the 2d the wind freshened W.S.W. to a gale, which obliged us to lie to; snow squalls were frequent, and having many ice-islands to pass, we had to make various courses, and changes in the quantity of sail on the vessels. I carefully avoided the tracks of Captains Cook and Furneaux: and I may here remark how narrowly Captain Furneaux in the Adventure, in December 1773 and January 1774, escaped seeing South Shetland and the South Orkneys. He passed within 45 miles of the east end of Shetland and 75 miles of the South Orkneys: hence 20 miles, we may presume, of a more southerly course, would have given us a knowledge of South Shetland 50 years ago.

Running east in this latitude of from 60° to 61° we were constantly accompanied by all the birds common in these latitudes. Great numbers of finned and hump-backed whales were also seen;

and penguins in large shoals, having for their resting-place some ice island.

Being determined to examine these latitudes thoroughly, we constantly hauled to the wind under close-reefed topsails during fogs and the darkest part of the night, bearing up to the eastward when daylight appeared. On the 4th in the morning land was believed to be seen in the N.E., resembling an island. The signal to that effect was made to our consort, and we carried all sail to ascertain the fact; but our pleasing hopes were again speedily dispelled by our illusive island sinking below the horizon. We returned to our former easterly course, and passed several ice islands, lying east and west. In fact, we found all the clusters to lie in that direction, which is caused, no doubt, by the prevalent westerly winds carrying them along to the eastward, and spreading them in proportion to their hold of the water and the surface they present above.

By the evening of the 4th we were within 100 miles of Sandwich Land, and within such a distance of the track of Captain Cook, as convinced me that no land lay between.

Our pursuit of land here, therefore, was now at an end, but I conceived it probable that a large tract might be found a little farther south than we had yet been. I accordingly informed Mr. Brisbane of my intention of standing to the southward, and he, with a boldness which greatly enhanced the respect I bore him, expressed his willingness to push our research in that direction, though we had been hitherto so unsuccessful.

The weather being dark and foggy we stood to the southward under close-reefed topsails only. At 10 o'clock the following morning the temperature of air was 37, that of water 36 degrees; our latitude at noon, by observation, was 61° 44', and longitude, by chronometers, 31° 13' 15".

From having had a long course of dense fogs and fresh gales, the decks of our vessels were constantly wet, which produced amongst our seamen colds, agues, and rheumatisms. To remedy this in some measure, I had the ship's cooking stove moved below for their comfort, and good fires kept for drying their clothes; and by attending to these matters, and administering a little medicine, their complaints were soon removed.

I had allowed them three wine-glasses of rum a day per man,

since we were in these seas; and their allowance of beef and pork was one pound and a quarter a man per day; five pounds of bread, two pints of flour, three of peas, and two of barley, a man per week. These allowances in a cold climate were rather scanty, but the uncertainty of the length of our voyage required the strictest economy.

During the 6th and 7th we passed many ice islands, one of which I estimated to be two miles in length, and 250 feet high. The wind prevailed between W.S.W. and W.N.W. with foggy and clear weather alternately. At noon we observed in latitude 64° 15′, and our longitude by chronometers was 30° 46′. The variation by azimuth in the forenoon was 8° 19′ easterly.

At 10 o'clock at night, the weather being foggy, we narrowly escaped striking an ice island in passing. We hailed our consort, but she was so close to our stern that she passed also very near to it. The temperature of air at 8 o'clock in the evening was 34°, that of water 36°. In the afternoon of the 9th, the fog clearing away, we saw an appearance of land in the N.W.; but, after the usual practice of pursuing all such appearances, we discovered it to be one of our delusive attendants, the fog banks. The wind now shifted to south and blew strong, accompanied by with snow squalls.

At daylight in the morning of the 10th the chief mate reported land within sight, in the shape of a sugar loaf; as soon as I saw it I believed it to be a rock, and fully expected to find *terra firma* a short distance to the southward.

It was 2 o'clock in the afternoon before we reached it; and not till then, when passing within 300 yards, could we satisfy ourselves that it was not land, but black ice. We found an island of clear ice lying close, and detached above water, though connected below, which made a contrast of colour that had favoured or rather completed the deception. In short, its north side was so thickly incorporated with black earth, that hardly any person at a distance would have hesitated to pronounce it a rock. This was a new disappointment, and seriously felt by several of our crew, whose hopes of having an immediate reward for their patience and perseverance were again frustrated.

The wind was at south and blowing a fresh gale, with which we might have gone rapidly to the northward; but the circumstance of having seen this ice island so loaded with earth, encouraged me to

66

expect that it had disengaged itself from land possessing a considerable quantity of soil; and that our arrival at that very desirable object might, perhaps, not be very distant. These impressions induced me to keep our wind, and we stood to the S.W.

I may here remark that many of the doubtful rocks laid down in the chart of the North Atlantic have been probably objects similar to what I have described; and still remain unascertained, to the great annoyance of all cautious navigators. Our latitude at noon was by account 66° 26', and our longitude by chronometers 32° 32'. The temperature of air was 35° 30', that of water 34°.

On the 11th in the morning the wind shifted to S.W. by S., and we stood to the S.E. At noon our latitude by observation was 65° 32', that of account 65° 53'; and the chronometers giving 44 miles more westing than the log. We had in 3 days experienced a current running N. 64° W. 48 miles: the difficulty, however, of keeping a correct reckoning, from the many changes made in the course and quantity of sail, must subject the error to a suspicion of arising more from bad observation than from a real current. We had evidently been set to the northward and westward, which is contrary to what is generally the case, as the current almost constantly sets to the eastward. In the afternoon I found the variation by azimuth 12° 2' east.

During the 12th and 13th we had the wind from S.S.W., and we stood to the S.E. Ice islands were numerous, and on the 14th at noon our latitude by account was 68° 28', and longitude by chronometers 29° 43' 15". In the afternoon, with the ship's head S.S.W. the variation by azimuth was 8° 5' east. At 4 o'clock ice islands were so numerous as almost to prevent our passing; sixty-six were counted around us, and for about 50 miles to the south we had seldom fewer in sight.

On the 15th at noon our latitude observed was 68° 44', by account 69°; this difference of 16 miles in the latitude with easting given by chronometers, makes a current in 4 days of N. 53° E. 27 miles. In the forenoon, with the ship's head S. by W., I took a set of azimuths, which to my great astonishment gave the variation but 1° 20' east; in the afternoon I took a second set, which gave 4° 58'. As I had taken great pains in making the observations, and the instruments were good, however unaccountable this great difference was, I could not do otherwise than abide by the result.

On the 16th at noon our latitude by account was 70° 26′, and longitude by chronometers 29° 58′; the wind was moderate from the westward, and the sea tolerably smooth. Ice islands had almost disappeared, and the weather became very pleasant. Through the afternoon we had the wind fresh from the N.E., and we steered S.W. by W.

In the morning of the 17th the water appearing discoloured, we hove a cast of the lead, but found no bottom. A great number of birds of the blue peterel kind were about us, and many hump and finned back whales.

In the morning I took an amplitude, which gave variation 12° 24′ east. The wind had shifted to the S.E. and became light. Our latitude at noon by account was 71° 34′, and longitude by chronometers 30° 12′. As the weather was now more settled, our consort sailed wide, in order to extend our view.

On the 18th the weather was remarkably fine, and the wind in the S.E. Having unfortunately broken my two thermometers, I could not exactly ascertain the temperature, but it was certainly not colder than we had found it in December (summer) in the latitude of 61°. With the ship's head S.W. by S. at about 8ʰ 30′ in the morning I took a set of azimuths, which gave variation 13° 23′ east. At noon our latitude by observation was 72° 38′, by account 72° 24′; hence, with chronometer difference of longitude, we had been set in three days S. 62° W., distance 30 miles. In the afternoon I took a long set of azimuths, which gave variation 19° 58′. This increase in so short a distance seemed unsatisfactory; on which account I neglected no opportunity of making observations in order to reconcile these irregularities. I had all the compasses brought upon deck, and I found them to agree, but rather inactive in traversing.

In the evening we had many whales about the ship, and the sea was literally covered with birds of the blue peterel kind. *Not a particle of ice of any description was to be seen.* The evening was mild and serene, and had it not been for the reflection that probably we should have obstacles to contend with in our passage northward, through the ice, our situation might have been envied. The wind was light and easterly during the night, and we carried all sail. The sun's amplitude in the morning of the 19th when the ship's head was S. by E. gave variation 15° 10′ east.

The weather being pleasant, our carpenter was employed in repairing a boat, and we were enabled to make several repairs on the sails and rigging. At noon our latitude by observation was 73° 17′, and longitude by chronometers 35° 54′ 45″. In the evening, by several sets of amplitudes, I found the variation to be but 5° 35′ east. About midnight it fell calm, but presently a breeze sprang up from the S.W. by W., and we hauled on a wind S. by E.

In the morning of the 20th the wind shifted to S. by W. and blew a fresh breeze, and seeing a clouded horizon, and a great number of birds in the S.E., we stood in that direction. At 10 o'clock in the forenoon, when the ship's head was E.S.E., I took a set of azimuths, which gave variation 11° 20′ east. The atmosphere now became very clear, and nothing like land was to be seen. Three ice islands were in sight from the deck, and one other from the mast-head. On one we perceived a great number of penguins roosted. Our latitude at this time, 20th February, 1822,[1] was 74° 15′, and longitude 34° 16′ 45″; the wind blowing fresh at south, prevented, what I most desired, our making farther progress in that direction. I would willingly have explored the S.W. quarter, but taking into consideration the lateness of the season, and that we had to pass homewards through 1000 miles of sea strewed with ice islands, with long nights, and probably attended with fogs, I could not determine otherwise than to take advantage of this favourable wind for returning.

I much regretted that circumstances had not allowed me to proceed to the southward, when in the latitude of 65°, on the 27th of January, as I should then have had sufficient time to examine this sea to my satisfaction.

Situated however as I actually was, my attention was naturally roused to observe any phenomena which might be considered interesting to science. I was well aware that the making of scientific observations in this unfrequented part of the globe was a very desirable object, and consequently the more lamented my not being well supplied with the instruments with which ships fitted out for discovery are generally provided.

As the exact longitude of the ship and of harbours, &c. is of the first consideration, I had expended 240*l*. in the purchase of three chronometers; all of these performed remarkably well, and, in par-

[1] Weddell means 1823.

ticular, one of eight days, (No. 820.) Murry, London, continued regular in its daily rate of gaining through an unparalleled trial by repeated shocks, which the vessel (but slightly built) sustained during a month among field ice. Such perfection in this most useful machine, cannot be too much appreciated by commanders of ships, who, by assistance of so precise a nature, can easily avoid embarrassment in critical situations, where many lives and much valuable property frequently depend on a true knowledge of the ship's place.

The laws to which the compass seems to be subject in regard to its variation have lately undergone such accurate investigation by eminent individuals, that the phenomena attending it are now, in great degree, ascertained.

My own actual observations with regard to the variation, are inserted at the end of the volume.

Those which I made about the latitude of 60 degrees, are corrected for local attraction from the table of experiments made with Mr. Barlow's plate, in H.M.S. Conway, by Captain Basil Hall, and by Mr. Foster; but the observations arrived at about the latitude of 70 degrees cannot be reconciled, as to quantity of local attraction, with the theory adopted on the subject; I therefore let them remain at the observed results. I found a difference of from 3 to 5 degrees between the variation taken at the binnacle and that on the main hatches; and I have found as great a difference when the observations were made, even on the same spot, an hour apart. In fact, it appeared evident that the magnetic energy of the earth upon the needle was much diminished when far to the southward; partly arising, no doubt, from the increased dip or diminution of horizontal action on the needle, which must be attracted in an increased degree by objects immediately about it. This, however, cannot be altogether decided till a more satisfactory theory in respect to the emanation of the magnetic influence has been demonstrated.

The Aurora Australis, which Mr. Foster saw in his voyage round the world with Captain Cook in the year 1773, I particularly looked for during the time the sun was beneath the horizon, which was more than six hours, but nothing of the kind was observable. As the twilight, however, was never out of the sky, that might be the cause of its not being visible.

The remarkable and distorted appearances which objects and the

horizon itself assume by refraction in high northern latitudes, occurred here but little more than in an ordinary way. The water
spouted by whales half an hour after sunrise in the morning of the
19th exhibited an increased refraction, but it soon disappeared.

The reason of this phenomenon not existing as singularly in the
south as it does in corresponding northern latitudes, may be attributed to this sea being clear of field ice.

It distinctly appears to me, that the conjecture of Captain Cook,
that field ice is formed and proceeds from land, and is not formed in
the open sea, is true. He latterly, however, changes his opinion from
having found ice solid in field in the latitude of 70 degrees to the
northward of Bhering's Straits. But I think it likely that the ice he fell
in with there proceeded from land in the north, not more distant, perhaps, than 150 miles. No person can doubt the probability of my
conjecture, when it is remembered, that in the latitude of 74° 15′
south, (which, according to the received opinion of former navigators that the southern hemisphere is proportionably colder by 10
degrees of latitude than the northern, would be equal to 84° 15′
north) I found a sea perfectly clear of field ice; whereas in the latitude
of 61° 30′, about 100 miles from the land, I was beset in heavy
packed ice. As in that situation we could not see the land, had I not
known of the existence of South Shetland, I might have fallen into
the commonly received error, that this ice proceeded continuously
from the South Pole. If, therefore, no land exist to the south of the
latitude at which I arrived, *viz.* seventy-four degrees, fifteen minutes,
—being three degrees and five minutes, or 214 geographical miles
farther south than Captain Cook, or any preceding navigator
reached, how is it possible that the South Pole should not be more
attainable than the North, about which we know there lies a great
deal of land?

The excessive cold of the southern hemisphere has been variously
accounted for, every philosopher adopting that theory which best
suited his own hydrographical system. Saint Pierre supposes it to
proceed from a cupola of ice surrounding the South Pole, and stretching far northward. We have now better *data* to go upon; for though
great exertions were used in the years 1773 and 1774 to discover the
*terra australis incognita* without success, yet we find there is a range
of land lying as far north as the latitude of 61 degrees. We may also

conjecture, without much fear of being in the wrong, that the land with which we are acquainted, lying in latitude of 61 degrees, and in longitude 54° 30', namely, the east end of South Shetland, stretches to the W.S.W., beyond the longitude in which Captain Cook penetrated to the latitude of 71° 10'. It is this land which, no doubt, ought to be looked upon as the source from which proceeds the excessive cold of these regions. The temperature of air and water in the latitude of 60 and 61 degrees, I have mentioned to be but little above the freezing point. The cold earthless land, and its immense ice islands, which are continually separating in the summer, and are made, by prevailing westerly winds, almost to girdle the earth, is evidently the cause of the very low temperature which prevails.

The part of the country which I have seen is without soil, reared in columns of impenetrable rock, inclosing and producing large masses of ice, even in the low latitude of 60° 45'.

It is certain that ice islands are formed only in openings or recesses of land; and field ice, I think, is not readily formed in a deep sea.

On soundings, the water is soon cooled down to the freezing point; hence field ice is found at the distance of many miles from any shore. These considerations induce me to conclude, that from having but three ice islands in sight, in latitude 74° degrees, the range of land, of which I have spoken, does not extend more southerly than the 73d degree. If this be true, and if there be no more land to the southward, the antarctic polar sea may be found less icy than is imagined, and a clear field of discovery, even to the South Pole, may therefore be anticipated.

Having now determined on returning, I made the signal to our consort to bear up and steer N.W., and we made all possible sail.

Our crews were naturally much disappointed at our ill success in not finding a southern land, as their interest in the voyage was to be a proportion of the cargo procured. In order, therefore, to reanimate them by acknowledging their merit, I expressed my approbation of their patient and orderly behaviour, and informed them that they were now to the southward of the latitude to which any former navigator had penetrated. Our colours were hoisted, and a gun was fired, and both crews gave three cheers. These indulgences, with an allowance of grog, dispelled their gloom, and infused a hope that fortune might yet be favourable.

□   *In the United States, a bizarre pseudoscientific theory was the motivating force for the first American scientific expedition to the Antarctic. A retired soldier named John Cleves Symmes had conceived the notion that the world was hollow and could be entered through openings at the poles. Symmes petitioned Congress to provide funds for an exploratory expedition to the Antarctic. He failed to attract support, but he did win the collaboration of Jeremiah N. Reynolds, an ambitious young newspaper editor from Ohio. Reynolds took charge of the Symmes crusade and soon Symmes himself, as well as the holes-in-the-poles idea, receded into the background.*

*Reynolds joined forces with the major sealing and whaling men, Edmund Fanning and Nat Palmer, who were eager, for commercial reasons, to see the south polar region explored more fully. During the John Quincy Adams administration in 1827 they nearly won government backing for their project, but the following year the plan was smothered by governmental wrangling. The undaunted promoters launched their own privately financed expedition instead.*

*Two vessels, the brigs Seraph and Annawan, sailed southward commanded by a pair of Antarctic veterans, Nat Palmer and Benjamin Pendleton. Jeremiah Reynolds went along as a "scientist." There was also a genuine scientist aboard, the Albany naturalist James Eights, who had received a $500 grant from the New York Lyceum of Natural History for Antarctic research.*

*The enterprise was a failure. The ships reached the South Shetlands safely late in 1829, but found the ice pack to the south impenetrable. After thirty-five days of waiting for conditions to improve, Pendleton and Palmer decided to abandon the Antarctic quest and sail westward into the Pacific—a decision hurried by a near-mutiny among the sailors. Many of the crewmen were put ashore at Val-*

*paraiso, Chile, and the expedition returned home soon afterward.*

*Two years after his return, James Eights published a short article in the* Transactions of the Albany Institute, *under the title, "A Description of a New Crustaceous Animal Found on the Shores of the South Shetlands, with Remarks on their Natural History." It has the distinction of being the first purely scientific treatise on this subantarctic region by an American. Eights also contributed a chapter to a book of Fanning's called* Voyages to the South Seas, Indian and Pacific Oceans, China Sea, North-West Coast, Feejee Islands, South Shetlands, etc. *(New York, William H. Vermilye, 1838). That chapter is reprinted here.* □

# JAMES EIGHTS

*A description of the New South Shetland Isles, by James Eights, Esq., M.D., naturalist in the scientific corps in the American exploring expedition, of brigs Seraph and Annawan under the command of Captain B. Pendleton, and N. B. Palmer, sent out to the South Seas under the directive agency of the author of this work, and the patronage of government in the years 1829 and 1830.*

The new South Shetland Isles are situated between 61° and 63° south latitude, and 54° and 63° west longitude. They are formed by an extensive cluster of rocks rising abruptly from the ocean, to a considerable height above its surface. Their true elevation cannot be easily determined, in consequence of the heavy masses of snow which lie over them, concealing them almost entirely from the sight. Some of them, however, rear their glistening summits, to an altitude of about three thousand feet, and when the heavens are free from clouds, imprint a sharp and well defined outline upon the intense blueness of the sky. They are divided every where by straits, and indented by deep bays, or coves: many of which afford to vessels a comfortable shelter from the rude gales to which these high latitudes are so subject. When the winds have ceased to blow, and the ocean is at rest, nothing can exceed the beautiful clearness of the atmosphere in these elevated regions. The numerous furrows and ravines which every where impress the snowy acclivity of the hills, are distinctly visible for fifty or sixty miles; and the various sea-fowl, resting upon the slight eminences, and brought in strong relief against the sky, ofttimes deceive the experienced eye of the mariner, by having their puny dimensions magnified in size to those of human form.

The ocean in the vicinity, so far as the eye has vision, is here and there studded with icebergs, varying in magnitude from a few feet to more than a mile in extent, and not unfrequently rising two hundred feet in the air, presenting every variety of form, from the snug white-washed cottage of the peasant, to the enormous architectural piles, containing either broadly expanded Grecian domes, or having the many lofty and finely attenuated spires of some Gothic structure.

The sun, even at midsummer, attains but a moderate altitude in these dreary regions, and when its horizontal beams illumine these masses of ice, their numerous angles and indentations, catching the light as they move along, exhibit all the beautiful gradations of colour, from an emerald green, to that of the finest blue. Some of them, whose sloping sides will admit of their ascent, are tenanted by large assemblies of Penguins, whose chattering noise may be heard on a still day at an incredible distance over the clear smooth surface of the sea.

When the storms rage and the ocean rolls its mountain wave against their slippery sides, the scene is truly sublime. Tall columns of spray shooting up far above their tops, soon become dissipated in clouds of misty white; gradually descending, they envelop the whole mass for a short time, giving to it much the appearance of being covered with a veil of silvery gauze. When thus agitated, they not unfrequently explode with the noise of thunder, scattering their fragments far and wide over the surrounding surface of the deep. These hills of ice are borne onwards at a considerable rate by the wind and the velocity of the current—when so, they sweep along with a majesty that nothing else can equal.

The sky, too, in these latitudes, presents a very singular aspect; being, most generally filled with innumerable clouds, torn into ragged and irregular patches by the wild gales which every where race over the Antarctic Seas: the sun, as it rises or sets slowly and obliquely in the northern horizon, sends its rays through the many

75

openings between, tinging them here and there with every variety of hue and colour, from whence they are thrown in mild and beautiful reflection upon the extensive fields of snow which lie piled on the surrounding hills, giving to the whole scene for a greater part of the long summer day, the ever-varying effect of a most gorgeous sunset.

Although many of the scenes about these islands are highly exciting, the effect produced on the mind, by their general aspect, is cold and cheerless to an unusual degree, for on their lonely shores the voice of man is seldom heard; the only indication of his ever having trod the soil, is the solitary grave of some poor seaman near the beach, and the only wood that any where meets the eye, are the staves that mark its dimensions; no sound for years disturb the silence of the scene, save the wild screech of the sea-birds as they wing their way in search of their accustomed food—the incessant chattering of the congregated penguins—the rude blasts, tearing among the icy hills—the sullen roar of the waves, tumbling and dashing along the shores, or the heavy explosions of the large masses of snow falling into the waves beneath, to form the vast icebergs which every where drift through the southern ocean. The shores of these islands are generally formed by the perpendicular cliffs of ice, frequently reaching for many miles, and rising from ten feet to several hundred in height. In many places at their base, the continued action of the water has worn out deep caves with broadly arched roofs, under which the ocean rolls its waves with a subterranean sound that strikes most singularly on the ear, and when sufficiently undermined, extensive portions crack off with an astounding report, creating a tremendous surge in the sea below, which, as it rolls over its surface, sweeps every thing before it, from the smallest animal that feeds upon its bottom, to those of the greatest bulk. . . .

The existence of a southern continent within the antarctic circle is, I conceive, a matter of much doubt and uncertainty; but, that there are extensive groups, or chains of islands, yet unknown, I think we have many indications to prove; and were I to express an opinion, I would say, that our course from the South Shetlands to the S. W., until we reached the 101° of west longitude, was at no great distance along the northern shores of one of these chains. The heavy clouds of mist which encircled us so often, could arise from no other cause than that of the influence of large quantities of snow or ice, on the temperature of the atmosphere; the hills of floating ice we encountered, could not form elsewhere than on the land. The drifting fuci we daily saw, grow only in the vicinity of rocky shores, and the penguins and terns that were almost at all times about us, from my observation of their habits, I am satisfied never leave the land at any great distance.

During our cruise to the south-west, above the 60° of south latitude, we found the current setting continually at a considerable rate towards the north-east, bearing the plants and ice along in its course, some of the latter embracing fragments of a rock, the existence of which we could discover no where on the islands we visited. When the westerly winds drew well towards the south, we were most generally enveloped in banks of fog, so dense that it was with difficulty we could distinguish objects at the distance of the vessel's length. When Palmer's Land becomes properly explored, together with the known islands, situated between the longitude of Cape Horn and that of Good Hope, I think they will prove to be the north-eastern termination of an extensive chain, passing near where Captain Cook's progress was arrested by the firm fields of ice, in latitude, 71° 10' S., and west longitude, about 105°; had that skilful navigator succeeded in penetrating this mass of ice, he would unquestionably, in a short time, have made the land upon which it was formed. Captain Weddel, after passing the icy barrier to the east of the South Shetlands, succeeded in reaching the 74° 15' south, (the highest latitude ever obtained by man,) and found, in crossing this chain, and progressing towards the south, that the sea became more free of ice, and the weather almost as mild as summer; evidently proving, I think, that the south pole can be nearly approached, without incurring any great degree of hazard in the attempt. But, for further information on the practicability of reaching the south pole, I must refer to the judicious remarks of Captain Edmund Fanning, of New-York, contained in his account of several voyages to the southern ocean, with which I perfectly coincide; and will conclude with regret, that the Government of the United States, with a population whose daring enterprise has already carried our flag into the remotest corners of the globe, could not yet (October, 1835,) be induced to forward an expedition, the expense of which would little exceed that of a vessel doubling Cape Horn.

They might thus settle this interesting question, and also determine, with certainty, the situation, magnitude, and extent of these lands, and by that means open a new source of revenue to the country, in the oil and fur of animals which must necessarily exist in these high southern regions.

□   *The lure of wealth drew many men to the seal rookeries of the subantarctic islands. As we have seen, such men as Weddell maintained a scientific curiosity while they hunted for salable pelts, and later skippers continued that tradition, particularly those employed by the British firm of Enderby Brothers. The Enderbys, who sent many sealing ships to the Antarctic in the first half of the nineteenth century, were frequently willing to place the pursuit of knowledge above that of profit.*

*One of the best known of the Enderby skippers was John Biscoe, who left England in July, 1830, commanding the schooner* Tula *and accompanied by the cutter* Lively. *On January 22, 1831, Biscoe crossed the Antarctic Circle, unknowingly following Bellingshausen's route of ten years before. Biscoe was able to sail well south of Bellingshausen's halting point, and in February caught a glimpse of the ice cliffs of Antarctica in the distance. Attempting to approach, the two ships were trapped in an icy bay, and it was a week before they escaped.*

*Despite severe storms and the onset of scurvy among his men, Biscoe continued to follow the Antarctic coast for hundreds of miles, finally retreating when winter drew near. The* Tula *limped back to Tasmania, with only three able-bodied men aboard, the rest down with scurvy. The* Lively *had become separated from Biscoe's ship during a storm some weeks before, and had reached Australia with only her captain, a seaman, and a cabin boy still alive.*

*In February, 1832, Biscoe was back in the Antarctic, this time exploring a different side of the continent—the Antarctic Peninsula side, which he charted in some detail. After moving on to the South*

*Shetlands for seals, Biscoe returned to London in January, 1833, aboard the* Tula; *the* Lively *was lost at sea on the homeward voyage. Biscoe brought little cargo back, and the Enderbys took a heavy loss on the enterprise, but he had covered thousands of miles in Antarctic waters, discovering land at many points and adding to the growing confidence that a body of land of continental size lay beyond the ice that covered the southern sea. Biscoe received the gold medal of the Royal Geographic Society and made several later voyages to high southern latitudes on behalf of the Enderbys. His final years are somewhat mysterious; he retired from the sea and settled in England, falling into such poverty that on his death in 1848 his widow and four children were left penniless and had to be cared for through funds raised by other seamen.*

*Extracts from Biscoe's log were published in* The Journal of the Royal Geographical Society, *1833. A more extensive selection appeared in* The Antarctic Manual, *a volume prepared for the use of the Scott Antarctic Expedition of 1901. It was edited by George Murray and published in London by the Royal Geographical Society in 1901. The extract that follows, from John Biscoe's "Journal of a Voyage toward the South Pole on board the brig* Tula, *with the cutter* Lively *in Company," is reprinted from that book.* □

# JOHN BISCOE

I have long been anxious to ascertain as nearly as possible the origin of icebergs. It is the given opinion of most navigators that they are formed contiguous to land, and Captain Weddell mentions one in his southern voyage, which had so much black earth about it that he could scarcely satisfy himself it was not a rock. But of all the icebergs I have seen, which are many hundreds, I could never discern the least trace of their having ever been connected with land, and had formed the opinion in my mind that they originated from a vast body of ice, frozen on the surface of the water, and accumulating with time, and I should have regretted much had I been obliged to leave these southern parallels, from the advanced state of the season, without satisfying myself in this particular, and having seen nothing but the field-ice. However, this morning has completely satisfied me in this respect, for I have not the least doubt that the whole spaces, from the latitudes I have visited to the Pole, are one solid mass; land may intervene, or winds, where they are strong and prevalent, may have prevented its forming in some parts more than others, but I have found such frequent calms and light airs with smooth water, that I see no reason why ice should not be formed to any extent during the winter seasons, and if, as I have before observed in my remarks, it could form in the month of January, in latitude 68° S., of the substance of half an inch in one night, what might it not do in the month of July under the same circumstances? As to the icebergs being formed on shore, I do not think it possible or probable for this reason, their own weight would prevent their accumulating on any prominent part of land. It would break off at different times and form what is called field-ice, for should it once become so extensive a mass as an iceberg, and which could only be when there was shallow water, it is utterly impossible it could even separate from the land where it was first formed, as it is well known that ice swims at least two-thirds under water; indeed I have been astonished at some pieces which were not more than six or seven feet above the surface, that swam so deep I could scarcely trace their bottoms in the water; as to the ragged tops of icebergs, it may be accounted for in this way: after a portion of ice has been separated from the main body by a gale of wind, or some eruption, or other natural cause, its surface, as I apprehend, is always perfectly smooth, at least all those which appeared recently separated were so, while the others which were sodden with salt water had smooth parts in them with occasional peaks, and in other parts completely honey-combed, which in my opinion is to be accounted for in this way: that as the water is generally found to be one or two degrees warmer than the atmosphere, together with the continual motion of the iceberg, which is sometimes considerable—at least the water has great motion near its edges, and breaks over it with great force—the lower part becomes sodden and undermined, and its softer parts give way to the force of the sea, break off and rise to the surface, which forms the field-ice.

After this continual decay below has gone on for some time, the lower part becomes unable to sustain the weight of the upper; it becomes too heavy and capsizes, which shows that rugged appearance

I have before mentioned, and should it be blown far to the north-ward, it turns over and over occasionally until it entirely dissolves, but I don't think the upper parts decay. I have observed several where the sun at times had the power to dissolve them a little, but from a change of wind or other circumstances it was again frozen into an icicle, which had a beautiful effect when the sun was shining on it; some have appeared to have been a long time drifting about, as several distinct layers of snow were perceptible on them, and those which appeared to be turned over were washed in places as smooth as a vessel's bottom, and sometimes not unlike the shape of one, with a smooth layer of snow over it, which froze as it fell, some forming arches, &c. Field-ice is I believe, likewise formed from the upper parts of icebergs, as on Sunday, the 20th inst., the vessels were very near a large ice-island, and while looking at it I observed a large mass of ice break off from one of its upper projections and fall into the water with a tremendous noise, and which floated in large lumps on the surface, so that the breaking up of one or two of these icebergs would make a considerable patch of field-ice.

Observing a large range of complete arches in this iceberg with many other cavities, I fired a cannon shot at it to see what effect it might have; but the motion of the vessel at the time of firing carried the shot just over its surface, when a complete cloud of snow birds rose from it, which in all probability had laid their eggs there. The second shot was more successful, but had no other effect than knock-ing off a few small pieces of ice. I pulled round this iceberg in a boat very close, but could observe no symptom of its having ever been in any way attached to the land.

I have been likewise much surprised at the constant easterly winds which prevail on these meridians, as it is generally understood to the southward strong westerly winds prevail, but I have a beating pas-sage of it, which with the frequent calm, now and then a strong blow from the S.E., with generally a heavy swell from the quarter for some time before and after, together with the thick weather, incom-mode me very much.

*Feb. 26* [1831].—A.M. Squally and cloudy. Wind southerly. At noon latitude 65° 57′, longitude 46° 17′. Passed some straggling ice. Many icebergs in sight. P.M., winds more easterly. Stood to the southward. 8 p.m., thick weather with an easterly swell. Tacked to the northward, it being too thick to venture among the ice. Cutter in close company.

*Feb. 27.*—Moderate breezes from the S.S.E., with a most distressing E.S.E. sea, which made the vessels pitch and strain very much, and were enabled in consequence to carry but little canvas, accompanied by thick weather. Repeated showers of snow. Many small birds about us.

*Feb. 28.*—In the morning more regular sea. Tacked to the southward. Wind S.E. Noon, more clear. Latitude 65° 57′ S., longitude 47° 20′ 30″ E. P.M., passed to the southward through much broken field-ice. 4 p.m. saw several hummocks to the southward, which much resembled tops of mountains, and at 6 p.m. clearly distinguished it to be land, and to considerable extent; to my great satisfaction what we had first seen being the black tops of mountains showing themselves through the snow on the lower land, which, however, appeared to be a great distance off, and completely beset with close field-ice and icebergs. The body of the land bearing S.E.

*March 1.*—During the whole of this day, and the 2nd, we were employed in endeavouring to work a passage through the ice, but after many fruitless attempts and some heavy blows, were always frustrated. P.M. As our attempts to near the land every hour opens some new object to us, and seeing a bluff point in S.E. which has every appearance of a cape, I still have hopes of accomplishing my wish. Latitude, at noon, 66° 7′, longitude, 49° 6′ 30″ E. The main body from S.W. to S.E. about twelve leagues (nearly calm), having stood far in among the ice, I found some difficulty in clearing it again, and as the calm had lasted several hours, the sea froze to that excess that on the morning of the 3rd we found it at least an inch thick over the whole surface of the water, and which impeded our progress through it very much.

*March 3.*—Thermometer, air 32½°, water 30°. At the same time, nearly the whole night, the Aurora Australis showed the most brilliant appearance, at times rolling itself over our heads in beautiful columns, then as suddenly forming itself as the unrolled fringe of a curtain, and again suddenly shooting to the form of a serpent, and at times appearing not many yards above us; it was decidedly transacted in our own atmosphere, and was without exception the grandest phenomenon of nature of its kind I ever witnessed. At this time we were completely beset with broken ice, and although the vessels were in considerable danger in running through it with a smart breeze, which had now sprung up, I could hardly restrain the people from looking at the Aurora Australis instead of the vessel's course. Having on the 3rd, in the morning, hauled round to appearance the easternmost part of the firm ice, with the wind at S.W., and after a run of about fifteen miles due S., having entered a narrow channel of about three miles broad, formed on the west side by an immense chain of ice-islands and on the east by firm field-ice, and seeing an opening ahead from the mast-head, was in great hopes to find a passage direct to the land, but at 6 p.m. found it blocked up in every direction, nor have I been able in any one place to come within 30° of it; hauled out to the northward, and at 10 p.m. came into clear water, and on the 4th steered along the edge of the field-ice. Our latitude by observation at noon, 65° 42′ S., longitude 49° 29′ E. The cape, which I have named Cape Ann, by bearings at 4 p.m., being in latitude 66° 25′ S., longitude 49° 17′ 45″ E. At 6.30 a breeze sprung up from S.E. with squalls. At midnight freshened to a stiff breeze, and at 4 p.m. of the 5th blew a fresh gale with thick weather shortly after. We lost sight of the cutter, bearing about west by north two miles. The gale increased, and at 12 blew a perfect hurricane, which lasted without intermission until the morning of the 8th. The weather during the whole time was so thick that we could scarcely see twice our own length in any direction, and being so close to ice of every description, were in a very dangerous situation, the vessel being at the same time a complete mass of ice, and the wind blowing so intensely cold, it was impossible for the people to hold anything in their hands for more than a minute or two at a time. Our larboard quarter-boat was washed away. Our bulwarks, starboard quarter-boats, quarter-deck rail stove in, the boats being up at least above four feet above rail cloths, but by the blessing of God we drove clear of all the icebergs, only seeing one close on our weather bow, our head the whole time of the gale from E.N.E. to N.E., and had we fallen a little to windward of any large iceberg, or any quantity of field-ice, must have all inevitably perished, as the vessel was unmanageable, and when the weather moderated on the morning of the 8th, left us almost a wreck. At 8 a.m. wore round to the southward. At noon our latitude by observation, 63° 49′, longitude 47° 00′ 00″

E., having made a drift of 120 miles N.N.W. during the gale. P.M. The weather still wearing a threatening appearance, the wind at N.E. I stood to the southward under easy sail, not to run the risk of being caught on a lee shore should it blow hard from the northward. I have had several men hurt [and] have now four or five on my list for cure. I am under much apprehension for the cutter, as I think this is the hardest blow I have ever known with the exception of the hurricane of 1814.

From the 8th to the 14th, strong S.E. gales, with generally one in 24 hours, a few hours interval of calms. Snow and sleet in great abundance nearly the whole time, so that when we had a few hours fair wind the weather was too thick to make much way towards the land, as the gales succeeded the calms very suddenly.

*March 15.*—P.M. Dry weather. Passed very close to large piece of ice about a ship's length, but thank God cleared it safely. At noon, latitude 64° 43′ S., thermometer shade 25°, wind S.W. by S. Clear weather.

*March 16.*—Stood to the southward. Latitude, at noon, 65° 16′; longitude, dead reckoning, 49° 27′ E.; temperature, air 24°, water 30°. P.M. It freshened to a gale at S.E. Wore to the northward. At midnight stood to the southward, the weather being moderate, and at 8 a.m. saw the land bearing south by compass, which was a very high mountain. Cape Ann was shortly after observed to bear S.W. At 6 p.m. made field-ice, and thick clusters of icebergs ahead, and 4 points on each bow, but am sorry to say could see nothing of the cutter. Our latitude at this time was 65° 44′ S., longitude 50° 09′ E. Cape Ann W. by S. High land about ten leagues south by compass. Temperature, air 22°, water 29°. Wind, N.E. and moderate, and as I observed little or no difference in the position of the field-ice since the S.E. gales, I feel myself absolutely obliged to give up all further pursuit in this part. The land inaccessible, heavy gales frequent every day, some of the people getting sick, the carpenter for some time past having lost the use of his legs, and two others at this time in the same situation, and two or three more under medicine for the same complaint, although every attention has been paid to their health and comfort.

◻  *Another celebrated Enderby captain was John Balleny, who set out on July 16, 1838, in command of the schooner* Eliza Scott, *accompanied by the cutter* Sabrina. *Sailing southward from New Zealand, Balleny encountered the islands that now bear his name, 450 miles off the Antarctic coast, and later found an iceberg in which was embedded a large block of stone—providing proof that there definitely was land, and not simply drifting ice, within the Antarctic Circle south of New Zealand. Thus another section of the Antarctic coastline was sighted, and given the name of Sabrina Land. In late March, 1839, a gale separated the two ships; the* Sabrina *was never seen again, while Balleny's* Eliza Scott *survived only with great difficulties. Balleny returned to London in September, just in time to confer with Captain James Clark Ross, then about to depart on a government expedition to Antarctica. Balleny's log was published as "Discoveries in the Antarctic Ocean in February, 1839" in* The Journal of the Royal Geographical Society, *1839, from which it is here reprinted.*  ◻

# JOHN BALLENY

*March 1* [1839].—With a steady breeze from the S.E. continued standing to the westward—passed several icebergs, and numerous flocks of penguins, petrels, and mutton-birds.

*March 2, A.M.*—Squally from the S.E., with snow and sleet. At 8 cleared off a little. At noon, latitude observed, 64° 58', longitude 121° 8', thermometer 35°. P.M., strong winds, and showers of snow and sleet; saw a great many birds. At 8, the water becoming smooth all at once, shortened sail and hove-to. Saw land to the southward, the vessel surrounded by drift-ice. At midnight strong breezes with snow.

*March 3, A.M.*—Found the ice closing and becoming more compact; stood through the drift-ice to the southward. At 8 found ourselves surrounded by icebergs of immense size; to the S.W. the ice was quite fast, with every appearance of land at the back of it, but, the weather coming on thick, were obliged to steer to the northward along the edge of the pack. At noon, latitude by observation 65° 10', longitude 117° 4'. P.M., fresh breezes from the S.S.E. and clear; numerous icebergs in sight.

*March 4.*—Moderate and cloudy weather. At 5 hauled to the westward; several icebergs in sight, and a great many birds and whales. At noon, wind increasing, with a heavy sea from the N.W. Latitude by observation 63° 56'; longitude by chronometer, at 4 p.m., 115° 30'. At sunset, found the variation by amplitude, with the ship's head N.E., to be 44° 11' W. At 9, being surrounded by icebergs, with thick weather and heavy snow squalls, hove the ship to for the night.

The two following days continued standing to the N.W., with variable winds. At sunrise on the morning of the 6th, in latitude 62° 40', longitude 164°, the variation by amplitude, with the ship's head to the N.N.W., was found to be 42° 21' W. During the next four days, stormy weather, with snow and sleet from the N.E.; stood to the N.W. whenever the numerous icebergs would allow the vessels to run. At midnight on the 10th, in latitude 61° 20', the Aurora Australis shone with great splendour. The following day was very fine, with the wind from the N.N.E.; innumerable icebergs in sight. In the afternoon, in latitude 61° 27', longitude 105° 30', the variation by azimuth was found to be 34° 30' W.

During the next few days the vessels slowly made their way to the W.N.W., constantly surrounded by icebergs; saw whales, penguins, several sea-birds and one albatross, the first seen since leaving Campbell Island; this occurred in latitude 61° 30'. . . .

*March 13.*—Light variable winds from the eastward; surrounded by icebergs; in latitude 61°, longitude 103° 40', passed ¼ of a mile of an iceberg about 300 feet high, with a block of rock attached to it.

□ *Charles Darwin is not noted for his part in the exploration of Antarctica, and indeed the closest he came to the frozen continent was on his journey around the world in the* Beagle, *which passed*

*through the Strait of Magellan in 1834. Five years later, Darwin was
still no more than a young gentleman with scientific inclinations, his
great work on evolution yet twenty years away from publication.
Icebergs interested him, though, and when he learned of the block
of stone sighted by Balleny he set out to interview a member of the
Eliza Scott's crew for further details.*

*The problem of the icebergs had occupied many minds over the
previous three generations. We have seen Cook, Bellingshausen,
Weddell, and Biscoe speculating on their cause, with greater or lesser
degrees of scientific accuracy. All but Biscoe had been of the opinion
that the presence of earth or rock in the icebergs indicated land to the
south—the still unreached Antarctic continent. Darwin now lent
himself to the debate, in a brief but historically important note. It
appeared in the same 1839 volume of* The Journal of the Royal Geographical Society *that contained Balleny's log.*   □

# CHARLES DARWIN

*Note on a Rock seen on an Iceberg in 61° S. Lat.*

Having been informed by Mr. Enderby that a block of rock, embedded in ice, had been seen during the voyage of the schooner *Eliza
Scott* in the Antarctic Seas, I procured through his means an interview with Mr. Macnab, one of the mates of the vessel, and I learnt
from him the following facts: On the 13th of March, when in latitude
61° S., and longitude 103° 40′ E., a black spot was seen on a distant
iceberg, which when the vessel had run within a quarter of a mile of
it, was clearly perceived to be an irregularly-shaped but angular fragment of dark-coloured rock. It was embedded in a perpendicular
face of ice, at least 20 feet above the level of the sea. That part which
was visible, Mr. Macnab estimated at about 12 feet in height, and
from 5 to 6 in width; the remainder (and from the dark colour of the
surrounding ice, probably the greater part) of the stone was concealed. He made a rough sketch of it at the time. The iceberg which
carried this fragment was between 250 and 300 feet high.

Mr. Macnab informs me that on one other occasion (about a week
afterwards) he saw on the summit of a low, flat iceberg a black mass,

which he thinks, but will not positively assert, was a fragment of rock. He has repeatedly seen, at considerable heights on the bergs, both reddish-brown and blackish-brown ice. Mr. Macnab attributes this discolouration to the continued washing of the sea; and it seems probable that decayed ice, owing to its porous texture, would filter every impurity from the waves which broke over it.

Every fact on the transportation of fragments of rock by ice is of importance, as throwing light on the problem of "erratic boulders," which has so long perplexed geologists; and the case first described possesses in some respects peculiar interest. The part of the ocean where the iceberg was seen is 450 miles distant from *Sabrina* land (if such land exists), and 1400 miles from any certainly known land. The tract of sea, however, due south, has not been explored; but assuming that land, if it existed there, would have been seen at some leagues' distance from a vessel, and considering the southerly course which the schooner *Eliza Scott* pursued immediately prior to meeting with the iceberg, and that of Cook in the year 1773, it is exceedingly improbable that any land will hereafter be discovered within 100 miles of this spot. The fragment of rock must, therefore, have travelled at least thus far from its parent source; and, from being deeply imbedded, it probably sailed many miles farther on before it was dropped from the iceberg in the depths of the sea, or was stranded on some distant shore. In my journal, during the voyage of H.M.S. *Beagle*, I have stated, on the authority of Captain Biscoe, that, during his several cruises in the Antarctic seas, he never once saw a piece of rock in the ice. An iceberg, however, with a considerable block lying on it, was met with to the east of South Shetland by Mr. Sorrell (the former boatswain of the *Beagle*) when in a sealing vessel. The case, therefore, here recorded is the second; but it is in many respects much the most remarkable one. Almost every voyager in the Southern Ocean has described the extraordinary number of icebergs, their vast dimensions, and the low latitudes to which they are drifted. Horsburgh has reported the case of several which were seen by a ship in her passage from India, in latitude 35° 55′ S. If, then, but one iceberg in a thousand, or in ten thousand, transports its fragment, the bottom of the Antarctic Sea, and the shores of its islands, must already be scattered with masses of foreign rock—the counterpart of the "erratic boulders" of the northern hemisphere.

# PART III

**TOWARD
THE MAGNETIC
POLE
1841-1874**

◻   *Balleny was virtually the last of the sealing captains to explore the Antarctic regions. The rookeries were nearly exhausted after four decades of intensive hunting. The next ships to go southward would sail on missions of science.*

*The search for the South Magnetic Pole was beginning. It had been known for some time that compass needles did not point toward the geographic poles, but rather to the so-called magnetic poles, which wandered through various positions around the Arctic and Antarctic regions. In 1831, a British expedition led by an officer named James Clark Ross reached the North Magnetic Pole. Scientists in many countries called next for an expedition to its southern counterpart, so that the earth's magnetic field could be accurately mapped for the first time.*

91

National pride entered the race for the South Magnetic Pole. Three countries organized expeditions practically simultaneously: Great Britain, France, and the United States. Since these were great public enterprises, the planning was extensive and the scope for political interference great, so that each of the expeditions was vastly delayed in getting to sea.

The French were the first to depart. In command was the scholarly and studious Jules Sebastien Cesar Dumont D'Urville, an explorer whose main interests lay in the fields of linguistics and ethnology, and who had remarkably little enthusiasm for making an Antarctic journey. It was D'Urville who, while visiting the Greek island of Melos in 1820 on a naval mission, had purchased the statue familiar to millions of Louvre visitors as the Venus de Milo; later, he helped to organize the Paris Geographical Society, and from 1822 to 1829 spent much of his time on expeditions in the South Pacific gathering ethnological information. D'Urville was planning a new expedition to that region in 1836, and when King Louis Philippe of France heard of the British plans for finding the South Magnetic Pole, he ordered D'Urville to detour to the south, hoping thus to anticipate the British explorers.

Somewhat glumly, D'Urville obeyed, observing, "whatever be the result it must at least give occasion for interesting observations." With two ships, the Astrolabe and the Zélée, he left France in September, 1837. An attempt to enter the Weddell Sea ended unsuccessfully when ice blocked an advance in 63°39' S., considerably short of Weddell's record of 74°15'. D'Urville spent the Antarctic summer of 1838 charting the South Shetlands and the Antarctic Peninsula, departing for the Pacific on March 5 and not returning to polar waters until late in 1839.

D'Urville's second thrust was made on the far side of Antarctica —the region south of 60° S., between 120° and 160° E. where Balleny had been in 1839. D'Urville did not know that, however, and he regarded himself as the discoverer of the coast there. In mid-January, 1840, he approached the shore and managed a landing on an offshore island, as described in the passage below. Unable to reach the mainland, the French continued eastward along the coast, and on January 29 took part in one of those odd coincidental meetings that were so strangely frequent in Antarctic exploration. They had a brief and *unpleasant encounter with the* Porpoise, *one of the American expedition's ships, which had set out for the Antarctic long after D'Urville's departure from France. There was mutual misunderstanding, each captain regarding the other as an interloper, and some international coolness resulted.*

*The French explorers returned to their homeland in November, 1840, after an absence of more than three years. D'Urville had not found the South Magnetic Pole, nor had he landed on the Antarctic continent, but he had charted a previously unknown coastline with great accuracy and added to the growing store of knowledge about the south polar region. A year and a half after his return D'Urville was killed in a railway accident as he rode back to Paris from an outing to Versailles.*

*The record of his expedition was published at Paris between 1841 and 1845 in twenty-three volumes, with six additional volumes of plates, as* Voyage au Pole Sud et dans l'Oceanie sur les corvettes l'Astrolabe et la Zélée execute par ordre du Roi pendant 1837–40. *The sections dealing with Antarctica were translated into English by Ethel S. Barton and first published in 1901 in* The Antarctic Manual, *edited by George Murray (London, the Royal Geographical Society). That translation is used here.*   □

# DUMONT D'URVILLE

Jan. 18 [1840].—On the evening of the 18th we had reached 64° S. lat. The weather was damp, the temperature fairly mild, and we were full of hope we might soon pass the 70th parallel; but at midnight we found ourselves suddenly surrounded by five enormous blocks shaped like a table. These icebergs (*glaces*) had exactly the same appearance as those we had encountered in such large numbers near the Powel Islands. From that moment my foreboding that we were near some unknown land increased; I reluctantly gave up the hope I had cherished of penetrating to a high latitude, for I thought that I should soon be stopped by the land which presumably was in front of us, and this in any case would form the nucleus of a solid and insuperable iceberg by offering a solid base for floating ice. The weather was cloudy; snow fell abundantly, and, notwithstanding the danger of sailing by night in these latitudes, we took advantage of a fair easterly breeze which was blowing to advance further to the south.

*Jan. 19.*—At 6 o'clock in the morning we counted 6 ice-islands floating round us. At 8 a.m. we distinguished 16. All the blocks were on the whole larger than those we had already encountered. They were all of the same shape, being flat with perpendicular sides. Their height varied from thirty to forty metres; as regards their horizontal dimensions, we noticed several which were more than 1000 metres broad, and one of them was admittedly a mile from end to end. They were all alike, and similar to those we had seen in the neighbourhood of land on our first polar expedition. There seemed to be no trace of fusion nor of decomposition; in none of them were to be seen those vast hollows formed by the sea at their edge, which imitate to perfection the arches of a bridge, especially when the light shines on them obliquely. These floating islands seemed to have been detached the night before from an ice-bound coast at a short distance.

Our corvettes were surrounded by white and grey petrels, petrels tachetés (*damiers*), some penguins, a whale, and two or three seals. This was another indication of being near land. At 9 a.m. we saw in the E.S.E. a great black cloud which seemed stationary and had the appearance of a raised island. For a long time we followed it with our eyes, always thinking we saw some indication which would prove we had made a new discovery. But at 10 a.m. the sky, hitherto cloudy, suddenly cleared. The sun appeared in all its glory, and quickly dispersed this deceptive apparition. Towards 3 p.m. M. Gervaize, who was officer of the watch, thought he saw once more an indication of land in the east. For some time he had noticed in this direction a greyish spot which appeared stationary; but we had already been so often misled by false appearances, so frequent in these latitudes, that we had become very sceptical. M. Dumoulin, who was on the poop, occupied at the moment in taking the bearing of the different ice-islands in sight, hastily climbed into the rigging to clear up all doubt; he assured himself that the indication given by M. Gervaize referred to a cloud which, seen from the height of the mizzen top, appeared to be above the horizon. On coming down he also announced to me that right before us there was an appearance of land much more distinct and sharply cut; this was in fact Adélie Land. Thanks to this circumstance, M. Dumoulin was the first among us all to see this land. But he had been so often deceived by illusions of this kind that he was himself far from believing in his discovery, and he was one of the very last to recognise the reality of its existence.

At 6 p.m. we counted 59 great icebergs round us and a great number of others in sight. The wind had quite dropped; the sea, beaten down under the weight of the enormous blocks which crowded it, was calm and smooth as a lake. The sun was shining in all its glory, and its rays, reflected on the crystal walls which surrounded us, produced a magical and charming effect. We had not a single man on the sick list. M. Dumoutier had warned me that he thought he recognised signs in some of the men of an approaching epidemic of scurvy; but happily all danger of this sort had rapidly disappeared, thanks to the precautions of the doctors. Thus our crews were full of courage and spirit and appeared happy and contented. They had been preparing for some time a ceremony similar to that practised on board ship when crossing the equator, and the actors, having asked my permission, were ready to appear on the scene as soon as we arrived at the polar circle. I have always thought that the practical jokes which the sailors are in the habit of playing off on those who cross the equator for the first time, have a good effect on board ship, where any distraction for the sailors is so rare, and where want of employment and the consequent boredom spread depression among the crew. Therefore, far from opposing the buffoonery, for which our men were preparing, I declared myself ready to be the first to submit to it; only, on account of the temperature, I forbade all throwing of water on the deck or of subjecting anyone to ablutions which are only supportable under the torrid zone. For the rest, I left them to invent the kind of ceremony to which they wished to subject those on board the *Astrolabe*, and it will be seen later that in this respect their powers did not fail. We had attained the 66° S. lat., everything led us to hope that we should soon pass the Antarctic circle, and according to custom I was officially warned that the next day I should receive a visit from Father Antarctic. After a rain of rice and beans hurled from the top, I received a postilion mounted on a seal, who brought me the message from his fantastic sovereign. I will spare the reader the costume of this singular ambassador and the contents of his letter; I observed with pleasure that the sailors had changed the ceremony of baptism, customary on the line, to one of communion in one element, that of wine, and as this would be better for them, I had no objection to make. We all hoped that the next day we should have passed the polar circle, but the calms which succeeded the wind arrested our progress. We were at the season when the days are longest in the glacial zone, so that at 9 p.m. the sun was still above the horizon and its luminous disc set slowly behind the land, whose existence was for several of us still very doubtful. At 10.50 this luminary disappeared, and showed up the raised contour of the land in all its sharpness. Everyone had run together on to the deck to enjoy the magnificent spectacle which offered itself to our gaze. It would have been impossible indeed to paint the grandeur of the sight. The calm of night gave to the enormous masses of ice which surrounded us a grander but also a more severe aspect; all the crew watched the sun disappearing behind the land and leaving behind him a long train of light. At midnight there was still twilight, and we could easily read on the deck. The night lasted only half-an-hour; I took advantage of it to snatch some rest, postponing till the next day the task of clearing up doubts as to the existence of the land in front of us.

*Jan. 20.*—At 4 a.m. I counted 72 large icebergs round us. I knew that during the night we had hardly changed our position, and yet among all these enormous blocks surrounding us, each with its own peculiar shape, although presenting an aspect of uniformity, I hardly recognised one of the floating islands I had noticed the night before. The sun had been up a long time, and although the atmosphere was misty its warmth could be felt, and all the icebergs around us seemed to be undergoing an active disintegration. One of them, which was only a short distance from us, attracted my notice especially. Numerous streams flowed from its summit, making deep hollows in its side, and hurled themselves into the sea in cascades. The weather was magnificent; but unfortunately there was no wind; before us rose the land: one could distinguish the details of it. Its aspect was very uniform. Entirely covered with snow, it stretched from east to west and seemed to drop towards the sea by an easy incline. In the midst of the uniform greyish tint which it presented we could see no peak, no single black spot. Thus there still remained more than one among us who doubted its existence. However, at midday all doubt vanished. A boat from the *Zélée*, which came to visit us, announced that land had been seen by those on board ever since the evening before. Less sceptical than ourselves, all the officers of the *Zélée* were already persuaded of the reality of this discovery. Unfortunately an unbroken calm prevented us from approaching it to make the matter certain. Nevertheless, joy reigned on board; henceforth the success of our enterprise was assured; for the expedition could report in any case the discovery of a new land.

The day was entirely devoted to the sports of the crew. Although we had not yet reached the polar circle, our men did not wait for that to produce the Antarctic sovereign on the bridge. They represented, as usual, all kinds of strange scenes; there was a show of mummers, a sermon, and a banquet. The whole closed with dancing and singing. The entire crew were cheery and full of fun. Indeed, since leaving Hobart Town, our men had rarely enjoyed more flourishing health. Numerous sea-birds surrounded us; we saw a great number of penguins floundering about in the water, and several fur seals, but not a single one of those giant petrels which we had found in such abundance on the icebergs during our first circumpolar expedition; they used to come, when our corvettes were hemmed in the ice, and fight under our very eyes for the remains of the seals killed by our hunters. We picked up on the surface of the sea a long whitish girdle of most singular appearance. It was more than 2 metres long, round, and uniform. Later we found it was formed by an agglomeration of molluscs; we found similar girdles later on, but shorter.

*Jan. 21.*—Ever since we had recognised land we were impatiently awaiting a wind which should enable us to approach; at last, at 3 a.m., it rose in the S.S.E., but it was so light that we hardly made one knot. As we approached nearer we distinctly saw crevasses on the ice crust which covered the earth, giving it a very uniform grey tint. Here and there we saw deep ravines hollowed out by the water which arose from the melting of the snow; but the details of the coast were hidden from us by the islands of floating ice which, in all probability, had but lately been detached.

At last the wind settled in the S.S.E., and we began to advance rapidly; but the nearer we came the more numerous and menacing became the ice-islands. Soon they really became an alarming mass, divided by narrow, winding channels. Nevertheless, I did not hesitate to steer towards it. At 8 o'clock we were so shut in by these floating masses that I feared every minute to see our corvettes dashed to pieces on them. We were by no means free from danger, for the sea produced around these masses considerable eddies, which could not fail to bring a ship to destruction if she were for a moment sheltered from the wind by the high cliffs of ice. In passing at their base we were well able to judge of the height which these icebergs attain. Their perpendicular walls towered above our masts; they overhung our ships, whose dimensions seemed ridiculously diminutive compared with these enormous masses. The spectacle which presented itself to our gaze was at once grand and terrifying. One could imagine oneself in the narrow streets of a city of giants. At the foot of these immense masses we perceived vast caverns hollowed out by the sea, where the waves rushed in with a roar. The sun darted oblique rays on the immense walls of ice, which resembled crystal. The effects of light and shade were truly magical and striking. From the top of these ice mountains there leaped into the sea numerous streams, caused by the apparently very active melting of the snow. We often saw in front of us two icebergs so near each other that we lost sight of the land towards which we were steering. We could then only see two straight, threatening walls rising up beside us. The orders of the officers were echoed several times by these gigantic masses, which threw the sounds of the voice from one to the other; when our eyes fell on the *Zélée*, following us at a short distance, she looked so small and her masts seemed so slender, that we could not suppress a feeling of alarm. For nearly an hour we saw nothing round us but vertical walls of ice. Then we reached a vast basin formed by the land on one side, and on the other by the chain of floating islands through which we had just passed. At midday we were not more than three or four miles from our new discovery.

The land which was in sight showed now such irregularities as it possessed; it stretched as far as one could see to south-east and north-west, and in these two directions its limits were invisible. It was entirely covered with snow, and might reach a height of 1000 to 1200 metres. Nowhere was there any striking peak. Nowhere was any spot to be seen which indicated soil, and one could almost believe that we had before us an ice-pack considerably larger than any we

had met, granting the possibility of any pack attaining such a prodigious height. The shore presented everywhere a vertical cliff of ice,
like those we had noticed in the floating islands we had just passed.
This aspect of the coast was so like that presented by the floating
icebergs that we had never hesitated about their formation. Besides
this, at several points along the shore we noticed a great quantity of
floating ice, apparently scarcely separated from the shore where they
had been formed, and only waiting for the winds and currents to
gain the open sea. The higher parts of the land presented everywhere
a uniform hue, reaching the sea by a gentle incline; owing to this
formation we could see at a glance a considerable stretch of land. At
several points we noticed that the surface of the snow which covered
the land was ploughed up. One could distinguish regular waves like
those hollowed out by wind in the sand deserts. It was especially in
the least sheltered places that the irregularities were more marked.
At other points this ice crust seemed also traversed by ravines or
hollowed by water. The sun was shining brilliantly, adding greatly
to the already very imposing aspect of this mass of ice. With our
glasses we were gazing curiously on this mysterious land, the existence of which no longer seemed doubtful, but which had not as yet
offered any undeniable proof of it. Before long the man on the look-
out thought he could distinguish a dark spot on the coast line, and
hastened to announce his discovery; several officers who had run up
the rigging also thought they could see the longed-for signs across a
mass of floating islands which bordered the coast. But as we approached, the black spot which had been sighted suddenly disappeared. We recognised among the floating islands one which had an
earthy colour, and this might have given rise to the mistake. We
supposed that this was the dark spot seen by the man on the look-
out. It is possible, however, that there was in this part an island or
a bare summit, which might have appeared in a given direction, but
which had disappeared later behind the icebergs which bordered the
coast. The events of the next few hours show that this hypothesis
was very probable.

The wind, although light, was favorable for sailing along the coast
westwards. All day was occupied in exploring it. We noticed several
projecting headlands and some rather shallow bays choked by an
immense quantity of floating islands; everywhere the coast pre-

sented the same aspect, terminating towards the sea in an ice-wall which rendered all landing impossible. For some time MM. Dumoulin and Coupvent, who were anxious to obtain magnetic observations more conclusive than those they had made on board, had asked me to land either on the coast or some ice-island sufficiently large to be absolutely steady. In vain during the day had I sought an opportunity to satisfy this laudable desire; all the ice-islands that we met with were inaccessible. But towards 6 p.m. one of them, having a fairly easy incline on one side, seemed to unite all the conditions necessary for this kind of work. Immediately the whale-boat was lowered in order to convey the officers who were to take their observations. In the meantime our corvettes lay-to, in order not to drift from this spot. It was at this moment that we verified irrefutably the existence of land. M. Duroch, who was officer of the watch, had already fixed his glass on a point where for a moment he thought he saw dark spots; but every mark of the sort immediately disappeared as our corvettes began to move. Suddenly, he again noticed rocks, the sombre hue of which contrasted with the whiteness of the snow, but they disappeared immediately behind the icebergs; this time, however, the land had been recognised in an unmistakable manner. I decided to have a boat got ready to go and verify this important fact. At this advanced hour of the day, the sending of a boat to so great a distance was not without danger. Besides our boats were very inferior in sailing qualities to the whaler, which I had already dispatched to make the physical observations. However, as I was anxious to profit by the fortunate circumstances which might never occur again, I confided the large boat to M. Duroch, with the order to collect palpable fragments of our discovery. The *Zélée* also sent a boat under the command of M. Dubouzet. Like ourselves, the officers of this ship had noticed bare islets, and were also keenly anxious to go and examine them. . . .

The two boats which had gone ashore did not return till 10.30, laden with fragments of rocks detached from the shore. The following is an account of this interesting excursion from the journal of M. Dubouzet:—"During the whole day all eyes had been fixed on the coast to try and discover something other than snow and ice. At last, when we were beginning to despair, after having passed a mass of floating islands which quite blocked out the shore, we noticed several little islets the sides of which, destitute of snow, showed us that blackish earth so ardently desired. Several minutes later we saw the large boat of the *Astrolabe* leave the corvette and start towards the shore with an officer and two naturalists. Immediately I requested Commander Jacquinot to embark me in his yawl, which he ordered to be lowered to send ashore. The *Astrolabe* boat had already got a good start on us; after 2½ hours hard rowing we reached the nearest islet. Our men were so full of ardour that they hardly noticed the effort they had just been making, in covering more than seven miles in so short a time. Going along, we passed quite close to immense ice-islands. Their perpendicular sides, eaten away by the sea, were crowned on the top by long needles of greenish ice formed after a thaw. Their appearance was to the last degree imposing. They seemed to form an insurmountable barrier to the east of the islets to which we were bound; and this made me think that they were perhaps fixed 80–100 fathoms down. Their height indicated about this draught of water. The sea was covered with débris of ice, which obliged us to take a very winding course. On the icebergs we noticed a crowd of penguins, who with a stupid air quietly watched us pass.

"It was nearly 9 o'clock when, to our great joy, we landed on the western part of the most westerly and the loftiest islet. The *Astrolabe's* boat had arrived a moment before, and already the men had climbed up the steep sides of this rock. They hurled down the penguins, who were much astonished to find themselves so brutally dispossessed of the island, of which they were the sole inhabitants. We also jumped on shore armed with pickaxes and hammers. The surf rendered this operation very difficult. I was forced to leave several men in the boat to look after her. I then immediately sent one of our men to unfurl the tricolour flag on this land, which no human creature had either seen or stepped on before. Following the ancient custom, faithfully kept up by the English, we took possession of it in the name of France, as well as of the adjacent coast, which the ice prevented us from approaching. Our enthusiasm and joy were such that it seemed to us we had just added a province to French territory, by this wholly pacific conquest. If the abuse which has been born of such acts of possession has caused them to be often regarded as ridiculous and worthless, in this case at any rate we believed ourselves sufficiently in the right to maintain the ancient custom in favour of our country. For we dispossessed none and our titles were incontestable. We regarded ourselves, therefore, at once as being on French soil; and there is at least this advantage that it will never raise up war against our country.

"The ceremony ended, as it should, with a libation. To the glory of France, which concerned us deeply just then, we emptied a bottle of the most generous of her wines, which one of our companions had had the presence of mind to bring with him. Never was Bordeaux wine called on to play a more worthy part; never was bottle emptied more fitly. Surrounded on all sides by eternal ice and snow, the cold was extreme. This generous liquor reacted with advantage against the rigours of the temperature. All this happened in less time than it takes to write it. We then all set to work immediately to collect everything of interest in natural history that this barren land could offer. The animal kingdom was only represented by the penguins. Notwithstanding all my search we did not find a single shell. The rock was entirely bare, and did not even offer the least trace of lichens. We found only one single seaweed, and that was dry; so it had been brought there by currents or birds. We were obliged to fall back on the mineral kingdom. Each of us took a hammer and began to hew at the rock. But it was so hard, being of a granite nature, that we could only detach very small pieces. Happily, while wandering on the summit of the island, the sailors discovered large fragments of rock detached by frost, and these they took into our boats. In a short time we had enough to supply specimens to all our museums and to others besides. In examining them closely, I recognised a perfect resemblance between these rocks and some small fragments that we had found in the stomach of a penguin killed the evening before. These fragments could, if necessary, have given an exact idea of the geological formation of this land, if it had been impossible to go on shore there. However extraordinary may be this way of doing geology, it proves how much interest the smallest observations may have for the naturalist, often even helping him in his researches, by leading him sometimes on to the track of discoveries to which they seem to be the most foreign. The small islet on which we landed is one of a group of eight or ten small islands rounded above, and all presenting pretty much the same form. These islands are separated from the nearest coast by a distance of 500–600 metres. We noticed

along the shore several more tops quite bare, and one cape of which
the base was also free from snow; but we noticed also a great quantity of ice which made the approach to it very difficult. All these
islets, very close to each other, seemed to form a continuous chain
parallel to the coast from east to west. All the ice islands, accumulated in the eastern part, which seemed to me fixed, probably cover
other islets similar to those on which we had landed. It is certain that
many rocks must be buried every year by enormous masses of ice, of
which they form the nucleus. Perhaps even the great land in front of
us was cut up by numerous channels. The hydrographical records
which were made in these latitudes can have no other object than to
determine the form of the glaciers at the moment of our passage
without showing the contour of the coast, which must rarely be free
from the thick crust covering the soil.

"We did not leave these islets till 9.30; we were entranced by the
treasures we carried away. Before hoisting sail we saluted our discovery with a general hurrah, to bid it a last good-bye. The echoes
of these silent regions, for the first time disturbed by human voices,
repeated our cries and then returned to their habitual silence, so
gloomy and so imposing; favoured by a good easterly breeze, we
took our course to the ships, which were bearing off from land,
often disappearing in their tacks behind the great ice-islands. We
reached them only at 11 p.m. The cold was then extremely sharp.
The thermometer registered 5° below zero. The outsides of our
boats, as well as the oars, were covered with a coating of ice. We
were glad to get back on board the corvettes, happy to have thus
completed our discovery without accident, for in this glacial and
capricious climate it is not good to leave one's ship for long at a time.
The least wind overtaking a ship on such a coast would force it to
go out to sea at once and abandon its boats."

After this excursion, which left no more doubt as to the reality
of our discovery, it remained only for me to extend the examination
of it as far as possible. The weather seemed to lend itself favourably
to this difficult course. The wind was east and blew us slowly westwards. Up to that time, and while any doubt remained, I did not
wish to give any name to our discovery; but on the return of our
boats I gave it the name of Adélie Land. The very projecting cape
which we had seen in the morning when we were trying to get near

the land, received the name of Cape Découverte. The point near to which our boats landed, and where they collected the geological specimens, was named Point Geology. . . .

*Jan. 29.*—The next day, the wind being apparently steady in the east, I thought I ought to give up all attempts to penetrate further in this direction, and I then began to consider how to direct my course in the best possible way towards the discovery of the magnetic pole. After consulting M. Dumoulin, the order was given to sail south-west, in order that we might cross all the magnetic meridians whose curves seem to approach most nearly those of the terrestrial meridians. At midday we were about 64° 48′ S. latitude: only two or three ice-islands were in sight. The sea was still running very high, but the weather was fine though foggy, and our corvettes under full sail, having the wind astern, moved rapidly. At 4 o'clock the man on watch signalled an iceberg of immense extent in front of us and not far off. Indeed, we soon saw through the fog a long line of ice, stretching from south-east to north-west, and apparently continuous. Accordingly I gave the order to bring her closer to the wind. This had hardly been done, and the officer of the watch was about to give the order to board the main tack, which had meantime been clewed up for the moment, when the man on the watch signalled a ship running towards us before the wind. Immediately everyone was on the poop. We were all in fact very glad to assure ourselves of the truth of news so unexpected in such latitudes. The ship was moving quickly, and it was already very near us when the man on watch had announced it. Till that moment it had been hidden by the fog. The same moment as we distinguished her form, we could recognise the flag she had at once run up on seeing us. It was an American brig, and the national pennant which floated at her mainmast showed that she was a man-o'-war. As I have already said, we knew when we left Hobart Town that the American expedition, which was composed of several ships under command of Captain Wilkes and destined for a voyage of circumnavigation, was at Sydney in December making preparations for a new polar expedition. Therefore, we were certain that the brig we saw belonged to this expedition; and she, on seeing our corvettes, had perhaps hoped we were part of the American expedition. However that may be, although we had hoisted our colours the ship continued to come towards us, and I hoped that she intended to speak us. In order to help her, I gave the order to wait a few moments before boarding the tack.

The American brig was soon no more than a cable's length behind us, and I thought her captain intended to pass to port of the *Astrolabe* and to remain a short distance to leeward. Now, since the ship under full sail had maintained a great speed compared with our own, and would rapidly have passed us, if at that moment she had gone to windward, I gave the order to board the main tack in order that the *Astrolabe* might remain longer alongside. This manoeuvre was probably misunderstood by the Americans, for the brig instantly bore off to the south, and went away quickly. Afterwards, the reports of Captain Wilkes which reached me, in mentioning this meeting, attributed intentions to me which were very far from my thoughts. Certainly, if I had not wished to communicate just then with the ship which had signalled to me, I should not have delayed so long the boarding the tack, to keep off a little from the ice-barrier we had met, as the fog had prevented us from seeing the way. We had no object in keeping secret the result of our operations, and the discoveries for which we had nearly paid so heavily. Besides, these are no longer the days when navigators, impelled by the interests of commerce, think themselves obliged to hide carefully their route and their discoveries in order to avoid the concurrence of rival nations. On the contrary, I should have been glad to give to our co-explorers the result of our researches, in the hope that it would have been useful to them, and enlarge the circle of our geographical knowledge. If I can believe what was told me in Hobart Town, it seems that the Americans were far from sharing these feelings. They have always maintained the greatest secrecy concerning their operations at all the points where they landed, and they have refrained from giving the slightest indication of the work which they accomplished.

◻ *The Americans were as surprised to see D'Urville's ships as the French were to find Yankees in the Antarctic. The American commander, Lieutenant Ringgold, had thought the ships belonged to the*

British expedition under James Clark Ross, and was, he said, "preparing to cheer the discoverer of the North Magnetic Pole" when the French flag was hoisted.

Ringgold was one of the officers serving in what became known as the Wilkes Expedition—the first Antarctic venture sponsored by the Government of the United States. It grew out of the Symmes holes-in-the-poles affair and out of Jeremiah Reynolds' ceaseless propagandizing for an American polar exploration. In 1835, Reynolds succeeded in getting $150,000 appropriated by Congress for the journey, and President Andrew Jackson expressed enthusiasm; but political bickering kept the mariners in the harbor for many years. The original commander resigned in disgust when no action had been taken by the end of 1837, and one experienced naval officer after another declined to accept the appointment as his replacement, until at last the Government had to turn to a junior officer, forty-year-old Charles Wilkes.

Wilkes, who held the rank of lieutenant, had specialized in mathematics and surveying, and had more scientific knowledge than the average Navy man of his day. He had been in charge of procuring scientific instruments for the expedition in 1836, when it seemed as though departure was near; the actual date of sailing, August 18, 1838, saw him in command of the entire operation, probably somewhat to his own surprise.

Wilkes had six ships at the outset. The Vincennes, his flagship, was a large sloop-of-war, as was its companion the Peacock; also in the fleet were the brig Porpoise, the supply ship Relief, and two pilot boats, the Gull and the Flying Fish. The expedition included 83 officers, 345 crewmen, and a dozen scientists and artists.

By March, 1839, Wilkes was in the South Shetlands; like D'Urville the year before, he failed to get far into the Weddell Sea, and the onset of Antarctic winter forced him back to harbor at Valparaiso. After a tour of Samoa, Fiji, and other Pacific islands, Wilkes left Sydney, Australia, late in 1839 for a second entry into the south frigid zone. Battered by icebergs, buffeted by storms, Wilkes' leaky, poorly equipped vessels neared the unapproachable Antarctic shore, sighting land some ten hours ahead of D'Urville, whose ships were four hundred miles to the west. The extract below describes this part of Wilkes' journey and records his opinion—still subject to debate at *that time—that Antarctica merited the name of "continent." In March, 1840, faced with mutiny by his scurvy-racked, fatigued men, Wilkes returned to Australia, but it was not until June, 1842, that the expedition reached the United States—where the controversial, outspoken Wilkes quickly found himself enmeshed in legal proceedings, a court-martial, and disgrace. He was accused of having exceeded his authority and of being unduly harsh to his crew, among many other things. Eventually he was cleared, though given a minor reprimand on one count.*

*After his clearance, Wilkes prepared a five-volume report on his expedition, which appeared between 1847 and 1849. From then until the outbreak of the Civil War, he busied himself editing the voluminous scientific findings of the journey for publication, and in 1861 returned to active service as commander of the sloop San Jacinto. After indulging in an independent naval maneuver that nearly brought Great Britain into the war on the side of the Confederacy (he intercepted a British mail steamer carrying two Confederate commissioners to London), he was again court-martialed, was found guilty, and was placed on the retired list. He spent the rest of his life working on the unpublished reports of his voyage to Antarctica, but Congress refused to appropriate funds for the publication of most of them. Wilkes died in 1877, and, no longer a thorny public figure, was hailed posthumously for his great Antarctic achievements. He had traveled fifteen hundred miles along the coast of an unknown continent in rotting ships, showing conclusively Antarctica's continental nature.*

*The passages that follow are from* Narrative of the United States Exploring Expedition During the Years 1838, 1839, 1840, 1841, 1842, *by Charles Wilkes, U.S.N. (Philadelphia, Lea & Blanchard, 1849).*  □

# CHARLES WILKES

On the 22d of January [1840] . . . the Vincennes passed a remarkable collection of tabular icebergs, for whose existence I can account in no other manner than by supposing them to be attached to a rocky islet, which formed a nucleus to which they adhered. It was quite obvious that they had not been formed in the place where they were seen, and must, therefore, have grounded, after being adrift.

On the 23d January, after passing around this group of icebergs, the sea was found comparatively clear, and a large open space showed itself to the southward. Into this space the course of the Vincennes was immediately directed. While thus steering to the south, the appearance of land was observed on either hand, both to the eastward and westward.

Pursuing this course, we by midnight reached the solid barrier, and all approach to the land on the east and west was entirely cut off by the close packing of the icebergs. I was, therefore, reluctantly compelled to return, not a little vexed that we were again foiled in our endeavour to reach the Antarctic Continent. This was a deep indentation in the coast, about twenty-five miles wide: we explored it to the depth of about fifteen miles, and did not reach its termination. This bay I have called Disappointment Bay: it is in latitude 67° 04′ 30″ S., longitude 147° 30′ E. The weather was remarkably fine, with a bracing air: the thermometer in the air 22°, in the water 31°.

The next day, 24th, we stood out of the bay, and continued our course to the westward. About noon, to my surprise, I learnt that one of the officers, Lieutenant Underwood, had marked on the log-slate that there was an opening of clear water, subtending three points of the compass, at the bottom of Disappointment Bay. Though confident that this was not the fact, in order to put this matter at rest, I at once determined to return, although forty miles distant, and ordered the ship about, to refute the assertion by the officer's own testimony. This was most effectually done the next morning, 25th, when the ship reached the identical spot, and all were fully convinced that no opening existed. The whole bay was enclosed by a firm barrier of ice, from north-north-west to east-northeast.

The weather proved delightful, with light airs from the southward, and I determined to take this opportunity to fill up the water-tanks with ice. The ship was hove-to, a hawser got in readiness, the boats lowered, and brought alongside of an iceberg well adapted to our purpose.

The same opportunity was also taken to make the magnetic observations on the ice, and to try the local attraction of the ship.

Many birds were seen about the ship, of which we were fortunate in obtaining specimens. The day was remarkably clear, and the same appearance of land was seen that had been witnessed on the 24th. We filled nineteen of our tanks with ice, after having allowed it to remain for some time on deck for the salt water to drain off in part, and it proved very potable.

At about 5 P.M., we had completed our required store of ice, and cast off, making sail to the northward.

In order that no further mistakes should take place as to the openings being passed, I issued an order, directing the officer of the deck on being relieved to go to the masthead, and report to me the exact situation of the ice, and this was continued during the remainder of our cruise among it. . . .

The dip observed on the ice was 87° 30′, and the variation 12° 46′ easterly. The compasses were found to be very sluggish, having but little horizontal directive force.

About half an hour after we cast off from the iceberg, a thick snowstorm came up, with the wind from the southeast. Although there were very many ice-islands around us, on our way out, I felt that I understood the ground well, having passed over it twice, and knowing I had a space of a few miles, only thinly sprinkled with icebergs, I hove-to with shortened sail. This was the first southeast wind we had had since being on this coast. I had been disappointed in not finding it from that quarter before; for I had been informed, by those who had navigated in high southern latitudes, that southeast would be the prevailing wind, and would be attended with fine weather. Now, however, with a fair wind, I was unable to run, for the weather was unfavourable.

At 6 A.M. on the 26th, we again made sail, and at 8 A.M. we discovered the Porpoise, to whom we made signals to come within hail. We found them all well, and compared chronometers.

As it still blew fresh from the southeast, and the weather became a little more clear, we both bore away, running through much drift-ice, at the rate of nine knots an hour. We had the barrier in sight; it was, however, too thick to see much beyond it. Sailing in this way I felt to be extremely hazardous; but our time was so short for the examination of this icy coast that while the barrier was to be seen, I deemed it my duty to proceed. We fortunately, by good look-outs, and carefully conning the ship, were enabled to avoid any heavy thumps.

On the 27th, we again had the wind from south-southwest. The floe-ice had become so thick, that we found it impossible to get through it in the direction I wished to go, and we were compelled to pass round it. The Porpoise was in sight until noon. The weather proved beautifully clear. A long range of tabular icebergs was in sight to the southward, indicating, as I have before observed, that the coast was near. I passed through these, losing sight of the Porpoise to the northwest about noon, when we were in longitude 142° 40′ E., latitude 65° 54′ 21″ S., variation 5° 08′ easterly.

On the 28th, I found myself completely surrounded by the tabular icebergs, through which we continued to pass. Towards midnight the wind shifted to the southeast, and enabled me to haul more to the southward. At 9½ A.M. we had another sight of the land ahead, and every prospect of nearing it, with a fine breeze. The sight of the icebergs around us, all of large dimensions, was beautiful. The greatest number in sight at one time was noted, and found to be more than a hundred, varying from a quarter of a mile to three miles in length. We took the most open route, and by eleven o'clock had run upwards of forty miles through them. We had the land now in plain view, but the weather soon began to thicken and the breeze to freshen. At noon it was so thick that every thing was hidden, and no observation was obtained. The ship was hove-to, but shortly after again put under way, making several tacks to keep my position, which I felt was becoming a critical one, in case a gale should ensue. I therefore looked carefully over my chart, and was surprised at the vast number of icebergs that appeared on it. At 2 P.M. the barometer began to fall, and the weather to change for the worse. At 5 P.M. a gale was evidently coming on, so we took three reefs in the topsails. It appeared now that certain wreck would ensue, should we remain where we were; and after much consideration, I made up my mind to retrace my way, and seek the open space forty miles distant, taking for a landmark a remarkable berg that had been the last entered on the chart, and which would be a guide to my course out. I therefore stood for its position. The weather was so thick, that it was necessary to run close to it, to be quite sure of recognising it, for on this seemed to depend our safety. About the estimated time we would take to pass over the distance, an iceberg was made (we were within one thousand feet of it) which, at first view, I felt confident was the one sought, but was not altogether satisfied afterwards. I therefore again consulted my chart, and became more doubtful of it. Just at that moment I was called on deck by an officer, who informed me that there were icebergs a short distance ahead! Such proved to be the case; our path was beset with them, and it was evident we could not regain our route. To return was worse, so having but little choice left, I determined to keep on. To encounter these icebergs so soon after seeing the other, was in some respects satisfactory, for it removed all doubts, and showed me that we were not near the track by which we entered. Nothing, therefore, was to be done but to keep a good look-out, and the ship under sufficient way to steer well. My safest plan was to keep as near our former track as possible, believing it to be most free of these masses.

At 8 P.M. it began to blow very hard, with a violent snow-storm, circumscribing our view, and rendering it impossible to see more than two ship's-lengths ahead. The cold was severe, and every spray that touched the ship was immediately converted into ice. At 9 P.M., the barometer still falling and the gale increasing, we reduced sail to close-reefed fore and main-topsails, reefed foresail and trysails, under which we passed numerous icebergs, some to windward, and some to leeward of us. At $10^h$ $30^m$, we found ourselves thickly beset with them, and had many narrow escapes; the excitement became intense; it required a constant change of helm to avoid those close aboard; and we were compelled to press the ship with canvass in order to escape them, by keeping her to windward. We thus passed close along their weather sides, and distinctly heard the roar of the surf dashing against them. We had, from time to time, glimpses of their obscure outline, appearing as though immediately above us. After many escapes, I found the ship so covered with ice, and the watch so powerless in managing her, that a little after midnight, on the 29th, I had all hands called. Scarcely had they been reported on deck, when it was made known to me that the gunner, Mr. Williamson, had fallen, broken his ribs, and otherwise injured himself, on the icy deck.

The gale at this moment was awful. We found we were passing large masses of drift-ice, and ice-islands became more numerous. At a little after one o'clock it was terrific, and the sea was now so heavy, that I was obliged to reduce sail still further: the fore and main-top-sails were clewed up; the former was furled, but the latter being a new sail, much difficulty was found in securing it.

A seaman, by the name of Brooks, in endeavouring to execute the order to furl, got on the lee yardarm, and the sail having blown over the yard, prevented his return. Not being aware of his position until it was reported to me from the forecastle, he remained there some time. On my seeing him he appeared stiff, and clinging to the yard and lift. Spilling-lines were at once rove, and an officer with several men sent aloft to rescue him, which they succeeded in doing by passing a bowline around his body and dragging him into the top. He was almost frozen to death. Several of the best men were completely exhausted with cold, fatigue, and excitement, and were sent below. This added to our anxieties, and but little hope remained to me of escaping: I felt that neither prudence nor foresight could avail in protecting the ship and crew. All that could be done, was to be prepared for any emergency, by keeping every one at his station.

We were swiftly dashing on, for I felt it necessary to keep the ship under rapid way through the water, to enable her to steer and work quickly. Suddenly many voices cried out, "Ice ahead!" then, "On the weather bow!" and again, "On the lee bow and abeam!" All hope of escape seemed in a moment to vanish; return we could not, as large ice-islands had just been passed to leeward: so we dashed on, expecting every moment the crash. The ship, in an instant, from having her lee guns under water, rose upright; and so close were we passing to leeward of one of these huge islands, that our trysails were almost thrown aback by the eddy wind. The helm was put up to pay the ship off, but the proximity of those under our lee bade me keep my course. All was now still except the distant roar of the wild storm, that was raging behind, before, and above us; the sea was in great agitation, and both officers and men were in the highest degree excited. The ship continued her way, and as we proceeded, a glimmering of hope arose, for we accidentally had hit upon a clear passage between two large ice-islands, which in fine weather we should not dare to have ventured through. The suspense endured while making our way between them was intense, but of short duration; and my spirits rose as I heard the whistling of the gale grow louder and

112

louder before us, as we emerged from the passage. We had escaped an awful death, and were again tempest-tost.

We encountered many similar dangers that night. At half-past 4 A.M., I found we had reached the small open space laid down on my chart, and at five o'clock I hove-to the ship. I had been under intense excitement, and had not been off the deck for nine hours, and was now thankful to the Providence that had guided, watched over, and preserved us. Until 7 A.M., all hands were on deck, when there was some appearance of the weather moderating, and they were piped down. . . .

This gale was from the southeast, from which quarter it blew during the whole of its strength; and when it began to moderate, the wind veered to the southward. By noon we felt satisfied that the gale was over, and that we had escaped, although it was difficult to realize a sense of security when the perils we had just passed through were so fresh in our minds, and others still impending. Towards four o'clock, it cleared off, and we saw but few icebergs near us. Our longitude was found to be 140° E., latitude 63° 30′ S., and I again made call for the ice to the south, to pass over the very route we had just traversed through so many perils.

The wind had now hauled to the southwest. At 6 P.M., we again began to enter among ice-islands. The weather appeared settled; but I had so often been deceived by its fickleness, that I felt no reliance ought to be put in its continuance. A powerful inducement was held out to us, in the prospect of getting close enough to effect a landing; and this rendered us insensible to the dangers.

On the morning of the 30th the sun rose in great brilliancy, and the scene could hardly be realized as the same as that we had passed through only twenty-four hours before. All was now quiet; a brisk breeze blew from the eastward, all sail was set, and there was every prospect that we might accomplish our object; for the land was in sight, and the icebergs seemed floating in quiet. We wound our way through them in a sea so smooth that a yawl might have passed over it in safety. No straight line could have been drawn from us in any direction, that would not have cut a dozen icebergs in the same number of miles, and the wondering exclamations of the officers and crew were oft repeated,—"How could we have passed through them unharmed?" and, "What a lucky ship!" At eight o'clock, we had reached the icy barrier, and hove-to close to it. It was tantalizing, with the land in sight, to be again and again blocked out. Open water was seen near the land to the southwest of us, and a tortuous channel through the broken ice to leeward, apparently leading to it. All sail was immediately crowded; we passed rapidly through, and found ourselves again in clear water, which reached to the shores: the barrier extending in a line with our course, about two miles to windward, and a clear channel to the northwest, about two miles wide, as far as the eye could reach. Seeing this, I remarked to one of the officers that it would have been a good place to drift in during the last gale,—little thinking that in a few short hours it would serve us for that purpose, in still greater need. A brisk gale ensued, and the ship ran at the rate of nine or ten miles an hour; one reef was taken in the topsails, and we stood directly in for the most southerly part of the bay.

This bay was formed partly by rocks and partly by ice-islands. The latter were aground, and on the western side of the bay extended about five miles to the northward of our position.

While we stood on in this direction the gale increased, and our room became so circumscribed that we had not time on any one tack to reduce our canvass, before it became necessary to go about. In this way we approached within half a mile of the dark, volcanic rocks, which appeared on both sides of us, and saw the land gradually rising beyond the ice to the height of three thousand feet, and entirely covered with snow. It could be distinctly seen extending to the east and west of our position fully sixty miles. I make this bay in longitude 140° 02′ 30″ E., latitude 66° 45′ S.; and, now that all were convinced of its existence, I gave the land the name of the Antarctic Continent.

□   *Later in the same volume Wilkes set down Lieutenant Ring-gold's version of the unhappy meeting with the D'Urville expedi-tion.*   □

. . . Lieutenant-Commandant Ringgold says, in reference to their situation—

"I felt great anxiety to proceed, but the course was so perilous, the extent and trend of the barrier so uncertain, I could not reconcile it with prudence to advance. The frequent falling in with fields of drift-ice, the numerous and often closely-grouped chains of icebergs, were sufficient to point out discretion. The long-extended barrier was encountered in latitude 65° 08′ S.; at twelve to-day our position was 65° 16′ S.; it is easy to perceive the possibility of a trend northerly again, which would have placed us in a large and dangerous gulf, with a heavy gale blowing directly on, without a hope of escape.

"At 8 P.M., blowing very heavy; the snow falling rendered vision beyond a few yards impossible; I have seldom experienced a heavier blow, and towards the conclusion the squalls were severe and frequent."

The barometer at 3 A.M., stood at 28·200 in., the lowest point it reached during the gale. The temperature of the air was 26°.

The severe gale continued during the 29th [of January, 1840], with a heavy sea, and snow falling thickly; at 8 A.M. the gale abated, and the clouds broke away; through the day the sun occasionally out; the weather appeared unsettled; the sun set red and fiery; the latitude was observed 64° 46′ S., longitude 137° 16′ E.

On the 30th they stood again to the southwest; at 2 A.M. they made the barrier of field-ice, extending from southeast to west, when it became necessary to haul more to the northwest; the weather becoming thick with a heavy fall of snow, at four o'clock, the wind increasing, compelled them to shorten sail; at 7ʰ 30ᵐ the ice in fields was discovered close aboard, heading west; at this time hauled immediately on a wind to the northeast, and soon passed out of sight of the ice and out of danger; during the day blowing a gale of wind, and very heavy sea running, passing occasional ice-islands; at meridian, being clear of the barrier, the brig was hove-to under storm-sails, to await the clearing of the weather. In the afternoon the weather showed signs of clearing; the sun coming out, again made sail to approach the barrier; no ice in sight; great numbers of black petrels about.

At 4 P.M. discovered a ship ahead, and shortly after another was made, both standing to the northward; the brig hauled up to the northwest, intending to cut them off and speak them, supposing them to be the Vincennes and the Peacock; shortly afterwards they were seen to be strangers, being smaller ships than our own; at 4ʰ 30ᵐ the Porpoise hoisted her colours. Knowing that an English squadron under Captain Ross was expected in these seas, Lieutenant-Commandant Ringgold took them for his ships, and was, as he says, "preparing to cheer the discoverer of the North Magnetic Pole."

"At 4$^h$ 50$^m$, being within a mile and a half, the strangers showed French colours: the leeward and sternmost displayed a broad pennant; concluded now that they must be the French discovery ships under Captain D'Urville, on a similar service with ourselves: desirous of speaking and exchanging the usual and customary compliments incidental to naval life, I closed with the strangers, desiring to pass within hail under the flag ship's stern. While gaining fast, and being within musket-shot, my intentions too evident to excite a doubt, so far from any reciprocity being evinced, I saw with surprise sail making by boarding the main tack on board the flag-ship. Without a moment's delay, I hauled down my colours and bore up on my course before the wind."

It is with regret that I mention the above transaction, and it cannot but excite the surprise of all that such a cold repulse should have come from a French commander, when the officers of that nation are usually so distinguished for their politeness and attention. It was with no small excitement I heard the report of it,—that the vessels of two friendly powers, alike engaged upon an arduous and hazardous service, in so remote a region, surrounded with every danger navigators could be liable to, should meet and pass without even the exchange of common civilities, and exhibit none of the kind feelings that the situation would naturally awaken:—how could the French commander know that the brig was not in distress or in want of assistance? By refusing to allow any communication with him, he not only committed a wanton violation of all proper feeling, but a breach of the courtesy due from one nation to another. It is difficult to imagine what could have prompted him to such a course.

□  *The third, and most ambitious, of the expeditions searching for the South Magnetic Pole was that mounted by Great Britain. It was led by James Clark Ross, already the discoverer of the North Mag-*

*netic Pole and thus a veteran of cold-weather exploring. Ross had joined the Royal Navy in 1812 at the age of twelve, serving aboard the ship of his uncle, Admiral Sir John Ross. His first taste of high latitudes came in 1827, when he took part in Sir Edward Parry's unsuccessful attempt to reach the North Pole. Four years later, Ross and his uncle located the North Magnetic Pole.*

*For the Antarctic expedition Ross was given two sturdy, thick-hulled little ships, the* Erebus *and the* Terror. *They were equipped with the most advanced ice saws, scurvy remedies, and other polar necessities. Ross took no civilian scientists with him, but the four medical officers of the expedition had training in zoology, geology, botany, and other disciplines, and were capable of making scientific observations. They left in September, 1839.*

*After setting up stations for magnetic research on the Atlantic island of St. Helena and at the Cape of Good Hope, Ross proceeded westward to Tasmania, where he learned for the first time that both Wilkes and D'Urville had already entered the regions Ross had "reserved" for himself. Changing his plan, Ross set out for hitherto unknown territory far to the east of Wilkes' easternmost stop. Entering an ice-free sea at about 176° E., Ross sailed due south until he was brought to a halt by the ice-bound coast. On January 11, 1841, Ross landed on an island just off the coast, and gave the mainland vicinity the name of Victoria Land. Continuing onward into what is now called the Ross Sea, the explorers surpassed all previous records for southerly attainment, reaching 78° 4' S. by February 2. By that time they had made the startling discovery of an active volcano on a coastal island, and had encountered the awesome apron of ice, more than 700 feet thick and as large as California, that lies between the mainland and the open water of the Ross Sea. It was man's first sight of the great barrier known today as the Ross Ice Shelf.*

*When ice made further progress impossible, Ross turned back, discovering, as he retreated, the inlet he named McMurdo Sound, at the western end of the Ross Sea, which would be the site of so many later explorers' camps. Reaching Tasmania in April, 1841, Ross spent six months refitting his ships, returning to Antarctica in November to try to find the way around the ice barrier to the South Magnetic Pole. Both ships were punished by storms and barely escaped destruction; Ross was forced back to the Falkland Islands*

117

*and spent the winter near Cape Horn. In December, 1842, he made a
third attempt to approach the continent, this time via the Weddell
Sea, but again was thwarted by a wall of ice. Ross returned to England the following September, receiving a magnificent welcome, and
until his death in 1862 was occupied with editing the scientific reports of his journey. Ross did not believe in the existence of an
Antarctic continent, preferring to speak of "various patches of land"
separated by icy straits, and he found himself at odds with Wilkes
and others who supported the continental theory. Ross and Wilkes
quarrelled bitterly over matters of priority and over the actual details of their journeys, and Ross attacked Wilkes' reliability in blunt
words. Later examination of the records has shown that Wilkes was
generally correct in most of the disputed assertions, and that Ross
was too hasty in opposing him.*

*Ross' voyage achieved its most important results its first year,
1841. The discovery of the Ross Sea provided an approach to the
previously unapproachable continent, and later explorers followed
Ross' route in making the first landfalls on the Antarctic mainland.
Ross published a popular account of his expedition as* A Voyage of
Discovery and Research in the Southern and Antarctic Regions During the Year 1839-43 *(London, John Murray, 1847), from which the
following excerpt is taken.* □

# JAMES CLARK ROSS

1841.
Jan. 21.

The land ice, although not more than five or six feet above the surface, and therefore probably not more than forty feet in thickness,
blends so imperceptibly with the snow which descends from the
mountains at this part and extends far into the sea, that it was almost
impossible to form any idea of the exact position of the coast line;
thus from the edge of the land ice, it seemed at no great distance
from its margin gradually to ascend until it reached the summits of
the highest mountains. To the N.W. the space between Coulman
Island and the main land was occupied by a similar kind of land ice
that appeared not to have been broken away for many years: in
this particular more like the barrier described by Lieut. Wilkes, as

118

extending from the shores of the lands discovered by him near the Antarctic Circle. It was sufficiently evident that it was impossible to penetrate this mass of ice to the westward, as there was not even a crack or hole of water to be seen in any part of it. I therefore made up my mind to proceed along its edge to the southward, hoping to be able afterwards to pursue a westerly course to the Magnetic Pole, which we still continued to approach very considerably, the dip now amounting to 87° 39'.

At noon we were in lat. 74° 15' S. by our reckoning, but the observation gave only 74°, showing that we had been driven to the northward by a current, which was the more mortifying as we had already begun to congratulate ourselves in the belief that we had reached as high a south latitude as had ever before been attained, and with every prospect of being permitted to extend our researches very much further. In spite of all our exertions we found the ships unable to contend against the combined influence of the southerly wind and northerly current, which still carried us back to the northward, and when it fell calm in the afternoon, we could do nothing but watch the gradually retrograde motion of the ships.

It was the most beautiful night we had seen in these latitudes, the sky perfectly clear and serene. At midnight, when the sun was skimming along the southern horizon at an altitude of about two degrees, the sky over head was remarked to be of a most intense indigo blue, becoming paler in proportion to the distance from the zenith. Jan. 22.

We got soundings in three hundred fathoms, and the dredge being again put over, and allowed to trail along the bottom for two or three hours, brought up many animals, some corallines, and a quantity of sand, mud, and small stones. Amongst them we found several entirely new forms of creatures, of which accurate drawings were taken by Dr. Hooker, which, together with their descriptions, are now in course of publication, and constitute one of the most interesting features of our researches. It is well known that marine invertebrate animals are more susceptible of change of temperature than land animals; indeed they may be isothermally arranged with great accuracy. It will, however, be difficult to get naturalists and philosophers to believe that these fragile creatures could possibly exist at the depth of nearly two thousand fathoms below the surface: yet as we know they can bear the pressure of one thousand fathoms, why may they not of two? We also know that several of the same species of creatures inhabit the Arctic, that we have fished up from great depths in the Antarctic, Seas. The only way they could have got from the one pole to the other must have been through the tropics; but the temperature of the sea in those regions is such that they could not exist in it, unless at a depth of nearly two thousand fathoms. At that depth they might pass from the Arctic to the Antarctic Ocean without a variation of five degrees of temperature; whilst any land animal, at the most favourable season, must experience a difference of fifty degrees, and, if in the winter, no less than one hundred and fifty degrees, of Fahrenheit's thermometer—a sufficient reason why there are neither quadrupeds, nor birds, nor land-insects common to both regions.

Again a southerly breeze came on at 4 A.M.; we continued beating to windward under all sail, and thus regained some of the lost ground; but at noon we were still four miles to the northward of our yesterday's latitude. As the breeze freshened and the motion of the ship increased, the compasses became very uncertain in their indications; but the weather was beautifully clear, the sun shining in great splendour; and although the barometer was already above the mean pressure of the atmosphere of these latitudes, it continued to rise (the second instance of the kind we have observed) as the wind increased to a moderate gale about midnight, which prevailed the whole of the next day, accompanied by sharp squalls and continuous showers of snow. By our reckoning we made some southing, being at noon in lat. 74° 20′ S.; and by 7 P.M., having good grounds for believing that we had reached a higher southern latitude than that attained by our enterprising countryman, the late Captain James Weddell, and therefore beyond all our predecessors, an extra allowance of grog was issued to our very deserving crews; and, being Saturday night, the seaman's favourite toast of "Sweethearts and wives" was not forgotten in the general rejoicing on the occasion.

Jan. 23.   The gale, which rather freshened during the night, gradually veered more to the eastward; we therefore wore round and stood towards the land on the port tack; but, owing to the continuance of thick and snowy weather during the whole of Sunday, we did not get sight of it until 7 P.M., when it was indistinctly seen ahead of

the ship. At midnight we were in lat. 74° 29′ by observation. We car-   Jan. 24.
ried all sail, and both wind and sea abating, we approached the land
rapidly; the barometer which had been rising throughout the gale,
reached the unusual height of 29.33 at 4 A.M. the next morning; the
line of coast was at this time distinctly seen, but at a great distance: a
heavy pack extended at least forty or fifty miles from the shore, into
which we stood amongst the loose ice as far as we could without
getting beset; this I did not think proper to hazard, as it would assuredly have occasioned considerable loss of time without any equiv-
alent advantage, and every hour at this period of the season was of
much importance to us. I have no doubt that had it been our object,
we might have penetrated it several miles further, for although
heavy-looking ice, it was not very densely packed, nor any thing like
the solid land-ice we had seen further to the northward, and we
should certainly have made the attempt, had not the land imposed an
insuperable barrier to our reaching the Pole, which we still hoped to
accomplish by a more circuitous route; and we were not then in a
condition to be content with any thing short of complete success.
Observations at noon placed us in lat. 74° 44′, long. 169° 30′, dip   Jan. 25.
87° 54′ S., var. 67° 13′, from which we deduced the place of the magnetic pole to be distant two hundred and forty-nine miles. We had
penetrated the pack as far as the ice admitted to the westward by
half-past eight in the evening, when we tacked and obtained observations by which we found we had approached so much nearer
the Pole that the dip had increased to 88° 10′. We tried for soundings with three hundred fathoms line, but it did not reach the bottom. Mount Melbourne and Mount Monteagle were here seen to
great advantage; the immense crater of the former, and the more
pointed summit of the latter, rose high above the contiguous mountains; and they form two of the more remarkable objects of this
most wonderful and magnificent mass of volcanic land.

Whilst struggling to get through the pack, we found it drifting,
under the influence of the wind and current, rapidly to the northward, which seemed to encourage a hope, that, if defeated in our attempt to pass round its southern extremity, we might be able, at a
later period of the season when more of the land-ice should have
drifted away, to penetrate to the shore, and find some place wherein
to secure the ships for the winter. For several days past we had seen

very few whales, which was the more remarkable on account of the very great numbers we met with not more than sixty or seventy miles to the northward. There must be doubtless some cause for their absence from this spot, which perhaps future observation may supply; for it is desirable to know where they are not to be found as well as where they are, that valuable time may not be thrown away by those who go in pursuit of them.

Jan. 26.    On reaching the clear water, we found a short irregular sea, in which the ships pitched heavily under the easiest sail we could prevail on ourselves to carry, which seemed to indicate a change of tide to windward. As we pursued our way along the pack edge to the southward, we saw a great many of the beautiful snowy petrel, and some penguins. The temperature of the air varied only one degree during the twenty-four hours, from 25° to 26°, which was sufficiently low to freeze into ice the sprays that fell on board the ship, and soon accumulated such a load about our bows as to keep the watch continually at work clearing it away, and beating it off the running ropes. At noon we had increased the dip to 88° 33', so that the magnetic pole was now only one hundred and seventy-four miles from us in a W. by S. (true) bearing. Mount Melbourne bore W. by N. eighty miles.

In the afternoon, as we got further from the pack, the uneasy irregular sea subsided, and the wind becoming more westerly enabled us to stand direct for the east extreme of the "land blink," which bore S.W. by S. (true) from us; and at this time some strong indications of land appeared, which we all hoped would prove a "Cape Flyaway," as many others had done before. As we increased our distance from the pack, the temperature of the sea at its surface gradually rose from 28° to 31°, at about twelve miles off, although the air was at the time at 25°.5.

Jan. 27.    Light baffling winds, which prevailed for two or three hours, were succeeded by a moderate breeze from the eastward; all sail that the ships could spread was immediately set; and although the fog and rain came on so thick as to prevent our seeing more than half a mile before us, we continued to run with studding-sails on both sides set to the southwestward until nearly eight o'clock, when we were suddenly taken aback by the wind shifting to that quarter, and on the fog clearing away, we found that we had been steering into a deep

122

bight of the main ice, which we now saw stretching across from the extreme point of the main land to an island bearing (true) south of us, and thus preventing our proceeding any further to the westward in this part; after closely examining the pack, in which no opening was to be seen, we stood away to the southward to endeavour to land on the island.

At noon we were in lat. 75° 48′ S., long. 168° 33′ E., dip 88° 24′, variation 80° 50′ E. At 3 P.M. we sounded in 200 fathoms, on fine black sand and small black stones, about twelve miles north of the island. At five o'clock when we were within two or three miles of it, I left the ship, accompanied by several officers, and soon afterwards followed by Commander Crozier, and a party from the Terror, we pulled towards the shore. A high southerly swell broke so heavily against the cliffs, and on the only piece of beach we could see as we rowed from one end of the island to the other, as almost to forbid our landing; a mortification not to be endured if possible to be avoided: the Terror's whale boat being more fit for encountering such a surf than the heavy cutter of the Erebus, I got into her, and by the great skill and management of the officers and crew I succeeded, by watching the opportunity when the boat was on the crest of the breakers, in jumping on to the rocks. By means of a rope, some of the officers landed with more facility, but not without getting thoroughly wetted; and one having nearly lost his life in this difficult affair, I was obliged to forbid any more attempting to land, to their very great disappointment. The thermometer being at 22°, every part of the rocks which were washed by the waves was covered with a coating of ice, so that in jumping from the boat, he slipped from them into the water, between her stern and the almost perpendicular rock on which we had landed, and but for the promptitude of those in the boat, in instantly pulling off, he must have been crushed between it and the rocks. It was most mercifully ordered otherwise, and he was taken into the boat without having suffered any other injury than being benumbed with the cold. We proceeded at once therefore to take possession of the island in due form; and to the great satisfaction of every individual in the expedition, I named it "Franklin Island;" in compliment to His Excellency Captain Sir John Franklin of the Royal Navy, to whom, and his amiable lady, I have already had occasion to express the gratitude we all felt for the great kindness we received at their hands, and the deep interest they manifested in all the objects of the expedition. Having procured numerous specimens of the rocks of the island, we hastened our departure, in consequence of the perishing condition of our unlucky companion, and succeeded in embarking without any further accident; we gained the ships before nine o'clock, all of us thoroughly drenched to the skin, and painfully cold.

Franklin Island is situate in lat. 76° 8′ S., long. 168° 12′ E. It is about twelve miles long and six broad, and is composed wholly of igneous rocks; the northern side presents a line of dark precipitous cliffs, between five and six hundred feet high, exposing several longitudinal broad white, probably aluminous, bands of several feet thickness; two or three of them were of a red ochre colour, and gave a most strange appearance to the cliffs. We could not perceive the smallest trace of vegetation, not even a lichen or piece of sea-weed growing on the rocks; and I have no doubt from the total absence of it at both the places we have landed, that the vegetable kingdom has no representative in antarctic lands. We observed that the white petrel had its nests on the ledges of the cliffs, as had also the rapacious skua gull; several seals were seen, and it is by no means improbable that the beach on which we in vain attempted to land may, at the proper season, be one of their places of resort, or "rookeries" as they are termed by the seal fishers.

At between two and three miles distance from the land, the soundings were regular, in thirty-eight to forty-one fathoms, on a bed of fine sand and black stones, and probably good anchorage might be found near the shore with southerly winds. A high cliff of ice projects into the sea from the south and south-west sides, rendering it there quite inaccessible, and a dangerous reef of rocks extends from its southern cape at least four or five miles, with apparently a deep water passage between them and the cape; several icebergs of moderate size were aground on the banks to the northward and westward of the island. At midnight the bearings of eight separate islands are given in the log of the Erebus; but as these afterwards proved to be the summits of mountains, at a great distance, belonging to the mainland, they do not appear upon the chart as islands. With a favourable breeze, and very clear weather, we stood to the southward, close to some land which had been in sight since the preceding noon,

124

and which we then called the "High Island;" it proved to be a mountain twelve thousand four hundred feet of elevation above the level of the sea, emitting flame and smoke in great profusion; at first the smoke appeared like snow drift, but as we drew nearer, its true character became manifest.

The discovery of an active volcano in so high a southern latitude Jan. 28. cannot but be esteemed a circumstance of high geological importance and interest, and contribute to throw some further light on the physical construction of our globe. I named it "Mount Erebus," and an extinct volcano to the eastward, little inferior in height, being by measurement ten thousand nine hundred feet high, was called "Mount Terror."

A small high round island, which had been in sight all the morning, was named "Beaufort Island," in compliment to Captain Francis Beaufort, of the Royal Navy, Hydrographer to the Admiralty. . . . At 4 P.M. we were in lat. 76° 6' S., long. 168° 11' E. The magnetic dip 88° 27' S., and the variation 95° 31' E.: we were therefore considerably to the southward of the magnetic pole, without any appearance of being able to approach it on account of the land-ice, at a short distance to the westward, uniting with the western point of the "High Island," which, however, afterwards proved to be part of the main land, and of which Mount Erebus forms the most conspicuous object. As we approached the land under all studding-sails, we perceived a low white line extending from its eastern extreme point as far as the eye could discern to the eastward. It presented an extraordinary appearance, gradually increasing in height, as we got nearer to it, and proving at length to be a perpendicular cliff of ice, between one hundred and fifty and two hundred feet above the level of the sea, perfectly flat and level at the top, and without any fissures or . promontories on its even seaward face. What was beyond it we could not imagine; for being much higher than our mast-head, we could not see any thing except the summit of a lofty range of mountains extending to the southward as far as the seventy-ninth degree of latitude. These mountains, being the southernmost land hitherto discovered, I felt great satisfaction in naming after Captain Sir William Edward Parry, R.N., in grateful remembrance of the honour he conferred on me, by calling the northernmost known land on the globe by my name; and more especially for the encouragement, assistance, and friendship which he bestowed on me during the many years I had the honour and happiness to serve under his distinguished command, on four successive voyages to the arctic seas; and to which I mainly attribute the opportunity now afforded me of thus expressing how deeply I feel myself indebted to his assistance and example. Whether "Parry Mountains" again take an easterly trending, and form the base to which this extraordinary mass of ice is attached, must be left for future navigators to determine. If there be land to the southward, it must be very remote, or of much less elevation than any other part of the coast we have seen, or it would have appeared above the barrier. Meeting with such an obstruction was a great disappointment to us all, for we had already, in expectation, passed far beyond the eightieth degree, and had even appointed a rendezvous there, in case of the ships accidentally separating. It was, however, an obstruction of such a character as to leave no doubt upon my mind as to our future proceedings, for we might with equal chance of success try to sail through the Cliffs of Dover, as penetrate such a mass. When within three or four miles of this most remarkable object, we altered our course to the eastward, for the purpose of determining its extent, and not without the hope that it might still lead us much further to the southward. The whole coast here from the western extreme point, now presented a similar vertical cliff of ice, about two or three hundred feet high. The eastern cape at the foot of Mount Terror was named after my friend and colleague Commander Francis Rawdon Moira Crozier, of the Terror. . . . I named the western promontory at the foot of Mount Erebus, "Cape Bird." These two points form the only conspicuous headlands of the coast, the bay between them being of inconsiderable depth. At 4 P.M. Mount Erebus was observed to emit smoke and flame in unusual quantities, producing a most grand spectacle. A volume of dense smoke was projected at each successive jet with great force, in a vertical column, to the height of between fifteen hundred and two thousand feet above the mouth of the crater, when condensing first at its upper part, it descended in mist or snow, and gradually dispersed, to be succeeded by another splendid exhibition of the same kind in about half an hour afterwards, although the intervals between the eruptions were by no means regular. The diameter of the columns of smoke was between two and three

126

hundred feet, as near as we could measure it; whenever the smoke cleared away, the bright red flame that filled the mouth of the crater was clearly perceptible; and some of the officers believed they could see streams of lava pouring down its sides until lost beneath the snow which descended from a few hundred feet below the crater, and projected its perpendicular icy cliff several miles into the ocean. Mount Terror was much more free from snow, especially on its eastern side, where were numerous little conical crater-like hillocks, each of which had probably been, at some period, an active volcano; two very conspicuous hills of this kind were observed close to Cape Crozier. The land upon which Mount Erebus and Terror stand comprised between Cape Crozier and Cape Bird, had the appearance of an island from our present position; but the fixed ice, not admitting of our getting to the westward of Cape Bird, prevented our ascertaining whether it was so or not at this time.

The day was remarkably fine; and favoured by a fresh north-westerly breeze, we made good progress to the E. S. E., close along the lofty perpendicular cliffs of the icy barrier. It is impossible to conceive a more solid-looking mass of ice; not the smallest appearance of any rent or fissure could we discover throughout its whole extent, and the intensely bright sky beyond it but too plainly indicated the great distance to which it reached to the southward. Many small fragments lay at the foot of the cliffs, broken away by the force of the waves, which dashed their spray high up the face of them.

Having sailed along this curious wall of ice in perfectly clear water a distance of upwards of one hundred miles, by noon we found it still stretching to an indefinite extent in an E. S. E. direction. We were at this time in lat. 77° 47′ S., long. 176° 43′ E. The magnetic dip had diminished to 87° 22′ S., and the variation amounted to 104° 25′ E. The wind fell light shortly before noon, but we fortunately had time to increase our distance from the barrier before it fell calm; for the northerly swell, though by no means of any great height, drifted us gradually towards it without our being able to make any effort to avoid the serious consequences that must have resulted had we been carried against it. We had gained a distance of twelve or fourteen miles from it, and as the Terror was getting short of water, I made the signal to Commander Crozier to collect some of the numerous fragments of the barrier that were about us; whilst

Jan. 29.

127

in the Erebus we were engaged making observations on the depth and temperature of the sea. We sounded in four hundred and ten fathoms, the leads having sunk fully two feet into a soft green mud, of which a considerable quantity still adhered to them. The temperature of three hundred fathoms was 34° 2', and at one hundred and fifty fathoms, 33°; that of the surface being 31° and the air 28°. So great a depth of water seemed to remove the supposition that had been suggested, of this great mass of ice being formed upon a ledge of rock, and to show that its outer edge at any rate could not be resting on the ground.

We had closed it several miles during the calm, but all our anxiety on that account was removed on a breeze springing up from the south-east. I went on board the Terror for a short time, this afternoon, to consult with Commander Crozier, and compare our chronometers and barometers, and on my return at half-past four, we made all sail on the starboard tack to the eastward; but not being able to fetch along the barrier, and the weather becoming thick with snow, we lost sight of it before nine o'clock in the evening.

□    *Neither Ross nor Wilkes nor D'Urville succeeded in reaching their prime goal, the South Magnetic Pole, which lay somewhere inland behind a towering barrier of ice. The reports of the three expeditions did not tend to encourage further exploration south of the Antarctic Circle. The southern continent—if indeed a continent at all—was wrapped in fog and cold, and girdled by an icy wall no man could possibly climb.*

*Visits to the Antarctic region were sparse in the decades that followed. One polar historian, Hugh R. Mill, characterized that time as "the generation of averted interest." In 1845, H.M.S. Pagoda ventured as far south as 64° to complete Ross' magnetic observations, but did not sight land. An Enderby sealer, the Brisk, made a short Antarctic cruise in 1850. A quarter of a century passed before a full-scale expedition approached the Antarctic.*

*A British-sponsored scientific mission, making a worldwide oceanographic cruise, crossed the Antarctic Circle in 1874. This was the famous* Challenger *expedition, which left England in December, 1872. The* Challenger, *a 2300-ton wooden ship, was a sailing vessel outfitted with auxiliary steam power, and so steamships came to the Antarctic for the first time.*

*The expedition explored the many subantarctic islands early in 1874, studying the habits of penguins and taking readings of sea temperatures. The Antarctic Circle was crossed in February, and an open sea lay ahead; but this was not intended as a true Antarctic expedition, and the* Challenger's *commander, Captain George Nares, did not take advantage of the opportunity to continue southward. Instead, the ship cruised eastward along the margin of the iceberg zone, taking depth soundings and dredging up oceanic life-forms, and by March 17, 1874, left the Antarctic entirely for scientific work in other parts of the world.*

*Although no land was sighted, the* Challenger's *brief visit produced more scientific information about the south polar region than any of the previous expeditions but for Ross'. The biological findings showed how populous the Antarctic seas were, while the dredges also yielded fragments of granite, quartz, and other minerals that reinforced the theory of an Antarctic continent. One of the* Challenger *scientists, Sir John Murray, was able to prepare from these rock samples an outline map of Antarctica that later proved surprisingly accurate.*

*Many members of the* Challenger *expedition published memoirs of the voyage. One of the best, used here, is* Notes By a Naturalist on H.M.S. Challenger *(London, John Murray, 1892). Its author, H. N. Moseley (1844–91), was in charge of zoological research aboard the oceanographic vessel.* ◻

# H. N. MOSELEY

The colouring of the southern bergs is magnificent. The general mass has a loaf-sugar-like appearance, with a slight bluish tint, excepting where fresh snow resting on the tops and ledges is conspicuous as being absolutely white. On this ground-colour there are parallel streaks of cobalt blue, of various intensities, and more or less marked effect, according to the distance at which the berg is viewed. Some bergs with the blue streaks very definitely marked have, when seen from quite close, exactly the appearance of the common marbled blue soap.

The colouring of the crevasses, caves, and hollows is of the deepest and purest possible azure blue. None of our artists on board were able to approach a representation of its intensity. It seemed to me a much more powerful colour than that which is to be seen in the ice of Swiss glaciers. In the case of the bergs with all their sides exposed, no doubt a greater amount of light is able to penetrate than in glaciers where the light can usually only enter at the top. A large berg full of caves and crevasses, seen on a bright day, is a most beautiful and striking object.

One small berg was passed at a distance which was of remarkable colour. It looked just like a huge crystal of sulphate of copper, being all intensely blue, but it seemed as if attached to, and forming part of, another berg of normal colour. Possibly it was part of the formerly submerged base, and of more than ordinary density. Only one other such was seen. The intensity of the blue light is ordinarily such that the grey sky behind appears distinctly reddened, assuming the complementary tint, and the reddening appears most intense close to the berg.

At night bergs appear as if they had a very slight luminous glow, almost as if they were to very small extent phosphorescent.

The sea at the foot of the bergs usually looks of a dark indigo colour, partly, no doubt, out of contrast to the brighter blue of the ice. Where spurs and platforms run out under water from the bases of the cliffs, the shallow water is seen to be lighted up by reflection of the light from these.

The surf beats on the coast of an iceberg as on a rocky shore, and washes and dashes in and out of the gullies and caverns, and up against the cliffs. Washing in and out of the caves, it makes a resounding roar, which, when many bergs surrounded the ship, is very loud. So heavy is the surf, and so steep are their sides as a rule, that we did not see one on which we could well have landed from a boat.

As the waves wash up into the wash-lines they form icicles, which are to be seen hanging in rows from the upper border of these grooves.

A line of fragments is always to be seen drifting away from a large berg. These are termed wash-pieces. They are very instructive as showing the vast relative extent of submerged ice required to float a small portion above water; the parts of the fragments below water being visible from a ship's deck.

The scenic effects produced by large numbers of icebergs, some in the foreground, others scattered at all distances to the horizon and beyond it, are very varied and remarkable, depending on the varying effects of light and atmosphere.

On one occasion, as we were approaching the pack ice, some distant bergs were seen to assume a most intense black colour. This was due to their being thrown in shade by clouds passing between them and the sun, and the heightening of this effect by the contrast with brilliantly lighted up bergs around them. They looked like rocks of basalt.

On February 15th [1874], a remarkable twilight effect was seen to the southward at about 10 P.M. A narrow band or line of dazzling bright yellow light shone out through a long narrow gap intervening between the lower edge of a densely dark cloud bank and the equally dark, almost black, horizon line. The horizon line was uneven, showing minute black projections or jags, due to hummocky pack ice.

The distant flat-topped icebergs showed out black and sharp, with rectangular outlines against the bright band, and some of their dark bodies joined the dark cloud line to the dark horizon line, bridging over the band of light. The whole effect was very curious, and drew all on deck to gaze at it.

We frequently enjoyed the sight of brilliant red sunsets. Then the bergs directly between the observer and the illuminated sky show a hard, almost black outline. Those lying on the horizon, right and left of the setting sun, reflect the light from their entire faces, or from those parts of their faces which lie at the necessary angle. Hence, bright red bergs, and also fantastic red forms, due to reflection from very uneven surfaces, appear on the horizon. Those that are nearer take a salmon tint.

In one remarkably brilliant sunset, the sun just before its lower limb reached the horizon was of a brilliant golden-yellow, and lit

131

up the spars and shrouds of the ship with a dazzling light. Later on, the horizon became excessively dark. Above it was a streak of golden light, succeeded by a band of green sky, the two colours being separated by a narrow horizontal violet cloud. Above the green were dark clouds lighted up with bright crimson at the edges. The bergs reflected the crimson and yellow light, and assumed the brightest hues.

Bergs in the far distance, in ordinary daylight, when lighted up often have a pinkish tinge, and then look remarkably like land. The deception is very complete. No doubt Commodore Wilkes was deceived by it. Bergs often also, from the presence of deep shadows, have the appearance of having rocks upon them when they have not.

We entered the ice rather unexpectedly, on February 13th. I was on deck at 11.30 P.M. Two icebergs were then in sight ahead, only just visible in the dim foggy haze. They became gradually more plain, and then a berg was reported right ahead. Sail was shortened, and we glided slowly on. A line of mist, contrasting strongly with the dark water, seemed in the uncertain light to be creeping over the surface of the sea towards us; in reality we were approaching it. Its edge was most sharply defined. We passed it, and immediately the dark water showed a sprinkling over of white dots, which looked as if they had been snow-flakes, which for some reason had fallen on the water without melting. These white specks became larger and larger, and closer together, and all at once I realized that we were amongst the ice. The thin layer of mist was hanging over its edge.

The pieces increased rapidly in size and thickness, as we went farther and farther ahead, until, in a very few minutes, we were forcing our way through a sort of soup-like looking fluid, full of large pieces of ice. The pieces were as much as six feet long, and three or four broad, all flat slabs, and standing six inches or so out of the water. The pieces bumped and grated against the ship's side, and the water-line being near the level of the officers' heads, as they lay in their berths asleep, several came up on deck to see what had happened. We soon steered out of the edge of the pack again.

Next morning I viewed the ice from the foretop and made a sketch of its appearance. All along the horizon, southwards, was a white line of ice, broken here and there by the outlines of bergs fast in the pack at various distances from the ship; some partly beyond the horizon, and with only their tops showing; others at the outer edge of the vast expanse of ice; others at all intermediate positions.

The field of ice appeared continuous, except just near its edge, where meandering openings, like rivers, led into it, sometimes for a mile or so. The edge of the pack was very irregular, projecting as it were in capes and promontories, with bays between, as on a broken coast-line. The fields of ice were made up of large fragments closely packed together. The pieces were not, however, much tilted or heaped up upon one another, as commonly occurs in packs.

Off the edge of the pack, extended serpentine bands of floating ice which drifted before the wind; they are termed "stream ice." We dredged within one of the streams. All the packs which we saw were similar to the one described.

Sometimes, the smaller floating masses of ice at the edge of the pack were covered with fresh snow. The parts of them projecting above water were frequently of very fantastic shapes. Some were like the antlers of deer, others like two pairs of antlers with three or four upstanding and branching horns, all borne aloft by irregularly shaped submerged floats. The soft upper masses of loose or but slightly congealed snow often split off and fell away as the masses floated past.

The ice was frequently stained of the yellow ochreous tint described by Sir J. D. Hooker, and found by him to be caused by Diatoms washed up on to the ice by the waves, and hanging on its rough surface. The colouring was always most marked about the honeycombed wash-lines of the ice blocks. Pancake ice is similarly discoloured by Diatoms in the Arctic regions.

On February 25th we entered the edge of the pack, sailing amongst some loosened outliers of it. The sea was covered with masses of ice up to 10 feet in length. These consisted mostly of light snow ice, and did not project more than from two to four feet out of water. The upper parts of the masses were composed of white fresh snow, or honeycombed wet frozen snow, which had been partly melted by the waves. Very many of these ice masses were stained of an ochre tint, by Diatoms and other surface organisms.

The lower submerged ice was transparent, but extremely full of large air vesicles. The ice below the water line, and under the overhanging edges at that level, looked blue. The upper masses were quite opaque.

I went in a boat to collect discoloured ice. The discolouration appears far less marked when seen at close quarters. It became almost invisible when the porous snow-ice drains dry. When, however, a small piece of the ice is seen floating nearly submerged, it looks almost of a chocolate brown colour.

Mr. Buchanan made experiments on the melting point, and amount of salt contained in salt-water ice. He came to the conclusion from analyses of successive meltings and the varying of the melting point, that in salt-water ice "the salt is not contained in the form of mechanically enclosed brine only, but exists in the solid form, either as a single crystalline substance, or as a mixture of ice and salt crystals."

He thinks that by fractional melting, salt water ice might be made to yield water fit to drink, although when a lump is melted as a whole, the resulting water is undrinkable.

We crossed the Antarctic Circle on February 16th, passing about six miles to the south of it. There was open water ahead, but the "Challenger" was not strengthened for ice work, and we were not ordered to proceed further south, so we turned back. There seemed to be a deep opening in the pack here, nearly due south of Heard Island. We subsequently passed within six miles of what is marked on maps as Wilkes' Termination Land, and found that this did not exist. Wilkes no doubt was deceived by the land-like appearance of distant icebergs. It is to be noted that he merely says that he saw appearance of land here, sixty miles distant, but high and mountainous. Others have named it for him and placed it on the charts.

# PART IV

## THE HEROIC AGE 1896-1920

◻    *The closing years of the nineteenth century saw a revival of interest in the Antarctic. The first to return were hunters, now seeking not seals but whales. Whale oil and whalebone were still precious commodities and, with the whales of the Arctic nearly extinct, Norwegian and Scottish whaling men began to turn toward southern waters.*

*One of the first such expeditions was financed by Svend Foyn, the venerable head of the Norwegian whaling industry, at the urging of a young Norwegian named H. J. Bull. Its purpose was mainly commercial, but there was some intent to explore. When the whaling ship* Antarctic *left Norway in September, 1893, it was under the command of Captain Leonard Kristensen. On board was Carstens*

137

*Borchgrevink, a Norwegian polar enthusiast who had been teaching languages and sciences in Australia. Unable to buy his way on board as a passenger, Borchgrevink had persuaded Captain Kristensen to take him on as an ordinary seaman.*

*The Antarctic first crossed the Antarctic Circle on December 21, 1894. Entering the Ross Sea, Kristensen made for the coast of Victoria Land and on January 16, 1895, sighted the promontory known as Cape Adare. Eight days later, a party went ashore—the first recorded landing on the Antarctic mainland, but for John Davis' disputed and uncertain landfall more than seventy years earlier. The following account of that historic moment comes from* The Cruise of the 'Antarctic,' *by H. J. Bull (London and New York, Edward Arnold, 1896).*  □

# H. J. BULL

*January 24* [1895].—Cape Adare was made at midnight. The weather was now favourable for a landing, and at 1 a.m. a party, including the Captain, second mate, Mr. Borchgrevinck, and the writer, set off, landing on a pebbly beach of easy access, after an hour's rowing through loose ice, negotiated without difficulty. In the calm weather little or no swell was observed against the shore. Jelly fish of a considerable size were noticed in the sea, an extraordinary high latitude for this class of invertebrate.

The sensation of being the first men who had set foot on the real Antarctic mainland was both strange and pleasurable, although Mr. Foyn would no doubt have preferred to exchange this pleasing sensation on our part for a Right whale even of small dimensions.

The tide current had been setting north with a great speed, estimated at about four to five knots an hour, but it had now turned, its velocity in the opposite direction being much less.

Our surroundings and our hosts were as strange and unique as our feelings. The latter—myriads of penguins—fairly covered the flat promontory, many acres in extent, jutting out into the bay between Cape Adare and a more westerly headland; they further lined all accessible projections of the rocks to an altitude of 800 to 900 feet. The youngsters were now almost full-grown. In their thick, woolly, and gray down they exhibited a most remarkable and comical appearance. At a distance the confused din and screaming emanating from parents and children resembled the uproar of an excited human assembly, thousands in number.

Our presence was not much appreciated, considering the millions of years which must have elapsed since the last visit by prehistoric man or monkey—before the glacial period. Our sea-boots were bravely attacked as we passed along their ranks. The space covered by the colony was practically free from snow; but the layer of guano was too thin, and mixed with too many pebbles, to be of commercial value in these days of cheap phosphates. Unless the guano has been carried out to sea from time to time by rains and melting snow, the thinness of the layers compared with the massiveness of similar deposits in other climes would indicate that South Victoria Land has only during comparatively recent ages been made use of by the penguins during their breeding season. From this (assumed) fact interesting inferences may again be drawn regarding changes in the climate of Antarctica during recent times, but men of science must weigh the pros and cons of this theory, and the most permissible deductions to be made.

The mortality in the colony must be frightful, judging by the number of skeletons and dead birds lying about in all directions. A raptorial (skua) gull was present here, as everywhere in the neighbourhood of penguin nurseries, and was busily occupied with its mission in life—viz., prevention of over-population in the colony.

The patience and endurance of the penguins are beyond praise when it is considered that thousands of them have to scale ridges hundreds of feet in height to reach their nests, although their mode of locomotion ashore is painfully awkward and slow. Like so many other polar animals, the full-grown bird is able to subsist on its own fat for long periods; but the young birds require frequent and regular feeding, as in all other cases of animal life. The capacity of most polar inhabitants for stowing away incredible quantities of food at one meal, and bringing it up again at will, explains no doubt how the young can be fed with fair regularity, although the parents may go for days without an opportunity of eating.

To commemorate our landing, a pole was erected, carrying a box, on which was painted the Norwegian colours, the date, and the vessel's name.

Before leaving we made a collection of penguins, stones, etc. Someone had the good sense to bring a sledge-hammer, with which pieces of the original rock were detached and carried on board.

In searching the more sheltered clefts of the rock, Mr. Borchgrevinck discovered further patches of the lichen already met with on Possession Island. The sea-weed found on the shore was more doubtful evidence of vegetable life, as it may have drifted there from warmer latitudes, although no current going South is known to me, and no other evidence of such a current, as, for instance, driftwood, etc., was met with.

On the shore were observed two dead seals, in a perfectly mummified state. I am unable to say whether they had retired there simply to die from wounds or disease, or had been cut off from the open water by the ice of an early winter, and so perished. The hairs had all come away, but the skins were smooth and hard, and the bodies had kept their original form so perfectly that they looked as if artificially preserved.

A single sea-leopard was found basking on the shore, and killed by the Captain. It showed no more signs of 'uneasiness and anxiety to regain the water' than the two mummies.

That Antarctica can support no land mammal, 'huge' or small, is, to my mind, proved by the existence of these undisturbed remains. Even frozen seal-flesh must be a tit-bit about mid-winter in a climate so rigorous that only the lowest forms of vegetable life can survive from season to season. The unbroken ice must in winter-time extend an enormous distance from the shores, driving all higher forms of animal life up to, or beyond, the edge of the open water. No land animal like the Arctic bear has ever been observed by any Antarctic traveller—the 'mysterious tracks in the snow,' etc., mentioned by one of our number were not observed by anyone else at the time—and certainly the possibility of finding Antarctic nations, etc., is too imbecile to require serious discussion.

We bade farewell about 3 a.m. to those of our hosts which we did not take away with us for a trip to natural history museums, and passed two very anxious and troublesome hours before regaining the vessel, as they had omitted to keep a look-out for us on board.

We thus had the pleasure of seeing the ship working in towards the land in one direction, whilst we were compelled by the ice to take an opposite one. By shouting in chorus we at last attracted attention, and saw the course altered towards us.

The mate's excuse was the report by the man aloft that he had just observed three of us on shore going down to the boat, and so thought it best to stand in as close as possible. As we had at that time been afloat for a considerable time, this proves that penguins on the march can be easily mistaken through a telescope for human beings—at least, when Mr. M. H. is at the other end of it.

During our exploration ashore we got a strong impression that the bay at Cape Adare inside the low promontory would provide many advantages as a landing-place and station for a new expedition. It is probable, at least, that a vessel moored inside this promontory would lie protected against the outer floes, as well as the ice forming in the bay itself; the tide is no doubt very powerful along the whole shore, but presumably less so in this partly-closed bay. Among the rocks of Cape Adare, a shelter could be found for the house, and the low promontory would furnish plenty of space for moving about, for observatory, etc., as it occupies a space of about one mile in length, by a quarter of a mile in width.

□  *Several national expeditions were in the planning stage while Bull, Borchgrevink, and their two companions were disturbing the penguins. In England, the geographer Sir Clements Markham had stirred a movement toward an official voyage, declaring, "the exploration of the Antarctic Regions is the greatest piece of geographical exploration still to be undertaken."*

*The first of the new expeditions to leave was Belgian. Its leader, Adrien de Gerlache, was an officer of the Belgian navy. The first mate was a twenty-five-year-old Norwegian named Roald Amundsen, whose consuming ambition it was to reach the North Pole. Amundsen had taken this wrong-way journey to gain experience in cold-weather navigation. The captain of the ship and one of the scientists were Belgians; two Poles and a Romanian were also aboard. When the expedition reached Rio de Janeiro, an American surgeon and photographer joined the party. He was Dr. Frederick Cook, later to win an inglorious name as the perpetrator of a hoax in which he claimed to have reached the North Pole.*

*The expedition's ship, the* Belgica, *entered the Antarctic in January, 1898—late in the season for such exploration. After charting the Antarctic Peninsula, the explorers headed south, and were forced by pack ice into the Bellingshausen Sea. De Gerlache unwisely continued until, by March 4, the* Belgica *was caught by the pack ice and frozen in. Never before had men endured a winter in the Antarctic.*

*For almost a year the* Belgica *was locked in the ice. The men suffered severe psychological disturbances during the endless night, recorded vividly in Dr. Cook's account of the voyage. One man died of a heart attack; gloom and despair assailed the others. Not until February, 1899, did the* Belgica *break free of the ice, and it was March 28 when the explorers reached Tierra del Fuego, after the most grueling experience thus far in the history of Antarctic discovery.*

*The selections that follow are from* Through the First Antarctic Night, *by Frederick A. Cook, M.D. (New York, Doubleday and McClure, 1900).* □

# THE BELGICA EXPEDITION

We are now doomed to remain, and become the football of an unpromising fate. Henceforth we are to be kicked, pushed, squeezed, and ushered helplessly at the mercy of the pack. Our first duty is to prepare for the coming of the night, with its unknowable cold and its soul-depressing effects. Aboard, the crew are re-storing coal and re-arranging the store of provisions. The scientific men are making plans for a year of observations, while the cook is racking his brain to devise some new dishes to appease our fickle appetites. His soups are full of "mystery," and the "embalmed meats" are on every tongue for condemnation. Outside there has been a rapid transformation. The summer days of midnight suns are past, and the premonitory darkness of the long night is falling upon us with marvellous rapidity, for in this latitude the sun dips below the southern skies at midnight late in January. This dip increases, and sweeps more and more of the horizon every day until early in May, when the sun sets and remains below the horizon for seventy-one days. When we first skirted the pack-ice in February [1898] there were a few hours, at midnight, of bright twilight. The darkness then was not sufficient to prevent navigation throughout the night; but now it is really dark for eight hours. The temperature, too, is falling rapidly. We have been led to believe by the experiences of previous antarctic explorers that the temperature, compared with arctic, would be more moderate; but in this we are disappointed. An icy wind comes from the south, brushing the warm, moist air seaward and replacing it by a sharp, frigid atmosphere. The temperature falls to ten degrees below zero, then to twenty (and later it descends to thirty, forty, and finally forty-five).

Soon after we entered the main body of the pack a fortnight ago, it was discovered that we drifted with the ice in a south-westerly direction. We concluded, at that time, that we were in a current. The shallow sea and the speed with which we moved were in favour of this theory; but now we are drifting north-westerly, and we begin to doubt the existence of a current. The ease with which the entire horizon, with its numerous mountains and fields of ice, sails over the invisible sea makes us anxious as to our destiny. If we remain here, on this blank space of the globe, where will we find ourselves a year hence? Will it be north, south, east or west? In this drift it is possible that the ship may be dragged over a submerged reef, and it is also possible that we may be carried onto a rocky shore, or against the formidable land-ice. In each case destruction of our vessel and a miserable death for all must be the inevitable result.

To forestall such a future we now ascend to the crow's-nest daily and with the telescope search the horizon. New bergs come over one part of the circle, old ones disappear in other directions. Appearances of land are often noted, but such appearances are no longer credited. New crevasses form, old ones close, but on the whole it is, day after day, the same heaving sea of frozen whiteness. Nevertheless the views are encouraging, and they now and then revive the dying hope of release from the icy prison. There is promise in the movement of the bergs, the continued swell of the sea, and the slow mysterious turning of the floes, together with the present northerly drift. The fact that each floe persistently remains as a single individual, and refuses to unite with its neighbours to form a conglomerate mass, which would effectually and finally cut off all hope of a retreat this year, is a pleasant thought. A brisk storm would easily separate these floes, and the open water, but ninety miles north, would carry us on its stormy bosom to a more congenial climate for the winter.

Last night was clear and blue. We knew from the stillness of the air and crackle of the ice that it would be very cold, and so it proved. At six o'clock it was —14.6° C. (5.72° F.), at midnight, —20° C. (—4° F.). A number of royal and small penguins and some seals were led by curiosity to visit us. They called, and cried, and talked, and grunted, as they walked over the ice about the ship, and were finally captured by the naturalist and the cook, who had an equal interest in the entertainment of our animal friends and in their future destiny. A few nights past a sea leopard interviewed the meteorologist, Arctowski. The animal sprang suddenly from a new break in the ice onto the floe, upon which Arctowski had a number of delicate meteorological instruments, and without an introduction, or any signs of friendship, the animal crept rapidly over the snow and examined Arctowski and his paraphernalia with characteristic seal inquisitiveness. The meteorologist had nothing with which to defend himself, and he didn't appear to relish the teeth of the leopard as it advanced and separated its massive jaws with a bear-like snort. He walked around the floe, the leopard after him. The seal examined the instruments, but they were not to its liking, and as to Arctowski, it evidently did not regard him of sufficient interest to follow long, for after it had made two rounds the seal plunged into the waters, swam under the ice and around the floe, and then raised its head far out to get another glimpse of the meteorologist. Thinking that the creature contemplated another attack, Arctowski made warlike gestures, and uttered a volley of sulphureous Polish words, but the seal didn't mind that. It raised its head higher and higher out of the water, and displayed its teeth in the best possible manner. Now and then its lips moved, and there was audible a weird noise, with signs which we took to be the animal's manner of inviting its new acquaintance to a journey under the icy surface, where they might talk over the matter out of the cold blast of the wind, in the blue depths below.

*March 15.*—The weather is remarkably clear. There is no wind, no noise, and no motion in the ice. During the night we saw the first aurora australis. I saw it first at eight o'clock, but it was so faint then that I could not be positively certain whether it was a cloud with an unusual ice-blink upon it or an aurora; but at ten o'clock we all saw it in a manner which was unmistakable. The first phenomenon was like a series of wavy fragments of cirrus clouds, blown by strong, high winds across the zenith. This entirely disappeared a few minutes after eight o'clock. What we saw later was a trembling lace-work, draped like a curtain, on the southern sky. Various parts were now dark, and now light, as if a stream of electric sparks illuminated the fabric. The curtain seemed to move in response to these waves of light, as if driven by the wind which shook out old folds and created new ones, all of which made the scene one of new interest and rare glory.

That I might better see the new attraction and also experiment with my sleeping-bag, I resolved to try a sleep outside upon one of the floes. For several days I had promised myself the pleasure of this experience, but for one reason or another I had deferred it. At midnight I took my bag and, leaving the warmth and comfort of the cabin, I struggled out over the icy walls of the bark's embankment, and upon a floe three hundred yards east I spread out the bag. The temperature of the cabin was the ordinary temperature of a comfortable room; the temperature of the outside air was —20° C. (—4° F.). After undressing quickly, as one is apt to do in such temperatures, I slid into the fur bag and rolled over the ice until I found a depression suitable to my ideas of comfort. At first my teeth chattered and every muscle of my body quivered, but in a few minutes this passed off and there came a reaction similar to that after a cold bath. With this warm glow I turned from side to side and peeped past the fringe of accumulating frost, around my blow-hole through the bag, at the cold glitter of the stars. As I lay there alone, away from the noise of the ship, the silence and the solitude were curiously oppressive. There was not a breath of air stirring the glassy atmosphere, and not a sound from the ice-decked sea or its life to indicate movement or commotion. Only a day ago this same ice was a mass of small detached floes, moving and grinding off edges with a complaining squeak. How different it was now! Every fragment was cemented together into one heterogeneous mass and carpeted by a hard, ivory-like sheet of snow. Every move which I made in my bag was followed by a crackling complaint from the snow crust.

At about three o'clock in the morning a little wind came from the east. My blow-hole was turned in this direction, but the slow blast of air which struck my face kept my moustache and my whiskers, and every bit of fur near the opening, covered with ice. As I rolled over to face the leeward there seemed to be a misfit somewhere. The hood portion of the bag was as hard as if coated with sheet-iron, and my head was firmly encased. My hair, my face, and the under garments about my neck were frozen to the hood. With every turn I endured an agony of hair pulling. If I remained still my head became more and more fixed by the increasing condensation. In the morning my head was boxed like that of a deep sea-diver. But aside from this little discomfort I was perfectly at ease, and might have slept if the glory of the heavens and the charm of the scene about had not been too fascinating to permit restful repose.

The aurora, as the blue twilight announced the dawn, had settled into an arc of steady brilliancy which hung low on the southern sky, while directly under the zenith there quivered a few streamers; overhead was the southern cross, and all around the blue dome there were sparkling spots which stood out like huge gems. Along the horizon from south to east there was the glow of the sun, probably reflected from the unknown southern lands. This was a band of ochre tapering to gold and ending in orange red. At four o'clock the aurora was still visible but faint. The heavens were violet and the stars were now fading behind the increasing twilight. A zone of yellow extended from west around south to east, while the other half of the circle was a vivid purple. The ice was a dark blue. An hour late the highest icebergs began to glitter as if tipped with gold, and then the hummocks brightened. Finally, as the sun rose from her snowy bed, the whole frigid sea was coloured as if flooded with liquid gold. I turned over and had dropped into another slumber when I felt a peculiar tapping on the encasement of my face. I remained quiet, and presently I heard a loud chatter. It was uttered by a group of penguins who had come to interview their new companion. I hastened to respond to the call, and, after pounding my head and pulling out some bunches of hair, I jumped into my furs, bid the surprised penguins good morning, and went aboard. Here I learned that Lecointe, not knowing of my presence on the ice, had taken me for a seal, and was only waiting for better light to try his luck with the rifle.

*July 22* [1898].—After so much physical, mental, and moral depression, and after having our anticipations raised to a fever heat by the tempting increase of dawn at noon, it is needless to say that we are elated at the expectation of actual daylight once more. In these dreadful wastes of perennial ice and snow, man feels the force of the superstitions of past ages, and becomes willingly a worshipper of the eternal luminary. I am certain that if our preparations for greeting the returning sun were seen by other people, either civilised or savage, we would be thought disciples of heliolatry.

Every man on board has long since chosen a favourite elevation from which to watch the coming sight. Some are in the crow's nest, others on the ropes and spars of the rigging; but these are the men who do little travelling. The adventurous fellows are scattered over the pack upon icebergs and high hummocks. These positions were taken at about eleven o'clock. The northern sky at this time was nearly clear and clothed with the usual haze. A bright lemon glow was just changing into an even glimmer of rose. At about half-past eleven a few stratus clouds spread over the rose, and under these there was a play in colours, too complex for my powers of description. The clouds were at first violet, but they quickly caught the train of colours which was spread over the sky beyond. There were spaces of gold, orange, blue, green, and a hundred harmonious blends, with an occasional strip like a band of polished silver to set the colours in bold relief. Precisely at twelve o'clock a fiery cloud separated, disclosing a bit of the upper rim of the sun.

All this time I had been absorbed by the pyrotechnic-like display, but now I turned about to see my companions and the glory of the new sea of ice, under the first light of the new day. Looking towards the sun the fields of snow had a velvety aspect in pink. In the opposite direction the pack was noticeably flushed with a soft lavender light. The whole scene changed in colour with every direction taken by the eye, and everywhere the ice seemed veiled by a gauzy atmosphere in which the colour appeared to rest. For several minutes my companions did not speak. Indeed, we could not at that time have found words with which to express the buoyant feeling of relief, and the emotion of the new life which was sent coursing through our arteries by the hammer-like beats of our enfeebled hearts.

Lecointe and Amundsen were standing on an iceberg close to me. They faced the light, and watched the fragment of the sun slide under bergs, over hummocks, and along the even expanse of the frozen sea, with a worshipful air. Their eyes beamed with delight, but under this delight there was noticeable the accumulated suffering of seventy dayless nights. Their faces were drawn and thin, though the weight of their bodies was not reduced. The skin had a sickly, jaundiced colour, green, and yellow, and muddy. Altogether, we accused each other of appearing as if we had not been washed for months. The uncertainty of our exact latitude made it impossible to estimate just how much of the sun's disk would be visible. Our time, too, was uncertain, for our pocket timepieces were not reliable, and we were far from the chronometers. We watched and watched, expecting that the crest of fire would rise and give us an increased glow of light and some heat, but it only slid teasingly on the verge of the sea. It seemed as though our world of ice was not yet worthy of the blessings of the "sun-god." A few minutes after twelve the light was extinguished, a smoky veil of violet was drawn over the dim outline of the ice, and quickly the stars again twinkled in the gobelin-blue of the sky as they had done, without being outshone, for nearly seventeen hundred hours.

□   *While the men of the* Belgica *were struggling to break free of the ice that had bound them for a year, another party was about to begin a voluntary winter stay on the Antarctic mainland. H. J. Bull had suggested establishing a base at Cape Adare for overland explora-*

tion, and the idea had blossomed in the mind of his countryman Carstens Borchgrevink.

In August, 1898, Borchgrevink left England aboard a Norwegian sealer renamed the Southern Cross, backed by the magazine publisher George Newnes. Reaching Cape Adare on February 17, 1899, Borchgrevink went ashore to build a hut. With nine companions, he settled in to experience a winter at what he called "the last terra incognita on the globe."

Borchgrevink's party included several scientists and two Finnish Lapps in charge of the dog teams that were to be used for transportation. The polar night descended on May 15; the temperature fell far below zero, and the savage blizzards pinned the men into their quarters. Their health remained good, however, and all survived but a zoologist, Nicolai Hanson, who died in October.

When the sun reappeared late in July, Borchgrevink attempted some short sledge journeys, as related below. The Southern Cross, which had spent the year in New Zealand, returned in February, 1900, to pick up the mainland party. Borchgrevink was back in London by the middle of the year, having shown that men could survive a winter on the Antarctic mainland. The episode that follows is from his book, First on the Antarctic Continent (London, George Newnes, 1901). ▫

# CARSTENS BORCHGREVINK

On the 26th of July, 1899, eager for active service again, I started a fresh sledge journey with the intention of attempting to reach the coast land to the west of Robertson Bay. At 12 mid-day I started with Mr. Evans and both of the Lapps. I took provisions for thirty days, and twenty-nine dogs. We travelled among very heavy screwed ice. Large blocks heaped upon each other at times rendered our route almost impassable, and for miles we had very rough travelling. A strong gale from the S.S.E. started, and at 4 p.m. we pitched our tent in the worn cave of an iceberg, and spent a very cold night there. In the early morning I scaled the berg and viewed the ice conditions to the southward. As these conditions appeared promising, I decided to send Mr. Evans back to Camp Ridley for the purpose of making Mr. Colbeck, Mr. Fougner, and Mr. Evans follow me up with more sledges and provisions. Mr. Evans took four dogs and a sledge and left for Camp Ridley. I started at once further south, accompanied by the two Lapps. We travelled all that night without pitching camp; the temperature was —30°. We passed over very rough ice and struggled hard between the ice-blocks in the dark. At midnight we came across a seal (*Weddelli*), which was killed to feed the dogs. We lighted the skin and blubber, which shone like a lighthouse far away into the dark as we slowly drew further from it. In the morning the weather was misty. There was no appearance of land, and as I could get no observations I pitched the tent between two ice mounds in the pack. On the 28th July it was still misty, and had started to blow with a low barometer. Towards evening a violent gale commenced, with heavy drift from S.E. We all had to remain inside the silk tent in our sleeping-bags during the next three days. It was bitterly cold, —40°, and we suffered greatly from frost-bites. Our reindeer sleeping-bags were unmanageable comforts after they had been in use two or three times on a sledge journey. We got hot in them the first night, and the steam from our bodies made them damp; we packed them on the sledges in the morning, flat, with the provisions on top of them. Then they froze hard, and when suddenly a gale surprised us, we had to thaw ourselves gradually into the bag, feet first, and their temperature did not always much differ from that of the frozen bag. Later we used to get the dogs to thaw them for us—they always liked to roll upon anything that was not snow or ice, even if it were but a thrown-away match—and when we had laid our frozen reindeer bags on the snow they generally clustered together on them at once, and half-an-hour later we could get into them.

The silk tent was rapidly filled with dense fog as we three camped in it, both on account of our breath, and because of the heat given off by the lantern. A thick layer of frost covered the inner walls of the tent in a short time, and beautiful snow-crystals shone down on us through the ventilation hole in the bag. The snow-drift soon buried the tent, and the snow pressure just left us space enough for our sleeping-bags.

That dark little spot which we formed on those vast white fields was blotted out. Men, dogs, sledges, all, disappeared, and the Ant-

150

arctic gale found nothing new as it raged over us, only cold, white solitude.

For three nights and for three days we had to take turn in standing on all fours to prevent being smothered by the pressure of the snow.

We roasted the heart of a seal and the heart of another we ate raw.

The dogs were completely snowed down and froze fast to the ice. Some of them had eaten the straps of their harness to free themselves, but were still unable to move on account of being frozen to the ice. No land could be sighted anywhere. Up to the 31st July I had seen nothing of the party which was to have followed us up. It was a cold job that morning to dig ourselves and our tent out of the drift. The temperature was —32°, and we suffered from frostbites. We again proceeded onwards on comparatively good ice. In the evening I discovered an island to the south, and reached the western side of it an hour after dark. We were then very hungry and worn: —40° when we pitched camp. Early in the morning of the 1st August we killed two seals. Still nothing was seen of the party which was to assist us, and I anticipated rightly that they had been compelled to return to Camp Ridley by the violent gale which had nearly made an end of my two faithful companions and myself. I called the new camp Midwinter Camp, and the island I named, after H.R.H. the Duke of York, Duke of York Island. The island is situated in lat. 71° 35′ S., long. 170° 2¾′ E. On the 2nd August I resolved to investigate some of the coast-line of this island; I took with me the Finn Must, leaving Savio in camp to construct a kind of Finn tent out of provision bags, sealskins, and bags which he proposed stretching over our sledges, pitched on end; as we would then be enabled to utilize some of the seal blubber as fuel. The Finn Must and myself proceeded along the northern shore of Duke of York Island, and reached a bay which I named Crescent Bay. During the succeeding days I managed to make as thorough an investigation of the immediate surroundings of our camp as the cold weather permitted. As I began to get anxious about the party which was to have followed us, I took in stores of seal-beef and blubber. We suffered a good deal from frost-bites, although we managed to keep up a blubber fire in the conical tent, if it so may be called, constructed by Savio in the manner described above. It was not a question of being warm in the sleeping-bags then, but of being less cold.

I found that the Lapps' method of never using socks in their Finn boots answered well. Socks are never used in Finnarken in winter time, but "senne grass," which they, of course, through practice and tradition, had a special method of arranging in the "komager" (Finn boots). The "senne grass," of which we brought several bags, is dry, although fresh. It is a kind of wiry grass growing near the beach in the north of Norway, and which has obtained there a certain commercial importance because of its use instead of socks amongst the Lapps. If you get wet feet while wearing the grass in the "komager" you will be warmer than ever, as the fresh grass will, by the moisture and the heat of your feet, in a way start to burn, or produce its own heat by spontaneous combustion. The great thing seems to be to arrange the grass properly in the boots, and although we all tried to imitate the Finns in their skill at this work, none of us felt as warm on our feet as when they had helped us.

Must suffered a good deal from the cold, and I had at times to use medical stimulants to keep him from passing away. I kept him alive principally by giving him "Nao," a very fine essence of beef, which gradually became a necessary part of our sledge provisions. However, both of my brave comrades kept up their courage and were always cheerful. A very valuable geological collection was secured and brought to Midwinter Camp. In the middle of August we started back to Camp Ridley. The temperature continued then to fall, the nights were very dark, and the track heavy. On this journey we experienced the lowest temperature we recorded; it was $-52°$, or $84°$ of frost! At night we dug ourselves down in the snow, finding this warmer than being in the tent. We had to use our reserve hickory ski to make slides for our sledges.

On my return to Camp Ridley I decided to continue the explorations already begun in Robertson Bay, partly because I found that the locality in itself contained valuable scientific properties—not least in the geological department—and partly because I also hoped to find here a place whereby to reach further inland. Expeditions were despatched during the remainder of August and September under the alternate charge of members of my staff.

We had constructed a rough stone hut at Midwinter Camp some 10 ft. in diameter. The roof we covered with seal-skin, canvas and rocks, and used spare ski to support it. The hut was placed in a

corner where the rocks of Duke of York Island formed a comparatively sheltered place. It was a cold job building this hut. To get the
material we had to carry rocks from far off, and break loose pieces
from the mountain side, where successive frost and thaw through
ages had made our task possible. When we had finished the hut we
covered it over completely with snow, only leaving a small space
open to let the smoke out. The first gale with snow-drift buried it
all. Our provisions were placed in a large cave which the Finns carved
out of an immense drift. This cave was approachable through a winding tunnel some 30 ft. long, and would have formed a comparative
warm and safe place in case we should have been unable to keep the
passage to the stone hut clear.

In the vicinity of Robertson Bay the nature of the land, with its
great elevations reaching far above 12,000 ft. in height, sometimes at
an angle of about 50°, and crossed by innumerable crevasses, made
our expeditions on the coast-line both arduous and risky. Savio and
myself worked hard in the neighbourhood of Mount Sabine for more
than seven weeks. Our main camp was at the time the stone hut. By
burning blubber we managed to keep the temperature near freezing-point, but at night it varied generally inside the hut between
—35° and —45°. During the time we were settled here communication with Camp Ridley was continually kept up, and stores brought
from there to form a depôt at Duke of York Island.

The dogs were invaluable to us on these journeys; we fed them
principally on blubber and seal-meat, and at the coast we secured
enough fish both for specimens and food.

On 11th September I killed a female seal near the edge of Dugdale
Glacier. It was a leopard (*Stenorhynchus Leptonyx*). When I had
skinned it, I cut it open, and, to my surprise, found a nearly full-
grown male young one alive in her. After I had freed him he seemed
quite happy as he rolled about on the ice in his soft, smooth coat. I
put him on my sledge, and drove him to the stone hut, where we kept
him alive on condensed milk until we were later on able to send him
by sledge to Camp Ridley, where Dr. Klövstad fed him from the
bottle!

Mr. Bernacchi and Mr. Ellefsen were the last to bring food supplies
to the depôt. They had a hard experience on their way. When overtaken by a furious gale in the ice-pack, they had to take refuge in an

iceberg. The thermometer was very low, and the gale so strong that they were unable to creep against the wind on all fours, and although it was still winter, with the ice about four or five feet thick, they expected every minute to see it break up, and in the midst of the gale climbed the berg and camped in a cavity until light allowed them to descend.

On one of our journeys on the glaciers of Victoria Land, in the vicinity of Duke of York Island, Savio very nearly lost his life. Carelessly, he had walked on alone, out of sight, onwards on the glacier without a guiding rope. New snow had fallen, and I had already for a long time been using the utmost care in crossing the glaciers at this locality. The Finn, who had walked boldly along, suddenly felt the snow give way beneath his feet, and fell headlong into a crevasse, turning three somersaults in the air before he was jammed, sixty feet below, head downwards. A dog which had followed him stood howling at the edge of the treacherous crevasse. Although he had managed to turn himself head upwards, Savio remained for hours in despair in his difficult position; the ice curved over his head, and shut off the edge from which he had fallen. The crevasse, which narrowed off at the place where the Finn was jammed, opened up a little to the right in an abyss, dark, wide, and of unknown depth. Had he fallen two feet further to the right, Savio would have been lost. What saved him was his coolness, presence of mind, and his never-failing store of resource. He found in his pocket a strong penknife, with which he slowly and carefully began to carve small supports for his feet; then, pushing his back up against the opposite wall of the crevasse, he gradually worked his way upwards, much in the way a chimney-sweep in the days gone by ascended a London chimney. The different widths, and the slippery, smooth ice wall presented great difficulties. However, Savio at length arrived at the top, but in an exhausted condition, and on meeting us was unable to speak on account of weakness. I made a thorough investigation of the crevasse by means of safety ropes, and ascertained the depth to which the Finn had fallen; also I saw the marks of the ingenious way in which he had saved his life.

Towards the west of Duke of York Island a gentle slope led up to a height of about 70 ft., where we found ourselves on the top of a glacier, or rather, a junction of glaciers. Towards the south, in the

Admiralty Range, a dark, high land rose, which stood out conspicuously against the white walls of Mount Sabine. It proved excellent travelling on the top of this glacier for some few miles until near the high land, which, towards the east, rose from Sir John Murray Glacier, and towards the west from an enormous glacier which I named Dugdale Glacier. It was on the junction of these two that we travelled towards this new land, which I named Geikie Land, after Sir Archibald Geikie. When we were about a mile from it we struck medial moraine, consisting of large broken rocks, and following it in a somewhat easterly direction we crossed the moraine at about the middle of the base line of this new land. This was no easy task, as it was cut through everywhere by deep crevasses, covered over with snow, gravel, and rocks in a most treacherous way. In addition to these crevasses came the difficulty of conveying the loaded sledges onward safely on this cover. The rocks tore the slides of the sledges, and we had to carry most of our provisions over on to the solid rocks of Geikie Land roped together, and slowly feeling our way with alpenstocks.

A young dog, which had followed our sledges loose, fell into a crevasse. We heard it howl and went in search. Most of us had given him up for lost when we, through our glasses, discovered one of the Finns out in the middle of the glacier; he was lying flat on the ice, and evidently looking down a crevasse. Through our glasses we did not see more than one of them, so began to think that the other might have come to grief; however, we soon saw them both approach with the lost dog between them. The brave, faithful fellows had risked much in saving that dog. Unwisely, they had not been roped together, neither had they any rope with them, but when they discovered the dog in the crevasse, landed on a ledge some 15 ft. below, they unbuckled their belts, fastened them together, and Savio, lying on his stomach, lowered the Finn Must into the crevasse, from which he was luckily pulled up, together with the dog, by Savio. The crevasse was broad and seemed to be very deep, and had the dog not landed on the ledge he would have gone down some 80 or 100 ft. at least.

On 12th September the doctor, Lieut. Colbeck, Mr. Bernacchi, both Finns and myself, started at 7 o'clock in the morning from the stone hut. We scaled the glacier and traversed the distance to Geikie Land;

and by following the moraine on the eastern side of Dugdale Glacier we succeeded in bringing our sledges with the outfit a considerable distance upwards. But the gradient got steeper and the crevasses more numerous, until progress by sledge was impossible; then we packed ourselves, roped together the doctor, Colbeck, myself and the Finn Savio, and cut our way upwards in the hard blue glacier. Step by step we rose until we were a few thousand feet up as indicated by the aneroid. At last the ascent became so steep that further progress was impossible, we all of us were then roped together at a place where our only foothold was that cut by the pick of the alpenstock, about the size of our hand. Towards the left an almost perpendicular wall rose; and to the right the glacier precipitated itself into a crevasse at a degree of about seventy. A slip of the foot of one of us would then probably have sent us all into eternity, and as the small lumps of snow and ice, with accelerating speed loosened by our feet, rushed downwards towards the crevasse below us, we could not but consider our chances in case we should go the same way. The worst of it would have been that we should have had such a long time before we arrived at our destination, and still had the certainty of destruction in view all the time while sliding speedily down.

□   *Among the members of Borchgrevink's* Southern Cross *expedition was the physicist Louis Bernacchi, who also wrote a book about his experiences. Bernacchi was a witness to another historic moment of this enterprise, the first sledge journey atop the Ross Ice Shelf. After the return of the* Southern Cross *to Cape Adare in February, 1900, some time remained before it was necessary to leave Antarctic waters. Borchgrevink took the opportunity to scale the Ice Shelf, accompanied by Lieutenant Colbeck of the* Southern Cross *and the Finn Savio. It was only a brief trip, but it carried man farther south than he had ever been before, and foretold the heroic sledge journeys of the decade to come. Bernacchi described the trip in his* To the South Polar Regions (*London, Hurst and Blackett, 1901*).   □

# LOUIS BERNACCHI

Those days in the Antarctic when your little ship is driving through blinding snow, ice, icebergs, darkness and an angry sea, are days of deep anxiety. The remembrance of those experiences makes one almost fear to encourage good and brave men to penetrate those forbidding regions. But it is not all gloom and depression beyond the Polar Circles. Sunshine and lively hope soon return, especially on those days when the sun shines forth with great brilliancy from a perfectly serene and clear sky of a most intense indigo blue, upon those majestic peaks of eternal snow, and you gaze with feelings of indescribable delight upon a scene of grandeur and magnificence beyond anything you have seen or could have conceived.

At about three o'clock in the morning of February 17th [1900] we entered an indentation in the ice wall which formed a large bay well sheltered from all quarters, excepting from the north.

The ice-wall, just here, was no longer a barrier, for it fell gradually into the sea, and landing upon it was accomplished without any difficulty. The ice-barrier in this longitude, viz., 164° W., is distinctly different in appearance to that observed further west, near Mounts Erebus and Terror. Its outlines were more broken and full of indentations; the elevation, too, was no more than 60 ft. or 80 ft. The fact that the position of the ice-barrier where we landed upon it was found to be some miles further south than reported by Ross is possibly due to a large portion of the barrier having been broken off and drifted away in the form of huge icebergs. Or, again, Ross might not have approached the barrier very closely at this particular spot, his highest south point being thirty miles more to the east.

We moored to the ice, sledges and dogs were lowered over the side, and the Commander, Lieut. Colbeck, and one of the Lapps started upon a short excursion southwards. Just prior to their departure a photograph was procured of the whole of the ship's company upon the ice—an interesting group, for it is taken at the farthest south latitude ever reached by a ship.

The sledge party returned towards one o'clock, having been absent about five hours, and penetrated due south over ten miles across the great ice-sheet, which afforded absolutely no obstacle to travelling, being smooth and level, and but little crevassed. From their turning point farthest south nothing could be distinguished but the great level expanse of ice extending away out of sight to the south.

The temperature during the day was about 2° Fahr. The barometer was low, viz., 28·84 in. and the sea was rapidly freezing. A sounding was taken in the course of the day, which indicated bottom at a depth of 350 fathoms, the lead bringing up with it from the ocean bed a greenish-grey mud. Ross took soundings in between 200 and 300 fathoms a few miles off the barrier. So far as is known no really great depth has been found to exist in the Ross Sea; the deepest sounding taken by Ross, 2,700 feet without touching bottom, was in Latitude 74° 40'S. and longitude 166° W., far distant from any known land; in the neighbourhood of land, on the contrary, the soundings gave much lower, and at the same time extremely variable, measurements.

Thus the depth about six miles from Cape Adare was found to be 991 feet, while 135 miles east of Cape Phillips, the depth was only 1,082 feet. The greatest depth actually measured descends no farther than 2,450 feet, and this sounding was taken near the edge of the Great Ice Barrier, about 105 miles east of Mount Erebus, while the greatest depth measured nearer land was 2,150 feet, between Franklin Island and McMurdo Bay. A properly organised system of soundings within the Antarctic Ocean, extending right round the globe, will probably throw more light upon the structure of Antarctic lands than would isolated sledge expeditions across their surfaces.

We lay all next day fastened to the ice barrier, waiting for the weather to clear in order to get sights for our geographical position, but not a glimpse of the sun did we get. The ship at this time presented a very wintery appearance, her sides were covered thick with ice, the rigging and yards covered with frost-rime, and from the chains at the bows hung long picturesque icicles, formed by the plunging of the ship in the freezing sea.

The following morning [Feb. 19], however, was clear and bright; a light wind blew from the south, and the temperature sank to −12° 5 Fahr. (−24° 4 Cent.), and this was February, one of the summer months of the Antarctic regions. A pleasant kind of temperature one would experience there in midwinter. To all appearance we were frozen up, for what was the day before a dark green moving mass of water, was now a level white plain, firm enough to walk upon.

Very early in the morning, Fougner, Evans, the second engineer Johansen and I, set out upon *ski* for a spot about five miles to the south where some 200 seals (*Leptonychotes Weddelli*) had congregated. We took with us a sledge and some dogs for carrying the photographic apparatus. The conditions for sledge travelling were splendid. The snow upon the surface of the ice was quite firm; one could easily cover twenty miles a day under such favourable conditions. Indeed, I feel sure that the surface of this ice-sheet or glacier, for as far as we could see, was sufficiently level and firm for the passage of a motor-car. We reached the seals after about an hour's travelling; they were all lying close together in a deep hollow in the ice-sheet which communicated with the sea by way of a crevass in the ice. . . .

After taking some photographs we returned, the steamer having whistled for our recall, and we reached the ship a little before one o'clock. During our absence some crustaceous life, with which the water teemed, had been caught, and Lieut. Colbeck had succeeded in getting capital sights for latitude and longitude.

The observation for latitude of ship gave 78° 34′ 37″ S. and longitude 164° 32′ 45″ W., and the magnetic declination or variation of the compass observed on the summit of the barrier was 103° 39′ E.

As the sledge party covered a distance of over ten miles, the farthest south latitude attained may be taken as something between 78° 45′ and 78° 50′ S., or about 40 miles farther south than Sir James Clark Ross in 1842.

At one o'clock we cast off, but we had some difficulty in ramming the ship out through the frozen surface of the sea. Another twenty-four hours and we should have been tightly wedged in for another winter.

◻ *The long-heralded British Antarctic expedition, for which Clements Markham had agitated since 1895, finally got under way in August, 1901. Its leader was perhaps the noblest and certainly the most tragic figure in the history of Antarctic exploration, Robert Falcon Scott.*

*Markham had first seen Scott as an eighteen-year-old midshipman in 1887, and had been impressed "with his intelligence, information, and the charm of his manner." Though he had been frail and sickly in boyhood, Scott became a strong and active naval officer, somewhat reserved and cool of manner, but a good administrator, well liked by his men. In 1899, he met Markham by chance and was persuaded to apply for the command of the forthcoming Antarctic expedition, and in June, 1900, his request was granted.*

*There were five scientists aboard Scott's ship, the* Discovery, *when it sailed. One of them was Louis Bernacchi of the* Southern Cross *adventure. Another was Dr. Edward "Bill" Wilson, a biologist with an artistic gift. One of Scott's officers was twenty-year-old Ernest Henry Shackleton, a sturdy, venturesome seaman who was destined for later Antarctic immortality.*

*Shackleton did not distinguish himself on Scott's first expedition. On November 2, 1902, he set out with Scott and Wilson on a sledge journey across the Ross Ice Shelf, with the South Pole hopefully the destination. Food ran low and scurvy threatened; by December 30, they were 380 miles from the camp at Hut Point near McMurdo Sound, but it was impossible to go farther. They had reached 82° 17′ S., closer to the Pole than any previous explorers.*

*On the return journey the trio nearly perished, with Shackleton so weakened by scurvy that he was unable to bear his share of the work. Much to his chagrin, he had to be invalided home early in 1903.*

*Scott's attempt to reach the Pole was the most widely publicized feature of his first expedition, but late in 1903 he made a second sledge trip that in some ways was even more taxing—a fifty-nine-day round trip westward from Hut Point, covering 725 miles. It involved climbing a lofty glacier to a high plateau where the thin air 9,000 feet above sea level made sledging difficult. Accompanied by two crew men, Scott successfully completed the traverse of what he called "this silent, wind-swept immensity" with seeming ease. In February, 1904, the* Discovery *left the Antarctic, bringing back enough scientific information about the polar region to fill many volumes.*

*The account that follows is from* The Voyage of the 'Discovery,' *by Robert F. Scott (London, Smith, Elder & Co., 1905).*  □

# ROBERT FALCON SCOTT— FIRST EXPEDITION

*December 15* [1903].—We all agree that yesterday was the most adventurous day in our lives, and we none of us want to have another like it. It seems wonderful that I should be lying here in ease and comfort to write of it, but as it is so, I can give its incidents in some detail.

Very early in the morning I awoke to find that all storm had passed, and that the land was all around us; but the clouds hung about the higher summits, and I was still unable to recognise any peak with certainty. In this bewildered condition we packed our sledge, and I could see no better course than to continue our march due east. We had scarcely been going half an hour, however, when high ice hummocks and disturbances appeared ahead, and we found ourselves on a hard glazed surface, which was cracked in all directions. Hoping to avoid the disturbed area, we first made a circuit to the right and then another to the left, but in neither of these directions did the prospect look more hopeful; we stopped and had a council of war, but by this time the wind had sprung up again, it was bitterly cold, and the only result of our deliberations was to show more clearly that we did not know where we were. In this predicament I vaguely realised that it would be rash to go forward, as the air was once more becoming thick with snowdrift; but then to stop might mean another long spell in a blizzard camp, when starvation would soon stare us in the face. I asked the men if they were prepared to take the risk of going on; they answered promptly in the affirmative. I think that after our trying experiences we were all feeling pretty reckless.

At any rate, we marched straight on for the ice disturbances, and were soon threading our way amongst the hummocks and across numerous crevasses. After a bit the surface became smoother, but at the same time the slope grew steeper, and our sledge began to overrun us. At this juncture I put the two men behind the sledge to hold it back whilst I continued in front to guide its course; we were all wearing crampons, which at first held well, but within a few minutes, as the inclination of the surface increased, our foothold became less secure.

Suddenly Lashly slipped, and in an instant he was sliding downward on his back; directly the strain came on Evans, he too was thrown off his feet. It all happened in a moment, and before I had time to look the sledge and the two men hurtled past me; I braced myself to stop them, but might as well have attempted to hold an express train. With the first jerk I was whipped off my legs, and we all three lay sprawling on our backs and flying downward with an ever-increasing velocity.

For some reason the first thought that flashed into my mind was that someone would break a limb if he attempted to stop our mad career, and I shouted something to this effect, but might as well have saved my breath. Then there came a sort of vague wonder as to what would happen next, and in the midst of this I was conscious that we had ceased to slide smoothly, and were now bounding over a rougher incline, sometimes leaving it for several yards at a time; my thoughts flew to broken limbs again, for I felt we could not stand much of such bumping. At length we gave a huge leap into the air, and yet we travelled with such velocity that I had not time to think before we came down with tremendous force on a gradual incline of rough, hard, wind-swept snow. Its irregularities brought us to rest in a moment or two, and I staggered to my feet in a dazed fashion, wondering what had happened.

Then to my joy I saw the others also struggling to their legs, and in another moment I could thank heaven that no limbs were broken. But we had by no means escaped scatheless; our legs now show one black bruise from knee to thigh, and Lashly was unfortunate enough to land once on his back, which is bruised and very painful. At the time, as can be imagined, we were all much shaken. I, as the lightest, escaped the easiest, yet before the two men crawled painfully to their feet their first question was to ask if I had been hurt.

As soon as I could pull myself together I looked round, and now to my astonishment I saw that we were well on towards the entrance of our own glacier; ahead and on either side of us appeared well-remembered landmarks, whilst behind, in the rough broken ice-wall over which we had fallen, I now recognised at once the most elevated ice cascade of our valley. In the rude fashion which I have described we must have descended some 300 feet; above us the snow-drift was still being driven along, but the wind had not yet reached our present level, so that all around us the sky was bright and clear and our eyes could roam from one familiar object to another until far away to the eastward they rested on the smoke-capped summit of Erebus.

I cannot but think that this sudden revelation of our position was very wonderful. Half an hour before we had been lost; I could not have told whether we were making for our own glacier or for any other, or whether we were ten or fifty miles from our depot; it was more than a month since we had seen any known landmark. Now in this extraordinary manner the curtain had been raised; we found that our rule-of-thumb methods had accomplished the most accurate "land fall," and down the valley we could see the high cliffs of the Depot Nunatak where peace and plenty awaited us.

How merciful a view this was we appreciated when we came to count up the result of our fall. Our sledge had not capsized until we all rolled over together at the end, but the jolting had scattered many of our belongings and had burst open the biscuit box, so that all that had remained in it lay distributed over the cascade; we had no provisions left except the few scraps we could pick up and the very diminished contents of our food bag. As well as our stiffening limbs would allow we hastened to collect the scattered articles, to repack the sledge, and to march on towards the depot. Before us now lay a long plateau, at the edge of which I knew we should find a second cascade, and beneath it the region of our Desolation Camp and a more gradual icy surface down to the Nunatak. By lunch-time we were well across the plateau, and we decided that our shaken condition deserved a hot meal, so we brewed cocoa and felt vastly better after swallowing it. By this time the wind had reached us again, and I had cold work in taking a round of angles, but I got through it, and in an hour we were on the march once more. We soon found ourselves at the top of the second cascade, and under conditions which prevented us from looking for an easy descent; however, fortune

163

favoured us, and by going very slowly and carefully we managed to get down without accident.

Though we were all much shaken and tired, we congratulated ourselves on having overcome the worst difficulties, and started off briskly to cover the last five or six miles which lay between us and our goal. Feeling quite unsuspicious of danger, we all three joined up our harness to our usual positions ahead of the sledge; this brought me in the middle and a little in advance, with Lashly on my right and Evans on my left. After we had been tramping on in this way for a quarter of an hour the wind swept across from the south, and as the sledge began to skid I told Lashly to pull wide in order to steady it. He had scarcely moved out in response to this order when Evans and I stepped on nothing and disappeared from his view; by a miracle he saved himself from following, and sprang back with his whole weight on the trace; the sledge flashed by him and jumped the crevass down which we had gone, one side of its frame cracked through in the jerk which followed, but the other side mercifully held. Personally I remember absolutely nothing until I found myself dangling at the end of my trace with blue walls on either side and a very horrid-looking gulf below; large ice-crystals dislodged by our movements continued to shower down on our heads.

As a first step I took off my goggles; I then discovered that Evans was hanging just above me. I asked him if he was all right, and received a reassuring reply in his usual calm, matter-of-fact tones. Meanwhile I groped about on every side with my cramponed feet, only to find everywhere the same slippery smooth wall. But my struggles had set me swinging, and at one end of a swing my leg suddenly struck a projection. In a moment I had turned, and saw at a glance that by raising myself I could get foothold on it; with the next swing I clutched it with my steel-shod feet, and after a short struggle succeeded in partly transferring my weight to it. In this position, with my feet firmly planted and my balance maintained by my harness, I could look about me.

I found myself standing on a thin shaft of ice which was wedged between the walls of the chasm—how it came there I cannot imagine, but its position was wholly providential; to the right or left, above or below, there was not the vestige of another such support—nothing, in fact, but the smooth walls of ice. My next step was to get

Evans into the same position as myself, and when he had slipped his harness well up under his arms I found I could pilot his feet to the bridge.

All this had occupied some time, and it was only now that I realised what had happened above us, for there, some twelve feet over our heads, was the outline of the broken sledge. I saw at once what a frail support remained, and shouted to Lashly to ask what he could do, and then I knew the value of such a level-headed companion; for whilst he held on grimly to the sledge and us with one hand, his other was busily employed in withdrawing our ski. At length he succeeded in sliding two of these beneath the broken sledge and so making our support more secure. The device was well thought of, but it still left us without his active assistance; for, as he told us, directly he relaxed his strain the sledge began to slip, and he dared not trust only to the ski.

There remained no other course for Evans and me but to climb out by our own unaided efforts, and I saw that one of us would have to make the attempt without delay, for the chill of the crevasse was already attacking us and our faces and fingers were on the verge of freezing. After a word with Evans I decided to try the first climb myself, but I must confess I never expected to reach the top. It is some time since I swarmed a rope, and to have to do so in thick clothing and heavy crampons and with frost-bitten fingers seemed to me in the nature of the impossible. But it was no use thinking about it, so I slung my mits over my shoulders, grasped the rope, and swung off the bridge. I don't know how long I took to climb or how I did it, but I remember I got a rest when I could plant my foot in the belt of my harness, and again when my feet held on the rings of the belt. Then came a mighty effort till I reached the stirrup formed by the rope span of the sledge, and then, mustering all the strength that remained, I reached the sledge itself and flung myself panting on to the snow beyond. Lashly said, "Thank God!" and it was perhaps then that I realised that his position had been the worst of all.

For a full five minutes I could do nothing; my hands were white to the wrists, and I plunged them into my breast, but gradually their circulation and my strength came back, and I was able to get to work. With two of us on top and one below, things had assumed a very different aspect, and I was able to unhitch my own harness and lower it once more for Evans; then with our united efforts he also was landed on the surface, where he arrived in the same frost-bitten condition as I had. For a minute or two we could only look at one another, then Evans said, "Well, I'm blowed"; it was the first sign of astonishment he had shown.

But all this time the wind was blowing very chill, so we wasted no time in discussing our escape, but turning our broken sledge end for end, we were soon harnessed to it again and trudging on over the snow. After this, as can be imagined, we kept a pretty sharp look-out for crevasses, marching in such an order as prevented more than one of us going down at once, and so we eventually reached the bare blue ice once more, and at six o'clock found our depot beneath the towering cliffs of the Depot Nunatak.

As long as I live I can never forget last night. Our camp was in bright sunshine, for the first time for six weeks the temperature was above zero, but what we appreciated still more was the fact that it was perfectly calm; the canvas of our tent hung limp and motion-less, and the steam of our cooking rose in a thin, vertical shaft. All Nature seemed to say that our long fight was over, and that at length we had reached a haven of rest. And it had been a fight indeed; it is only now that I realise what discomforts we have endured and what a burden of anxiety we have borne during the past month. The relief of being freed from such conditions is beyond the power of my pen to describe, but perhaps what brought it home to us most completely was the fact that the worst of our troubles and adventures came at the end, and that in the brief space of half an hour we passed from abject discomfort to rest and peace. . . .

This morning the sun shines as brightly as ever, and there is still no breath of wind. It is so warm in the tent that as I write I have had to throw open my jacket. Meanwhile outside I can hear the tap of the hammer as my companions are arming our sledge-runners for the hard ice of the glacier.

We only found a very small quantity of food at the Depot Nuna-tak, but it was enough to carry us to the main depot, which lay several miles below, provided we marched hard, as we were quite prepared to do. Luckily, here also we found a new nine-foot sledge which had been left the previous year, and to which we could now transfer the greater part of our load. But one of our most pleasing discoveries at the Depot Nunatak was the small folded notes which told us of the movements of our fellow-travellers. By these I learnt to my relief that Skelton and his companions had safely reached the glacier, and that Ferrar's party was all well after it had left our Desolation Camp. According to previous arrangements I found these notes at various stated points in the glacier, and there were few pleasanter things for us returning wayfarers than to find these cheery documents.

Starting our downward march on the afternoon of the 15th, we stretched over the miles with ease. This sort of work was mere child's play to our hardened muscles, and that night we reached the broad amphitheatre below Finger Mountain. On the 16th we picked up the ample supply of food which we had left in our depot opposite the Solitary Rocks, and that evening took up our quarters in the Knob Head Moraine. I mention these movements because at this point I had determined to do a small piece of exploration which is of some interest. The reader will see that we were now in the large glacier basin which I described, and will remember that I mentioned amongst other outlets its northern arm. This arm of the glacier descended with a very steep incline to the right of the Solitary Rocks, and then its valley seemed to turn sharply to the eastward. The direction of flow of the ice-streams in the glacier basin had always been something of a mystery for us, and we had thought that the main portion of the ice must discharge through this valley.

On the 17th, therefore, we started to descend it to see what the conditions actually were, and after rattling down over a sharp gradient for several miles we found ourselves turning to the east. We followed a long string of morainic boulders through a deep valley on a moderate incline, but early in the afternoon the descent became steeper and the surface of the ice much rougher, until at length our sledge bumped so heavily that we thought it wise to camp.

Our camp life by this time had become wholly pleasant except to poor Lashly, who had a fierce attack of snow-blindness. We pitched our tent behind a huge boulder which must have weighed at least five hundred tons, and here we were pleasantly sheltered from the wind, whilst close by us trickled a glacier stream from which we were able to fill our cooking pot and obtain an unlimited quantity of drinking-water. We had a splendid view of the great ice masses sweeping down from above, but looking downward we were much puzzled, for the glacier surface descended steeply, and beyond it stood a lofty groin of rock which seemed a direct bar to its further passage. This sight made us very anxious to proceed with our exploration, and as we could not advance further with our sledge, it became necessary to arrange for a long absence from our camp. Accordingly we rose very early on the following day, and taking our coil of Alpine rope, with our crampons and a supply of food, we set off over the rough ice of the glacier. As this walk had several points of interest, I give its outline from my diary:

"Started at seven o'clock with a supply of pemmican, chocolate, sugar, and biscuit in our pockets, and our small provision measure to act as a drinking-cup. It is an extraordinary novelty in our sledging experience to find that one can get water by simply dipping it up. As we descended, the slope became steeper, and soon the ice grew so disturbed that we were obliged to rope ourselves together and proceed with caution. The disturbance was of very much the same nature as that which we had found on the south side of the Ferrar Glacier; the ice seemed to have broken down, leaving steep faces towards the south. Here and there we found scattered boulders and finer morainic material, and the channels of the glacial streams became visible in places, to vanish again under deep blue arches of ice.

"At length we descended into one of these water-courses and followed it for some distance, until, to our surprise, it came abruptly to an end, and with it the glacier itself, which had gradually dwindled to this insignificant termination. Before us was a shallow, frozen lake into which the thaw-water of the glacier was pouring. The channel in which we stood was about twenty feet above its surface, and the highest pinnacles of ice were not more than the same distance above our heads, whereas the terminal face of the glacier was about three or four hundred yards across. So here was the limit of the great ice-river which we had followed down from the vast basin of the interior; instead of pouring huge icebergs into the sea, it was slowly dwindling away in its steep-sided valley. It was, in fact, nothing but the remains of what had once been a mighty ice-flow from the inland.

"With a little difficulty we climbed down to the level of the lake, and then observed that the glacier rested on a deep ground moraine of mud, in some places as much as ten or twelve feet in thickness; this layer of mud extended beyond the face of the glacier, where it had been much worn by water; enough remained, however, for Lashly to remark, 'What a splendid place for growing spuds!' Skirting the lake below the glacier, we found ourselves approaching the high, rocky groin which puzzled us so much last night, but we now saw that a very narrow channel wound round its base. At its narrowest this channel was only seventeen feet across, and as we traversed this part, the high cliffs on either side towered above our heads and we seemed to be passing through a massive gateway; beyond this the valley opened out again, and its floor was occupied by a frozen lake a mile in breadth and three or four miles in length. As the snow surface of this lake was very rough, we were obliged to skirt its margin; we were now 1,300 feet below our camp, and about 300 feet above sea level. The shores of the lake for several hundred feet up the hillsides were covered with a coarse granitic sand strewn with numerous boulders, and it was curious to observe that these boulders, from being rounded and sub-angular below, gradually grew to be sharper in outline as they rose in level.

"At the end of the second lake the valley turned towards the north-east; it was equally clearly cut, but the floor rose on a mass of morainic material. At first there was a general tendency for this to be distributed in long ridges, but later the distribution was disturbed, and it was easy to see that broad water-channels had made clean breaches in these vast piles of sand and boulders. Quite suddenly these moraines ceased, and we stepped out on to a long stretch of undulating sand traversed by numerous small streams, which here and there opened out into small, shallow lakes quite free from ice.

"I was so fascinated by all these strange new sights that I strode forward without thought of hunger until Evans asked if it was any use carrying our lunch further; we all decided that it wasn't, and so sat down on a small hillock of sand with a merry little stream gurgling over the pebbles at our feet. It was a very cheery meal, and certainly the most extraordinary we have had. We commanded an extensive view both up and down the valley, and yet, except about the rugged mountain summits, there was not a vestige of ice or snow to be seen; and as we ran the comparatively warm sand through our fingers and quenched our thirst at the stream, it seemed almost impossible that we could be within a hundred miles of the terrible conditions we had experienced on the summit.

"Proceeding after lunch, we found that the valley descended to a deep and splendid gorge formed by another huge groin extending from the southern side, but as we approached the high cliffs we found our way again obstructed by confused heaps of boulders, amongst which for the first time we saw the exposed rocks of the floor of the valley smoothed and striated in a manner most typical of former ice action. My object in pressing on had been to get a view of the sea, and I now thought the best plan would be to ascend the neck of the groin on our right. It was a long climb of some 700 feet over rough, sharp boulders. We eventually reached the top, but, alas! not to catch any glimpse of the sea; for the valley continued to wind its way onward through deep gorges, and some five or six miles below yet another groin shut out our further view.

"But from our elevated position we could now get an excellent view of this extraordinary valley, and a wilder or in some respects more beautiful scene it would have been difficult to imagine. Below lay the sandy stretches and confused boulder heaps of the valley floor, with here and there the gleaming white surface of a frozen lake and elsewhere the silver threads of the running water; far above us towered the weather-worn, snow-splashed mountain peaks, between which in places fell in graceful curves the folds of some hanging glacier. The rocks at our feet were of every variety of colour and form, mixed in that inextricable confusion which ice alone can accomplish. The lower slopes of the mountains were thickly clothed with similar rocks, but the variety of colour was lost in the distance, and these steep slopes had a general tone of sober grey. This colour was therefore predominant, but everywhere at a height of 3,000 feet above the valley it ended in a hard line illustrating in the most beautiful manner the maximum extent to which the ice had once spread.

"I cannot but think that this valley is a very wonderful place. We have seen to-day all the indications of colossal ice action and considerable water action, and yet neither of these agents is now at work. It is worthy of record, too, that we have seen no living thing, not even a moss or a lichen; all that we did find, far inland amongst

170

the moraine heaps, was the skeleton of a Weddell seal, and how that came there is beyond guessing. It is certainly a valley of the dead: even the great glacier which once pushed through it has withered away.

"It was nearly four o'clock before we turned towards our camp, and nearly ten before we reached it, feeling that it was quite time for supper. The day's record, however, is pretty good tribute to our marching powers, for we have walked and climbed over the roughest country for more than fourteen hours with only one brief halt for lunch."

With this short expedition our last piece of exploration came to an end, and on the 19th we started to ascend the north arm. By the night of the 20th we had reached our second depot under Cathedral Rocks, and here for the first time, and with anxious eyes, we looked out towards the sea. Many a time we had discussed this prospect, and agreed that we should not have cared how far round we had to walk if only that stubborn sheet of ice in the strait would break away. But now, alas! it was evident that our homeward track might be as direct as we chose to make it, for the great unbroken plain of ice still bridged the whole strait. Only in the far distance could we see the open water, where a thin blue ribbon ran in from Cape Bird and ended abreast of the black rocks of Cape Royds. We saw with grief that there must be very many miles between it and our unfortunate ship.

On rounding Butter Point we had another blow on finding an entire absence of seals, but thanks to the kindness of Skelton and his party, we were not deprived of our long-expected feast of fresh meat, for close to our tin of butter we found a buried treasure in the shape of some tit-bits of an animal which they had killed. From Butter Point we turned our course south to those curious moraine heaps which we had called the 'Eskers,' and which I had not yet seen. We spent half a day in rambling amongst these steep little hills, and in trying to find skuas' eggs which were not hard set; but fortune was against us in this last respect, and we found that we were at least a week too late.

On the afternoon of the 23rd we started to cross the strait for the last time, and late on Christmas Eve we saw the masts of the 'Discovery,' and were soon welcomed by the four persons who alone remained on board. And so after all our troubles and trials we spent our Christmas Day in the snug security of our home quarters, and tasted once again those delights of civilised existence to which we had so long been strangers.

□   *The Swedish expedition that departed for Antarctica in October, 1901, began with high hopes, but ended in a kind of tragicomic confusion. Its leader was Otto Nordenskjöld, a geologist and mineralogist, who included eight other scientists in his party of twenty-nine. The ship was the* Antarctic, *the whaling vessel that had carried Bull and Borchgrevink to Cape Adare in 1895. Her captain this time was a veteran whaler, C. A. Larsen.*

*After exploring the ice-locked Weddell Sea early in 1902, Nordenskjöld and five other men set up a winter base in February at Snow Hill Island, just off the eastern coast of the Antarctic Peninsula. The* Antarctic *left them on February 21, intending to return and pick up the land party the following summer. Nordenskjöld and his companions made extensive sledge journeys, carried out geological and botanical studies, and visited the nearby islands. By February, 1903, it became apparent that the ice pack was too thick to permit the* Antarctic *to reach them, something that Nordenskjöld had anticipated, and the men at Snow Hill Island settled down to spend a second winter at their base.*

*They did not know that the ship had been trapped in the ice late in 1902. Three men, Andersson, Duse, and Grunden, had been put ashore to attempt an overland journey to Snow Hill Island with the news, but they, too, became stranded and had to establish an improvised winter base for themselves. Meanwhile, in January, 1903, an ice floe ripped a hole in the* Antarctic's *side, and the ship went down on February 13 after vain efforts to save her. All hands escaped in open boats, and after a sixteen-day journey through an ice-filled sea reached nearby Paulet Island and built a stone hut there.*

*Three Swedish parties thus were wintering within fifty miles of* one another, with no way of making contact. When the winter ended, the stranded explorers began to stir, and an improbable series of meetings followed. Captain Larsen and five other men from the Paulet Island group set out in search of Andersson, Duse, and Grunden, found their hut, and learned that they had gone on toward Snow Hill Island at the end of September. Larsen and his men followed. At Snow Hill, Nordenskjöld had met the Andersson party in October, and on November 8 a second group arrived at the base— four men from the Argentine navy, part of a rescue mission that had come to see what had become of the expedition. A few hours after the Argentinians arrived, Larsen and his five men came trekking into the Snow Hill Island camp, thus reuniting the expedition but for the men who had remained at Paulet Island. A few days later they were picked up by the rescue party, and by late 1903 the Swedish group was back in Stockholm.

One of the many accounts of this expedition tells the story from the viewpoint of the Paulet Island party. It is by C. J. Skottsberg, the expedition's botanist, and appeared in Otto Nordenskjöld's book, Antarctica (London, Macmillan, 1905).   □

# C. J. SKOTTSBERG—
# WINTER ON PAULET ISLAND

We were rather tired when we landed, for we had rowed uninterruptedly for 6½ hours, and without having eaten or drunk anything since the preceding evening. And we got no rest yet awhile, for we were obliged to move all our things farther up on to the land, as it was now low water. After an hour or two the cooks had managed to prepare a little dinner for us. It was a memorable meal, not because of the dishes—for we had only tinned meat, coffee, butter and ship's biscuits—but because it was the last time that we ate other meat than that procured by our "hunting parties"; it was the last time we had sugar with our coffee, and the last time we had as much butter and biscuits as we wished. It was with a certain solemnity that the sugar was dropped into the cup—I believe I took twice as many pieces as usual, although I prefer the smaller quantity.

The shore on to which we had drawn up our boats was not very broad; it was succeeded by a slope whither we transported our things. This slope was free from penguins, and lying between rather steep hills offered more protection from the wind than did the other habitable part of our island. After helping to erect the tent and to cover the floor with flat stones, I had time to make a little exploring expedition, of which the following report may be interesting.

Paulet Island lies in about 63° 35′ S. lat. (corresponding pretty nearly to the position of the Faroe Islands in the northern hemisphere) and long. 55° 50′ W. It is almost circular in form, being about three miles in circumference. The island consists entirely of recent volcanic rocks, basalt and such like, and has the appearance of a very typical crater-island, the middle of which is occupied by a little circular lake, towards which the sides of the hill fall very steeply. The highest point of the island lies 385 metres (1,250 feet) above the sea. The hill slopes are very steep, and it is only in a few places that the top can be reached.

The place was rather silent and deserted when we arrived, for, unfortunately, the greater number of the penguins had already left the island. Those who were left were old birds who were moulting; they sat there peaceably and quietly enough, although they were evidently irritated by our arrival. Nearly all of them belonged to the black and white Adélie penguins (*Pyogoscelis Adeliae*).

We look around in vain for seals. There ought to be some, and if they do not soon put in an appearance—! Raw penguin-meat is not very enticing.

Fancy being able to go to sleep, confident of waking in the same latitude and longitude where one dropped off. Our life seems quite full of enjoyment, though the stones are not soft to lie on.

*March 1st* [1903].—Now begins our Esquimaux life. We mark it at dinnertime, the meal consisting of penguin-soup, which is very good, being made from freshly-killed birds. Then we go out to look for seal, and find no less than eight, all of which are killed, the skins and the best part of the meat being brought home to the tent amidst rejoicing. Today is Sunday, and, therefore, we have done no other work than the killing of these seals, but there is much to be thought of. It is evident that we shall not be able to make shift with our weak tent. It has stood one storm, it is true, but who can say how it will fare on the next occasion? And besides it cannot, of course, keep out the cold in the least, and it would be impossible for us to dwell a whole winter as we are now doing.

So we must build a house. The first thing is to choose a site. The little plain near the shore, to the east of the tent, is level and enticing enough, but the winds blow more unhindered there, and it would be troublesome to take our building materials to the place. The slope on which we dwell is not quite level anywhere, but it is somewhat protected from the wind, and one of the hills close by is covered with the finest flat basalt-stones of an even thickness, which look as if they would make excellent building material. We determine to erect the hut at the foot of this little hill, and begin by taking some large, irregularly rounded blocks of basalt and rolling them down to the spot where the foundations are to be laid. Some of the men stand there ready to receive them, and place them in their proper positions, in double rows, with small stones and old and now inodorous guano to fill the spaces between. Almost before we are aware of the fact the foundations are ready, and we stop to cast a look of hopeful pride at our masterpiece. The style is quite new and might be called Paulet Island architecture. It is probably unrepresented elsewhere—and I hope that none of my readers will ever find themselves forced to adopt it.

The best stones near the hut are soon taken, and we are obliged to go some distance off and climb the hill in order to look for suitable material. It is hard work carrying slabs of stone on one's back, hour after hour. Building is much pleasanter—putting the blocks together as closely as possible and slipping in small pieces here and there, and filling in with earth. Naturally we build double walls everywhere, and we do not make rapid progress with the work, as we have to provide shelter for twenty men, and the walls must be built close, in order to exclude storm and snow. One grows both tired and thirsty—has to stop to take breath every now and then—must take a drink of water from the bucket. The water comes from the crater-lake. It is a little too greenish-yellow in colour, and has an unpleasant taste—for thousands of penguins have dwelt upon the steep slopes—but we do not attach importance to trifles, and when used for the soup the water does not taste so bad.

The house grew day by day. The doorway leading out into the

future kitchen was made ready after we had found a couple of slabs large enough to go quite across the top. On the opposite side we left place for two small windows. We had been hoping to escape snow until we had the roof ready, but we were not so fortunate, and a great deal of snow fastened in all the corners of our new building.

Our health is not quite as it should be. Our stomachs rebel against the constant meat diet. But we have nothing else, for no one can still his hunger with ship's biscuits and the coffee-cup. Most of us soon grow accustomed to the new diet, however, and scarcely anyone was as bad as I was for a period of several weeks.

The 6th and the 7th were very unpleasant days, but during the afternoon of the latter day we finished most of the work necessary inside of the house, and commenced the erection of the framework of the roof, consisting of two narrow tables in the middle, and, on each side of these, two roof-couples of tent-poles. The roof-tree consisted of two boat-hooks fastened together. The sails were laid over the ridge and built into the wall; the windows were stuffed up; a tarpaulin was hung before the door, and we moved in during the course of the evening. There was a considerable quantity of snow on the floor and in all the cracks of the walls, but now there was no help for it.

It already begins to be winter. The snow whirls about in shifting gusts, and snowdrifts accumulate inside the hut, for the entrance cannot be kept tightly closed, as there are twenty of us, and we must be able to go in and out freely. The thermometer outside the house shows about fourteen or eighteen degrees of frost the whole of the twenty-four hours. It is rather cold indoors, but we hope to improve matters as soon as we get the kitchen built outside the entrance, and have the roof-cloth covered with seal skins. We calculate that we need about thirty of these skins; some lie ready on the hill, but are frozen stiff. As soon as they thaw we intend sewing them fast to the canvas. And, in addition, when the windows and the doors are in their places, I imagine we need not freeze to death.

As an addition to our fare we have now commenced to eat blubber, boiled in the soup. We cannot afford to take much, but a little is always of some use. For my own part I believe we can thank the blubber for the good health we enjoyed during the time we wintered here, for I fancy the fat serves in some degree to make up for the vegetable foodstuffs of which we had such a small supply. At the beginning we swallowed the bits of blubber without daring to taste them, but at last one actually enjoyed masticating the fat, especially when it was quite fresh.

The bad weather continued, but it did not prevent us from building our kitchen, for the cook had really a miserable existence, and the snow came whirling in upon those of us who lay nearest the door, so that the satisfaction was general, therefore, when after a couple of days we had the kitchen ready. The building had only three single walls of equal height, covered with a roof made of a tarpaulin, canvas and some seal skins.

The total length of the house was about 34 feet, of which 24 were taken up by the dwelling-room. Its breadth was 22 feet or so, that of the kitchen being 12 feet, or a little more. The front and back walls were 3½ feet and 4 feet high respectively, as the floor sloped towards the shore; the side walls were 8 feet high. Tall as I am, I could walk erect along the middle line of the house, and no greater height than this was required, I fancy. The doors were low, and one was obliged to stoop on entering. The area of the floor in the living room was 20 feet by 18, and was almost entirely taken up by the sleeping bags. Low stone-beds, seven feet broad, were built along the two sides of the room, and here the bags lay in two rows, ten in each. Between the beds was a passage, four feet wide, which constituted the only common space in the room. We had not many domestic utensils. In the window recesses stood a couple of Primus petroleum-stoves; a pair of scales for bread hung on the wall—it had been constructed by Larsen out of the sides of a cocoa-tin; under them stood a sack, or a barrel, containing bread. Each one had his plate, knife, fork, spoon and cup. In the kitchen we kept all the provisions, with the exception of five barrels of ship's biscuits, which lay snowed-up lower down the hill, and the food supplies obtained on the island itself, these being buried in the snow below the hut.

The list of provisions brought to Paulet Island included, amongst other things, 600 kilogrammes ship's biscuits; 25 kg. sugar; 30 kg. coffee; 14 kg. tea; 70 kg. pease; 165 tins of preserved meat and fish (the greater part of the tinned meat was left behind us on the island when we were rescued); 16 tins condensed milk; 100 kg. margarine (Zenith's and Pellerin's); 600 portions preserved vegetables; 240

litres petroleum (140 litres of which still remained at the end of our stay here); and 300 candles and a supply of matches.

The supply may seem considerable to anyone who does not reflect how many there were of us. But it formed a small fraction of all that we consumed; in fact, we should have soon have been starved to death had we not been able to supplement these stores very considerably. While the house was building we killed a seal now and then, but seal-meat was unpopular at the time, the majority of the men thinking that the penguin-soup tasted much better. We had determined, from the very beginning, to collect a supply of penguins for the winter, and we calculated that we should require at least 3,000 or 4,000 of the birds.

The penguin-colony was growing smaller and smaller every day; an increasing number of the birds had already acquired their new feathers, after which they made no delay in taking their departure, but several thousands of the penguins were still left on the 11th of March, when we at last had an opportunity of beginning the work of massacre. But this was no easy task. It went well enough for the first few days, but it did not take long before the birds saw what our intentions were, and fled long ere we could come within reach. Still, it was very strange that they should have become shy so suddenly. We could not afford to throw away powder on them, but did the work with sticks. As I have said, it became at last almost impossible to catch any birds. Where the ground was free from snow we contrived to obtain some spoils of the chase, but where the snow lay we sank into it, while the penguins simply ran away from us, throwing themselves on their bellies and kicking themselves forward at a most astonishing rate. When the last of the birds had left the island we had killed about 1,100 of them.

A few words may be said about our clothes. Each of us had a couple of changes of underwear. Our clothes were, as a rule, of homespun; some of us had an extra coat or pair of trousers, although these were not made for winter use. Still, I think no one suffered from the cold on account of a scarcity of wearing-apparel.

We were worse off for shoes, our ordinary shoes and boots being anything but sufficiently warm, and complaints about cold feet were made every day, while nothing was said of any other part of the body suffering from the severity of the climate.

178

Winter had now made its appearance; some entries from my diary will show that it at once assumed despotic power.

*March 14th.*—"Bad weather, with a snowstorm from the west-southwest. All outdoor work interrupted." *March 15th.*—"Fresh south wind with snowstorm, and twenty-two degrees of frost the whole day. But K. Andersson and I took a walk, for one grows stupid lying in the bags all day." *March 18th.*—"Weather bad, and a snow-storm from the southwest in the evening, but I had my forenoon walk." *March 19th.*—"It began to blow hard at 11 last night, with increasing violence. The roof is not ready yet, and the gusts of wind attacked the frail structure with terrible power, causing the sails to thresh against the roof-poles. Strangely enough, the covering held. But when we looked out in the morning the kitchen roof had disap-peared. It had fluttered away for a couple of hundred yards, and had nearly continued its journey far away over the ice. The whole island has quite another look after the storm; immense masses of snow have fallen, in which we are obliged to wade up to the knees."

The days creep along at a snail's pace, the weather keeping us, as a rule, indoors. Scarcely a bird can be heard about the precipices; the little *chionis* (wattled sheathbill) alone comes hopping around our cottage, but goodness knows that it is not much he has thrown to him by the Paulet Island savages.

It is winter all around us. The ice lies fast between here and Dundee Island, so that the snow can now whirl direct to our hut from the glaciers of the latter place. But the cold has given us one advantage; it has extended the area available for walks, and we are no longer confined to a narrow strip of coast. Our new domain of ice is not so monotonous as the reader might believe. There we have chains of hills with intervening valleys, ridges and peaks, cliffs and precipices. There are fissures, and holes where the seal blows—his movements watched every day by vigilant eyes.

Unfortunately we were not aware of the wind conditions here, otherwise we should have placed the door in another part of the building. As it is, the entrance is continually blocked with snow, and every day we have endless trouble in making our way in and out.

The time goes a little slowly. But there is one thing in the world which is able, in a way, to make the days pass quickly, and that is the looking forward to something agreeable. And we go here longing, longing for Easter, and our longing grows the greater the nearer we approach the great event—rice porridge! What a trifle, is it not? But what do you think penguin-soup is when compared with the mere thought of rice-porridge?

Easter Eve, the great day, is come. There is great joy amongst us, for we have taken a seal. The work of flaying it is soon completed, and we creep into our bags and wait devoutly for the long-expected meal. The conversation turns wholly upon rice-porridge.

Amid laughter and jest each one takes out his table service; we even wipe our plates clean. I use a coal-black handkerchief, which shines with fat and soot. The day opens; the conversation dies away; there is a touch of reverence in the silence.

It is no every-day dish we are promised. Quite a number of *chionis* have been sacrificed, and we have indulged in the luxury of frying them in margarine. There is absolutely no end to the praises lavished on this prodigally prepared dish. But suddenly there comes a new silence over us; the kitchen door is thrown open for the second time and the cook enters heavily, toiling along with the big, heavy porridge-pot. A most delicious aroma spreads about in the hut; the steam fills the low room, and the plates are handed round. We sit and long for our turn to come.

Never in our lives have we eaten anything so good. But as it would be prodigality to take the whole at one meal, I put my plate on the shelf behind me, leaving a little bit for the morrow.

How we spent our everyday life during the following winter months can be realised by taking the description of one day—any one day. We may assume that the weather is calm, cold and clear, a condition of things which, unfortunately, did not often exist.

It is about 7:30 A.M. My watch has been out of order for a long time past, and so I poke my friend, K. A. Andersson—who lies on my left—in the side, and ask him what the time is. The ceiling is glitteringly white, for it is clothed with a very respectable layer of rime. This rime has dropped on to our bags during the night, so that they, too, lie white and beautiful in the day-dawn. The walls are also covered with frost, and all the cracks are filled with ice, which grows thicker after each touch of mild weather. Of course we have to keep our bags well closed over the head, in order to retain the warmth; one breathes through the blanket and the canvas, and, on awakening, there lies a vault of ice above the face.

At length it is eight o'clock, and, if the weather permit, Andersson or I go out to note the height of the thermometer. This *can* be a pleasure, but—after a snowstorm! *Then* the passage through the snowdrift to the door is filled with hard-packed snow and on looking outside one sees a smooth, white wall. If there happens to be a shovel inside, we make a hole and creep out, but sometimes there is nothing else one can do but go into the snowdrift head first, and wriggle out into the open. On coming in again, one hears hollow-sounding, questioning voices from the depths of the bags, for everyone is curious to know how the thermometer stands.

Or I have gone to bed at half-past seven the evening before, and have slept almost twelve hours, and am awakened by a rattling noise. It is the "waterman" knocking the ice out of the pail before he goes to fetch fresh water from the crater-lake.

Out of the way for the cook; here comes the coffee! Cups are held out, and the boiling hot drink is soon swallowed and warms the whole of one's frozen frame. We drink coffee and tea on alternate days, with cocoa on Sundays. This sounds fine, but one has either to keep a very careful count of the days, or else have a most delicate sense of taste, if one is to be able to distinguish between the various decoctions. The tea was undoubtedly the worst of them all.

We can suppose that the weather is fine, and so order the day accordingly. We make preparations for going out, and begin to dress ourselves. The boots always occasion the greatest difficulty, for they are as hard as sheet-iron. The coat has, of course, become wet on some occasion or another, and may now be best compared to a mail-shirt. But, at length, off we go to our various employments. Some take their fishing-lines and go down to the ice to stand and stamp by a hole for a couple of hours, cheered by faint visions of a fish-breakfast. My boots, which are thin, being intended to be filled with shoe-hay, do not permit my standing still so long when it is cold; so I go about, pick up the fish when any are caught, and take them home to be cleaned.

It may be that I go on the lookout for a seal. We go far over the ice, but, unfortunately, it is seldom that our efforts are crowned with success.

But in the end it grows wearisome, this going out and clambering about. The sleeping-bag is no very enticing bed, but we have no other place of refuge. So we go indoors and take off our outdoor clothes, and each one withdraws to his lair. Then begins a new period of waiting. A couple of hours elapse ere the food comes, consisting, it is true, of penguin-soup alone, but it gives occasion for a salutary interruption. It is no very agreeable odour that steams from the kettle when it is brought in, and when the fare comes on to the plates it does not look pleasanter than it smells, for it consists of a brownish-yellow, thin soup, with some thick penguin-bones lying in it and pieces of seal-blubber floating about. But we finish it all. And when one has swallowed the two platefuls we get, there are many who cast a look of regret towards the empty kettle as it is carried out.

Still, our dinners are not always such plain ones. Saturday is the best day in the week, for the man who does not eat his fill then has only himself to blame. Dinner that day consists of an endless number of seal-steaks, and a plate of what is alleged to be fruit-syrup soup. I shudder when I think of the portions we received: seven or eight enormous, black steaks, swimming in fried train-oil, and garnished with bits of blubber. There was not much taste to the soup, and great faith was necessary that water might be changed to syrup. But fortunately we were all of us believers, and we lavished unending praise on the decoction.

It is not more than six o'clock. How long the evenings are! If only we had enough tobacco, for now we think it much if we get a single whiff of a pipe! Old Haslum, the second mate, will always be present in my recollections; I can still see him comfortably sending out clouds of smoke which smell bad enough to make one's hair stand on end, for he used dried tea-leaves mixed with snuff. And Martin, who used to beg, in advance, for pipes that might eventually be broken, and who, when he received the treasure, would chew the bowl. It is a thankless task, the endeavour to keep a sailor and pig-tail tobacco apart!

And so we lie staring up at the roof where the rime-frost is gradually increasing, for it is growing colder and colder outside. Yet no one gives way to despondency—not at all; but each one does what he can to be cheerful and chatty; subjects of conversation never come to an end in Paulet Cottage, and Johansson never ceases trolling some tune. It is an advantage to be able to be in good humour at any time, even if deep down in our hearts we consider the situation desperate. A hang-gallows wit it is that flourishes in our midst.

A moment's reading livens one up considerably. But we have to be saving of that, too, although it is often hard to close the book. And so we lie and think a little while longer, and by-and-by it is time for bed. The process of undressing is not an arduous task; that of arranging the bed is much more tedious. The pillow is a mosaic composed of various articles of dress; the canvas bag shows a tendency to slip down; the blankets are twisted. At last everything is in order; we creep inside, draw the blankets and canvas over our heads and wish for nothing else but to be able to sleep. We have first to take up a position which is not too inconvenient, a thing easier said than done; the mattress consisting of stones—and knobbly and sharp ones into the bargain—covered by nothing but thin rags. Many a time when I have lain me down have I thought of Hamlet's words: "—to sleep. No more; and by a sleep to say we end the heartache and the thousand natural shocks that flesh is heir to. . . . To sleep—perchance to dream!"

Many hundred dreams have been dreamed in our island, but I do not know if they helped to brighten our existence. They grouped themselves around two objects—food and rescue. Why, we could dream through a whole dinner, from the soup to the dessert, and waken to be cruelly disappointed. How many times did one not see the relief vessel in our visions—sometimes as a large ship, sometimes as nothing but a little sloop? And we knew the persons on board; they spoke about our journey; took us in their arms; patted us on the back.

A train-oil lamp winks faintly through the smoky darkness. Nothing can be heard but the breathing of the sleepers. . . .

The Antarctic winter weather is not enticing. It is true that the cold in these latitudes is nothing nearly so great as it is within the northern hemisphere; but here, on the other hand, the wind becomes a much more important factor. And the changes in the weather come with extraordinary rapidity; in a couple of hours the temperature can rise from —20° C. (—4° F.) to freezing-point, and two hours later we have once more 20° (36°) of cold. But we rejoiced at the thunder of the wind which is doing good work out at sea by driving the ice east-wards and away from us. We must have ice-free water in the spring when the relief-boat comes.

In mild weather it was nice and warm indoors; that is, the tempera-ture was about +3° or 4° C. (37° to 39° F.), but the change was attended by several inconveniences, a dreadful smell arising from the kitchen-midden to which the passage between the rows of beds had been gradually transformed. And the rotting penguin-skins were still worse! In order to make their beds softer, several of our party had placed penguin-skins under the sleeping bags, and if anyone hap-pened to move the bundle, a terrible odour at once filled the room. When one came out of the fresh air into the hut it was at first almost impossible to breathe, so bad was the atmosphere. It seems very strange now that we enjoyed such good health as we did the whole time we were on the island, although it can easily be understood that the digestion of several of us was somewhat affected by our fare.

But we were not wholly preserved from sickness and death as we had hoped we should be. Wennersgaard had been a long time poorly, had violent attacks of coughing as soon as he went into the open air, and, as we thought at the time, showed other signs of consumption.

But what were his bodily sufferings compared with the mental anguish he must have felt! To sit there amid dirt and wretchedness and hear his comrades speak of rescue, of home, of friends, and to know within himself that he was doomed to rest here for ever, doomed never to see his native land again.

Sometimes it happened that he cheered up somewhat, recovered his good spirits and chatted with his companions. On the 17th of May, for example, the national day of Norway, when merriment and a festive feeling prevailed in the hut, Wennersgaard, too, felt better for the while, but a few days later he was worse again. It was touch-ing to see him writing a few words of farewell to his parents and his brothers and sisters. He would sit night after night, moaning softly and slowly, for he seldom had any rest, and if one happened to look up during the course of the night one met the terrified gaze of his large sorrowful eyes. We seldom heard him complain; he only moaned softly.

On the morning of the 7th of June he had said good-night to his attendant, Martin, with a "Now I shall sleep well." And he fell asleep in a sitting posture, the only one possible for him. Then his neighbour suddenly felt how Wennersgaard sank softly down upon his shoulder—a few rattling breaths, and life had fled.

It was dim and silent in the hut; cold, clear and silent in the open air. Death, the one guest who could reach us, had laid his hand heavily upon the circle of comrades who had so long striven together for life.

Slowly went the procession out through the low door. Sewn up in his sleeping bag, the only coffin we could give him, he was carried out to one of the boats. A couple of days later we buried his body in an immense snowdrift; not until the spring came could we build him a lasting resting-place. Slowly we wander home and assemble in the hut, where everything speaks of death and corruption; we assemble there—*nineteen* of us.

It is the 6th of November, and early in the morning I hear cries of exultation around me, and peep out from amidst my rag-bed and there stands Duus in the middle of the passage with his hat full of eggs; large, white, round penguin-eggs! How we shout and laugh all together; we possess a poultry yard worth having! But we must not care for the needs of the day alone; in a week or two there will be no more fresh eggs, and it is a matter of great importance for us to have a supply for the next few months; out here the eggs keep fresh for a long time without any special treatment.

Armed with buckets, off we go on our expedition. No strife, no palm! We have to submit to blows and pecks; the penguin is small but he is a jolly good fighter, and our legs are sore when the day's work is ended.

Oh, how we revel! Fried eggs, boiled eggs, raw eggs, eggs in soup, in coffee, in tea; I am a temperate man and never ate more than a score in one day, but I know of a sailor who ate three dozen in the same time.

It is the 10th of November. We lie indolently in our sleeping bags, contented with the day's work; our store of eggs now amounts to a total of 6,000. It is so very agreeable to always feel satisfied after meals; how many of my readers know what it means to lie in cold, and darkness, and hunger, week after week? But believe me when I say that a man learns to appreciate the day when he can eat his fill without being obliged to think of economising.

Our conversation that evening, as on so many other evenings, turned on the rescue—we speak of it now in the definite form. And suddenly one of us has a curious idea and asks the rest, "What should you do if a boat came and began to whistle here in the sound, without anyone being prepared for it?" What a question! We should probably go mad with joy, though we have had time to prepare ourselves for the arrival of the ship. But who could think at the moment that we should be put to the test the very same night?

I did not sleep at all quietly after going to bed, but crawled out of my bag just before 4 A.M. and crept softly outside. A deathly silence reigned; the sea was as smooth as a mirror. My gaze was directed as usual to the horizon, but there was nothing to be seen there—nothing. And why should there be anything? I went indoors with a sigh, shut the door behind me, crept into the bag again and made up my mind to sleep.

But what in all the world—! A discordant sound breaks the stillness of the night; a well-known sound, but one inconceivable just here. No; I must have been dreaming.—The sound is repeated—it must be so—it can be nothing else—*the boat is here!* I am out of the bag. I thump at the sleepers beside me: "Can't you hear it is the boat —*the boat*—THE BOAT!"—"A BOAT! HURRAH!" Arms wave wildly in the air; the shouts are so deafening that the penguins awake and join in the cries; the cat, quite out of her wits, runs round and round the walls of the room; everybody tries to be the first out of doors, and in a minute we are all out on the hillside, half-dressed and grisly to behold. Hurrah! There she is; we dare scarcely believe our eyes, but it must be true; we shall see home again; we shall be home for Christmas. There is an oar, carrying the yellow and the blue of Sweden, stuck in to a snowdrift near the corner of the hut; here we have a piece of Scandinavia that will soon be reunited to the mother country!

It is an iron boat down here amid the ice—a new wonder. An Argentine man-of-war—it is almost incomprehensible! Breathless with expectation we stand on the ice-wall by the shore; I cannot take the glass from my eye—the first boat is approaching. More and more clearly can I distinguish my comrades—there is Gunnar Andersson, there Karl Andreas Andersson, and, actually, it's Duse himself standing in the bows! They leap ashore; there is no end to our exultation; questions and answers fill the air. Here comes Karl Andreas and gives me a glass of "zoological" spirit; Bodman has some bits of sugar for me; Duse, a piece of chocolate and a cigarette! It is my first banquet after the rescue.

The hut is soon filled with provisions for a depot; the door is barred; I have passed over its threshold for the last time.

I am in a ship that moves—I can scarcely comprehend it. Slowly we glide away, away from the island, whose dark peak looms above us as threateningly as before. But I cannot take my eyes away from it. I can hardly grieve that our prison-doors have been opened, and yet it is with a sense of sadness and of regret that I see Paulet Island disappear behind the dazzling inland ice—disappear maybe for ever.

Has it not been my home?

□   *On November 2, 1902, a handsome steam-equipped sailing ship called the* Scotia *went down the River Clyde, Antarctic-bound. It was a former Norwegian whaler that now served as the vessel of the Scottish Antarctic Expedition, whose guiding spirit was the naturalist W. S. Bruce of Edinburgh. Bruce had visited the Antarctic aboard whaling ships a decade before, and organized a public subscription in Scotland to finance his expedition. With the exception of Monaco, Scotland is the smallest country ever to launch such a large-scale research voyage.*

*The* Scotia *carried a staff of six scientists. Crossing the Antarctic Circle in February, 1903, it entered the Weddell Sea and reached 70° 25′ S. before worsening ice conditions forced a retreat. The explorers spent the winter in the subantarctic South Orkney Islands, making a series of important meteorological and magnetic observations. Early in 1904 the* Scotia *set out for the Antarctic again, this time penetrating the Weddell Sea almost as far as Weddell himself had reached. Halting at 74° S., the Scots caught sight of land ahead, the first time land had been sighted south of the Weddell Sea. The excerpt that follows describes this climactic moment of the expedition. It is drawn from* The Voyage of the 'Scotia,' *by J. H. Harvey*

*Pirie, L. C. Mossman, and R. N. Rudmose Brown (Edinburgh and London, Blackwood & Sons, 1906).* ▫

# THE SCOTIA EXPEDITION

On February 22 [1904] we bade our final good-bye to the South Orkneys, Mossman remaining behind in charge of the Argentine party,—also Smith, who had volunteered to stay on as cook. We skirted the north coast of Laurie Island to fix the position of two outlying rocks, then the survey, so far as we were concerned, was finished.

We were once more southward bound—following the traditional policy of the inhabitants of Scotland, laid down at least as far back as the Old Red Sandstone days, and faithfully adhered to during successive aeons. Even in those early days of the world's history, if the geological record is to be believed, the fishes meditated invasions of England, for their fossil remains are found *all* with their heads turned southwards towards the border!

We did not, however, go due south, but south-east, with the object of cutting between our two tracks of the previous year. Within fifty miles of the land, in addition to Cape pigeons, Wilson's stormy petrels, and snowy petrels, we met in with sooty albatroses (*Phoebetria fuliginosa*), blue petrels (*Halobena cerulea*), and silver petrels (*Thalassoeca glacialoides*); the two former of these were never seen at the Orkneys, and the latter only very rarely.

On the 25th, when stopped for sounding, we obtained a specimen of Hutton's albatros (*Phoebetria cornicoides*). This species differs from the sooty albatros only slightly, in having the plumage of the back and breast greyer, and the stripe on the mandible is pale-blue, and not yellow as in the better known sooty albatros. Both these species range farther south than the great white or wandering albatros (*Diomedea exulans*), which always keeps some distance north of the ice-pack. It was the shooting of a sooty albatros, as narrated in Shelvocke's 'Voyage Round the World' (1726), that supplied Coleridge with the idea elaborated in 'The Ancient Mariner.' The bird hovering about them for days while they had tempestuous contrary winds was imagined from his colour to be of ill omen, and shot.

They often followed us and were occasionally shot, not as ill omens, but for museum specimens: their flight is not quite so graceful as that of the wandering albatros, as they not unfrequently flap their wings, which the wandering albatros never seems to do.

The weather was quiet, very few bergs were encountered, and no pack-ice seen until we came to the Antarctic circle in about 32° W. long. Here we met in with some loose streams of pack which appeared closer to the south, so that we were compelled to make a slight detour eastwards to round them. Sounding there on February 27, a curious incident occurred. When about 1000 fathoms of wire were out, the machine stopped dead as if the bottom had been reached, but then ran on again, touching bottom in 2630 fathoms. The probability is the sounder landed on some large fish or on a whale—there were some playing around the ship at the time, but it seems an impossible depth for them to descend to: whatever it was I expect it had rather a surprise when sixty pounds of iron dropped whack on its back—a novel form of bolt from the empyrean.

On the 28th we captured a youngish specimen of the Ross seal (*Ommatophoca rossi*). This seal, perhaps the rarest of all seals, only occurs singly in the open pack. On the *Scotia* only two were seen altogether, one on each trip, and one was observed in the summer at the Orkneys, but not captured. It has a somewhat striped hide, and is described by M. Racovitza of the Belgian Expedition as "le plus phoque des phoques, car chez lui toute forme de quadrupede a disparu. Son corps n'est plus qu'un sac fusiform pourvu de membres très reduites." Its most remarkable feature is the thick neck, giving it an appearance not unlike a pouter pigeon. This swelling is caused by a great development of the larynx, which, acting like a resonator, gives the animal a very curious voice.

On March 1 we crossed our track of the previous year, getting a clear run to the south under canvas only, where a year before there was impenetrable pack, and a sea freezing up for the winter. There is little doubt the summer 1903-04 was a very open one all over the Antarctic, and had circumstances been such that we could have struck south a month earlier, a much larger part of new coast-line might have been traced. But regrets were vain; there was nothing for it but to make the most of the time still remaining.

March 2 was a "Stratus 10" day—*i.e.*, completely overcast: with a strong northerly wind and considerable sea we still boomed merrily south-east, encountering a few bergs, but no pack until the following morning, when we were brought up short in 72° 18' S. lat., 17° 59' W. long. Taking a sounding, we found the depth to be only 1131 fathoms,—up till now it had seldom been under 2500. This sent the skipper up to the crow's nest with a run, and the excitement was great when he reported "Land ahead." Steaming towards this, we found it to be a lofty ice-barrier similar to that first discovered by Ross on the other side of the Pole: it stretched in a north-easterly and south-westerly direction, but heavy pack-ice prevented a nearer approach than two miles. This ice was much heavier than any we had hitherto seen, rivalling in thickness, if not in extent, the great ice-fields of the Arctic. Birds, which during the last day or two had been very scarce in the open, were now found in numbers, including antarctic and snowy petrels, giant petrels, terns, and emperor penguins; of the latter three were captured after an exciting chase on an ice-floe.

The wind coming away strong from the north with thick snow, we were compelled to retreat a little to avoid being nipped in the ice. This weather continued most of the next day while we dodged along to the westwards about one knot per hour, the coal-bunkers being refilled from the hold,—a proceeding which, though very necessary, made the usual lovely mess of dust on board, and rendered all other operations impossible.

The mist lifted a little in the evening, and we had a good distant view of the Barrier with a magnificent ice-blink over it—the bright reflection in the sky of the white surface of the great ice-sheet. The 5th of March was also overcast, and the Barrier still remained more or less of a mystery. Two hauls were taken with an eight-foot net within 100 fathoms of the surface: the catch included numerous pteropods (a form of soft-shelled mollusc with an expanded wing-like foot), some small crustaceans, brilliantly coloured bristly chaeto-pod worms, and fathoms of what we thought was a nemertine worm, but has turned out to be the tentacles of some unknown siphonophore jelly-fish, probably of great dimensions. Birds were abundant, and some grampus were seen playing in the open water. Large bergs were numerous, and one small piece of banded berg-ice was noted studded with rock fragments, but it proved impossible to geologise on account of the brash-ice surrounding it.

The 6th, being a Sunday, proved rather a better day, and we were enabled to trace the Barrier to a point about 150 miles south-west of where we had first encountered it. It was in sight practically all day, save once when we passed the mouth of a bight, the head of which was not visible. The surface of this great Inland Ice, of which the Barrier was the terminal face or seafront, seemed to rise up very gradually in undulating slopes, and faded away in height and distance into the sky, though in one place there appeared to be the outline of distant hills: if so, they were entirely ice-covered, no naked rock being visible. Pack-ice kept us always some distance off, but a sounding, two and a half miles from the Barrier by range-finder, gave a depth of only 159 fathoms. This made it certain that we were really off a new Antarctic land, which has been named "Coats' Land" in honour of Mr James Coats, jun., and Major Andrew Coats, the two chief subscribers to the Expedition. Whether this land is a large island or a part of the Antarctic continent remains for future explorers to finally decide, but the latter hypothesis seems the more probable one. Mr Bruce is of the opinion that the coast-line of "Antarctica" runs more or less continuously eastward from Coats' Land to Enderby Land, as there appears to be no other way of accounting for the obstructions which Cook, Bellingshausen, Biscoe, Ross, and Moore all met with in attempting to penetrate south in that region. Weddell, in 1823, was probably also not far from discovering the edge of the Antarctic continent when he turned homeward in 74° 15' S., for the large number of birds he observed there accords with the distribution we found in relation to the discovery of Coats' Land.

The skuas, terns, giant petrels, antarctic and snowy petrels, and the black-throated penguins which we had found retreating northward the previous summer, all go to show that not far distant were the beaches and rocky cliffs of some actual land where they could nest. The ice-barrier, a vertical cliff from 100 to 150 feet in height, stretching in unbroken majesty for at least 150 miles and probably for many more, is the seaward edge of part of the great Inland Ice of Antarctica, which covers an area probably larger than that of Australia. The accumulated snowfall of ages, altered into solid though plastic glacier ice, creeps slowly but steadily down off the land, pushing its way some distance over the sea-bottom until it reaches water deep enough to float in; then part breaks off and becomes one of the large tabular icebergs so typical of the Antarctic seas.

That the land is of a continental character is shown by the boulders brought up in the dredgings taken in the vicinity,—boulders which have been picked up by the ice-sheet from the underlying rock and deposited on the floor of the ocean by the melting of the bergs. Amongst others, granites, schist, gneiss, quartzite, sandstone, slate, and limestone were found, all rocks characteristic of an old continental land-surface.

Its discovery in this latitude was very unexpected. Sir John Murray, basing his calculations on Ross's sounding of 4000 fathoms no bottom (which we had still to prove fallacious), put the outline of Antarctica about 400 miles farther south in this longitude.

The Weddell sea has turned out to be considerably less in extent than was previously supposed, and our soundings also show that its depth is very much less.

Early on the morning of the 7th the *Scotia* was caught in a northeast blizzard, and despite all efforts to get free, was beset in slush and heavy pack-ice. During this and the following day the pressure from the driving pack became great, the ice piling up against the ship's sides almost level with the top of the bulwarks.

It happened to be my week as night meteorological observer, and it proved "dreich" and eerie sitting there alone in the watches of the night. Silent watches they were not, for the crushing of the ice made the good ship's timbers creak and groan, and every minute I was wondering whether the ice would not rise still farther and overwhelm us altogether—a fate which has overtaken many a ship ere now. Although not specially built with a rounded hull like the *Fram*, we found afterwards that the ice had gone right under the ship, lifting her bodily out of the water some four feet, and it was doubtless in consequence of this that the *Scotia* suffered no injury from the tremendous pressure.

At the end of two days the gale abated, and we then found we had been driven into a bight of the ice-barrier. To the westward was a low part of the great ice-sheet, probably soon to break off as a berg, and over it could be seen the tops of distant bergs where the line of

Captain James Cook.

The *Resolution* and the *Adventure* encounter icebergs on Cook's second expedition, 1772-75.

Captain Nathaniel Palmer.
(Bettmann Archive and
Peabody Museum of
Salem.)

Admiral Fabian Gottlieb von Bellingshausen.

The ships *Jane* and *Beaufoy* on Weddell's 1822–24 voyage.

Captain James Weddell.

Adélie penguins on the frozen sea ice, Hallett Station, Antarctica. (*Official U.S. Navy Photograph.*)

Admiral Dumont d'Urville.

Lieutenant Charles Wilkes.

Wilkes' men ashore on an Antarctic ice island.

James Clark Ross.

Ross' ships anchored off Mt. Erebus, 1841.

Two U.S. Navy ships moored to sea ice in McMurdo Sound; Mt. Erebus in background, 1963. (*Official U.S. Navy Photograph.*)

Dr. Frederick Cook ashore on the ice during the 1898 voyage of the *Belgica*.

Otto Nordenskjöld.

Men of the *Antarctica* chasing king penguins during the 1901–03
expedition.

Robert Falcon Scott wearing the famous wallet in which he carried his journals.

Scott's ship, the *Discovery*, on his first expedition, 1901–04.

Sir Ernest Shackleton.

Douglas Mawson.

Roald Amundsen.

Amundsen and his men at the South Pole,
December 16–17, 1911.

Admiral Richard E. Byrd.

Adélie penguin. (*Official U.S. Navy Photograph.*)

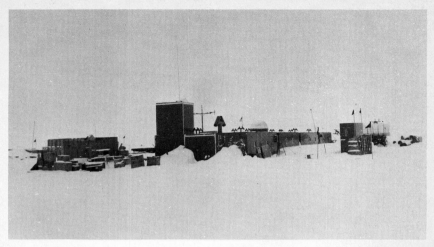

Eights Station, Antarctica, 1963. (*Official U.S. Navy Photograph.*)

"Moby Dick," a one-and-one-half-million-ton iceberg in McMurdo Sound, 1964. (*Official U.S. Navy Photograph.*)

Sir Vivian Fuchs at Shackleton Base, 1957.

USNS *Arneb* offloading cargo on Ross Ice Shelf, McMurdo Sound, 1962. (*Official U.S. Navy Photograph.*)

Antarctic landscape between McMurdo Station and South Pole, 1963. (*Official U.S. Navy Photograph.*)

USNS *John Towle* approaching mooring position cut and cleared by ice-cutter near McMurdo Station, 1963. (*Official U.S. Navy Photograph.*)

Weddell seal, up for a look around, McMurdo Sound, 1963. (*Official U.S. Navy Photograph.*)

the Barrier turned more sharply to the south just beyond our position. We were in lat. 74° 1′ S., long. 22° 0′ W., the farthest south point we attained.

The immediate danger was past, but there lay before us the prospect of having possibly to spend the winter there, frozen up in the pack. This was not altogether enticing: of the necessities, food and coal, we had sufficient to get along on, but our supply of light was limited, and the prospect of nearly three months' total darkness was not inviting. Also we thought, what would be the feelings of those at home: it was known we had no intention of spending another winter in the south, and if we did not turn up at Cape Town in May or June they would naturally imagine the worst.

Three days later our chance of escape looked even gloomier. There was no open water in sight to the north, and the temperature having dropped to near zero, the pack was freezing up hard.

Hope was not altogether given up, but the question of having to winter was seriously entertained. The topgallant yards were sent down from aloft so as to offer less resistance to the wind, light was at once cut down to a minimum, and a tally of stores taken preparatory to going on to strict rations.

Had the mental horizon not been somewhat cloudy, nothing could have been finer than our situation. The air was calm, crisp, and beautifully clear; from the crow's nest one could see to the north only huge bergs—"ice mast high going floating by"—and pack-ice, with every here and there a black dot where a seal or a penguin lay. To the south lay the Great Barrier, sublime and mysterious, inclining one to be in pensive mood brooding over its awful silent loneliness; but the hum of voices from the deck below, or the shouts ascending from the large floe nearbye, which served for the nonce as a football field, soon brought the wandering thoughts back to the worries of our microcosmos, stranded on the edge of the chaos of ice.

A large trap was sunk in a depth of 161 fathoms—two miles off the Barrier—and collections of the marine fauna made, including a fine specimen of feather-star (*Antedon*) and abundant small amphipod crustaceans, which soon cleared the flesh off the penguins used to bait the trap. A number of emperor penguins, which were here very numerous, were captured: in the event of wintering they would have served as food, but as it turned out it was only their skins that had to do duty. To test the effect of music on them, Piper Kerr played to one on his pipes,—we had no Orpheus to warble sweetly on a lute,—but neither rousing marches, lively reels, nor melancholy laments seemed to have any effect on these lethargic, phlegmatic birds; there was no excitement, no sign of appreciation or disapproval, only sleepy indifference. Some of them when weighed turned the scale at close on eighty pounds, and it was just all that one man could do to lead one up to the ship: with their beaks they bit fairly hard, and with their long flipper-like wings could hit out decidedly hard.

*March* 12.—"An exciting but tantalising day; the wind came away faintly from the south-west, and our hopes ran high. Under its influence, the ice being no longer pent up against the Barrier, the floe split into great fields separated by long leads of open water, the whole mass drifting westwards in front of the Barrier. The fields gradually cracked up into smaller pieces: about 4 P.M. a wide lead ran far to the north-east from the stern of the *Scotia*, but midships and at the bows she was still fast, and remained so despite futile efforts to blast the ice with tonite and gunpowder, and to break it by poling and by the whole ship's company jumping on it, Newfoundland sealer fashion. It was not till 8.30 P.M. that the ice split, and the *Scotia* slid down from her icy cradle and was once more afloat; but, alas! the lead had closed, and we could make nothing of our partial freedom, but wait in patience to see what the future had in store."

*March* 13.—"All morning we lay jammed in the ice, powerless to move or help ourselves, but in the afternoon the pack loosened a little, and after five hours' dodging, ramming, and butting our way 'twixt the floes, we were some two or three miles nearer the open water. It was risky work for the propeller, which frequently brought up sharp against projecting tongues of ice, but it was neck or nothing, and something had to be risked. A small piece was, indeed, snapped out of one blade, but luckily not enough to seriously interfere with its action.

"The uncertainty was very trying to our equanimity, every one being in a state of nervous tension, obvious or suppressed as the case might be."

On the 14th, with the first dawn the engines were again under way, and by breakfast-time our freedom was assured: we were out of the heavy pack into young pancake-ice, where the sea was just beginning to freeze over. It was none too soon, for the wind was again round to the north. How we blessed our engines!—without them we might have tacked till doomsday and not succeeded in forcing a passage through the maze of leads between the floes and hummocks.

◻ *The least heroic figure of Scott's first expedition was Ernest Shackleton, the burly young Irishman who came down with scurvy and had to be sent home. That humiliation rankled in him. He recovered quickly once back in a warm climate and, driven by the need to atone for his earlier failure, he pressed for a second chance to conquer the Antarctic.*

*Born in 1874, Shackleton served in the merchant service until Scott tapped him for the Antarctic voyage of 1901. After his return, he lectured, ran without success for Parliament, wrote magazine articles, and ceaselessly sought to organize a new Antarctic expedition. In 1907, borrowing $100,000 from a group of businessmen, Shackleton was able to make his second try.*

*He planned to use Scott's old base at Hut Point, but that plan had to be abandoned when Scott himself announced his intention to use the base on a forthcoming expedition. Shackleton agreed to make camp east of Hut Point. His ship, the* Nimrod, *sailed in July, 1907. The slow, overcrowded vessel carried dogs and ponies, skis, sledges, and a number of scientists, including two Australians, the physicist Douglas Mawson and the geologist Edgworth David. Setting up a base at Cape Royds on the Ross Sea, Shackleton planned ambitious sledge journeys in several directions.*

*In March, 1908, the fifty-year-old Edgworth David and five companions climbed the volcano Mount Erebus. They were the first to ascend the peak, which is more than 12,000 feet high. In October, David, Mawson, and a third man took part in a second great exploit, a grueling sledge journey that achieved the discovery of the South Magnetic Pole. The trip took 122 days and covered 1,260 miles, all of it done on foot, hauling heavy sledges.*

*While this adventure was unfolding, Shackleton himself was challenging the South Geographical Pole. He set out on October 29, 1908, taking with him a meteorologist named Adams, a cartographer named Marshall, and Frank Wild, like Shackleton a veteran of the Scott expedition. Hampered by blizzards and weakened by lack of food, they were further impeded by the loss of their four ponies as the trek proceeded. From December 7 onward, they had to continue on foot, dragging their sledges up the great glaciers that blocked the route to the Pole. As related below, they came within ninety-seven miles of the Pole before admitting defeat on January 9, 1909. Only through the most heroic measures did they get back to their base at the end of February, having come closer to the southernmost point of the globe than any men before them.*

*The polar journey is described in* The Heart of the Antarctic, *by Ernest Shackleton (Philadelphia, J. B. Lippincott, 1909).*  □

# ERNEST SHACKLETON

*21st December* [1908].—Midsummer Day, with 28° of frost! We have frost-bitten fingers and ears, and a strong blizzard wind has been blowing from the south all day, all due to the fact that we have climbed to an altitude of over 8,000 ft. above sea-level. From early morning we have been striving to the south, but six miles is the total distance gained, for from noon, or rather from lunch at 1 p.m., we have been hauling the sledges up, one after the other, by standing pulls across crevasses and over great pressure ridges. When we had advanced one sledge some distance, we put up a flag on a bamboo to mark its position, and then roped up and returned for the other. The wind, no doubt, has a great deal to do with the low temperature, and we feel the cold, as we are going on short commons. The altitude adds to the difficulties, but we are getting south all the time. We started away from camp at 6.45 a.m. today, and except for an hour's halt at lunch, worked on until 6 p.m. Now we are camped in a filled-up crevasse, the only place where snow to put round the tents can be obtained, for all the rest of the ground we are on is either névé or hard ice. We little thought that this particular pressure ridge was going to be such an obstacle; it looked quite ordinary, even a short way off, but we have now decided to trust nothing to eyesight, for the distances are so deceptive up here. It is a wonderful sight to look down over the glacier from the great altitude we are at, and to see the mountains stretching away east and west, some of them over 15,000 ft. in height. We are very hungry now, and it seems as cold almost as the spring sledging. Our beards are masses of ice all day long. Thank God we are fit and well and have had no accident, which is a mercy, seeing that we have covered over 130 miles of crevassed ice.

*22nd December.*—As I write of today's events, I can easily imagine I am on a spring sledging journey, for the temperature is minus 5° Fahr. and a chilly south-easterly wind is blowing and finds its way through the walls of our tent, which are getting worn. All day long, from 7 a.m., except for the hour when we stopped for lunch, we have been relaying the sledges over the pressure mounds and across crevasses. Our total distance to the good for the whole day was only four miles southward, but this evening our prospects look brighter, for we must now have come to the end of the great glacier. It is flattening out, and except for crevasses there will not be much trouble in hauling the sledges tomorrow. One sledge today, when coming down with a run over a pressure ridge, turned a complete somersault, but nothing was damaged, in spite of the total weight being over 400 lb. We are now dragging 400 lb. at a time up the steep slopes and across the ridges, working with the alpine rope all day, and roping ourselves together when we go back for the second sledge, for the ground is so treacherous that many times during the day we are saved only by the rope from falling into fathomless pits. Wild describes the sensation of walking over this surface, half ice and half snow, as like walking over the glass roof of a station. The usual query when one of us falls into a crevasse is: "Have you found it?" One gets somewhat callous as regards the immediate danger, though we are always glad to meet crevasses with their coats off, that is, not hidden by the snow covering. Tonight we are camped in a filled-in crevasse. Away to the north down the glacier a thick cumulus cloud is lying, but some of the largest mountains are standing out clearly.

Immediately behind us lies a broken sea of pressure ice. Please God, ahead of us there is a clear road to the Pole.

*23rd December.*—Eight thousand eight hundred and twenty feet up, and still steering upwards amid great waves of pressure and ice-falls, for our plateau, after a good morning's march, began to rise in higher ridges, so that it really was not the plateau after all. Today's crevasses have been far more dangerous than any others we have crossed, as the soft snow hides all trace of them until we fall through. Constantly today one or another of the party has had to be hauled out from a chasm by means of his harness, which had alone saved him from death in the icy vault below. We started at 6.40 a.m. and worked on steadily until 6 p.m., with the usual lunch hour in the middle of the day. The pony maize does not swell in the water now, as the temperature is very low and the water freezes. The result is that it swells inside after we have eaten it. We are very hungry indeed, and talk a great deal of what we would like to eat. In spite of the crevasses, we have done thirteen miles today to the south, and we are now in latitude 85° 41' South. The temperature at noon was plus 6° Fahr. and at 6 p.m. it was minus 1° Fahr., but it is much lower at night. There was a strong south-east to south-south-east wind blowing all day, and it was cutting to our noses and burst lips. Wild was frost-bitten. I do trust that tomorrow will see the end of this bad travelling, so that we can stretch out our legs for the Pole.

*24th December.*—A much better day for us; indeed, the brightest we have had since entering our Southern Gateway. We started off at 7 a.m. across waves and undulations of ice, with some one or other of our little party falling through the thin crust of snow every now and then. At 10.30 a.m. I decided to steer more to the west, and we soon got on to a better surface, and covered 5 miles 250 yards in the forenoon. After lunch, as the surface was distinctly improving, we discarded the second sledge, and started our afternoon's march with one sledge. It has been blowing freshly from the south and drifting all day, and this, with over 40° of frost, has coated our faces with ice. We get superficial frost-bites every now and then. During the afternoon the surface improved greatly, and the cracks and crevasses disappeared, but we are still going uphill, and from the summit of one ridge saw some new land, which runs south-south-east down to latitude 86° South. We camped at 6 p.m., very tired and with cold feet. We have only the clothes we stand up in now, as we depôted everything else, and this continued rise means lower temperatures than I had anticipated. Tonight we are 9,095 ft. above sea-level, and the way before us is still rising. I trust that it will soon level out, for it is hard work pulling at this altitude. So far there is no sign of the very hard surface that Captain Scott speaks of in connection with his journey on the Northern Plateau. There seem to be just here regular layers of snow, not much wind-swept, but we will see better the surface conditions in a few days. Tomorrow will be Christmas Day, and our thoughts turn to home and all the attendant joys of the time. One longs to hear "the hansoms slurring through the London mud." Instead of that we are lying in a little tent, isolated high on the roof of the end of the world, far, indeed, from the ways trodden of men. Still, our thoughts can fly across the wastes of ice and snow and across the oceans to those whom we are striving for and who are thinking of us now. And, thank God, we are nearing our goal. The distance covered today was 11 miles 250 yards.

*25th December.*—Christmas Day. There has been from 45° to 48° of frost, drifting snow and a strong biting south wind, and such has been the order of the day's march from 7 a.m. to 6 p.m. up one of the steepest rises we have yet done, crevassed in places. Now, as I write, we are 9,500 ft. above sea-level, and our latitude at 6 p.m. was 85° 55' South. We started away after a good breakfast and soon came to soft snow, through which our worn and torn sledge-runners dragged heavily. All morning we hauled along, and at noon had done 5 miles 250 yards. Sights gave us latitude 85° 51' South. We had lunch then, and I took a photograph of the camp with the Queen's flag flying and also our tent flags, my companions being in the picture. It was very cold, the temperature being minus 16° Fahr., and the wind went through us. All the afternoon we worked steadily uphill and we could see at 6 p.m. the new land plainly trending to the south-east. This land is very much glaciated. It is comparatively bare of snow, and there are well-defined glaciers on the side of the range, which seems to end up in the south-east with a large mountain like a keep. We have called it "The Castle." Behind these the mountains have more gentle slopes and are more rounded. They seem to fall away to the south-east, so that, as we are going south, the angle opens and we will soon miss them. When we camped at 6 p.m. the wind was decreasing. It is hard to understand this soft snow with such a persistent wind, and I can only suppose that we have not yet reached the actual plateau level, and that the snow we are travelling over just now is on the slopes, blown down by the south and south-east wind. We had a splendid dinner. First came hoosh, consisting of pony ration boiled up with pemmican and some of our emergency Oxo and biscuit. Then in the cocoa water I boiled our little plum pudding, which a friend of Wild's had given him. This, with a drop of medical brandy, was a luxury which Lucullus himself might have envied; then came cocoa, and lastly cigars and a spoonful of *creme de menthe* sent us by a friend in Scotland. We are full tonight, and this is the last time we will be for many a long day. After dinner we discussed the situation, and we have decided to still further reduce our food. We have now nearly 500 miles, geographical, to do if we are to get to the Pole and back to the spot where we are at the present moment. We have one month's food, but only three weeks' biscuit, so we are going to make each week's food last ten days. We will have one biscuit in the morning, three at midday, and two at night. It is the only thing to do. Tomorrow we will throw away everything except the most absolute necessities. Already we are, as regards clothes, down to the limit, but we must trust to the old sledge-runners and dump the spare ones. One must risk this. We are very far away from all the world, and home thoughts have been much with us today, thoughts interrupted by pitching forward into a hidden crevasse more than once. Ah, well, we shall see all our own people when the work here is done. Marshall took our temperatures tonight. We are all two degrees sub-normal, but as fit as can be. It is a fine open-air life and we are getting south.

*26th December.*—Got away at 7 a.m. sharp, after dumping a lot of gear. We marched steadily all day except for lunch, and we have done 14 miles 480 yards on an uphill march, with soft snow at times and a bad wind. Ridge after ridge we met, and though the surface is better and harder in places, we feel very tired at the end of ten hours' pulling. Our height tonight is 9,590 ft. above sea-level according to the hypsometer. The ridges we meet with are almost similar in appearance. We see the sun shining on them in the distance, and then the rise begins very gradually. The snow gets soft, and the weight of the sledge becomes more marked. As we near the top the soft snow gives place to a hard surface, and on the summit of the ridge we find small crevasses. Every time we reach the top of a ridge we say to ourselves: "Perhaps this is the last," but it never is the last; always there appears away ahead of us another ridge. I do not think that the land lies very far below the ice-sheet, for the crevasses on the summits of the ridges suggest that the sheet is moving over land at no great depth. It would seem that the descent towards the glacier proper from the plateau is by a series of terraces. We lost sight of the land today, having left it all behind us, and now we have the waste of snow all around. Two more days and our maize will be finished. Then our hooshes will be more woefully thin than ever. This shortness of food is unpleasant, but if we allow ourselves what, under ordinary circumstances, would be a reasonable amount, we would have to abandon all idea of getting far south.

*27th December.*—If a great snow plain, rising every seven miles in a steep ridge, can be called a plateau, then we are on it at last, with an altitude above the sea of 9,820 ft. We started at 7 a.m. and marched till noon, encountering at 11 a.m. a steep snow ridge which pretty well cooked us, but we got the sledge up by noon and camped. We are pulling 150 lb. per man. In the afternoon we had a good going till 5 p.m. and then another ridge as difficult as the previous one, so that our backs and legs were in a bad way when we reached the top at 6 p.m., having done 14 miles 930 yards for the day. Thank heaven it has been a fine day, with little wind. The temperature is minus 9° Fahr. This surface is most peculiar, showing layers of snow with little sastrugi all pointing south-south-east. Short food make us think of plum puddings, and hard half-cooked maize gives us indigestion, but we are getting south. The latitude is 86° 19' South tonight. Our thoughts are with the people at home a great deal.

*28th December.*—If the Barrier is a changing sea, the plateau is a changing sky. During the morning march we continued to go up hill steadily, but the surface was constantly changing. First there was soft snow in layers, then soft snow so deep that we were well over our ankles, and the temperature being well below zero, our feet were cold through sinking in. No one can say what we are going to find next, but we can go steadily ahead. We started at 6.55 a.m., and had done 7 miles 200 yards by noon, the pulling being very hard. Some of the snow is blown into hard sastrugi, some that looks perfectly smooth and hard has only a thin crust through which we break when pulling; all of it is a trouble. Yesterday we passed our last crevasse, though there are a few cracks or ridges fringed with shining crystals like diamonds, warning us that the cracks are open. We are now 10,199 ft. above sea-level, and the plateau is gradually flattening out, but it was heavy work pulling this afternoon. The high altitude, and a temperature of 48° of frost made breathing and work difficult. We are getting south—latitude 86° 31' South tonight. The last sixty miles we hope to rush, leaving everything possible, taking one tent only and using the poles of the other as marks every ten miles, for we will leave all our food sixty miles off the Pole except enough to carry us there and back. I hope with good weather to reach the Pole on 12th January, and then we will try and rush it to get to Hut Point by 28th February. We are so tired after each hour's pulling that we throw ourselves on our backs for a three minutes' spell. It took us over ten hours to do 14 miles 450 yards today, but we did it all right. It is a wonderful thing to be over 10,000 ft. up at the end of the world almost. The short food is trying, but when we have done the work we will be happy. Adams had a bad headache all yesterday, and to-day I had the same trouble, but it is better now. Otherwise we are all fit and well. I think the country is flattening out more and more, and hope tomorrow to make fifteen miles, at least.

*29th December.*—Yesterday I wrote that we hoped to do fifteen miles today, but such is the variable character of this surface that one cannot prophesy with any certainty an hour ahead. A strong southerly wind, with from 44° to 49° of frost, combined with the effect of short rations, made our distance 12 miles 600 yards instead. We have reached an altitude of 10,310 ft., and an uphill gradient gave us one of the most severe pulls for ten hours that would be possible. It looks serious, for we must increase the food if we are to get on at all, and we must risk a depot at seventy miles off the Pole and dash for it then. Our sledge is badly strained, and on the abominably bad surface of soft snow is dreadfully hard to move. I have been suffering from a bad headache all day, and Adams also was worried by the cold. I think that these headaches are a form of mountain sickness, due to our high altitude. The others have bled from the nose, and that must relieve them. Physical effort is always trying at a high altitude, and we are straining at the harness all day, sometimes slipping in the soft snow that overlies the hard sastrugi. My head is very bad. The sensation is as though the nerves were being twisted up with a corkscrew and then pulled out. Marshall took our temperatures tonight, and we are all at about 94°, but in spite of this we are getting south. We are only 198 miles off our goal now. If the rise would stop the cold would not matter; but it is hard to know what is man's limit. We have only 150 lb. per man to pull, but it is more severe work than the 250 lb. per man up the glacier was. The Pole is hard to get.

*30th December.*—We only did 4 miles 100 yards today. We started at 7 a.m., but had to camp at 11 a.m., a blizzard springing up from the south. It is more than annoying. I cannot express my feelings. We were pulling at last on a level surface, but very soft snow, when at about 10 a.m. the south wind and drift commenced to increase, and at 11 a.m. it was so bad that we had to camp. And here all day we have been lying in our sleeping-bags trying to keep warm and listening to the threshing drift on the tent-side. I am in the cooking-tent, and the wind comes through, it is so thin. Our precious food is going and the time also, and it is so important to us to get on. We lie here and think of how to make things better, but we cannot reduce food now, and the only thing will be to rush all possible at the end. We will do, and are doing all humanly possible. It is with Providence to help us.

*31st December.*—The last day of the old year, and the hardest day we have had almost, pushing through soft snow uphill and with a strong head wind and drift all day. The temperature is minus 7° Fahr., and our altitude is 10,477 ft. above sea-level. The altitude is trying. My head has been very bad all day, and we are all feeling the short food, but still we are getting south. We are in latitude 86° 54′ South tonight, but we have only three weeks' food and two weeks' biscuits to do nearly 500 geographical miles. We can only do our best. Too tired to write more tonight. We all get iced-up about our faces, and are on the verge of frost-bite all the time. Please God the weather will be fine during the next fourteen days. Then all will be well. The distance today was eleven miles.

If we had only known that we were going to get such cold weather as we were at this time experiencing, we would have kept a pair of scissors to trim our beards. The moisture from the condensation of one's breath accumulated on the beard and trickled down on to the Burberry blouse. Then it froze into a sheet of ice inside, and it became very painful to pull the Burberry off in camp. Little troubles of this sort would have seemed less serious to us if we had been able to get a decent feed at the end of the day's work, but we were very hungry. We thought of food most of the time. The chocolate certainly seemed better than the cheese, because the two spoonfuls of cheese per man allowed under our scale of diet would not last as long as the two sticks of chocolate. We did not have both at the same meal. We had the bad luck at this time to strike a tin in which the biscuits were thin and overbaked. Under ordinary circumstances they would probably have tasted rather better than the other biscuits, but we wanted bulk. We soaked them in our tea so that they would swell up and appear larger, but if one soaked a biscuit too much, the sensation of biting something was lost, and the food seemed to disappear much too easily.

*1st January.*—Head too bad to write much. We did 11 miles 900 yards (statute) today, and the latitude at 6 p.m. was 87° 6½′ South, so we have beaten North and South records. Struggling uphill all day in very soft snow. Every one done up and weak from want of food. When we camped at 6 p.m. fine warm weather, thank God. Only 172½ miles from the Pole. The height above sea-level, now 10,755 ft., makes all work difficult. Surface seems to be better ahead. I trust it will be so tomorrow.

*2nd January.*—Terribly hard work today. We started at 6.45 a.m. with a fairly good surface, which soon became very soft. We were sinking in over our ankles, and our broken sledge, by running sideways, added to the drag. We have been going uphill all day, and tonight are 11,034 ft. above sea-level. It has taken us all day to do 10 miles 450 yards, though the weights are fairly light. A cold wind, with a temperature of minus 14° Fahr., goes right through us now, as we are weakening from want of food, and the high altitude makes every movement an effort, especially if we stumble on the march. My head is giving me trouble all the time. Wild seems the most fit of us. God knows we are doing all we can, but the outlook is serious if this surface continues and the plateau gets higher, for we are not travelling fast enough to make our food spin out and get back to our depot in time. I cannot think of failure yet. I must look at the matter sensibly and consider the lives of those who are with me. I feel that if we go on too far it will be impossible to get back over this surface, and then all the results will be lost to the world. We can now definitely locate the South Pole on the highest plateau in the world, and our geological work and meteorology will be of the greatest use to science; but all this is not the Pole. Man can only do his best, and we have arrayed against us the strongest forces of nature. This cutting south wind with drift plays the mischief with us, and after ten hours of struggling against it one pannikin of food with two biscuits and a cup of cocoa does not warm one up much. I must think over the situation carefully tomorrow, for time is going on and food is going also.

*3rd January.*—Started at 6.55 a.m., cloudy but fairly warm. The temperature was minus 8° Fahr. at noon. We had a terrible surface all the morning, and did only 5 miles 100 yards. A meridian altitude gave us latitude 87° 22' South at noon. The surface was better in the afternoon, and we did six geographical miles. The temperature at 6 p.m. was minus 11° Fahr. It was an uphill pull towards the evening, and we camped at 6.20 p.m., the altitude being 11,220 ft. above the sea. Tomorrow we must risk making a depot on the plateau, and make a dash for it, but even then, if this surface continues, we will be two weeks in carrying it through.

*4th January.*—The end is in sight. We can only go for three more days at the most, for we are weakening rapidly. Short food and a blizzard wind from the south, with driving drift, at a temperature of 47° of frost have plainly told us today that we are reaching our limit, for we were so done up at noon with cold that the clinical thermometer failed to register the temperature of three of us at 94°. We started at 7.40 a.m., leaving a depot on this great wide plateau, a risk that only this case justified, and one that my comrades agreed to, as they have to every one so far, with the same cheerfulness and regardlessness of self that have been the means of our getting as far as we have done so far. Pathetically small looked the bamboo, one of the tent poles, with a bit of bag sown on as a flag, to mark our stock of provisions, which has to take us back to our depot, one hundred and fifty miles north. We lost sight of it in half an hour, and are now trusting to our footprints in the snow to guide us back to each bamboo until we pick up the depot again. I trust that the weather will keep clear. Today we have done 12½ geographical miles, and with only 70 lb. per man to pull it is as hard, even harder, work than the 100 odd lb. was yesterday, and far harder than the 250 lb. were three weeks ago, when we were climbing the glacier. This, I consider, is a clear indication of our failing strength. The main thing against us is the altitude of 11,200 ft. and the biting wind. Our faces are cut, and our feet and hands are always on the verge of frost-bite. Our fingers, indeed, often go, but we get them round more or less. I have great trouble with two fingers on my left hand. They have been badly jammed when we were getting the motor up over the ice face at winter quarters, and the circulation is not good. Our boots now are pretty well worn out, and we have to halt at times to pick the snow out of the soles. Our stock of sennegrass is nearly exhausted, so we have to use the same frozen stuff day after day. Another trouble is that the lamp-wick with which we tie the finnesko is chafed through, and we have to tie knots in it. These knots catch the snow under our feet, making a lump that has to be cleared every now and then. I am of the opinion that to sledge even in the height of summer on this plateau, we should have at least forty ounces of food a day per man, and we are on short rations of the ordinary allowance of thirty-two ounces. We depoted our extra underclothing to save weight about three weeks ago, and are now in the same clothes night and day. One suit of underclothing, shirt and guernsey, and our thin Burberries, now all patched. When we get up in the morning, out of the wet bag, our Burberries become like a coat of mail at once, and our heads and beards get iced-up with the moisture when breathing on the march. There is half a gale blowing dead in our teeth all the time. We hope to reach within 100 geographical miles of the Pole; under the circumstances we can expect to do very little more. I am confident that the Pole lies on the great plateau we have discovered, miles and miles from any outstanding land. The temperature tonight is minus 24° Fahr.

   *5th January.*—Today head wind and drift again, with 50° of frost, and a terrible surface. We have been marching through 8 in. of snow, covering sharp sastrugi, which plays hell with our feet, but we have done 13⅓ geographical miles, for we increased our food, seeing that it was absolutely necessary to do this to enable us to accomplish anything. I realize that the food we have been having has not been sufficient to keep up our strength, let alone supply the wastage caused by exertion, and now we must try to keep warmth in us, though our strength is being used up. Our temperatures at 5 a.m. were 94° Fahr. We got away at 7 a.m. sharp and marched till noon, then from 1 p.m. sharp till 6 p.m. All being in one tent makes our camp-work slower, for we are so cramped for room, and we get up at 4.40 a.m. so as to get away at 7 a.m. Two of us have to stand outside the tent at night until things are squared up inside, and we find it cold work. Hunger grips us hard, and the food-supply is very small. My head still gives me great trouble. I began by wishing that my worst enemy had it instead of myself, but now I don't wish even my worst enemy to have such a headache; still, it is no use talking about it. Self is a subject that most of us are fluent on. We find the utmost difficulty in carrying through the day, and we can only go for two or three more days. Never once has the temperature been above zero since we got on to the plateau, though this is the height of summer. We have done our best, and we thank God for having allowed us to get so far.

*6th January.*—This must be our last outward march with the sledge and camp equipment. Tomorrow we must leave camp with some food, and push as far south as possible, and then plant the flag. Today's story is 57° of frost, with a strong blizzard and high drift; yet we marched 13¼ geographical miles through soft snow, being helped by extra food. This does not mean full rations, but a bigger ration than we have been having lately. The pony maize is all finished. The most trying day we have yet spent, our fingers and faces being frost-bitten continually. Tomorrow we will rush south with the flag. We are at 88° 7' South tonight. It is our last outward march. Blowing hard tonight. I would fail to explain my feelings if I tried to write them down, now that the end has come. There is only one thing that lightens the disappointment, and that is the feeling that we have done all we could. It is the forces of nature that have prevented us from going right through. I cannot write more.

*7th January.*—A blinding, shrieking blizzard all day, with the temperature ranging from 60° to 70° of frost. It has been impossible to leave the tent, which is snowed up on the lee side. We have been lying in our bags all day, only warm at food time, with fine snow making through the walls of the worn tent and covering our bags.

We are greatly cramped. Adams is suffering from cramp every now and then. We are eating our valuable food without marching. The wind has been blowing eighty to ninety miles an hour. We can hardly sleep. Tomorrow I trust this will be over. Directly the wind drops we march as far south as possible, then plant the flag, and turn homeward. Our chief anxiety is lest our tracks may drift up, for to them we must trust mainly to find our depot; we have no land bearings in this great plain of snow. It is a serious risk that we have taken, but we had to play the game to the utmost, and Providence will look after us.

*8th January.*—Again all day in our bags, suffering considerably physically from cold hands and feet, and from hunger, but more mentally, for we cannot get on south, and we simply lie here shivering. Every now and then one of our party's feet go, and the unfortunate beggar has to take his leg out of the sleeping-bag and have his frozen foot nursed into life again by placing it inside the shirt, against the skin of his almost equally unfortunate neighbour. We must do something more to the south, even though the food is going, and we weaken lying in the cold, for with 72° of frost, the wind cuts through our thin tent, and even the drift is finding its way in and on to our bags, which are wet enough as it is. Cramp is not uncommon every now and then, and the drift all round the tent has made it so small that there is hardly room for us at all. The wind has been blowing hard all day; some of the gusts must be over seventy or eighty miles an hour. This evening it seems as though it were going to ease down, and directly it does we shall be up and away south for a rush. I feel that this march must be our limit. We are so short of food, and at this high altitude, 11,600 ft., it is hard to keep any warmth in our bodies between the scanty meals. We have nothing to read now, having depoted our little books to save weight, and it is dreary work lying in the tent with nothing to read, and too cold to write much in the diary.

*9th January.*—Our last day outwards. We have shot our bolt, and the tale is latitude 88° 23' South, longitude 162° East. The wind eased down at 1 a.m., and at 2 a.m. were up and had breakfast. At 4 a.m. started south, with the Queen's Union Jack, a brass cylinder containing stamps and documents to place at the furthest south point, camera, glasses and compass. At 9 a.m. we were in 88° 23'

South, half running and half walking over a surface much hardened by the recent blizzard. It was strange for us to go along without the nightmare of a sledge dragging behind us. We hoisted her Majesty's flag and the other Union Jack afterwards, and took possession of the plateau in the name of his Majesty. While the Union Jack blew out stiffly in the icy gale that cut us to the bone, we looked south with our powerful glasses, but could see nothing but the dead white snow plain. There was no break in the plateau as it extended towards the Pole, and we feel sure that the goal we have failed to reach lies on this plain. We stayed only a few minutes, and then, taking the Queen's flag and eating our scanty meal as we went, we hurried back and reached our camp about 3 p.m. We were so dead tired that we only did two hours' march in the afternoon and camped at 5.30 p.m. The temperature was minus 19° Fahr. Fortunately for us, our tracks were not obliterated by the blizzard; indeed, they stood up, making a trail easily followed. Homeward bound at last. Whatever regrets may be, we have done our best.

□   *Shackleton had beaten Robert Falcon Scott's southward record by 366 miles, but he had failed to reach that symbolic goal, the South Pole. Less than a year after Shackleton's return to London in 1909, Scott was en route to Antarctica for his second and fatal expedition.*

*The voyage seemed foredoomed. One omen came on October 12, 1910, when Scott's* Terra Nova *reached Melbourne, Australia. A telegram waited there from the Norwegian Roald Amundsen, announcing that he, too, was about to make an assault on the Pole. Willy-nilly Scott found himself in a race against a man who had trained all his life for the high prize of the Pole, albeit the North Pole.*

*The* Terra Nova *entered McMurdo Sound in January, 1911. Scott set up camp fifteen miles south of his old base at Hut Point, and spent the next few months laying depots where food was stored for* the trek to the Pole. The key depot was One Ton Camp, about 130 miles south of the new base, called Cape Evans. The coming of winter ended these preparations, and on November 1, 1911, Scott set out for the South Pole. Amundsen, whose base was 450 miles to the east, had started Poleward two weeks before.

The trip was slowed by blizzards, and by warm air that turned the snow to slush. Scott began to fall behind Shackleton's timetable of 1908-09; he was following Shackleton's route, and knew that he had to better the pace if he hoped to reach the Pole and return before winter descended. Many supporting parties accompanied Scott in the early stages of the journey, but he sent them back, as planned, when each depot point was reached. On January 4, 1912, 146 miles from the Pole, Scott sent the last support party back. The four-man polar team chosen for the final stretch consisted of Scott, Dr. Edward "Bill" Wilson, a sailor named Edgar Evans, and an army officer, Lawrence Oates, nicknamed "Titus" or "Soldier." Impulsively, Scott added a fifth man to the party, H. R. "Birdie" Bowers. That proved a fatal miscalculation, for Bowers had no skis and would slow the others.

Storms assailed them. Weakened by the cold and by the onset of scurvy, they made slow progress, and barely staggered on to the Pole. They reached it on January 17, only to find that Amundsen had been there, leaving the Norwegian flag fluttering over his tent. The great effort had been pointless, since no scientific knowledge could be gained by reaching the Pole; it was purely a stunt, and there was little satisfaction in being the second to achieve it. Scott and his four companions began the return trip in low spirits. They were frostbitten and dazed; Evans seemed to break down entirely, and died on February 17. As their strength ebbed, they struggled to get back to One Ton Camp, where they hoped a relief party was waiting. Able to travel only a few miles a day, they reached a point eleven miles from safety on March 21, but there a blizzard penned them for eight days, until their food was gone. The following October, searchers from the main base found the frozen bodies of the explorers.

Scott's diary of his polar journey was included in the posthumous book, Scott's Last Expedition, edited by Leonard Huxley (New York, Dodd, Mead, 1913). The section that follows describes the final

210

*month of Scott's life during the return journey from the Pole. It is*
*reprinted by permission of Dodd, Mead & Company.* ▫

# ROBERT FALCON SCOTT— SECOND EXPEDITION

*Friday, March 2* [1912].—Lunch. Misfortunes rarely come singly. We marched to the (Middle Barrier) depôt fairly easily yesterday afternoon, and since that have suffered three distinct blows which have placed us in a bad position. First we found a shortage of oil; with most rigid economy it can scarce carry us to the next depôt on this surface (71 miles away). Second, Titus Oates disclosed his feet, the toes showing very bad indeed, evidently bitten by the late temperatures. The third blow came in the night, when the wind, which we had hailed with some joy, brought dark overcast weather. It fell below —40° in the night, and this morning it took 1½ hours to get our foot gear on, but we got away before eight. We lost cairn and tracks together and made as steady as we could N. by W., but have seen nothing. Worse was to come—the surface is simply awful. In spite of strong wind and full sail we have only done 5½ miles. We are in a *very* queer street since there is no doubt we cannot do the extra marches and feel the cold horribly.

*Saturday, March 3.*—Lunch. We picked up the track again yesterday, finding ourselves to the eastward. Did close on 10 miles and things looked a trifle better; but this morning the outlook is blacker than ever. Started well and with good breeze; for an hour made good headway; then the surface grew awful beyond words. The wind drew forward; every circumstance was against us. After 4¼ hours things so bad that we camped, having covered 4½ miles. One cannot consider this a fault of our own—certainly we were pulling hard this morning—it was more than three parts surface which held us back—the wind at strongest, powerless to move the sledge. When the light is good it is easy to see the reason. The surface, lately a very good hard one, is coated with a thin layer of woolly crystals, formed by radiation no doubt. These are too firmly fixed to be removed by the wind and cause impossible friction on the runners. God help us, we can't keep up this pulling, that is certain. Amongst ourselves we are unendingly cheerful, but what each man feels in his heart I can only guess. Pulling on foot gear in the morning is getter slower and slower, therefore every day more dangerous.

*Sunday, March 4.*—Lunch. Things looking *very* black indeed. As usual we forgot our trouble last night, got into our bags, slept splendidly on good hoosh, woke and had another, and started marching. Sun shining brightly, tracks clear, but surface covered with sandy frostrime. All the morning we had to pull with all our strength, and in 4½ hours we covered 3½ miles. Last night it was overcast and thick, surface bad; this morning sun shining and surface as bad as ever. One has little to hope for except perhaps strong dry wind—an unlikely contingency at this time of year. Under the immediate surface crystals is a hard sastrugi surface, which must have been excellent for pulling a week or two ago. We are about 42 miles from the next depôt and have a week's food, but only about 3 to 4 days' fuel—we are as economical of the latter as one can possibly be, and we cannot afford to save food and pull as we are pulling. We are in a very tight place indeed, but none of us despondent *yet*, or at least we preserve every semblance of good cheer, but one's heart sinks as the sledge stops dead at some sastrugi behind which the surface sand lies thickly heaped. For the moment the temperature is on the — 20° —an improvement which makes us much more comfortable, but a colder snap is bound to come again soon. I fear that Oates at least will weather such an event very poorly. Providence to our aid! We can expect little from man now except the possibility of extra food at the next depôt. It will be real bad if we get there and find the same shortage of oil. Shall we get there? Such a short distance it would have appeared to us on the summit! I don't know what I should do if Wilson and Bowers weren't so determinedly cheerful over things.

*Monday, March 5.*—Lunch. Regret to say going from bad to worse. We got a slant of wind yesterday afternoon, and going on 5 hours we converted our wretched morning run of 3½ miles into something over 9. We went to bed on a cup of cocoa and pemmican solid with the chill off. The result is telling on all, but mainly on Oates, whose feet are in a wretched condition. One swelled up tremendously last night and he is very lame this morning. We started march on tea and pemmican as last night—we pretend to prefer the pemmican this way. Marched for 5 hours this morning over a slightly better surface covered with high moundy sastrugi. Sledge capsized twice; we pulled on foot, covering about 5½ miles. We are two pony marches and 4 miles about from our depôt. Our fuel dreadfully low and the poor Soldier nearly done. It is pathetic enough because we can do nothing for him; more hot food might do a little, but only a little, I fear. We none of us expected these terribly low temperatures, and of the rest of us Wilson is feeling them most; mainly, I fear, from his self-sacrificing devotion in doctoring Oates' feet. We cannot help each other, each has enough to do to take care of himself. We get cold on the march when the trudging is heavy, and the wind pierces our warm garments. The others, all of them, are unendingly cheerful when in the tent. We mean to see the game through with a proper spirit, but it's tough work to be pulling harder than we ever pulled in our lives for long hours, and to feel that the progress is so slow. One can only say 'God help us!' and plod on our weary way, cold and very miserable, though outwardly cheerful. We talk of all sorts of subjects in the tent, not much of food now, since we decided to take the risk of running a full ration. We simply couldn't go hungry at this time.

*Tuesday, March 6.*—Lunch. We did a little better with help of wind yesterday afternoon, finishing 9½ miles for the day, and 27 miles from depôt. But this morning things have been awful. It was warm in the night and for the first time during the journey I overslept myself by more than an hour; then we were slow with foot gear; then, pulling with all our might (for our lives) we could scarcely advance at rate of a mile an hour; then it grew thick and three times we had to get out of harness to search for tracks. The result is something less than 3½ miles for the forenoon. The sun is shining now and the wind gone. Poor Oates is unable to pull, sits on the sledge when we are track-searching—he is wonderfully plucky, as his feet must be giving him great pain. He makes no complaint, but his spirits only come up in spurts now and he grows more silent in the tent. We are making a spirit lamp to try and replace the primus when our oil is exhausted. It will be a very poor substitute and we've not got much spirit. If we could have kept up our 9-mile days we might have got within reasonable distance of the depôt before running out, but nothing but a strong wind and good surface can help us now, and though we had quite a good breeze this morning, the sledge came as heavy as lead. If we were all fit I should have hopes of getting through, but the poor Soldier has become a terrible hindrance, though he does his utmost and suffers much I fear.

*Wednesday, March 7.*—A little worse I fear. One of Oates' feet *very* bad this morning; he is wonderfully brave. We still talk of what we will do together at home.

We only made 6½ miles yesterday. This morning in 4½ hours we did just over 4 miles. We are 16 from our depôt. If we only find the correct proportion of food there and this surface continues, we may get to the next depôt [Mt. Hooper, 72 miles farther] but not to One Ton Camp. We hope against hope that the dogs have been to Mt. Hooper; then we might pull through. If there is a shortage of oil again we can have little hope. One feels that for poor Oates the crisis is near, but none of us are improving, though we are wonderfully fit considering the really excessive work we are doing. We are only kept going by good food. No wind this morning till a chill northerly air came ahead. Sun bright and cairns showing up well. I should like to keep the track to the end.

*Tuesday, March 8.*—Lunch. Worse and worse in morning; poor Oates' left foot can never last out, and time over foot gear something awful. Have to wait in night foot gear for nearly an hour before I start changing, and then am generally first to be ready. Wilson's feet giving trouble now, but this mainly because he gives so much help to others. We did 4½ miles this morning and are now 8½ miles from the depôt—a ridiculously small distance to feel in difficulties, yet on this surface we know we cannot equal half our old marches, and that for that effort we expend nearly double the energy. The great question is, What shall we find at the depôt? If the dogs have visited it we may get along a good distance, but if there is another short allowance of fuel, God help us indeed. We are in a very bad way, I fear, in any case.

*Saturday, March 10.*—Things steadily downhill. Oates' foot worse. He has rare pluck and must know that he can never get through. He asked Wilson if he had a chance this morning, and of course Bill had to say he didn't know. In point of fact he has none. Apart from him, if he went under now, I doubt whether we could get through. With great care we might have a dog's chance, but no more.

214

The weather conditions are awful, and our gear gets steadily more icy and difficult to manage. At the same time of course poor Titus is the greatest handicap. He keeps us waiting in the morning until we have partly lost the warming effect of our good breakfast, when the only wise policy is to be up and away at once; again at lunch. Poor chap! it is too pathetic to watch him; one cannot but try to cheer him up.

Yesterday we marched up the depôt, Mt. Hooper. Cold comfort. Shortage on our allowance all round. I don't know that anyone is to blame. The dogs which would have been our salvation have evidently failed. Meares had a bad trip home I suppose.

This morning it was calm when we breakfasted, but the wind came from W.N.W. as we broke camp. It rapidly grew in strength. After travelling for half an hour I saw that none of us could go on facing such conditions. We were forced to camp and are spending the rest of the day in a comfortless blizzard camp, wind quite foul.

*Sunday, March 11.*—Titus Oates is very near the end, one feels. What we or he will do, God only knows. We discussed the matter after breakfast; he is a brave fine fellow and understands the situation, but he practically asked for advice. Nothing could be said but to urge him to march as long as he could. One satisfactory result to the discussion; I practically ordered Wilson to hand over the means of ending our troubles to us, so that anyone of us may know how to do so. Wilson had no choice between doing so and our ransacking the medicine case. We have 30 opium tabloids apiece and he is left with a tube of morphine. So far the tragical side of our story.

The sky completely overcast when we started this morning. We could see nothing, lost the tracks, and doubtless have been swaying a good deal since—3·1 miles for the forenoon—terribly heavy dragging—expected it. Known that 6 miles is about the limit of our endurance now, if we get no help from wind or surfaces. We have 7 days' food and should be about 55 miles from One Ton Camp tonight, 6 × 7 = 42, leaving us 13 miles short of our distance, even if things get no worse. Meanwhile the season rapidly advances.

*Monday, March 12.*—We did 6·9 miles yesterday, under our necessary average. Things are left much the same, Oates not pulling much, and now with hands as well as feet pretty well useless. We did 4 miles this morning in 4 hours 20 min.—we may hope for 3 this afternoon, $7 \times 6 = 42$. We shall be 47 miles from the depôt. I doubt if we can possibly do it. The surface remains awful, the cold intense, and our physical condition running down. God help us! Not a breath of favourable wind for more than a week, and apparently liable to head winds at any moment.

*Wednesday, March 14.*—No doubt about the going downhill, but everything going wrong for us. Yesterday we woke to a strong northerly wind with temp. $-37°$. Couldn't face it, so remained in camp till 2, then did 5¼ miles. Wanted to march later, but party feeling the cold badly as the breeze (N.) never took off entirely, and as the sun sank the temp. fell. Long time getting supper in dark.

This morning started with southerly breeze, set sail and passed another cairn at good speed; half-way, however, the wind shifted to W. by S. or W.S.W., blew through our wind clothes and into our mits. Poor Wilson horribly cold, could not get off ski for some time. Bowers and I practically made camp, and when we got into the tent at last we were all deadly cold. Then temp. now midday down $-43°$ and the wind strong. We *must* go on, but now the making of every camp must be more difficult and dangerous. It must be near the end, but a pretty merciful end. Poor Oates got it again in the foot. I shudder to think what it will be like to-morrow. It is only with greatest pains rest of us keep off frostbites. No idea there could be temperatures like this at this time of year with such winds. Truly awful outside the tent. Must fight it out to the last biscuit, but can't reduce rations.

*Friday, March 16 or Saturday 17.*—Lost track of dates, but think the last correct. Tragedy all along the line. At lunch, the day before yesterday, poor Titus Oates said he couldn't go on; he proposed we should leave him in his sleeping-bag. That we could not do, and induced him to come on, on the afternoon march. In spite of its awful nature for him he struggled on and we made a few miles. At night he was worse and we knew the end had come.

Should this be found I want these facts recorded. Oates' last thoughts were of his Mother, but immediately before he took pride in thinking that his regiment would be pleased with the bold way in which he met his death. We can testify to his bravery. He has borne intense suffering for weeks without complaint, and to the very last was able and willing to discuss outside subjects. He did not—would

216

not—give up hope to the very end. He was a brave soul. This was the end. He slept through the night before last, hoping not to wake; but he woke in the morning—yesterday. It was blowing a blizzard. He said, 'I am just going outside and may be some time.' He went out into the blizzard and we have not seen him since.

I take this opportunity of saying that we have stuck to our sick companions to the last. In case of Edgar Evans, when absolutely out of food and he lay insensible, the safety of the remainder seemed to demand his abandonment, but Providence mercifully removed him at this critical moment. He died a natural death, and we did not leave him till two hours after his death. We knew that poor Oates was walking to his death, but though we tried to dissuade him, we knew it was the act of a brave man and an English gentleman. We all hope to meet the end with a similar spirit, and assuredly the end is not far.

I can only write at lunch and then only occasionally. The cold is intense, —40° at midday. My companions are unendingly cheerful, but we are all on the verge of serious frostbites, and though we constantly talk of fetching through I don't think anyone of us believes it in his heart.

We are cold on the march now, and at all times except meals. Yesterday we had to lay up for a blizzard and to-day we move dreadfully slowly. We are at No. 14 pony camp, only two pony marches from One Ton Depôt. We leave here our theodolite, a camera, and Oates' sleeping-bags. Diaries, &c., and geological specimens carried at Wilson's special request, will be found with us or on our sledge.

*Sunday, March 18.*—To-day, lunch, we are 21 miles from the depôt. Ill fortune presses, but better may come. We have had more wind and drift from ahead yesterday; had to stop marching; wind N.W., force 4, temp. —35°. No human being could face it, and we are worn out *nearly*.

My right foot has gone, nearly all the toes—two days ago I was proud possessor of best feet. These are the steps of my downfall. Like an ass I mixed a small spoonful of curry powder with my melted pemmican—it gave me violent indigestion. I lay awake and in pain all night; woke and felt done on the march; foot went and I didn't know it. A very small measure of neglect and have a foot which is not pleasant to contemplate. Bowers takes first place in condition, but there is not much to choose after all. The others are still confident of getting through—or pretend to be—I don't know! We have the last *half* fill of oil in our primus and a very small quantity of spirit—this alone between us and thirst. The wind is fair for the moment, and that is perhaps a fact to help. The mileage would have seemed ridiculously small on our outward journey.

*Monday, March 19.*—Lunch. We camped with difficulty last night, and were dreadfully cold till after our supper of cold pemmican and biscuit and a half a pannikin of cocoa cooked over the spirit. Then, contrary to expectation, we got warm and all slept well. Today we started in the usual dragging manner. Sledge dreadfully heavy. We are 15½ miles from the depôt and ought to get there in three days. What progress! We have two days' food but barely a day's fuel. All our feet are getting bad—Wilson's best, my right foot worst, left all right. There is no chance to nurse one's feet till we get hot food into us. Amputation is the least I can hope for now, but will the trouble spread? That is the serious question. The weather doesn't give us a chance—the wind from N. to N.W. and —40° temp. today.

*Wednesday, March 21.*—Got within 11 miles of depôt Monday night; had to lay up all yesterday in severe blizzard. To-day forlorn hope, Wilson and Bowers going to depôt for fuel.

*Thursday, March 22 and 23.*—Blizzard bad as ever—Wilson and Bowers unable to start—to-morrow last chance—no fuel and only one or two of food left—must be near the end. Have decided it shall be natural—we shall march for the depôt with or without our effects and die in our tracks.

*Thursday, March 29.*—Since the 21st we have had a continuous gale from W.S.W. and S.W. We had fuel to make two cups of tea apiece and bare food for two days on the 20th. Every day we have been ready to start for our depôt *11 miles* away, but outside the door of the tent it remains a scene of whirling drift. I do not think we can hope for any better things now. We shall stick it out to the end, but we are getting weaker, of course, and the end cannot be far.

It seems a pity, but I do not think I can write more.

R. SCOTT.

For God's sake look after our people.

□   *Two of the men who died with Scott at the Pole had taken part, a few months before, in an exploit nearly as difficult. They were Dr. Edward "Bill" Wilson and H. R. "Birdie" Bowers, who, with a young zoologist named Apsley Cherry-Garrard, made the first extensive sledge journey through an Antarctic winter.*

*On his first visit to the Antarctic in 1901, Wilson had discovered a rookery of penguins at the eastern end of Ross Island. He had concluded that the nesting season for the Emperor penguin of Antarctica must be June or July—the depth of winter. To study these birds in the nesting season, Wilson and his two companions persuaded Scott to let them make the difficult 65-mile journey even though it was the harshest season of a harsh continent.*

*As the narrative reprinted here indicates, the journey was a strenuous one. The temperature sank to —65° on July 3, and it was even colder a few days later. They reached the rookery, carried out their studies, and returned on August 2, 1911, after a trip lasting more than a month. It produced valuable information about penguins and about man's ability to withstand the most brutal conditions of cold. Cherry-Garrard told the story some years later in an aptly-named book,* The Worst Journey in the World *(London, Chatto & Windus, 1922). The selection that follows is reprinted through the courtesy of the late Mr. Cherry-Garrard's widow, Mrs. Angela Mathias.*   □

# APSLEY CHERRY-GARRARD

The view from eight hundred feet up the mountain was magnificent and I got my spectacles out and cleared the ice away time after time to look. To the east a great field of pressure ridges below, looking in the moonlight as if giants had been ploughing with ploughs which made furrows fifty or sixty feet deep: these ran right up to the Barrier edge, and beyond was the frozen Ross Sea, lying flat, white and peaceful as though such things as blizzards were unknown. To the north and north-east the Knoll. Behind us Mount Terror on which we stood, and over all the grey limitless Barrier seemed to cast a spell of cold immensity, vague, ponderous, a breeding-place of wind and drift and darkness. God! What a place!

There was now little moonlight or daylight, but for the next forty-eight hours we used both to their utmost, being up at all times by day and night, and often working on when there was great difficulty in seeing anything; digging by the light of the hurricane lamp. By the end of two days we had the walls built, and banked up to one or two feet from the top; we were to fit the roof cloth close before banking up the rest. The great difficulty in banking was the hardness of the snow, it being impossible to fill in the cracks between the blocks which were more like paving-stones than anything else. The door was in, being a triangular tent doorway, with flaps which we built close in to the walls, cementing it with snow and rocks. The top folded over a plank and the bottom was dug into the ground.

Birdie was very disappointed that we could not finish the whole thing that day: he was nearly angry about it, but there was a lot to do yet and we were tired out. We turned out early the next morning (Tuesday [June] 18th [1911]) to try and finish the igloo, but it was blowing too hard. When we got to the top we did some digging but it was quite impossible to get the roof on, and we had to leave it. We realized that day that it blew much harder on the top of the slope than where our tent was. It was bitterly cold up there that morning with a wind force 4-5 and a minus thirty temperature.

The oil question was worrying us quite a lot. We were now well in to the fifth of our six tins, and economizing as much as possible, often having only two hot meals a day. We had to get down to the Emperor penguins somehow and get some blubber to run the stove which had been made for us in the hut. The 19th being a calm fine day we started at 9.30, with an empty sledge, two ice-axes, Alpine rope, harnesses and skinning tools.

Wilson had made this journey through the Cape Crozier pressure ridges several times in the Discovery days. But then they had daylight, and they had found a practicable way close under the cliffs which at the present moment were between us and the ridges.

As we neared the bottom of the mountain slope, farther to the north than we had previously gone, we had to be careful about crevasses, but we soon hit off the edge of the cliff and skirted along it until it petered out on the same level as the Barrier. Turning left handed we headed towards the sea-ice, knowing that there were some two miles of pressure between us and Cape Crozier itself. For about half a mile it was fair going, rounding big knobs of pressure but always managing to keep more or less on the flat and near the ice-cliff which soon rose to a very great height on our left. Bill's idea was to try and keep close under this cliff, along that same Discovery way which I have mentioned above. They never arrived there early enough for the eggs in those days: the chicks were hatched. Whether we should now find any Emperors, and if so whether they would have any eggs, was by no means certain.

However, we soon began to get into trouble, meeting several crevasses every few yards, and I have no doubt crossing scores of others of which we had no knowledge. Though we hugged the cliffs as close as possible we found ourselves on the top of the first pressure ridge, separated by a deep gulf from the ice-slope which we wished to reach. Then we were in a great valley between the first and second ridges: we got into huge heaps of ice pressed up in every shape on every side, crevassed in every direction: we slithered over snow-slopes and crawled along drift ridges, trying to get in towards the cliffs. And always we came up against impossible places and had to crawl back. Bill led on a length of Alpine rope fastened to the toggle of the sledge; Birdie was in his harness also fastened to the toggle, and I was in my harness fastened to the rear of the sledge, which was of great use to us both as a bridge and a ladder.

Two or three times we tried to get down the ice-slopes to the comparatively level road under the cliff, but it was always too great a drop. In that dim light every proportion was distorted; some of the places we actually did manage to negotiate with ice-axes and Alpine rope looked absolute precipices, and there were always crevasses at the bottom if you slipped. On the way back I did slip into one of these and was hauled out by the other two standing on the wall above me.

We then worked our way down into the hollow between the first and second large pressure ridges, and I believe on to the top of the second. The crests here rose fifty or sixty feet. After this I don't know where we went. Our best landmarks were patches of crevasses, sometimes three or four in a few footsteps. The temperatures were lowish ($-37°$), it was impossible for me to wear spectacles, and this was a tremendous difficulty to me and handicap to the party: Bill would find a crevasse and point it out; Birdie would cross; and then time after time, in trying to step over or climb over on the sledge, I put my feet right into the middle of the cracks. This day I went well in at least six times; once, when we were close to the sea, rolling into and out of one and then down a steep slope until brought up by Birdie and Bill on the rope.

We blundered along until we got into a great cul-de-sac which probably formed the end of the two ridges, where they butted on to the sea-ice. On all sides rose great walls of battered ice with steep snow-slopes in the middle, where we slithered about and blundered into crevasses. To the left rose the huge cliff of Cape Crozier, but we could not tell whether there were not two or three pressure ridges between us and it, and though we tried at least four ways, there was no possibility of getting forward.

And then we heard the Emperors calling.

Their cries came to us from the sea-ice we could not see, but which must have been a chaotic quarter of a mile away. They came echoing back from the cliffs, as we stood helpless and tantalized. We listened and realized that there was nothing for it but to return, for the little light which now came in the middle of the day was going fast, and to be caught in absolute darkness there was a horrible idea. We started back on our tracks and almost immediately I lost my footing and rolled down a slope into a crevasse. Birdie and Bill kept their balance and I clambered back to them. The tracks were very faint and we soon began to lose them. Birdie was the best man at following tracks that I have ever known, and he found them time after time. But at last even he lost them altogether and we settled we must just go ahead. As a matter of fact, we picked them up again, and by then were out of the worst: but we were glad to see the tent.

The next morning (Thursday, June 20) we started work on the igloo at 3 A.M. and managed to get the canvas roof on in spite of a wind which harried us all that day. Little did we think what that roof had in store for us as we packed it in with snow blocks, stretching it over our second sledge, which we put athwartships across the middle of the longer walls. The windward (south) end came right down to the ground and we tied it securely to rocks before packing it in. On the other three sides we had a good two feet or more of slack all round, and in every case we tied it to rocks by lanyards at intervals of two feet. The door was the difficulty, and for the present we left the cloth arching over the stones, forming a kind of portico. The whole was well packed in and over with slabs of hard snow, but there was no soft snow with which to fill up the gaps between the blocks. However, we felt already that nothing could drag that roof out of its packing, and subsequent events proved that we were right.

It was a bleak job for three o'clock in the morning before breakfast, and we were glad to get back to the tent and a meal, for we meant to have another go at the Emperors that day. With the first glimpse of light we were off for the rookery again.

But we now knew one or two things about that pressure which we had not known twenty-four hours ago; for instance, that there was a lot of alteration since the Discovery days and that probably the pressure was bigger. As a matter of fact it has been since proved by photographs that the ridges now ran out three-quarters of a mile farther into the sea than they did ten years before. We knew also that if we entered the pressure at the only place where the ice-cliffs came down to the level of the Barrier, as we did yesterday, we could neither penetrate to the rookery nor get in under the cliffs where formerly a possible way had been found. There was only one other thing to do—to go over the cliff. And this was what we proposed to try and do.

Now these ice-cliffs are some two hundred feet high, and I felt uncomfortable, especially in the dark. But as we came back the day before we had noticed at one place a break in the cliffs from which there hung a snow-drift. It *might* be possible to get down that drift.

And so, all harnessed to the sledge, with Bill on a long lead out in front and Birdie and myself checking the sledge behind, we started down the slope which ended in the cliff, which of course we could not see. We crossed a number of small crevasses, and soon we knew we must be nearly there. Twice we crept up to the edge of the cliff with no success, and then we found the slope: more, we got down it without great difficulty and it brought us out just where we wanted to be, between the land cliffs and the pressure.

Then began the most exciting climb among the pressure that you can imagine. At first very much as it was the day before—pulling ourselves and one another up ridges, slithering down slopes, tumbling into and out of crevasses and holes of all sorts, we made our way along under the cliffs which rose higher and higher above us as we neared the black lava precipices which form Cape Crozier itself. We straddled along the top of a snow ridge with a razor-backed edge, balancing the sledge between us as we wriggled: on our right was a drop of great depth with crevasses at the bottom, on our left was a smaller drop also crevassed. We crawled along, and I can tell you it was exciting work in the more than half darkness. At the end was a series of slopes full of crevasses, and finally we got right in under the rock on to moraine, and here we had to leave the sledge.

We roped up, and started to worry along under the cliffs, which had now changed from ice to rock, and rose 800 feet above us. The tumult of pressure which climbed against them showed no order here. Four hundred miles of moving ice behind it had just tossed and twisted those giant ridges until Job himself would have lacked words to reproach their Maker. We scrambled over and under, hanging on with our axes, and cutting steps where we could not find a foothold with our crampons. And always we got towards the Emperor penguins, and it really began to look as if we were going to do it this time, when we came up against a wall of ice which a single glance told us we could never cross. One of the largest pressure ridges had been thrown, end on, against the cliff. We seemed to be stopped, when Bill found a black hole, something like a fox's earth, disappearing into the bowels of the ice. We looked at it: "Well, here goes!" he said, and put his head in, and disappeared. Bowers likewise. It was a longish way, but quite possible to wriggle along, and presently I found myself looking out of the other side with a deep gully below me, the rock face on one hand and the ice on the other. "Put your back against the ice and your feet against the rock and level yourself along," said Bill, who was already standing on firm ice at the far end in a snow pit. We cut some fifteen steps to get out of that hole. Excited by now, and thoroughly enjoying ourselves, we found the way ahead easier, until the penguins' call reached us again and we stood, three crystallized ragamuffins, above the Emperors' home. They were there all right, and we were going to reach them, but where were all the thousands of which we had heard?

We stood on an ice-foot which was really a dwarf cliff some twelve feet high, and the sea-ice, with a good many ice-blocks strewn upon it, lay below. The cliff dropped straight, with a bit of an over-hang and no snow-drift. This may have been because the sea had only frozen recently; whatever the reason may have been it meant that we should have a lot of difficulty in getting up again without help. It was decided that some one must stop on the top with the Alpine rope, and clearly that one should be I, for with short sight and fogged spectacles which I could not wear I was much the least useful of the party for the job immediately ahead. Had we had the sledge we could have used it as a ladder, but of course we had left this at the beginning of the moraine miles back.

We saw the Emperors standing all together huddled under the Barrier cliff some hundreds of yards away. The little light was going fast: we were much more excited about the approach of complete darkness and the look of wind in the south than we were about our triumph. After indescribable effort and hardship we were witnessing a marvel of the natural world, and we were the first and only men who had ever done so; we had within our grasp material which might prove of the utmost importance to science; we were turning theories into facts with every observation we made,—and we had but a moment to give.

The disturbed Emperors made a tremendous row, trumpeting with their curious metallic voices. There was no doubt they had eggs, for they tried to shuffle along the ground without losing them off their feet. But when they were hustled a good many eggs were dropped and left lying on the ice, and some of these were quickly picked up by eggless Emperors who had probably been waiting a long time for the opportunity. In these poor birds the maternal side seems to have necessarily swamped the other functions of life. Such is the struggle for existence that they can only live by a glut of maternity, and it would be interesting to know whether such a life leads to happiness or satisfaction.

I have told how the men of the Discovery found this rookery where we now stood. How they made journeys in the early spring but never arrived early enough to get eggs and only found parents and chicks. They concluded that the Emperor was an impossible kind of bird who, for some reason or other, nests in the middle of the

Antarctic winter with the temperature anywhere below seventy degrees of frost, and the blizzards blowing, always blowing, against his devoted back. And they found him holding his precious chick balanced upon his big feet, and pressing it maternally, or paternally (for both sexes squabble for the privilege) against a bald patch in his breast. And when at last he simply must go and eat something in the open leads near by, he just puts the child down on the ice, and twenty chickless Emperors rush to pick it up. And they fight over it, and so tear it that sometimes it will die. And, if it can, it will crawl into any ice-crack to escape from so much kindness, and there it will freeze. Likewise many broken and addled eggs were found, and it is clear that the mortality is very great. But some survive, and summer comes; and when a big blizzard is going to blow (they know all about the weather), the parents take the children out for miles across the sea-ice, until they reach the threshold of the open sea. And there they sit until the wind comes, and the swell rises, and breaks that ice-floe off; and away they go in the blinding drift to join the main pack-ice, with a private yacht all to themselves.

You must agree that a bird like this is an interesting beast, and when, seven months ago, we rowed a boat under those great black cliffs, and found a disconsolate Emperor chick still in the down, we knew definitely why the Emperor has to nest in mid-winter. For if a June egg was still without feathers in the beginning of January, the same egg laid in the summer would leave its produce without practical covering for the following winter. Thus the Emperor penguin is compelled to undertake all kinds of hardships because his children insist on developing so slowly, very much as we are tied in our human relationships for the same reason. It is of interest that such a primitive bird should have so long a childhood.

But interesting as the life history of these birds must be, we had not travelled for three weeks to see them sitting on their eggs. We wanted the embryos, and we wanted them as young as possible, and fresh and unfrozen, that specialists at home might cut them into microscopic sections and learn from them the previous history of birds throughout the evolutionary ages. And so Bill and Birdie rapidly collected five eggs, which we hoped to carry safely in our fur mitts to our igloo upon Mount Terror, where we could pickle them in the alcohol we had brought for the purpose. We also wanted oil for our blubber stove, and they killed and skinned three birds—an Emperor weighs up to 6½ stones.

The Ross Sea was frozen over, and there were no seal in sight. There were only 100 Emperors as compared with 2000 in 1902 and 1903. Bill reckoned that every fourth or fifth bird had an egg, but this was only a rough estimate, for we did not want to disturb them unnecessarily. It is a mystery why there should have been so few birds, but it certainly looked as though the ice had not formed very long. Were these the first arrivals? Had a previous rookery been blown out to sea and was this the beginning of a second attempt? Is this bay of sea-ice becoming unsafe?

Those who previously discovered the Emperors with their chicks saw the penguins nursing dead and frozen chicks if they were unable to obtain a live one. They also found decomposed eggs which they must have incubated after they had been frozen. Now we found that these birds were so anxious to sit on something that some of those which had no eggs were sitting on ice! Several times Bill and Birdie picked up eggs to find them lumps of ice, rounded and about the right size, dirty and hard. Once a bird dropped an ice nest egg as they watched, and again a bird returned and tucked another into itself, immediately forsaking it for a real one, however, when one was offered.

Meanwhile a whole procession of Emperors came round under the cliff on which I stood. The light was already very bad and it was well that my companions were quick in returning: we had to do everything in a great hurry. I hauled up the eggs in their mitts (which we fastened together round our necks with lampwick lanyards) and then the skins, but failed to help Bill at all. "Pull," he cried, from the bottom: "I am pulling," I said. "But the line's quite slack down here," he shouted. And when he had reached the top by climbing up on Bowers' shoulders, and we were both pulling all we knew Birdie's end of the rope was still slack in his hands. Directly we put on a strain the rope cut into the ice edge and jammed—a very common difficulty when working among crevasses. We tried to run the rope over an ice-axe without success, and things began to look serious when Birdie, who had been running about prospecting and had meanwhile put one leg through a crack into the sea, found a place where the cliff did not overhang. He cut steps for himself, we hauled, and at last we were all together on the top—his foot being by now surrounded by a solid mass of ice.

We legged it back as hard as we could go: five eggs in our fur mitts, Birdie with two skins tied to him and trailing behind, and myself with one. We were roped up, and climbing the ridges and getting through the holes was very difficult. In one place where there was a steep rubble and snow slope down I left the ice-axe half way up; in another it was too dark to see our former ice-axe footsteps, and I could see nothing, and so just let myself go and trusted to luck. With infinite patience Bill said: "Cherry, you *must* learn how to use an ice-axe." For the rest of the trip my wind-clothes were in rags.

We found the sledge, and none too soon, and now had three eggs left, more or less whole. Both mine had burst in my mitts: the first I emptied out, the second I left in my mitt to put into the cooker; it never got there, but on the return journey I had my mitts far more easily thawed out than Birdie's (Bill had none) and I believe the grease in the egg did them good. When we got into the hollows under the ridge where we had to cross, it was too dark to do anything but feel our way. We did so over many crevasses, found the ridge and crept over it. Higher up we could see more, but to follow our tracks soon became impossible, and we plugged straight ahead and luckily found the slope down which we had come. All day it had been blowing a nasty cold wind with a temperature between −20° and 30°, which we felt a good deal. Now it began to get worse. The weather was getting thick and things did not look very nice when we started up to find our tent. Soon it was blowing force 4, and soon we missed our way entirely. We got right up above the patch of rocks which marked our igloo and only found it after a good deal of search.

I have heard tell of an English officer at the Dardanelles who was left, blinded, in No Man's Land between the English and Turkish trenches. Moving only at night, and having no sense to tell him which were his own trenches, he was fired at by Turk and English alike as he groped his ghastly way to and from them. Thus he spent days and nights until, one night, he crawled towards the English trenches, to be fired at as usual. "Oh God! what can I do!" some one heard him say, and he was brought in.

Such extremity of suffering cannot be measured: madness or death may give relief. But this I know: we on this journey were already beginning to think of death as a friend. As we groped our way back that night, sleepless, icy, and dog-tired in the dark and the wind and the drift, a crevasse seemed almost a friendly gift.

"Things must improve," said Bill next day, "I think we reached bed-rock last night." We hadn't, by a long way.

It was like this.

We moved into the igloo for the first time, for we had to save oil by using our blubber stove if we were to have any left to travel home with, and we did not wish to cover our tent with the oily black filth which the use of blubber necessitates. The blizzard blew all night, and we were covered with drift which came in through hundreds of leaks: in this wind-swept place we had found no soft snow with which we could pack our hard snow blocks. As we flensed some blubber from one of our penguin skins the powdery drift covered everything we had.

Though uncomfortable this was nothing to worry about over-much. Some of the drift which the blizzard was bringing would collect to leeward of our hut and the rocks below which it was built, and they could be used to make our hut more weather-proof. Then with great difficulty we got the blubber stove to start, and it spouted a blob of boiling oil into Bill's eye. For the rest of the night he lay, quite unable to stifle his groans, obviously in very great pain: he told us afterwards that he thought his eye was gone. We managed to cook a meal somehow, and Birdie got the stove going afterwards, but it was quite useless to try and warm the place. I got out and cut the green canvas outside the door, so as to get the roof cloth in under the stones, and then packed it down as well as I could with snow, and so blocked most of the drift coming in.

It is extraordinary how often angels and fools do the same thing in this life, and I have never been able to settle which we were on this journey. I never heard an angry word: once only (when this same day I could not pull Bill up the cliff out of the penguin rookery) I heard an impatient one: and these groans were the nearest approach to complaint. Most men would have howled. "I think we reached bed-rock last night," was strong language for Bill. "I was incapaci-tated for a short time," he says in his report to Scott. Endurance was tested on this journey under unique circumstances, and always these two men with all the burden of responsibility which did not fall upon

229

myself, displayed that quality which is perhaps the only one which may be said with certainty to make for success, self-control.

We spent the next day—it was July 21—in collecting every scrap of soft snow we could find and packing it into the crevasses between our hard snow blocks. It was a pitifully small amount but we could see no cracks when we had finished. To counteract the lifting tendency the wind had on our roof we cut some great flat hard snow blocks and laid them on the canvas top to steady it against the sledge which formed the ridge support. We also pitched our tent outside the igloo door. Both tent and igloo were therefore eight or nine hundred feet up Terror: both were below an outcrop of rocks from which the mountain fell steeply to the Barrier behind us, and from this direction came the blizzards. In front of us the slope fell for a mile or more down to the ice-cliffs, so wind-swept that we had to wear crampons to walk upon it. Most of the tent was in the lee of the igloo, but the cap of it came over the igloo roof, while a segment of the tent itself jutted out beyond the igloo wall.

That night we took much of our gear into the tent and lighted the blubber stove. I always mistrusted that stove, and every moment I expected it to flare up and burn the tent. But the heat it gave, as it burned furiously, with the double lining of the tent to contain it, was considerable.

It did not matter, except for a routine which we never managed to keep, whether we started to thaw our way into our frozen sleeping-bags at 4 in the morning or 4 in the afternoon. I think we must have turned in during the afternoon of that Friday, leaving the cooker, our finnesko, a deal of our foot-gear, Bowers' bag of personal gear, and many other things in the tent. I expect we left the blubber stove there too, for it was quite useless at present to try and warm the igloo. The tent floor-cloth was under our sleeping-bags in the igloo.

"Things must improve," said Bill. After all there was much for which to be thankful. I don't think anybody could have made a better igloo with the hard snow blocks and rocks which were all we had: we would get it air-tight by degrees. The blubber stove was working, and we had fuel for it: we had also found a way down to the penguins and had three complete though frozen eggs: the two which had been in my mitts smashed when I fell about because I could not wear spectacles. Also the twilight given by the sun below the horizon at noon was getting longer.

But already we had been out twice as long in winter as the longest previous journeys in spring. The men who made those journeys had daylight where we had darkness, they had never had such low temperatures, generally nothing approaching them, and they had seldom worked in such difficult country. The nearest approach to healthy sleep we had had for nearly a month was when during blizzards the temperature allowed the warmth of our bodies to thaw some of the ice in our clothing and sleeping-bags into water. The wear and tear on our minds was very great. We were certainly weaker. We had a little more than a tin of oil to get back on, and we knew the conditions we had to face on that journey across the Barrier: even with fresh men and fresh gear it had been almost unendurable.

And so we spent half an hour or more getting into our bags. Cirrus cloud was moving across the face of the stars from the north, it looked rather hazy and thick to the south, but it is always difficult to judge weather in the dark. There was little wind and the temperature was in the minus twenties. We felt no particular uneasiness. Our tent was well dug in, and was also held down by rocks and the heavy tank off the sledge which were placed on the skirting as additional security. We felt that no power on earth could move the thick walls of our igloo, nor drag the canvas roof from the middle of the embankment into which it was packed and lashed.

"Things must improve," said Bill.

I do not know what time it was when I woke up. It was calm, with that absolute silence which can be so soothing or so terrible as circumstances dictate. Then there came a sob of wind, and all was still again. Ten minutes and it was blowing as though the world was having a fit of hysterics. The earth was torn in pieces: the indescribable fury and roar of it all cannot be imagined.

"Bill, Bill, the tent has gone," was the next I remember—from Bowers shouting at us again and again through the door. It is always these early morning shocks which hit one hardest: our slow minds suggested that this might mean a peculiarly lingering form of death. Journey after journey Birdie and I fought our way across the few yards which had separated the tent from the igloo door. I have never

understood why so much of our gear which was in the tent remained, even in the lee of the igloo. The place where the tent had
been was littered with gear, and when we came to reckon up afterwards we had everything except the bottom piece of the cooker, and
the top of the outer cooker. We never saw these again. The most
wonderful thing of all was that our finnesko were lying where they
were left, which happened to be on the ground in the part of the
tent which was under the lee of the igloo. Also Birdie's bag of personal gear was there, and a tin of sweets.

Birdie brought two tins of sweets away with him. One we had to
celebrate our arrival at the Knoll: this was the second, of which we
knew nothing, and which was for Bill's birthday, the next day. We
started eating them on Saturday, however, and the tin came in useful to Bill afterwards.

To get that gear in we fought against solid walls of black snow
which flowed past us and tried to hurl us down the slope. Once
started nothing could have stopped us. I saw Birdie knocked over
once, but he clawed his way back just in time. Having passed everything we could find in to Bill, we got back into the igloo, and started
to collect things together, including our very dishevelled minds.

There was no doubt that we were in the devil of a mess, and it was
not altogether our fault. We had had to put our igloo more or less
where we could get rocks with which to build it. Very naturally we
had given both our tent and igloo all the shelter we could from the
full force of the wind, and now it seemed we were in danger not because they were in the wind, but because they were not sufficiently
in it. The main force of the hurricane, deflected by the ridge behind,
fled over our heads and appeared to form by suction a vacuum below.
Our tent had either been sucked upwards into this, or had been
blown away because some of it was in the wind while some of it was
not. The roof of our igloo was being wrenched upwards and then
dropped back with great crashes: the drift was spouting in, not it
seemed because it was blown in from outside, but because it was
sucked in from within: the lee, not the weather, wall was the worst.
Already everything was six or eight inches under snow.

Very soon we began to be alarmed about the igloo. For some time
the heavy snow blocks we had heaved up on to the canvas roof
kept it weighted down. But it seemed that they were being gradually

moved off by the hurricane. The tension became well-nigh unendurable: the waiting in all that welter of noise was maddening. Minute after minute, hour after hour—those snow blocks were off now anyway, and the roof was smashed up and down—no canvas ever made could stand it indefinitely.

We got a meal that Saturday morning, our last for a very long time as it happened. Oil being of such importance to us we tried to use the blubber stove, but after several preliminary spasms it came to pieces in our hands, some solder having melted; and a very good thing too, I thought, for it was more dangerous than useful. We finished cooking our meal on the primus. Two bits of the cooker having been blown away we had to balance it on the primus as best we could. We then settled that in view of the shortage of oil we would not have another meal for as long as possible. As a matter of fact God settled that for us.

We did all we could to stop up the places where the drift was coming in, plugging the holes with our socks, mitts and other clothing. But it was no real good. Our igloo was a vacuum which was filling itself up as soon as possible: and when snow was not coming in a fine black moraine dust took its place, covering us and everything. For twenty-four hours we waited for the roof to go: things were so bad now that we dare not unlash the door.

Many hours ago Bill had told us that if the roof went he considered that our best chance would be to roll over in our sleeping-bags until we were lying on the openings, and get frozen and drifted in.

Gradually the situation got more desperate. The distance between the taut-sucked canvas and the sledge on which it should have been resting became greater, and this must have been due to the stretching of the canvas itself and the loss of the snow blocks on the top: it was not drawing out of the walls. The crashes as it dropped and banged out again were louder. There was more snow coming through the walls, though all our loose mitts, socks and smaller clothing were stuffed into the worst places: our pyjama jackets were stuffed between the roof and the rocks over the door. The rocks were lifting and shaking here till we thought they would fall.

We talked by shouting, and long before this one of us proposed to try and get the Alpine rope lashed down over the roof from outside.

But Bowers said it was an absolute impossibility in that wind. "You could never ask men at sea to try such a thing," he said. He was up and out of his bag continually, stopping up holes, pressing against bits of roof to try and prevent the flapping and so forth. He was magnificent.

And then it went.

Birdie was over by the door, when the canvas which was bent over the lintel board was working worse than anywhere else. Bill was practically out of his bag pressing against some part with a long stick of some kind. I don't know what I was doing but I was half out of and half in my bag.

The top of the door opened in little slits and that green Willesden canvas flapped into hundreds of little fragments in fewer seconds than it takes to read this. The uproar of it all was indescribable. Even above the savage thunder of that great wind on the mountain came the lash of the canvas as it was whipped to little tiny strips. The highest rocks which we had built into our walls fell upon us, and a sheet of drift came in.

Birdie dived for his sleeping-bag and eventually got in, together with a terrible lot of drift. Bill also—but he was better off: I was already half into mine and all right, so I turned to help Bill. "Get into your own," he shouted, and when I continued to try and help him, he leaned over until his mouth was against my ear. "*Please*, Cherry," he said, and his voice was terribly anxious. I know he felt responsible: feared it was he who had brought us to this ghastly end.

The next I knew was Bowers' head across Bill's body. "We're all right," he yelled, and we answered in the affirmative. Despite the fact that we knew we only said so because we knew we were all wrong, this statement was helpful. Then we turned our bags over as far as possible, so that the bottom of the bag was uppermost and the flaps were more or less beneath us. And we lay and thought, and sometimes we sang.

◻   *It was the* North *Pole that Roald Amundsen dreamed of conquering. Amundsen, born in 1872 near Oslo, Norway, planned his exploring career in boyhood. He prepared himself systematically for his great ambition, visiting the Antarctic with the* Belgica *expedition in 1897, then becoming the first man to navigate the Northwest Passage from Atlantic to Pacific, between 1903 and 1906. Three years after that success, he began to organize his North Pole expedition, but before he could get under way there came the news of Robert Peary's attainment of the Pole.*

*Amundsen changed plans swiftly. One Pole remained; and on August 9, 1910, Amundsen's ship, the* Fram, *turned southward. No one aboard but Amundsen knew the true destination. Nor did Robert Falcon Scott, then heading for Antarctica himself, realize that he had a competitor until Amundsen's jolting telegram reached him in Australia later that year.*

*The Norwegian chose as his base the Bay of Whales, an inlet along the Ross Ice Shelf well to the east of Scott's headquarters at McMurdo Sound. Amundsen thus began his polar quest sixty-nine miles closer to the Pole than Scott. After spending the early part of 1911 laying depots, Amundsen waited out the winter and set out for the Pole on October 19, having made a false start in September. The polar party consisted of four men in all, with four sledges drawn by fifty-two dogs. The skilled, capable Norwegian explorers carried out their journey with precision, nearly everything going according to plan, and they reached the Pole after an anticlimactically undramatic trip on December 14. The return trip was equally uneventful. The Norwegians had left a message in their tent for Scott, who was then launched on his far more arduous polar trek. Scott arrived at the Pole a month after Amundsen—too late in the season for him to survive the return.*

*Amundsen's dash to the South Pole was his last encounter with the Antarctic. He turned back to his first love, Arctic exploration, making pioneering flights by plane and dirigible over the North Pole. He disappeared in 1928 while taking part in an air search for another explorer.*

*The account of the polar journey included here is taken from* South Pole, *by Roald Amundsen, translated from the Norwegian by A. G. Chater (London, John Murray, 1913).*   ◻

# ROALD AMUNDSEN

In lat. 87° S.—according to dead reckoning—we saw the last of the land to the north-east. The atmosphere was then apparently as clear as could be, and we felt certain that our view covered all the land there was to be seen from that spot. We were deceived again on this occasion, as will be seen later. Our distance that day (December 4 [1911]) was close upon twenty-five miles; height above the sea, 10,100 feet.

The weather did not continue fine for long. Next day (December 5) there was a gale from the north, and once more the whole plain was a mass of drifting snow. In addition to this there was thick falling snow, which blinded us and made things worse, but a feeling of security had come over us and helped us to advance rapidly and without hesitation, although we could see nothing. That day we encountered new surface conditions—big, hard snow-waves (*sastrugi*). These were anything but pleasant to work among, especially when one could not see them. It was of no use for us "forerunners" to think of going in advance under these circumstances, as it was impossible to keep on one's feet. Three or four paces was often the most we managed to do before falling down. The *sastrugi* were very high, and often abrupt; if one came on them unexpectedly, one required to be more than an acrobat to keep on one's feet. The plan we found to work best in these conditions was to let Hanssen's dogs go first; this was an unpleasant job for Hanssen, and for his dogs too, but it succeeded, and succeeded well. An upset here and there was, of course, unavoidable, but with a little patience the sledge was always righted again. The drivers had as much as they could do to support their sledges among the *sastrugi*, but while supporting the sledges, they had at the same time a support for themselves. It was worse for us who had no sledges, but by keeping in the wake of them we could see where the irregularities lay, and thus get over them. Hanssen deserves a special word of praise for his driving on this surface in such weather. It is a difficult matter to drive Eskimo dogs forward when they cannot see; but Hanssen managed it well, both getting the dogs on and steering his course by compass. One would not think it possible to keep an approximately right course when the uneven ground gives such violent shocks that the needle flies several times round the compass, and is no sooner still again than it recommences the same dance; but when at last we got an observation, it turned out that Hanssen had steered to a hair, for the observations and dead reckoning agreed to a mile. In spite of all hindrances, and of being able to see nothing, the sledge-meters showed nearly twenty-five miles. The hypsometer showed 11,070 feet above the sea; we had therefore reached a greater altitude than the Butcher's [the previous campsite].

December 6 brought the same weather: thick snow, sky and plain all one, nothing to be seen. Nevertheless we made splendid progress. The *sastrugi* gradually became levelled out, until the surface was perfectly smooth; it was a relief to have even ground to go upon once more. These irregularities that one was constantly falling over were a nuisance; if we had met with them in our usual surroundings it would not have mattered so much; but up here on the high ground, where we had to stand and gasp for breath every time we rolled over, it was certainly not pleasant.

That day we passed 88° S., and camped in 88° 9′ S. A great surprise awaited us in the tent that evening. I expected to find, as on the previous evening, that the boiling-point had fallen somewhat; in other words, that it would show a continued rise of the ground, but to our astonishment this was not so. The water boiled at exactly the same temperature as on the preceding day. I tried it several times, to convince myself that there was nothing wrong, each time with the same result. There was great rejoicing among us all when I was able to announce that we had arrived on the top of the plateau.

December 7 began like the 6th, with absolutely thick weather, but, as they say, you never know what the day is like before sunset. Possibly I might have chosen a better expression than this last—one more in agreement with the natural conditions—but I will let it stand. Though for several weeks now the sun had not set, my readers will not be so critical as to reproach me with inaccuracy. With a light wind from the north-east, we now went southward at a good speed over the perfectly level plain, with excellent going. The uphill work had taken it out of our dogs, though not to any serious extent. They had turned greedy—there is no denying that—and the half kilo of pemmican they got each day was not enough to fill their stomachs. Early and late they were looking for something—no matter what—to devour. To begin with they contented themselves with such loose objects as ski-bindings, whips, boots, and the like; but as we came to know their proclivities, we took such care of everything that they found no extra meals lying about. But that was not the end of the matter. They then went for the fixed lashings of the sledges, and—if we had allowed it—would very quickly have resolved the various sledges into their component parts. But we found a way of stopping that: every evening, on halting, the sledges were buried in the snow, so as to hide all the lashings. That was successful; curiously enough, they never tried to force the "snow rampart."

I may mention as a curious thing that these ravenous animals, that devoured everything they came across, even to the ebonite points of our ski-sticks, never made any attempt to break into the provision cases. They lay there and went about among the sledges with their noses just on a level with the split cases, seeing and scenting the pemmican, without once making a sign of taking any. But if one raised a lid, they were not long in showing themselves. Then they all came in a great hurry and flocked about the sledges in the hope of getting a little extra bit. I am at a loss to explain this behaviour; that bashfulness was not at the root of it, I am tolerably certain.

During the forenoon the thick, grey curtain of cloud began to grow thinner on the horizon, and for the first time for three days we could see a few miles about us. The feeling was something like that one has on waking from a good nap, rubbing one's eyes and looking around. We had become so accustomed to the grey twilight that this positively dazzled us. Meanwhile, the upper layer of air seemed obstinately to remain the same and to be doing its best to prevent the sun from showing itself. We badly wanted to get a meridian altitude, so that we could determine our latitude. Since 86° 47′ S. we had had no observation, and it was not easy to say when we should get one. Hitherto, the weather conditions on the high ground had not been particularly favourable. Although the prospects were not very promising, we halted at 11 a.m. and made ready to catch the sun if it should be kind enough to look out. Hassel and Wisting used one sextant and artificial horizon, Hanssen and I the other set.

I don't know that I have ever stood and absolutely pulled at the sun to get it out as I did that time. If we got an observation here which agreed with our reckoning, then it would be possible, if the worst came to the worst, to go to the Pole on dead reckoning; but if we got none now, it was a question whether our claim to the Pole would be admitted on the dead reckoning we should be able to produce. Whether my pulling helped or not, it is certain that the sun appeared. It was not very brilliant to begin with, but, practised as we now were in availing ourselves of even the poorest chances, it was good enough. Down it came, was checked by all, and the altitude written down. The curtain of cloud was rent more and more, and before we had finished our work—that is to say, caught the sun at its highest, and convinced ourselves that it was descending again— it was shining in all its glory. We had put away our instruments and were sitting on the sledges, engaged in the calculations. I can safely say that we were excited. What would the result be, after marching blindly for so long and over such impossible ground, as we had been doing? We added and subtracted, and at last there was the result. We looked at each other in sheer incredulity: the result was as astonishing as the most consummate conjuring trick—88° 16′ S., precisely to a minute the same as our reckoning, 88° 16′ S. If we were forced to go to the Pole on dead reckoning, then surely the most exacting would admit our right to do so. We put away our observation books, ate one or two biscuits, and went at it again.

We had a great piece of work before us that day: nothing less than carrying our flag farther south than the foot of man had trod. We had our silk flag ready; it was made fast to two ski-sticks and laid on Hanssen's sledge. I had given him orders that as soon as we had covered the distance to 88° 23′ S., which was Shackleton's farthest south, the flag was to be hoisted on his sledge. It was my turn as fore-runner, and I pushed on. There was no longer any difficulty in holding one's course; I had the grandest cloud-formations to steer by, and everything now went like a machine. First came the forerunner for the time being, then Hanssen, then Wisting, and finally Bjaaland. The forerunner who was not on duty went where he liked: as a rule he accompanied one or other of the sledges. I had long ago fallen into a reverie—far removed from the scene in which I was moving; what I thought about I do not remember now, but I was so preoccupied that I had entirely forgotten my surroundings. Then suddenly I was roused from my dreaming by a jubilant shout, followed by ringing cheers. I turned round quickly to discover the reason of this unwonted occurrence, and stood speechless and overcome.

I find it impossible to express the feelings that possessed me at this moment. All the sledges had stopped, and from the foremost of them the Norwegian flag was flying. It shook itself out, waved and flapped so that the silk rustled; it looked wonderfully well in the pure, clear air and the shining white surroundings. 88° 23' was past; we were farther south than any human being had been. No other moment of the whole trip affected me like this. The tears forced their way to my eyes; by no effort of will could I keep them back. It was the flag yonder that conquered me and my will. Luckily I was some way in advance of the others, so that I had time to pull myself together and master my feelings before reaching my comrades. We all shook hands, with mutual congratulations; we had won our way far by holding together, and we would go farther yet—to the end.

We did not pass that spot without according our highest tribute of admiration to the man, who—together with his gallant companions—had planted his country's flag so infinitely nearer to the goal than any of his precursors. Sir Ernest Shackleton's name will always be written in the annals of Antarctic exploration in letters of fire. Pluck and grit can work wonders, and I know of no better example of this than what that man has accomplished.

The cameras of course had to come out, and we got an excellent photograph of the scene which none of us will ever forget. We went on a couple of miles more, to 88° 25', and then camped. The weather had improved, and kept on improving all the time. It was now almost perfectly calm, radiantly clear, and, under the circumstances, quite summer-like: —0·4° F. Inside the tent it was quite sultry. This was more than we had expected.

After much consideration and discussion we had come to the conclusion that we ought to lay down a depot—the last one—at this spot. The advantages of lightening our sledges were so great that we should have to risk it. Nor would there be any great risk attached to it, after all, since we should adopt a system of marks that would lead even a blind man back to the place. We had determined to mark it not only at right angles to our course—that is, from east to west—

but by snow beacons at every two geographical miles to the south.

We stayed here on the following day to arrange this depot. Hanssen's dogs were real marvels, all of them; nothing seemed to have any effect on them. They had grown rather thinner, of course, but they were still as strong as ever. It was therefore decided not to lighten Hanssen's sledge, but only the two others; both Wisting's and Bjaaland's teams had suffered, especially the latter's. The reduction in weight that was effected was considerable—nearly 110 pounds on each of the two sledges; there was thus about 220 pounds in the depot. The snow here was ill-adapted for building, but we put up quite a respectable monument all the same. It was dogs' pemmican and biscuits that were left behind; we carried with us on the sledges provisions for about a month. If, therefore, contrary to expectation, we should be so unlucky as to miss this depot, we should nevertheless be fairly sure of reaching our depot in 86° 21' before supplies ran short. The cross-marking of the depot was done with sixty splinters of black packing case on each side, with 100 paces between each. Every other one had a shred of black cloth on the top. The splinters on the east side were all marked, so that on seeing them we should know instantly that we were to the east of the depot. Those on the west had no marks.

The warmth of the past few days seemed to have matured our frost-sores, and we presented an awful appearance. It was Wisting, Hanssen, and I who had suffered the worst damage in the last south-east blizzard; the left side of our faces was one mass of sore, bathed in matter and serum. We looked like the worst type of tramps and ruffians, and would probably not have been recognized by our nearest relations. These sores were a great trouble to us during the latter part of the journey. The slightest gust of wind produced a sensation as if one's face were being cut backwards and forwards with a blunt knife. They lasted a long time, too; I can remember Hanssen removing the last scab when we were coming into Hobart—three months later. We were very lucky in the weather during this depot work; the sun came out all at once, and we had an excellent opportunity of taking some good azimuth observations, the last of any use that we got on the journey.

December 9 arrived with the same fine weather and sunshine. True, we felt our frost-sores rather sharply that day, with —18·4° F.

and a little breeze dead against us, but that could not be helped. We at once began to put up beacons—a work which was continued with great regularity right up to the Pole. These beacons were not so big as those we had built down on the Barrier; we could see that they would be quite large enough with a height of about 3 feet, as it was very easy to see the slightest irregularity on this perfectly flat surface. While thus engaged we had an opportunity of becoming thoroughly acquainted with the nature of the snow. Often—very often indeed—on this part of the plateau, to the south of 88° 25', we had difficulty in getting snow good enough—that is, solid enough for cutting blocks. The snow up here seemed to have fallen very quietly, in light breezes or calms. We could thrust the tent-pole, which was 6 feet long, right down without meeting resistance, which showed that there was no hard layer of snow. The surface was also perfectly level; there was not a sign of *sastrugi* in any direction.

Every step we now took in advance brought us rapidly nearer the goal; we could feel fairly certain of reaching it on the afternoon of the 14th. It was very natural that our conversation should be chiefly concerned with the time of arrival. None of us would admit that he was nervous, but I am inclined to think that we all had a little touch of that malady. What should we see when we got there? A vast, endless plain, that no eye had yet seen and no foot yet trodden; or—— No, it was an impossibility; with the speed at which we had travelled, we must reach the goal first, there could be no doubt about that. And yet—and yet—— Wherever there is the smallest loophole, doubt creeps in and gnaws and gnaws and never leaves a poor wretch in peace. "What on earth is Uroa scenting?" It was Bjaaland who made this remark, on one of these last days, when I was going by the side of his sledge and talking to him. "And the strange thing is that he's scenting to the south. It can never be——" Mylius, Ring, and Suggen, showed the same interest in the southerly direction; it was quite extraordinary to see how they raised their heads, with every sign of curiosity, put their noses in the air, and sniffed due south. One would really have thought there was something remarkable to be found there.

From 88° 25' S. the barometer and hypsometer indicated slowly but •urely that the plateau was beginning to descend towards the other side. This was a pleasant surprise to us; we had thus not only found the very summit of the plateau, but also the slope down on the far side. This would have a very important bearing for obtaining an idea of the construction of the whole plateau. On December 9 observations and dead reckoning agreed within a mile. The same result again on the 10th: observation 2 kilometres behind reckoning. The weather and going remained about the same as on the preceding days: light south-easterly breeze, temperature —18·4° F. The snow surface was loose, but ski and sledges glided over it well. On the 11th, the same weather conditions. Temperature —13° F. Observation and reckoning again agreed exactly. Our latitude was 89° 15' S. On the 12th we reached 89° 30', reckoning 1 kilometre behind observation. Going and surface as good as ever. Weather splendid— calm with sunshine. The noon observation on the 13th gave 89° 37' S. Reckoning 89° 38·5' S. We halted in the afternoon, after going eight geographical miles, and camped in 89° 45', according to reckoning.

The weather during the forenoon had been just as fine as before; in the afternoon we had some snow-showers from the south-east. It was like the eve of some great festival that night in the tent. One could feel that a great event was at hand. Our flag was taken out again and lashed to the same two ski-sticks as before. Then it was rolled up and laid aside, to be ready when the time came. I was awake several times during the night, and had the same feeling that I can remember as a little boy on the night before Christmas Eve—an intense expectation of what was going to happen. Otherwise I think we slept just as well that night as any other.

On the morning of December 14 the weather was of the finest, just as if it had been made for arriving at the Pole. I am not quite sure, but I believe we despatched our breakfast rather more quickly than usual and were out of the tent sooner, though I must admit that we always accomplished this with all reasonable haste. We went in the usual order—the forerunner, Hanssen, Wisting, Bjaaland, and the reserve forerunner. By noon we had reached 89° 53' by dead reckoning, and made ready to take the rest in one stage. At 10 a.m. a light breeze had sprung up from the south-east, and it had clouded over, so that we got no noon altitude; but the clouds were not thick, and from time to time we had a glimpse of the sun through them. The going on that day was rather different from what it had been; sometimes the ski went over it well, but at others it was pretty bad. We advanced that day in the same mechanical way as before; not much was said, but eyes were used all the more. Hanssen's neck grew twice as long as before in his endeavour to see a few inches farther. I had asked him before we started to spy out ahead for all he was worth, and he did so with a vengeance. But, however keenly he stared, he could not descry anything but the endless flat plain ahead of us. The dogs had dropped their scenting, and appeared to have lost their interest in the regions about the earth's axis.

At three in the afternoon a simultaneous "Halt!" rang out from the drivers. They had carefully examined their sledge-meters, and they all showed the full distance—our Pole by reckoning. The goal was reached, the journey ended. I cannot say—though I know it would sound much more effective—that the object of my life was attained. That would be romancing rather too barefacedly. I had better be honest and admit straight out that I have never known any man to be placed in such a diametrically opposite position to the goal of his desires as I was at that moment. The regions around the North Pole—well, yes, the North Pole itself—had attracted me from childhood, and here I was at the South Pole. Can anything more topsy-turvy be imagined?

We reckoned now that we were at the Pole. Of course, every one of us knew that we were not standing on the absolute spot; it would be an impossibility with the time and the instruments at our disposal to ascertain that exact spot. But we were so near it that the few miles which possibly separated us from it could not be of the slightest importance. It was our intention to make a circle round this camp, with a radius of twelve and a half miles (20 kilometres), and to be satisfied with that. After we had halted we collected and congratulated each other. We had good grounds for mutual respect in what had been achieved, and I think that was just the feeling that was expressed in the firm and powerful grasps of the fist that were exchanged. After this we proceeded to the greatest and most solemn act of the whole journey—the planting of our flag. Pride and affection shone in the five pairs of eyes that gazed upon the flag, as it unfurled itself with a sharp crack, and waved over the Pole. I had determined that the act of planting it—the historic event—should be equally divided among us all. It was not for one man to do this; it was for *all* who had staked their lives in the struggle, and held together through thick and thin. This was the only way in which I could show my gratitude to my comrades in this desolate spot. I could see that they understood and accepted it in the spirit in which it was offered. Five weather-beaten, frost-bitten fists they were that grasped the pole, raised the waving flag in the air, and planted it as the first at the geographical South Pole. "Thus we plant thee, beloved flag, at the South Pole, and give to the plain on which it lies the name of King Haakon VII.'s Plateau." That moment will certainly be remembered by all of us who stood there.

One gets out of the way of protracted ceremonies in those regions —the shorter they are the better. Everyday life began again at once. When we had got the tent up, Hanssen set about slaughtering Helge, and it was hard for him to have to part from his best friend. Helge had been an uncommonly useful and good-natured dog; without making any fuss he had pulled from morning to night, and had been a shining example to the team. But during the last week he had quite fallen away, and on our arrival at the Pole there was only a shadow of the old Helge left. He was only a drag on the others, and did absolutely no work. One blow on the skull, and Helge had ceased to live. "What is death to one is food to another," is a saying that can scarcely find a better application than these dog meals. Helge was portioned out on the spot, and within a couple of hours there was nothing left of him but his teeth and the tuft at the end of his tail. This was the second of our eighteen dogs that we had lost. The Major, one of Wisting's fine dogs, left us in 88° 25' S., and never returned. He was fearfully worn out, and must have gone away to die. We now had sixteen dogs left, and these we intended to divide into two equal teams, leaving Bjaaland's sledge behind.

Of course, there was a festivity in the tent that evening—not that champagne corks were popping and wine flowing—no, we contented ourselves with a little piece of seal meat each, and it tasted well and did us good. There was no other sign of festival indoors. Outside we heard the flag flapping in the breeze. Conversation was lively in the tent that evening, and we talked of many things. Perhaps, too, our thoughts sent messages home of what we had done.

Everything we had with us had now to be marked with the words "South Pole" and the date, to serve afterwards as souvenirs. Wisting proved to be a first-class engraver, and many were the articles he had to mark. Tobacco—in the form of smoke—had hitherto never made its appearance in the tent. From time to time I had seen one or two of the others take a quid, but now these things were to be altered. I had brought with me an old briar pipe, which bore inscriptions from many places in the Arctic regions, and now I wanted it marked "South Pole." When I produced my pipe and was about to mark it, I received an unexpected gift: Wisting offered me tobacco for the rest of the journey. He had some cakes of plug in his kit-bag, which he would prefer to see me smoke. Can anyone grasp what such an offer meant at such a spot, made to a man who, to tell the truth, is very fond of a smoke after meals? There are not many who can understand it fully. I accepted the offer, jumping with joy, and on the way home I had a pipe of fresh, fine-cut plug every evening. Ah! that Wisting, he spoiled me entirely. Not only did he give me tobacco, but every evening—and I must confess I yielded to the temptation after a while, and had a morning smoke as well—he undertook the disagreeable work of cutting the plug and filling my pipe in all kinds of weather.

But we did not let our talk make us forget other things. As we had got no noon altitude, we should have to try and take one at midnight. The weather had brightened again, and it looked as if midnight would be a good time for the observation. We therefore crept into our bags to get a little nap in the intervening hours. In good time— soon after 11 p.m.—we were out again, and ready to catch the sun; the weather was of the best, and the opportunity excellent. We four navigators all had a share in it, as usual, and stood watching the course of the sun. This was a labour of patience, as the difference of altitude was now very slight. The result at which we finally arrived was of great interest, as it clearly shows how unreliable and valueless a single observation like this is in these regions. At 12.30 a.m. we put our instruments away, well satisfied with our work, and quite convinced that it was the midnight altitude that we had observed. The calculations which were carried out immediately afterwards gave us 89° 56′ S. We were all well pleased with this result.

The arrangement now was that we should encircle this camp with a radius of about twelve and a half miles. By encircling I do not, of course, mean that we should go round in a circle with this radius;

that would have taken us days, and was not to be thought of. The encircling was accomplished in this way: Three men went out in three different directions, two at right angles to the course we had been steering, and one in continuation of that course. To carry out this work I had chosen Wisting, Hassel, and Bjaaland. Having concluded our observations, we put the kettle on to give ourselves a drop of chocolate; the pleasure of standing out there in rather light attire had not exactly put warmth into our bodies. As we were engaged in swallowing the scalding drink, Bjaaland suddenly observed: "I'd like to tackle this encircling straight away. We shall have lots of time to sleep when we get back." Hassel and Wisting were quite of the same opinion, and it was agreed that they should start the work immediately. Here we have yet another example of the good spirit that prevailed in our little community. We had only lately come in from our day's work—a march of about eighteen and a half miles—and now they were asking to be allowed to go on another twenty-five miles. It seemed as if these fellows could never be tired. We therefore turned this meal into a little breakfast—that is to say, each man ate what he wanted of his bread ration, and then they began to get ready for the work. First, three small bags of light windproof stuff were made, and in each of these was placed a paper, giving the position of our camp. In addition, each of them carried a large square flag of the same dark brown material, which could be easily seen at a distance. As flag-poles we elected to use our spare sledge-runners, which were both long—12 feet—and strong, and which we were going to take off here in any case, to lighten the sledges as much as possible for the return journey.

Thus equipped, and with thirty biscuits as an extra ration, the three men started off in the directions laid down. Their march was by no means free from danger, and does great honour to those who undertook it, not merely without raising the smallest objection, but with the greatest keenness. Let us consider for a moment the risk they ran. Our tent on the boundless plain, without marks of any kind, may very well be compared with a needle in a haystack. From this the three men were to steer out for a distance of twelve and a half miles. Compasses would have been good things to take on such a walk, but our sledge-compasses were too heavy and unsuitable for carrying. They therefore had to go without. They had the sun to go by, certainly, when they started, but who could say how long it would last? The weather was then fine enough, but it was impossible to guarantee that no sudden change would take place. If by bad luck the sun should be hidden, then their own tracks might help them. But to trust to tracks in these regions is a dangerous thing. Before you know where you are the whole plain may be one mass of driving snow, obliterating all tracks as soon as they are made. With the rapid changes of weather we had so often experienced, such a thing was not impossible. That these three risked their lives that morning, when they left the tent at 2.30, there can be no doubt at all, and they all three knew it very well. But if anyone thinks that on this account they took a solemn farewell of us who stayed behind, he is much mistaken. Not a bit; they all vanished in their different directions amid laughter and chaff.

The first thing we did—Hanssen and I—was to set about arranging a lot of trifling matters; there was something to be done here, something there, and above all we had to be ready for the series of observations we were to carry out together, so as to get as accurate a determination of our position as possible. The first observation told us at once how necessary this was. For it turned out that this, instead of giving us a greater altitude than the midnight observation, gave us a smaller one, and it was then clear that we had gone out of the meridian we thought we were following. Now the first thing to be done was to get our north and south line and latitude determined, so that we could find our position once more. Luckily for us, the weather looked as if it would hold. We measured the sun's altitude at every hour from 6 a.m. to 7 p.m., and from these observations found, with some degree of certainty, our latitude and the direction of the meridian.

By nine in the morning we began to expect the return of our comrades; according to our calculation they should then have covered the distance—twenty-five miles. It was not till ten o'clock that Hanssen made out the first black dot on the horizon, and not long after the second and third appeared. We both gave a sigh of relief as they came on; almost simultaneously the three arrived at the tent. We told them the result of our observations up to that time; it looked as if our camp was in about 89° 54′ 30″ S., and that with our encircling we had therefore included the actual Pole. With this result we might very well have been content, but as the weather was so good and gave the impression that it would continue so, and our store of provisions proved on examination to be very ample, we decided to go on for the remaining ten kilometres (five and a half geographical miles), and get our position determined as near to the Pole as possible. Meanwhile the three wanderers turned in—not so much because they were tired, as because it was the right thing to do—and Hanssen and I continued the series of observations.

In the afternoon we again went very carefully through our provision supply before discussing the future. The result was that we had food enough for ourselves and the dogs for eighteen days. The surviving sixteen dogs were divided into two teams of eight each, and the contents of Bjaaland's sledge were shared between Hanssen's and Wisting's. The abandoned sledge was set upright in the snow, and proved to be a splendid mark. The sledge-meter was screwed to the sledge, and we left it there; our other two were quite sufficient for the return journey; they had all shown themselves very accurate. A couple of empty provision cases were also left behind. I wrote in pencil on a piece of case the information that our tent—"Polheim" —would be found five and a half geographical miles north-west quarter west by compass from the sledge. Having put all these things in order the same day, we turned in, very well satisfied.

Early next morning, December 16, we were on our feet again. Bjaaland, who had now left the company of the drivers and been received with jubilation into that of the forerunners, was immediately entrusted with the honourable task of leading the expedition forward to the Pole itself. I assigned this duty, which we all regarded as a distinction, to him as a mark of gratitude to the gallant Telemarkers for their pre-eminent work in the advancement of ski sport. The leader that day had to keep as straight as a line, and if possible to follow the direction of our meridian. A little way after Bjaaland came Hassel, then Hanssen, then Wisting, and I followed a good way behind. I could thus check the direction of the march very accurately, and see that no great deviation was made. Bjaaland on this occasion showed himself a matchless forerunner; he went perfectly straight the whole time. Not once did he incline to one side or the other, and

249

when we arrived at the end of the distance, we could still clearly see the sledge we had set up and take its bearing. This showed it to be absolutely in the right direction.

It was 11 a.m. when we reached our destination. While some of us were putting up the tent, others began to get everything ready for the coming observations. A solid snow pedestal was put up, on which the artificial horizon was to be placed, and a smaller one to rest the sextant on when it was not in use. At 11.30 a.m. the first observation was taken. We divided ourselves into two parties—Hanssen and I in one, Hassel and Wisting in the other. While one party slept, the other took the observations, and the watches were of six hours each. The weather was altogether grand, though the sky was not perfectly bright the whole time. A very light, fine, vaporous curtain would spread across the sky from time to time, and then quickly disappear again. This film of cloud was not thick enough to hide the sun, which we could see the whole time, but the atmosphere seemed to be disturbed. The effect of this was that the sun appeared not to change its altitude for several hours, until it suddenly made a jump.

Observations were now taken every hour through the whole twenty-four. It was very strange to turn in at 6 p.m., and then on turning out again at midnight to find the sun apparently still at the same altitude, and then once more at 6 a.m. to see it still no higher. The altitude had changed, of course, but so slightly that it was imperceptible with the naked eye. To us it appeared as though the sun made the circuit of the heavens at exactly the same altitude. The times of day that I have given here are calculated according to the meridian of Framheim: we continued to reckon our time from this. The observations soon told us that we were not on the absolute Pole, but as close to it as we could hope to get with our instruments. . . .

On December 17 at noon we had completed our observations, and it is certain that we had done all that could be done. In order if possible to come a few inches nearer to the actual Pole, Hanssen and Bjaaland went out four geographical miles (seven kilometres) in the direction of the newly found meridian.

Bjaaland astonished me at dinner that day. Speeches had not hitherto been a feature of this journey, but now Bjaaland evidently thought the time had come, and surprised us all with a really fine oration. My amazement reached its culmination when, at the conclusion of his speech, he produced a cigar-case full of cigars and offered it round. A cigar at the Pole! What do you say to that? But it did not end there. When the cigars had gone round, there were still four left. I was quite touched when he handed the case and cigars to me with the words: "Keep this to remind you of the Pole." I have taken good care of the case, and shall preserve it as one of the many happy signs of my comrades' devotion on this journey. The cigars I shared out afterwards, on Christmas Eve, and they gave us a visible mark of that occasion.

When this festival dinner at the Pole was ended, we began our preparations for departure. First we set up the little tent we had brought with us in case we should be compelled to divide into two parties. It had been made by our able sailmaker, Rönne, and was of very thin windproof gabardine. Its drab colour made it easily visible against the white surface. Another pole was lashed to the tent-pole, making its total height about 13 feet. On the top of this a little Norwegian flag was lashed fast, and underneath it a pennant, on which "Fram" was painted. The tent was well secured with guy-ropes on all sides. Inside the tent, in a little bag, I left a letter, addressed to H.M. the King, giving information of what he had accomplished. The way home was a long one, and so many things might happen to make it impossible for us to give an account of our expedition. Besides this letter, I wrote a short epistle to Captain Scott, who, I assumed, would be the first to find the tent. Other things we left there were a sextant with a glass horizon, a hypsometer case, three reindeer-skin foot-bags, some kamiks and mits.

When everything had been laid inside, we went into the tent, one by one, to write our names on a tablet we had fastened to the tent-pole. On this occasion we received the congratulations of our companions on the successful result, for the following messages were written on a couple of strips of leather, sewed to the tent: "Good luck," and "Welcome to 90°." These good wishes, which we suddenly discovered, put us in very good spirits. They were signed by Beck and Rönne. They had good faith in us. When we had finished this we came out, and the tent-door was securely laced together, so that there was no danger of the wind getting a hold on that side.

And so good-bye to Polheim. It was a solemn moment when we bared our heads and bade farewell to our home and our flag. And then the travelling tent was taken down and the sledges packed. Now the homeward journey was to begin—homeward, step by step, mile after mile, until the whole distance was accomplished. We drove at once into our old tracks and followed them. Many were the times we turned to send a last look to Polheim. The vaporous, white air set in again, and it was not long before the last of Polheim, our little flag, disappeared from view.

□ *An Australian-sponsored Antarctic expedition brought Douglas Mawson back to the polar regions in 1912. Mawson, born in England in 1882 but raised in Australia, had been a member of Shackleton's expedition in 1907-09, and had taken part in the climb of Mount Erebus and the trek to the South Magnetic Pole. Now, the physicist and geologist was leading his own expedition. The goal was Wilkes Land, directly south of Australia. Mawson's purpose was to make scientific and geographical investigations along an almost unknown stretch of coastland.*

*His ship, the* Aurora, *was the first Antarctic exploration vessel equipped with radio. Mawson also brought the first airplane to the Antarctic, but it crashed on a trial flight and was never used. Setting up a base at Commonwealth Bay, at about 144° E., in January, 1912, Mawson directed several reconnoitering trips before the onset of winter. In November, the expedition leader set out on a sledging journey to map the shoreline east of his base, accompanied by Lieutenant B. E. S. Ninnis, a young English army officer, and Dr. Xavier Mertz, a Swiss lawyer and explorer. What began as a routine tour turned into an epic of endurance as unexpectedly difficult conditions hampered the men. Ninnis and Mertz both lost their lives on the journey, and Mawson barely returned to tell the story. He got back to the base too late in the season to be picked up by the relief ship, and was forced to spend a second winter in Antarctica, notwithstanding his impaired state of health. Mawson made a full recovery in the years that followed, and led a second Antarctic expedition in 1929. He died in 1958.*

*The following account of Mawson's sledge journey is from* The Home of the Blizzard, *by Sir Douglas Mawson (London, William Heinemann, 1915). It is reprinted by permission of the publishers.* □

# SIR DOUGLAS MAWSON

Mertz appeared to be depressed and, after the short meal, sank back into his bag without saying much. Occasionally, during the day, I would ask him how he felt, or we would return to the old subject of food. It was agreed that on our arrival on board the *Aurora* Mertz was to make penguin omelettes, for we had never forgotten the excellence of those we had eaten just before leaving the Hut.

Reviewing the situation, I found that we were one hundred miles south-east of Winter Quarters where food and plenty awaited us. At the time we had still ordinary rations for several days. How short a distance it would seem to the vigorous, but what a lengthy journey for the weak and famished!

The skin was peeling off our bodies and a very poor substitute remained which burst readily and rubbed raw in many places. One day, I remember, Mertz ejaculated, "Just a moment," and, reaching over, lifted from my ear a perfect skin-cast. I was able to do the same for him. As we never took off our clothes, the peelings of hair and skin from our bodies worked down into our under-trousers and socks, and regular clearances were made.

During the evening of the 6th I made the following note in my diary:

"A long and wearisome night. If only I could get on; but I must stop with Xavier. He does not appear to be improving and both our chances are going now."

"*January 7* [1913].—Up at 8 A.M., it having been arranged last night that we would go on to-day at all costs, sledge-sailing, with Xavier in his bag on the sledge." It was a sad blow to me to find that Mertz was in a weak state and required helping in and out of his bag. He needed rest for a few hours at least before he could think of travelling. "I have to turn in again to kill time and also to keep warm, for I feel the cold very much now."

"At 10 A.M. I get up to dress Xavier and prepare food, but find him in a kind of fit." Coming round a few minutes later, he exchanged a few words and did not seem to realize that anything had happened. ". . . Obviously we can't go on to-day. It is a good day though the light is bad, the sun just gleaming through the clouds. This is terrible; I don't mind for myself but for others. . . . I pray to God to help us."

"I cook some thick cocoa for Xavier and give him beef-tea; he is better after noon, but very low—I have to lift him up to drink."

During the afternoon he had several more fits, then became delirious and talked incoherently until midnight, when he appeared to fall off into a peaceful slumber. So I toggled up the sleeping-bag and retired worn out into my own. After a couple of hours, having felt no movement from my companion, I stretched out an arm and found that he was stiff.

My comrade had been accepted into "the peace that passeth all understanding." It was my fervent hope that he had been received where sterling qualities and a high mind reap their due reward. In his life we loved him; he was a man of character, generous and of noble parts.

For hours I lay in the bag, rolling over in my mind all that lay behind and the chance of the future. I seemed to stand alone on the wide shores of the world—and what a short step to enter the unknown future!

My physical condition was such that I felt I might collapse in a moment. The gnawing in the stomach had developed there a permanent weakness, so that it was not possible to hold myself up in certain positions. Several of my toes commenced to blacken and fester near the tips and the nails worked loose.

Outside, the bowl of chaos was brimming with drift-snow and I wondered how I would manage to break and pitch camp single-handed. There appeared to be little hope of reaching the Hut. It was easy to sleep on in the bag, and the weather was cruel outside. But inaction is hard to brook, and I thought of Service's lines:

> Buck up, do your damndest and fight,
> It's the plugging away that will win you the day.

If I failed to reach the Hut it would be something done to reach some prominent point likely to catch the eye of a search party, where a cairn might be erected and our diaries cached. And so I commenced to modify the sledge and camping gear to meet fresh requirements.

The sky remained clouded, but the wind fell off to a calm which lasted for several hours. I took the opportunity to set to work on the sledge, sawing it in halves with a pocket tool. A mast was made out of one of the rails of the discarded half of the sledge and a spar was cut from the other rail. The sledge-meter, very much battered, was still serviceable. Lastly, the load was cut down to a minimum by the elimination of all but the barest necessities.

Late on the evening of the 8th I took the body of Mertz, wrapped up in his sleeping-bag, outside the tent, piled snow blocks around it and raised a rough cross made of the two half-runners of the sledge.

On January 9 the weather was overcast and fairly thick drift was flying in a wind reaching about fifty miles an hour. As certain matters still required attention and my chances of re-erecting the tent were rather doubtful, if I had decided to move on, the start was delayed.

"I read the Burial Service over Xavier this afternoon. As there is little chance of my reaching human aid alive, I greatly regret inability at the moment to set out the detail of coastline met with for three hundred miles travelled and observations of glacier and ice-formations, etc.; the most of which latter are, of course, committed to my head.

"The approximate location of the camp is latitude 68° 2′ S., longitude 145° 9′ E. This is dead reckoning, as the theodolite legs have been out of action for some time, splinted together to form tent-props. I believe the truth lies nearer latitude 67° 57′ S., longitude 145° 20′ E., as the wind must have drifted us to the north."

During the afternoon I cut up Mertz's burberry jacket and roughly sewed it to a large canvas clothes-bag, making a sail which could be readily set or furled, so as to save delay in starting out or in camping.

January 10 was an impossible day for travelling on account of thick drift and high wind. I spent part of the time in reckoning up the amount of food remaining and in cooking the rest of the dogs' meat; the last device enabling me to leave behind some of the kerosene, of which there was still a good supply. Late in the afternoon the wind fell and the sun peered amongst the clouds just as I was in the middle of a long job riveting and lashing the broken shovel.

It was on January 11—a beautiful, calm day of sunshine—that I set out over a good surface with a slight down grade. From the start my feet felt lumpy and sore. They had become so painful after a mile of walking that I decided to make an examination of them on the spot, sitting in the sun on the sledge. The sight of my feet gave me quite a shock, for the thickened skin of the soles had separated in each case as a complete layer, and abundant watery fluid had escaped into the socks. The new skin underneath was very much abraded and raw.

I did what appeared to be the best thing under the circumstances: smeared the new skin with lanoline, of which there was a good store, and with bandages bound the skin soles back in place, as they were comfortable and soft in contact with the raw surfaces. Outside the bandages I wore six pairs of thick woollen socks, fur boots and a crampon over-shoe of soft leather. Then I removed most of my clothing and bathed in the glorious heat of the sun. A tingling sensation seemed to spread throughout my whole body, and I felt stronger and better.

When the day commenced with ideal weather I thought I would cover a long distance, but at 5:30 P.M., after six and a quarter miles, I felt nerve-worn and had to camp, "so worn that had it not been a delightful evening, I should not have found strength to erect the tent."

Though the medical outfit was limited, there were a fair number of bandages and on camping I devoted much time to tending raw patches all over the body, festering fingers and inflamed nostrils.

High wind and much drift put travelling out of the question on January 12, and in any case my feet needed a rest.

"*January 13.*—The wind subsided and the snow cleared off at noon. The afternoon was beautifully fine. Descended hard ice-slopes over many crevasses—almost all descent—but surfaces cut my feet up; at 8 P.M. camped, having done five and three-quarter miles—painful feet—on camping find feet worse than ever; things look bad but shall persevere. It is now 11 P.M. and the glacier is firing off like artillery—appears to send up great jets of imprisoned air."

During the march Aurora Peak showed up to the west, about twenty miles away, across the Mertz Glacier. I felt happy at thus

256

fixing my position, and at the sight of the far plateau which led onwards to Winter Quarters.

The glacier was the next obstacle to advance. To the south-west it descended from the plateau in immense broken folds. Pressing northward it was torn into the jumbled crush of sérac-ice, sparkling beneath an unclouded sun. The idea of diverging to the west and rounding the ice-falls occurred to me, but the detours involved other difficulties, so I strove to pick out the best track across the valley.

A high wind which blew on the morning of the 14th diminished in strength by noon and allowed me to get away. The sun was so warm that the puckered ice underfoot was covered with a film of water and in some places small trickles ran away to disappear into crevasses.

Though the course was downhill to the Mertz Glacier, the sledge required a good deal of pulling owing to the wet runners. At 9 P.M., after travelling five miles, I pitched camp in the bed of the glacier.

Between 9.30 P.M. and 11 P.M. the "cannonading" heard on the previous night recommenced. The sounds, resembling the explosions of heavy guns, usually started higher up the glacier and ended down towards the sea. When I first heard them, I put my head outside the tent to see what was going on. The reports came at random from every direction, but there was no visible evidence as to how they were produced. Without a doubt they had something to do with the re-freezing and splitting of the ice owing to the evening chill; but the sounds seemed far too loud to be explained by this cause alone.

January 15—the date on which all the summer sledging parties were due at the Hut! It was overcast and snowing early in the day, and in a few hours the sun broke out and shone warmly. The travelling was so heavy over a soft snowy surface, partly melting, that I gave up, after one mile, and camped.

At 7 P.M. the surface had not improved, the sky was thickly obscured and snow fell. At 10 P.M. the snow was coming down heavily, and, since there were many crevasses in the vicinity, I resolved to wait.

On the 16th at 2 A.M. the snow was as thick as ever, but at 5 A.M. the atmosphere lightened and the sun appeared.

Without delay I broke camp. A favourable breeze sprang up, and with sail set I managed to proceed through the snowy "deluge" in short stages. The snow clung in lumps to the runners, which had to be scraped frequently. I passed some broken ridges and sank into several holes leading down to crevasses out of which it was possible to scramble easily.

After laboriously toiling up one long slope, I was just catching my breath at the top and the sledge was running easily when I noticed that the surface beneath my feet fell away steeply in front. I suddenly realized that I was on the brink of a great blue hole like a quarry. The sledge was following of its own accord and was rapidly gaining speed, so I turned and, exerting every effort, was just able to hold it back by means of the hauling-line from the edge of the abyss. I should think that there must have been an interval of quite a minute during which I held my ground without being able to make it budge. Then it slowly came my way, and the imminent danger was past.

The day's march was an extremely hard five miles. Before turning in I had an extra supper of jelly soup, made by boiling down some of the dogs' sinews, strengthened with a little pemmican. The acute enjoyment of eating under these circumstances compensates in a slight measure for the suffering of starvation.

January 17 was another day of overcast weather and falling snow. Delay meant a reduction in the ration which was low enough already, so there was nothing to do but go on.

When I got away at 8 A.M. I found that the pulling was easier than it had been on the previous day. Nevertheless I covered only two miles and had to consider myself fortunate in not winding up the whole story then and there. This is what happened, following the account in my diary:

"Going up a long, fairly steep slope, deeply covered with soft snow, broke through lid of crevasse but caught myself at thighs, got out, turned fifty yards to the north, then attempted to cross trend of crevasse, there being no indication of it; a few moments later found myself dangling fourteen feet below on end of rope in crevasse—sledge creeping to mouth—had time to say to myself, 'so this is the end,' expecting the sledge every moment to crash on my head and all to go to the unseen bottom—then thought of the food uneaten on the sledge; but as the sledge pulled up without letting

258

me down, thought of Providence giving me another chance." The chance was very small considering my weak condition. The width of the crevasse was about six feet, so I hung freely in space, turning slowly round.

A great effort brought a knot in the rope within my grasp, and, after a moment's rest, I was able to draw myself up and reach another, and, at length, hauled myself on to the overhanging snow-lid into which the rope had cut. Then, when I was carefully climbing out on to the surface, a further section of the lid gave way, precipitating me once more to the full length of the rope.

Exhausted, weak and chilled (for my hands were bare and pounds of snow had got inside my clothing) I hung with the firm conviction that all was over except the passing. Below was a black chasm; it would be but the work of a moment to slip from the harness, then all the pain and toil would be over. It was a rare situation, a rare temptation—a chance to quit small things for great—to pass from the petty exploration of a planet to the contemplation of vaster worlds beyond. But there was all eternity for the last and, at its longest, the present would be but short. I felt better for the thought.

My strength was fast ebbing; in a few minutes it would be too late. It was the occasion for a supreme attempt. New power seemed to come as I addressed myself to one last tremendous effort. The struggle occupied some time, but by a miracle I rose slowly to the surface. This time I emerged feet first, still holding on to the rope, and pushed myself out, extended at full length, on the snow—on solid ground. Then came the reaction, and I could do nothing for quite an hour.

The tent was erected in slow stages and I then had a little food. Later on I lay in the sleeping-bag, thinking things over. It was a time when the mood of the Persian philosopher appealed to me:

> *Unborn To-morrow and dead Yesterday,*
> *Why fret about them if To-day be sweet?*

I was confronted with this problem: whether it was better to enjoy life for a few days, sleeping and eating my fill until the provisions gave out, or to "plug on" again in hunger with the prospect of plunging at any moment into eternity without the great luxury and pleasure of the food. And then an idea presented itself which greatly improved my prospects. It was to construct a ladder from alpine rope; one end of which was to be secured to the bow of the sledge and the other carried over my left shoulder and loosely attached to the sledge harness. Thus, if I fell into a crevasse again, it would be easy for me, even though weakened by starvation, to scramble out again by the ladder, provided the sledge was not also engulphed.

Notwithstanding the possibilities of the rope ladder, I could not sleep properly at all; my nerves had been so over-taxed. All night considerable wind and drift continued.

On the 19th it was overcast and light snow was falling. I resolved "to go ahead and leave the rest to Providence."

As they wallowed through the deep snow my feet and legs kept breaking through into space. Then I went right under, but the sledge was held back and the ladder "proved trumps." A few minutes later I was down again, but I emerged again without much exertion, half-smothered with snow. Faintness overcame me and I stopped to camp, though only a short distance had been covered.

All around was a leaden glare, the snow-clouds "corralling" me in. The sun had not shown up for some days and I was eager to see it once more, not only that it might show up the landscape but for its cheerful influence and life-giving energy. A few days previously my condition had been improving, but now it was going back.

During the night of the 18th loud booming noises, sharp cracks and muffled growls issued from the neighbouring crevasses and kept waking me up. At times one could feel a vibration accompanying the growling sounds, and I concluded that the ice was in rapid motion.

The sun at last appeared on the 19th, and I was off by 8.30 A.M. The whole surface was a network of crevasses, some very wide. Along one after another of these I dragged the sledge until a spot was reached where the snow-bridge looked to be firm. Here I plunged across, risking the consequences.

After three hours' marching nothing serious had happened and I found myself on safer ground with a "pimply" surface visible ahead, close under the slopes of the highlands. Once on this I became over-reliant, and in consequence sank several times into narrow fissures.

At 1 P.M. the Mertz Glacier was at last crossed and I had reached the rising hills on its western side. Overlooking the camp, five hundred feet above the glacier, were beetling, crevassed crags, but I could trace out a good road, free from pitfalls, leading to the plateau, at an elevation of three thousand feet.

To lighten my load for the climb I threw away alpine rope, finnesko crampons, sundry pairs of worn crampons and socks, while I rubbed a composition on the sledge-runners which prevented them from sticking to wet snow.

January 20 was a wretched day; overcast, with wind and light drift. In desperation I got away at 2 P.M. in a wind which proved to be of considerable assistance. I could see nothing of my surroundings; one thing was certain, and that was that the ascent had commenced and every foot took me upward. The day's work amounted to about two and a half miles.

On the 21st the sun shone brightly and there was a good following wind. Through deep snow I zigzagged up for three miles before deciding to camp.

Wind and drift prevailed early on the 22nd but fell away towards noon, and I was then favoured with a glorious sunny day. Away to the north was a splendid view of the open sea; it looked so beautiful and friendly that I longed to be down near it. Six miles had been covered during the day, but I felt very weak towards the end on account of the heavy pulling.

During the early hours of the 23rd the sun was visible, but about 8 A.M. the clouds sagged low, the wind rose and everything became blotted out in a swirl of driving snow.

I wandered on through it for several hours, the sledge capsizing at times owing to the strength of the wind. It was not possible to keep an accurate course, for even the wind changed direction as the day wore on. Underfoot there was soft snow which I found comfortable for my sore feet, but which made the sledge drag heavily at times.

When camp was pitched at 4 P.M. I reckoned that the distance covered in a straight line had been three and a half miles.

Erecting the tent single-handed in the high wind was a task which required much patience and some skill. The poles were erected first and then the tent was gathered up in the proper form and taken to the windward side of the legs where it was weighted down. The flounce on the windward side was got into position and piled up with snow blocks. Other blocks of snow had previously been placed in a ring round the legs in readiness to be tumbled on to the rest of the flounce when the tent was quickly slipped over the apex of the poles. In very windy weather it was often as much as two hours after halting before I would be cosy within the shelter of the tent.

High wind and dense driving snow persisted throughout the 24th and I made five and a half miles, sitting on the sledge most of the time with the sail up.

The blizzard continued on the 25th, but after the trying experience of the previous two days, I did not feel well enough to go on. Outside, the snow fell in "torrents," piled up round the tent and pressed in until it was no bigger than a coffin, of which it reminded me.

I passed most of the day doctoring myself, attending to raw and inflamed places. Tufts of my beard and hair came out, and the snowy floor of the tent was strewn with it at every camp.

"*January 26.*—I went on again in dense, driving snow. There was no need of the sail. The wind, which was behind, caught the sledge and bundled it along so that, though over a soft surface of snow, the travelling was rapid. The snow was in large, rounded grains, and beat on the tent like hail. Altogether nine miles were covered.

"*January 27.*—Blizzard-bound again. The previous day's exertions were too much for me to undertake the same again without a long rest.

"*January 28.*—In the morning the wind had moderated very much but the sky remained overcast and snow continued to fall. It was a long job digging the tent out. Soon after the start the sun gleamed and the weather improved. The three-thousand-foot crest of the plateau had been crossed and I was bearing down rapidly on Commonwealth Bay, the vicinity of which showed up as a darker patch on the clouds of the north-west horizon.

"The evening was fine and I really began to feel that Winter Quarters were approaching. To increase my excitement Madigan Nunatak came into view for a time in the clear, evening light. Distance covered, over eight miles."

The calm of the previous evening was broken again, and I started on the morning of January 29 in considerable drift and a fairly strong wind. After going five miles I had miraculous good fortune.

I was travelling along on an even down grade and was wondering how long the two pounds of food which remained would last, when something dark loomed through the drift a short distance away to the right. All sorts of possibilities fled through my mind as I headed the sledge for it. The unexpected happened—it was a cairn of snow erected by McLean, Hodgeman and Hurley, who had been out searching for us. On the top of the mound was a bag of food, left on the chance that it might be picked up, while in a tin was a note stating the bearing and distance of the mound from Aladdin's Cave (E. 30° S., distance twenty-three miles), that the Ship had arrived at the Hut and was waiting, that Amundsen had reached the Pole, and that Scott was remaining another year in Antarctica.

It was rather a singular fact that the search party only left this mound at eight o'clock on the morning of that very day (January 29). It was about 2 P.M. when I found it. Thus, during the night of the 28th, our camps had been only about five miles apart.

With plenty of food, I speedily felt stimulated and revived, and anticipated reaching the Hut in a day or two, for there was then not more than twenty-three miles to cover. Alas, however, there was to be another delay. I was without crampons—they had been thrown away on the western side of Mertz Glacier—and in the strong wind was not able to stand up on the slippery ice of the coastal slopes. The result was that I sat on the sledge and ran along with the wind, nibbling at the food as I went. The sledge made so much leeway that near the end of the day, after fourteen miles, I reckoned that I had been carried to the east of Aladdin's Cave. The course was therefore changed to the west, but the wind came down almost broadside-on to the sledge, and it was swept away. The only thing to do was to camp.

On the 30th I cut up the box of the theodolite and into two pieces of wood stuck as many screws and tacks as I could procure from the sledge-meter. In the repair-bag there were still a few ice-nails which at this time were of great use. Late in the day the wind fell off, and I started westward over the ice-slopes with the pieces of nail-studded wood lashed to my feet.

After six miles these improvised crampons broke up, and the increasing wind got me into difficulties. Finally, the sledge slipped sideways into a narrow crevasse and was caught by the boom (which crossed from side to side at the lower part of the mast). I was not strong enough for the job of extricating it straight away, and by the time I had got it safely on the ice, the wind had increased still more. So I pitched camp.

The blizzard was in full career on January 31 and I spent all day and until late at night trying to make the crampons serviceable, but without success.

On February 1 the wind and drift subsided late in the afternoon, and I clearly saw to the west the beacon which marked Aladdin's Cave.

At 7 P.M. I reached this haven within the ice, and never again was I to have the ordeal of pitching the tent. Inside the cave were three oranges and a pineapple which had been brought from the Ship. It was wonderful once more to be in the land of such things!

I waited to mend one of the crampons and then started off for the Hut; but a blizzard had commenced. To descend the five miles of steep icy slopes with my miserable crampons, in the weak state in which I found myself, would only have been as a last resort. So I camped in the comfortable cave and hoped for better weather next day.

The high wind, rising to a hurricane at times, continued for a whole week with dense drift until the 8th. I spent the long hours making crampons of a new pattern, eating and sleeping. Eventually I became so anxious that I used to sit outside the cave for long spells, watching for a lull in the wind.

At length I resolved to go down in the blizzard, sitting on the sledge as long as possible, blown along by the wind. I was making preparations for a start when the wind suddenly decreased and my opportunity had come.

In a couple of hours I was within one mile and a half of the Hut. There was no sign of the Ship lying in the offing, but I comforted myself with the thought that she might be still at the anchorage and have swung inshore so as to be hidden by the ice-cliffs, or on the other hand that Captain Davis might have been along the coast to the east searching there.

But even as I gazed about seeking for a clue, a speck on the northwest horizon caught my eye and my hopes went down. It looked like a distant ship; it might well have been the *Aurora*. Well, what matter! the long journey was at an end—a terrible chapter of my life was finished!

Then the rocks around Winter Quarters began to come into view, part of the basin of the boat harbour appeared, and lo! there were human figures! They almost seemed unreal—I was in a dream—but after a brief moment one of them saw me and waved an arm, I replied, there was a commotion and they all ran towards the Hut. Then they were lost, for the crest of the first steep slope hid them. It almost seemed to me that they had run away to hide.

Minutes passed, and I slowly went along with the sledge. Then a head rose over the brow of the hill and there was Bickerton, breathless after a long run. I expect he considered for a while which one of us it was. Soon we had shaken hands and he knew all in a few brief words, and I learned that the Ship had left earlier in the day. Madigan, McLean, Bage and Hodgeman arrived, and then a newcomer—Jeffryes. Five men had remained behind to make a search for our party, and Jeffryes was a new wireless operator brought down by Captain Davis.

We were soon at the Hut where I found that full preparations had been made for wintering a second year. The weather was calm and the Ship was no distance away so I decided to recall her by wireless. The masts at the Hut had been re-erected during the summer, and on board the *Aurora* Hannam was provided with a wireless receiving set. Jeffryes had arranged with Hannam to call up at 8, 9 and 10 P.M. for several evenings while the *Aurora* was "within range" in case there were any news of my party. A message recalling the Ship was therefore sent off and repeated at frequent intervals till past midnight.

Next morning there was a forty-mile wind when we went outside, but away across Commonwealth Bay to the west the *Aurora* could be seen close to the face of the ice-cliffs. She had returned in response to the call and was steaming up and down, waiting for the wind to moderate.

We immediately set to work getting all the records, instruments and personal gear ready to be taken down to the boat harbour in anticipation of calm weather during the day.

The wind chose to continue and towards evening was in the

sixties, while the barometer fell. During the afternoon Hodgeman went across to the western ridge and saw that the Ship was still in the Bay. The sea was so heavy that the motor-boat could never have lived through it.

That night Jeffryes sent another message, which we learned afterwards was not received, in which Captain Davis was given the option of remaining until calm weather supervened or of leaving at once for the Western Base. I felt that the decision should be left to him, as he could appreciate exactly the situation of the Western Base and what the Ship could be expected to do amid the ice at that season of the year. The time was already past when, according to my written instructions left for him on arrival at Commonwealth Bay, the *Aurora* should sail west to relieve Wild and his party.

On the morning of the 10th there was no sign of the Ship and evidently Captain Davis had decided to wait no longer, knowing that further delay would endanger the chances of picking up the eight men who had elected to winter on the shelf-ice one thousand five hundred miles to the west. At such a critical moment determination, fearless and swift, was necessary, and, in coming to his momentous decision, Captain Davis acted well and for the best interests of the Expedition.

A long voyage lay before the *Aurora* through many miles of ice-strewn sea, swept by intermittent blizzards and shrouded now in midnight darkness. We still fostered the hope that the vessel's coal supply would be sufficient for her to return to Adelie Land and make an attempt to pick us up. But it was not to be.

The long Antarctic winter was fast approaching and we turned to meet it with resolution, knowing that if the *Aurora* failed us in early March, that the early summer of the same year would bring relief.

□ *In August, 1914, war engulfed Europe just as Ernest Shackleton was about to depart on a new Antarctic expedition. Immediately,*

*he offered to place his ships and crew at the service of the war effort,
but a one-word answer from Winston Churchill, First Lord of the
Admiralty, sent the expedition to sea. "Proceed," Churchill said.
Britain would manage to fight on without Shackleton, for the conquest of Antarctica had to continue.*

*Shackleton's Imperial Trans-Antarctic Expedition of 1914 had
an impressive goal: to execute a trek cutting completely across the
Antarctic continent. One party would land at the Ross Shelf, the
other at the southern end of the Weddell Sea, and both would march
inland to meet at the Pole, while two other teams carried out scientific research. Half the cost of this enterprise was underwritten by
Sir James Caird, a Scottish industrialist, and the rest came from public and private donations. But Shackleton's plan fell far short of
accomplishment.*

*His ship, the* Endurance, *struck unusually severe ice conditions
in the Weddell Sea, and by January 19, 1915, at a latitude of 76°34'
S., the vessel was frozen into the pack, never to be freed. After
drifting all winter in a slab of ice three miles long and two and a
half miles wide, the* Endurance *was crushed by moving ice floes in
October, and had to be abandoned. Shackleton and his men made
camp on ice floes, and, after the ship sank in November, they set out
to reach Paulet Island, 346 miles away, where part of the Nordenskjöld expedition had taken refuge in 1903. It proved impossible
to reach Paulet Island, and the marooned explorer finally came
ashore at Elephant Island in the South Shetlands. The nearest place
to seek help was the island of South Georgia, 870 miles away.
Shackleton chose to make the journey himself, in an open boat 23
feet long, the* James Caird. *He selected five companions, including
Thomas Crean, a veteran of Scott's last expedition, and Frank Worsley, who had been captain of the* Endurance. *The narrative of that
boat journey is reprinted here. After reaching South Georgia, Shackleton led a Chilean relief mission to Elephant Island to pick up the
rest of his men, and all returned to England in 1917. Four years later
Shackleton organized his final Antarctic expedition, but he died of
a heart attack near South Georgia in January, 1922, at the age of
forty-seven, and was buried not far from the place where he had
come ashore at the end of his memorable boat trip.*

*The excerpt that follows is from* South: The Story of Shackleton's

Last Expedition, *by Ernest Shackleton (New York, Macmillan, 1920), and is reprinted by permission of the publishers.*   □

# SHACKLETON'S BOAT JOURNEY

By midday [April 24, 1916] the *James Caird* was ready for the voyage. Vincent and the carpenter had secured some dry clothes by exchange with members of the shore party (I heard afterwards that it was a full fortnight before the soaked garments were finally dried), and the boat's crew was standing by waiting for the order to cast off. A moderate westerly breeze was blowing. I went ashore in the *Stancomb Wills* and had a last word with Wild, who was remaining in full command, with directions as to his course of action in the event of our failure to bring relief, but I practically left the whole situation and scope of action and decision to his own judgment, secure in the knowledge that he would act wisely. I told him that I trusted the party to him and said good-bye to the men. Then we pushed off for the last time, and within a few minutes I was aboard the *James Caird*. The crew of the *Stancomb Wills* shook hands with us as the boats bumped together and offered us the last good wishes. Then, setting our jib, we cut the painter and moved away to the north-east. The men who were staying behind made a pathetic little group on the beach, with the grim heights of the island behind them and the sea seething at their feet, but they waved to us and gave three hearty cheers. There was hope in their hearts and they trusted us to bring the help that they needed.

I had all sails set, and the *James Caird* quickly dipped the beach and its line of dark figures. The westerly wind took us rapidly to the line of pack, and as we entered it I stood up with my arm around the mast, directing the steering, so as to avoid the great lumps of ice that were flung about in the heave of the sea. The pack thickened and we were forced to turn almost due east, running before the wind towards a gap I had seen in the morning from the high ground. I could not see the gap now, but we had come out on its bearing and I was prepared to find that it had been influenced by the easterly drift. At four o'clock in the afternoon we found the channel, much narrower than it had seemed in the morning but still navigable. Dropping sail, we rowed through without touching the ice anywhere, and by 5.30 p.m. we were clear of the pack with open water before us. We passed one more piece of ice in the darkness an hour later, but the pack lay behind, and with a fair wind swelling the sails we steered our little craft through the night, our hopes centred on our distant goal. The swell was very heavy now, and when the time came for our first evening meal we found great difficulty in keeping the Primus lamp alight and preventing the hoosh splashing out of the pot. Three men were needed to attend to the cooking, one man holding the lamp and two men guarding the aluminum cooking-pot, which had to be lifted clear of the Primus whenever the movement of the boat threatened to cause a disaster. Then the lamp had to be protected from water, for sprays were coming over the bows and our flimsy decking was by no means water-tight. All these operations were conducted in the confined space under the decking, where the men lay or knelt and adjusted themselves as best they could to the angles of our cases and ballast. It was uncomfortable, but we found consolation in the reflection that without the decking we could not have used the cooker at all.

The tale of the next sixteen days is one of supreme strife amid heaving waters. The sub-Antarctic Ocean lived up to its evil winter reputation. I decided to run north for at least two days while the wind held and so get into warmer weather before turning to the east and laying a course for South Georgia. We took two-hourly spells at the tiller. The men who were not on watch crawled into the sodden sleeping-bags and tried to forget their troubles for a period; but there was no comfort in the boat. The bags and cases seemed to be alive in the unfailing knack of presenting their most uncomfortable angles to our rest-seeking bodies. A man might imagine for a moment that he had found a position of ease, but always discovered quickly that some unyielding point was impinging on muscle or bone. The first night aboard the boat was one of acute discomfort for us all, and we were heartily glad when the dawn came and we could set about the preparation of a hot breakfast.

This record of the voyage to South Georgia is based upon scanty notes made day by day. The notes dealt usually with the bare facts of distance, positions, and weather, but our memories retained the incidents of the passing days in a period never to be forgotten. By running north for the first two days I hoped to get warmer weather and also to avoid lines of pack that might be extending beyond the main body. We needed all the advantage that we could obtain from the higher latitude for sailing on the great circle, but we had to be cautious regarding possible ice-streams. Cramped in our narrow quarters and continually wet by the spray, we suffered severely from cold throughout the journey. We fought the seas and the winds and at the same time had a daily struggle to keep ourselves alive. At times we were in dire peril. Generally we were upheld by the knowledge that we were making progress towards the land where we would be, but there were days and nights when we lay hove to, drifting across the storm-whitened seas and watching with eyes interested rather than apprehensive the uprearing masses of water, flung to and fro by Nature in the pride of her strength. Deep seemed the valleys when we lay between the reeling seas. High were the hills when we perched momentarily on the tops of giant combers. Nearly always there were gales. So small was our boat and so great were the seas that often our sail flapped idly in the calm between the crests of two waves. Then we would climb the next slope and catch the full fury of the gale where the wool-like whiteness of the breaking water surged around us. We had our moments of laughter—rare, it is true, but hearty enough. Even when cracked lips and swollen mouths checked the outward and visible signs of amusement we could see a joke of the primitive kind. Man's sense of humour is always most easily stirred by the petty misfortunes of his neighbours, and I shall never forget Worsley's efforts on one occasion to place the hot aluminium stand on top of the Primus stove after it had fallen off in an extra heavy roll. With his frost-bitten fingers he picked it up, dropped it, picked it up again, and toyed with it gingerly as though it were some fragile article of lady's wear. We laughed, or rather gurgled with laughter.

The wind came up strong and worked into a gale from the north-west on the third day out. We stood away to the east. The increasing seas discovered the weaknesses of our decking. The continuous blows shifted the box-lids and sledge-runners so that the canvas sagged down and accumulated water. Then icy trickles, distinct from

the driving sprays, poured fore and aft into the boat. The nails that
the carpenter had extracted from cases at Elephant Island and used
to fasten down the battens were too short to make firm the decking.
We did what we could to secure it, but our means were very limited,
and the water continued to enter the boat at a dozen points. Much
baling was necessary, and nothing that we could do prevented our
gear from becoming sodden. The searching runnels from the canvas
were really more unpleasant than the sudden definite douches of the
sprays. Lying under the thwarts during watches below, we tried
vainly to avoid them. There were no dry places in the boat, and at
last we simply covered our heads with our Burberrys and endured
the all-pervading water. The baling was work for the watch. Real
rest we had none. The perpetual motion of the boat made repose
impossible; we were cold, sore, and anxious. We moved on hands
and knees in the semi-darkness of the day under the decking. The
darkness was complete by 6 p.m., and not until 7 a.m. of the following day could we see one another under the thwarts. We had a few
scraps of candle, and they were preserved carefully in order that we
might have light at meal-times. There was one fairly dry spot in the
boat, under the solid original decking at the bows, and we managed
to protect some of our biscuit from the salt water; but I do not think
any of us got the taste of salt out of our mouths during the voyage.

The difficulty of movement in the boat would have had its humor-
ous side if it had not involved us in so many aches and pains. We
had to crawl under the thwarts in order to move along the boat, and
our knees suffered considerably. When a watch turned out it was
necessary for me to direct each man by name when and where to
move, since if all hands had crawled about at the same time the result would have been dire confusion and many bruises. Then there
was the trim of the boat to be considered. The order of the watch
was four hours on and four hours off, three men to the watch. One
man had the tiller-ropes, the second man attended to the sail, and
the third baled for all he was worth. Sometimes when the water in
the boat had been reduced to reasonable proportions, our pump
could be used. This pump, which Hurley had made from the Flinder's
bar case of our ship's standard compass, was quite effective, though
its capacity was not large. The man who was attending the sail could
pump into the big outer cooker, which was lifted and emptied over-

board when filled. We had a device by which the water could go direct from the pump into the sea through a hole in the gunwale, but this hole had to be blocked at an early stage of the voyage, since we found that it admitted water when the boat rolled.

While a new watch was shivering in the wind and spray, the men who had been relieved groped hurriedly among the soaked sleeping-bags and tried to steal a little of the warmth created by the last occupants; but it was not always possible for us to find even this comfort when we went off watch. The boulders that we had taken aboard for ballast had to be shifted continually in order to trim the boat and give access to the pump, which became choked with hairs from the moulting sleeping-bags and finneskoe. The four reindeer-skin sleeping-bags shed their hair freely owing to the continuous wetting, and some became quite bald in appearance. The moving of the boulders was weary and painful work. We came to know every one of the stones by sight and touch, and I have vivid memories of their angular peculiarities even to-day. They might have been of considerable interest as geological specimens to a scientific man under happier conditions. As ballast they were useful. As weights to be moved about in cramped quarters they were simply appalling. They spared no portion of our poor bodies. Another of our troubles, worth mention here, was the chafing of our legs by our wet clothes, which had not been changed now for seven months. The insides of our thighs were rubbed raw, and the one tube of Hazeline cream in our medicine-chest did not go far in alleviating our pain, which was increased by the bite of the salt water. We thought at the time that we never slept. The fact was that we would dose off uncomfortably, to be aroused quickly by some new ache or another call to effort. My own share of the general unpleasantness was accentuated by a finely developed bout of sciatica. I had become possessor of this originally on the floe several months earlier.

Our meals were regular in spite of the gales. Attention to this point was essential, since the conditions of the voyage made increasing calls upon our vitality. Breakfast, at 8 a.m., consisted of a pannikin of hot hoosh made from Bovril sledging ration, two biscuits, and some lumps of sugar. Lunch came at 1 p.m., and comprised Bovril sledging ration, eaten raw, and a pannikin of hot milk for each man. Tea, at 5 p.m., had the same menu. Then during the night we had a hot drink, generally of milk. The meals were the bright beacons in those cold and stormy days. The glow of warmth and comfort produced by the food and drink made optimists of us all. We had two tins of Virol, which we were keeping for an emergency; but, finding ourselves in need of an oil-lamp to eke out our supply of candles, we emptied one of the tins in the manner that most appealed to us, and fitted it with a wick made by shredding a bit of canvas. When this lamp was filled with oil it gave a certain amount of light, though it was easily blown out, and was of great assistance to us at night. We were fairly well off as regarded fuel, since we had 6½ gallons of petroleum.

A severe south-westerly gale on the fourth day out forced us to heave to. I would have liked to have run before the wind, but the sea was very high and the *James Caird* was in danger of broaching to and swamping. The delay was vexatious, since up to that time we had been making sixty or seventy miles a day, good going with our limited sail area. We hove to under double-reefed mainsail and our little jigger, and waited for the gale to blow itself out. During that afternoon we saw bits of wreckage, the remains probably of some unfortunate vessel that had failed to weather the strong gales south of Cape Horn. The weather conditions did not improve, and on the fifth day out the gale was so fierce that we were compelled to take in the double-reefed mainsail and hoist our small jib instead. We put out a sea-anchor to keep the *James Caird's* head up to the sea. This anchor consisted of a triangular canvas bag fastened to the end of the painter and allowed to stream out from the bows. The boat was high enough to catch the wind, and, as she drifted to leeward, the drag of the anchor kept her head to windward. Thus our boat took most of the seas more or less end on. Even then the crests of the waves often would curl right over us and we shipped a great deal of water, which necessitated unceasing baling and pumping. Looking out abeam, we would see a hollow like a tunnel formed as the crest of a big wave toppled over on to the swelling body of water. A thousand times it appeared as though the *James Caird* must be engulfed; but the boat lived. The south-westerly gale had its birthplace above the Antarctic Continent, and its freezing breath lowered the temperature far towards zero. The sprays froze upon the boat and gave bows, sides, and decking a heavy coat of mail. This accumulation of ice reduced the buoyancy of the boat, and to that extent was an added peril; but it possessed a notable advantage from one point of view. The water ceased to drop and trickle from the canvas, and the spray came in solely at the well in the after part of the boat. We could not allow the load of ice to grow beyond a certain point, and in turns we crawled about the decking forward, chipping and picking at it with the available tools.

When daylight came on the morning of the sixth day out we saw and felt that the *James Caird* had lost her resiliency. She was not rising to the oncoming seas. The weight of the ice that had formed in her and upon her during the night was having its effect, and she was becoming more like a log than a boat. The situation called for immediate action. We first broke away the spare oars, which were encased in ice and frozen to the sides of the boat, and threw them overboard. We retained two oars for use when we got inshore. Two of the fur sleeping-bags went over the side; they were thoroughly wet, weighing probably 40 lbs. each, and they had frozen stiff during the night. Three men constituted the watch below, and when a man went down it was better to turn into the wet bag just vacated by another man than to thaw out a frozen bag with the heat of his unfortunate body. We now had four bags, three in use and one for emergency use in case a member of the party should break down permanently. The reduction of weight relieved the boat to some extent, and vigorous chipping and scraping did more. We had to be very careful not to put axe or knife through the frozen canvas of the decking as we crawled over it, but gradually we got rid of a lot of ice. The *James Caird* lifted to the endless waves as though she lived again.

About 11 a.m. the boat suddenly fell off into the trough of the sea. The painter had parted and the sea-anchor had gone. This was serious. The *James Caird* went away to leeward, and we had no chance at all of recovering the anchor and our valuable rope, which had been our only means of keeping the boat's head up to the seas without the risk of hoisting sail in a gale. Now we had to set the sail and trust to its holding. While the *James Caird* rolled heavily in the trough, we beat the frozen canvas until the bulk of the ice had cracked off it and then hoisted it. The frozen gear worked protestingly, but after a struggle our little craft came up to the wind again, and we breathed more freely. Skin frost-bites were troubling us, and we had developed large blisters on our fingers and hands. I shall always carry the scar of one of these frost-bites on my left hand, which became badly inflamed after the skin had burst and the cold had bitten deeply.

We held the boat up to the gale during that day, enduring as best we could discomforts that amounted to pain. The boat tossed interminably on the big waves under grey, threatening skies. Our thoughts did not embrace much more than the necessities of the hour. Every surge of the sea was an enemy to be watched and circumvented. We ate our scanty meals, treated our frost-bites, and hoped for the improved conditions that the morrow might bring. Night fell early, and in the lagging hours of darkness we were cheered by a change for the better in the weather. The wind dropped, the snow-squalls became less frequent, and the sea moderated. When the morning of the seventh day dawned there was not much wind. We shook the reef out of the sail and laid our course once more for South Georgia. The sun came out bright and clear, and presently Worsley got a snap for longitude. We hoped that the sky would remain clear until noon, so that we could get the latitude. We had been six days out without an observation, and our dead reckoning naturally was uncertain. The boat must have presented a strange appearance that morning. All hands basked in the sun. We hung our sleeping-bags to the mast and spread our socks and other gear all over the deck. Some of the ice had melted off the *James Caird* in the early morning after the gale began to slacken, and dry patches were appearing in the decking. Porpoises came blowing round the boat, and Cape pigeons wheeled and swooped within a few feet of us. These little black-and-white birds have an air of friendliness that is not possessed by the great circling albatross. They had looked grey against the swaying sea during the storm as they darted about over our heads and uttered their plaintive cries. The albatrosses, of the black or sooty variety, had watched with hard, bright eyes, and seemed to have a quite impersonal interest in our struggle to keep afloat amid the battering seas. In addition to the Cape pigeons an occasional stormy petrel flashed overhead. Then there was a small bird, unknown to me, that appeared always to be in a fussy, bustling state, quite out of keeping with the surroundings. It irritated me. It had practically no tail, and it flitted about vaguely as though in search of the lost member. I used to find myself wishing it would find its tail and have done with the silly fluttering.

We revelled in the warmth of the sun that day. Life was not so bad, after all. We felt we were well on our way. Our gear was drying, and we could have a hot meal in comparative comfort. The swell was still heavy, but it was not breaking and the boat rode easily. At noon Worsley balanced himself on the gunwale and clung with one hand to the stay of the mainmast while he got a snap of the sun. The result was more than encouraging. We had done over 380 miles and were getting on for half-way to South Georgia. It looked as though we were going to get through.

The wind freshened to a good stiff breeze during the afternoon, and the *James Caird* made satisfactory progress. I had not realized until the sunlight came how small our boat really was. There was some influence in the light and warmth, some hint of happier days, that made us revive memories of other voyages, when we had stout decks beneath our feet, unlimited food at our command, and pleasant cabins for our ease. Now we clung to a battered little boat, "alone, alone—all, all alone; alone on a wide, wide sea." So low in the water were we that each succeeding swell cut off our view of the sky-line. We were a tiny speck in the vast vista of the sea—the ocean that is open to all and merciful to none, that threatens even when it seems to yield, and that is pitiless always to weakness. For a moment the consciousness of the forces arrayed against us would be almost overwhelming. Then hope and confidence would rise again as our boat rose to a wave and tossed aside the crest in a sparkling shower like the play of prismatic colours at the foot of a waterfall. My double-barrelled gun and some cartridges had been stowed aboard the boat as an emergency precaution against a shortage of food, but we were not disposed to destroy our little neighbours, the Cape pigeons, even for the sake of fresh meat. We might have shot an albatross, but the wandering king of the ocean aroused in us something of the feeling that inspired, too late, the Ancient Mariner. So the gun remained among the stores and sleeping-bags in the narrow quarters beneath our leaking deck, and the birds followed us unmolested.

The eighth, ninth, and tenth days of the voyage had few features worthy of special note. The wind blew hard during those days, and the strain of navigating the boat was unceasing; but always we made some advance towards our goal. No bergs showed on our horizon, and we knew that we were clear of the ice-fields. Each day brought its little round of troubles, but also compensation in the form of food and growing hope. We felt that we were going to succeed. The odds against us had been great, but we were winning through. We still suffered severely from the cold, for, though the temperature was rising, our vitality was declining owing to shortage of food, exposure, and the necessity of maintaining our cramped positions day and night. I found that it was now absolutely necessary to prepare hot milk for all hands during the night, in order to sustain life till dawn. This meant lighting the Primus lamp in the darkness and involved an increased drain on our small store of matches. It was the rule that one match must serve when the Primus was being lit. We had no lamp for the compass and during the early days of the voyage we would strike a match when the steersman wanted to see the course at night; but later the necessity for strict economy impressed itself upon us, and the practice of striking matches at night was stopped. We had one water-tight tin of matches. I had stowed away in a pocket, in readiness for a sunny day, a lens from one of the telescopes, but this was of no use during the voyage. The sun seldom shone upon us. The glass of the compass got broken one night, and we contrived to mend it with adhesive tape from the medicine-chest. One of the memories that comes to me from those days is of Crean singing at the tiller. He always sang while he was steering, and nobody ever discovered what the song was. It was devoid of tune and as monotonous as the chanting of a Buddhist monk at his prayers; yet somehow it was cheerful. In moments of inspiration Crean would attempt "The Wearing of the Green."

On the tenth night Worsley could not straighten his body after his spell at the tiller. He was thoroughly cramped, and we had to drag him beneath the decking and massage him before he could unbend himself and get into a sleeping-bag. A hard north-westerly gale came up on the eleventh day (May 5) and shifted to the south-west in the late afternoon. The sky was overcast and occasional snow-squalls added to the discomfort produced by a tremendous cross-sea—the worst, I thought, that we had experienced. At midnight I was at the tiller and suddenly noticed a line of clear sky between the south and south-west. I called to the other men that the sky was clearing, and then a moment later I realized that what I had seen was not a rift in the clouds but the white crest of an enormous wave. During twenty-six years' experience of the ocean in all its moods I had not encountered a wave so gigantic. It was a mighty upheaval of the ocean, a thing quite apart from the big white-capped seas that had been our tireless enemies for many days. I shouted "For God's sake, hold on! It's got us." Then came a moment of suspense that seemed drawn out into hours. White surged the foam of the breaking sea around us. We felt our boat lifted and flung forward like a cork in breaking surf. We were in a seething chaos of tortured water; but somehow the boat lived through it, half full of water, sagging to the dead weight and shuddering under the blow. We baled with the energy of men fighting for life, flinging the water over the sides with every receptacle that came to our hands, and after ten minutes of uncertainty we felt the boat renew her life beneath us. She floated again and ceased to lurch drunkenly as though dazed by the attack of the sea. Earnestly we hoped that never again would we encounter such a wave.

The conditions in the boat, uncomfortable before, had been made worse by the deluge of water. All our gear was thoroughly wet again. Our cooking-stove had been floating about in the bottom of the boat, and portions of our last hoosh seemed to have permeated everything. Not until 3 a.m., when we were all chilled almost to the limit of endurance, did we manage to get the stove alight and make ourselves hot drinks. The carpenter was suffering particularly, but he showed grit and spirit. Vincent had for the past week ceased to be an active member of the crew, and I could not easily account for his collapse. Physically he was one of the strongest men in the boat. He was a young man, he had served on North Sea trawlers, and he should have been able to bear hardships better than McCarthy, who, not so strong, was always happy.

The weather was better on the following day (May 6), and we got a glimpse of the sun. Worsley's observation showed that we were not more than a hundred miles from the north-west corner of South Georgia. Two more days with a favourable wind and we would sight the promised land. I hoped that there would be no delay, for our supply of water was running very low. The hot drink at night was essential, but I decided that the daily allowance of water must be cut down to half a pint per man. The lumps of ice we had taken aboard had gone long ago. We were dependent upon the water we had brought from Elephant Island, and our thirst was increased by the fact that we were now using the brackish water in the breaker that had been slightly stove in in the surf when the boat was being loaded. Some sea-water had entered at that time.

Thirst took possession of us. I dared not permit the allowance of water to be increased since an unfavourable wind might drive us away from the island and lengthen our voyage by many days. Lack of water is always the most severe privation that men can be condemned to endure, and we found, as during our earlier boat voyage, that the salt water in our clothing and the salt spray that lashed our faces made our thirst grow quickly to a burning pain. I had to be very firm in refusing to allow any one to anticipate the morrow's allowance, which I was sometimes begged to do. We did the necessary work dully and hoped for the land. I had altered the course to the east so as to make sure of our striking the island, which would have been impossible to regain if we had run past the northern end. The course was laid on our scrap of chart for a point some thirty miles down the coast. That day and the following day passed for us in a sort of nightmare. Our mouths were dry and our tongues were swollen. The wind was still strong and the heavy sea forced us to navigate carefully, but any thought of our peril from the waves was buried beneath the consciousness of our raging thirst. The bright moments were those when we each received our one mug of hot milk during the long, bitter watches of the night. Things were bad for us in those days, but the end was coming. The morning of May 8 broke thick and stormy, with squalls from the north-west. We searched the waters ahead for a sign of land, and though we could see nothing more than had met our eyes for many days, we were cheered by a sense that the goal was near at hand. About ten o'clock that morning we passed a little bit of kelp, a glad signal of the proximity of land. An hour later we saw two shags sitting on a big mass of kelp, and knew then that we must be within ten or fifteen miles of the shore. These birds are as sure an indication of the proximity of land as a lighthouse is, for they never venture far to sea. We gazed ahead with increasing eagerness, and at 12.30 p.m., through a rift in the clouds,

McCarthy caught a glimpse of the black cliffs of South Georgia, just fourteen days after our departure from Elephant Island. It was a glad moment. Thirst-ridden, chilled, and weak as we were, happiness irradiated us. The job was nearly done.

We stood in towards the shore to look for a landing-place, and presently we could see the green tussock-grass on the ledges above the surf-beaten rocks. Ahead of us and to the south, blind rollers showed the presence of uncharted reefs along the coast. Here and there the hungry rocks were close to the surface, and over them the great waves broke, swirling viciously and spouting thirty and forty feet into the air. The rocky coast appeared to descend sheer to the sea. Our need of water and rest was well-nigh desperate, but to have attempted a landing at that time would have been suicidal. Night was drawing near, and the weather indications were not favourable. There was nothing for it but to haul off till the following morning, so we stood away on the starboard tack until we had made what appeared to be a safe offing. Then we hove to in the high westerly swell. The hours passed slowly as we waited the dawn, which would herald, we fondly hoped, the last stage of our journey. Our thirst was a torment and we could scarcely touch our food; the cold seemed to strike right through our weakened bodies. At 5 a.m. the wind shifted to the north-west and quickly increased to one of the worst hurricanes any of us had ever experienced. A great cross-sea was running, and the wind simply shrieked as it tore the tops off the waves and converted the whole seascape into a haze of driving spray. Down into valleys, up to tossing heights, straining until her seams opened, swung our little boat, brave still but labouring heavily. We knew that the wind and set of the sea was driving us ashore, but we could do nothing. The dawn showed us a storm-torn ocean, and the morning passed without bringing us a sight of the land; but at 1 p.m., through a rift in the flying mists, we got a glimpse of the huge crags of the island and realized that our position had become desperate. We were on a dead lee shore, and we could gauge our approach to the unseen cliffs by the roar of the breakers against the sheer walls of rock. I ordered the double-reefed mainsail to be set in the hope that we might claw off, and this attempt increased the strain upon the boat. The *Caird* was bumping heavily, and the water was pouring in everywhere. Our thirst was forgotten in the realization of our imminent danger, as we baled unceasingly, and adjusted our weights from time to time; occasional glimpses showed that the shore was nearer. I knew that Annewkow Island lay to the south of us, but our small and badly marked chart showed uncertain reefs in the passage between the island and the mainland, and I dared not trust it, though as a last resort we could try to lie under the lee of the island. The afternoon wore away as we edged down the coast, with the thunder of the breakers in our ears. The approach of evening found us still some distance from Annewkow Island, and, dimly in the twilight, we could see a snow-capped mountain looming above us. The chance of surviving the night, with the driving gale and the implacable sea forcing us on to the lee shore, seemed small. I think most of us had a feeling that the end was very near. Just after 6 p.m., in the dark, as the boat was in the yeasty backwash from the seas flung from this iron-bound coast, then, just when things looked their worst, they changed for the best. I have marvelled often at the thin line that divides success from failure and the sudden turn that leads from apparently certain disaster to comparative safety. The wind suddenly shifted, and we were free once more to make an offing. Almost as soon as the gale eased, the pin that locked the mast to the thwart fell out. It must have been on the point of doing this throughout the hurricane, and if it had gone nothing could have saved us; the mast would have snapped like a carrot. Our backstays had carried away once before when iced up and were not too strongly fastened now. We were thankful indeed for the mercy that had held that pin in its place throughout the hurricane.

We stood off shore again, tired almost to the point of apathy. Our water had long been finished. The last was about a pint of hairy liquid, which we strained through a bit of gauze from the medicine-chest. The pangs of thirst attacked us with redoubled intensity, and I felt that we must make a landing on the following day at almost any hazard. The night wore on. We were very tired. We longed for day. When at last the dawn came on the morning of May 10 there was practically no wind, but a high cross-sea was running. We made slow progress towards the shore. About 8 a.m. the wind backed to the north-west and threatened another blow. We had sighted in the meantime a big indentation which I thought must be King Haakon Bay, and I decided that we must land there. We set the bows of the boat towards the bay and ran before the freshening gale. Soon we had angry reefs on either side. Great glaciers came down to the sea and offered no landing-place. The sea spouted on the reefs and thundered against the shore. About noon we sighted a line of jagged reef, like blackened teeth, that seemed to bar the entrance to the bay. Inside, comparatively smooth water stretched eight or nine miles to the head of the bay. A gap in the reef appeared, and we made for it. But the fates had another rebuff for us. The wind shifted and blew from the east right out of the bay. We could see the way through the reef, but we could not approach it directly. That afternoon we bore up, tacking five times in the strong wind. The last tack enabled us to get through, and at last we were in the wide mouth of the bay. Dusk was approaching. A small cove, with a boulder-strewn beach guarded by a reef, made a break in the cliffs on the south side of the bay, and we turned in that direction. I stood in the bows directing the steering as we ran through the kelp and made the passage of the reef. The entrance was so narrow that we had to take in the oars, and the swell was piling itself right over the reef into the cove; but in a minute or two we were inside, and in the gathering darkness the *James Caird* ran in on a swell and touched the beach. I sprang ashore with the short painter and held on when the boat went out with the backward surge. When the *James Caird* came in again three of the men got ashore, and they held the painter while I climbed some rocks with another line. A slip on the wet rocks twenty feet up nearly closed my part of the story just at the moment when we were achieving safety. A jagged piece of rock held me and at the same time bruised me sorely. However, I made fast the line, and in a few minutes we were all safe on the beach, with the boat floating in the surging water just off the shore. We heard a gurgling sound that was sweet music in our ears, and, peering around, found a stream of fresh water almost at our feet. A moment later we were down on our knees drinking the pure ice-cold water in long draughts that put new life into us. It was a splendid moment.

# PART V

## THE AGE OF MECHANIZED EXPLORATION 1930-PRESENT

□   *Richard Evelyn Byrd (1888-1957) is the American whose name is most closely associated with the exploration of Antarctica. Scion of a historic family, brother to Virginia's Senator Harry Byrd, he set a high standard of leadership and bravery.*

*The North Pole was his first goal. After serving in the U.S. Navy before World War I, and as an aviation instructor during that war, Byrd took part in several Arctic expeditions, and in 1926 he and another naval aviator, Floyd Bennett, were the first to fly over the North Pole. The following year, he, Bennett, and a third man attracted attention by flying nonstop from New York to Paris.*

*Turning next to Antarctica, Byrd raised $800,000 in the boom year of 1928 to finance an expedition. His ambitiously conceived scheme* required the use of four airplanes, a motor tractor, radio transmitters, and four ships. The age of mechanized exploration of the Antarctic had begun. Reaching the Ross Ice Shelf on Christmas Day, 1928, Byrd supervised the construction of a village on the ice barrier —the first Little America, three miles from the site of Amundsen's base of 1911. Three large buildings and more than a dozen smaller ones held Byrd's forty-two men, his ninety-five sledge dogs, and his wealth of special equipment.

The highlight of Byrd's first expedition was his flight to the South Pole, described in the account following. Byrd's co-pilot was the veteran aviator Bernt Balchen; also aboard were Ashley McKinley, a photographer, and Harold June, a radio engineer. The hazardous undertaking brought men to the South Pole for the first time since Scott's death, though the aviators did not attempt a landing. Other flights and sledge trips yielded valuable data on previously unexplored parts of Antarctica, such as the plateau that Byrd named Marie Byrd Land, east of known territory. After fourteen successful months, the expedition departed for home in February, 1930.

The narrative of the first flight to the South Pole is from Little America, by Richard E. Byrd (New York, G. P. Putnam's Sons, 1930). It is reprinted by permission of the publisher.  □

# BYRD'S FLIGHT
# TO THE SOUTH POLE

Thanksgiving Day, November 25th [1929], gave us what we wanted. At noon the Geological Party radioed a final weather report: "Unchanged. Perfect visibility. No clouds anywhere." Harrison finished with his balloon runs, Haines with his weather charts. The sky was still somewhat overcast, and the surface wind from the east-southeast. Haines came into the library, his face very grave and determined. Dear old Bill, he always takes his responsibilities seriously. Together we went out for a walk and a last look at the weather. What he said exactly I have forgotten, but it was in effect: "If you don't go now you may never have another chance as good as this." And that was that.

There were a few things to be done. Every possible thing that could happen and some that could not possibly happen we had attempted to anticipate and prepare for. First, I delivered to Haines, who would be in charge of the camp during our absence and until the return of Gould, a set of instructions suggesting his procedure in case we should fail. It was, of course, necessary to anticipate this contingency. There were, besides, a number of sealed instructions, to be opened only if no word came from us within a fixed period. These provided for the organization of a relief expedition, the allocation of responsibility, the return of part of the expedition to the United States and the messages which a thoughtful man must leave behind before undertaking such a flight. These last I gave to Lofgren, who had served the expedition faithfully and than whom there is no squarer or truer man.

The mechanics, Bubier, Roth and Demas, went over the plane for the last time, testing everything with scrupulous care. A line of men passed five-gallon cans of gasoline to several men standing on the wing, who poured them into the wing tanks. Another line fed the stream of gear which flowed into the plane. Black weighed each thing before passing it on to McKinley and June, who were stowing the stuff in the cabin. Hanson went over the radio equipment. With de Ganahl I made a careful check of the sextant and the watches and chronometers, which were among the last things put aboard. For days de Ganahl and I had nursed the chronometers, checking them against the time tick which was broadcast every night from the United States. We knew their exact loss or gain. We had to know. An error in time would put the Bumstead sun compass off and our geographical position as well.

No thoroughbred went into a race more carefully, scrupulously groomed than was the Floyd Bennett before the polar flight. Responsibility for its performance rested with no single man. It lay on the shoulders of the whole camp. It was a sobering responsibility, and I think that every man felt it in his heart.

We were done with these details shortly after three o'clock. At the last moment we decided to take aboard an additional 100 gallons of gasoline. There was no telling what kind of winds we would meet. If head winds, then the extra quantity of fuel would be invaluable. If not, we could dump it overboard before we reached the "Hump."

The total weight was approximately 15,000 pounds.

Haines came up with a final report on the weather. "A twenty-mile wind from the south at 2,000 feet." It meant clear skies to the south. I went into my office and picked up a flag weighted with a stone from Floyd Bennett's grave. It seemed fitting that something connected with the spirit of this noble friend who stood with me over the North Pole, on May 9, 1926, should rest as long as stone endures at the bottom of the world.

There were handshakes all around, and at 3:29 o'clock we were off. The skis were in the air after a run of 30 seconds—an excellent take-off. I was greatly relieved. A calm expectation took hold of my mind. Having started, we were certainly going to get somewhere.

There was a flashing glimpse of the men clustered near the run-way—those splendid fellows whose willing help and indestructible spirit have never faltered, no, not once—and we faced the south.

The moment the Ford leveled off the impalpable haze with which we had contended so often confused the vision, and we lost several precious minutes before we found the trail. But if Haines' predictions were correct, this would not last for long.

Our course was laid along the meridian of the trail, which at that point was 143° 45' W. Although the trail did not always follow that meridian, it would bring us finally to Axel Heiberg Glacier.

The sky began to clear, under the sweeping movements of a south-easterly wind, and presently blue sky showed ahead. Haines was right, as always. Slowly gaining altitude, we passed 20 Mile Depot, then 44 Mile Depot.

From time to time we lost the trail, as our altitude changed or our distance from it varied slightly. But invariably by steering a straight course with the Bumstead sun compass we picked it up again.

Presently the northern edge of the crevasses was underneath. The trail then followed meridian 163° 42' W. The wind was still from the east and it was necessary to nose the plane 10° to the left of the course, to make good a straight course to the south. Had there been any one below to see, he must have been surprised at the sight of a plane headed well to the east but flying steadily to the south. With this diagonal push tending to press us from our course it was neces-sary to check the course frequently with the drift indicator.

Had you been there to glance over the cabin of this modern ma-chine which has so revolutionized polar travel, I think you would have been impressed most of all—perhaps first of all—with the profusion of gear in the cabin. There was a small sledge, rolled masses of sleeping bags, bulky food sacks, two pressure gasoline stoves, rows of cans of gasoline packed about the main tank forward, funnels for draining gasoline and oil from the engine, mounds of clothing, tents and so on, *ad infinitum*. There was scarcely room in which to move.

June had his radio in the after bulkhead on the port side. From time to time he flashed reports on our progress to the base. From the ear phones strapped to his helmet ran long cords, so that he might move freely about the cabin without being obliged to take them off. His duties were varied and important. He had to attend to the motion picture camera, the radio and the complicated valves of the six gasoline tanks. Every now and then he relieved Balchen at the wheel, or helped him to follow the elusive trail.

McKinley had his mapping camera ready to go into action either on port or starboard side. It was for him and the camera he so sedulously served that the flight was made. The mapping of the corridor between Little America and the South Pole was one of the major objectives of the expedition.

Balchen was forward, bulking large in the narrow compartment, his massive hands on the wheel, now appraising the engines with a critical eye, now the dozen flickering fingers on the dials on the instrument board. Balchen was in his element. His calm fine face bespoke his confidence and sureness. He was anticipating the struggle at the "Hump" almost with eagerness.

It was quite warm forward, behind the engines. But a cold wind swept aft through the cabin, causing one to be thankful for the protection of heavy clothes. When the skies cleared, the cabin was flooded with a golden light. The sound of the engines and propellers filled it. One had to shout to make oneself heard. From the navigation table aft, where my charts were spread out, a trolley ran to the control cabin. Over it I shot to Balchen the necessary messages and courses. On receiving them, he turned and smiled his understanding.

That, briefly, is the picture, and a startling one it makes in contrast with that of Amundsen's party which had pressed along this same course eighteen years before. A wing, pistons and flashing propellers had taken the place of runners, dogs and legs. Amundsen was delighted to make 25 miles per day. We had to average 90 miles per hour to accomplish our mission. We had the advantages of swiftness and comfort, but we had as well an enlarged fallibility. A flaw in a piece of steel, a bit of dirt in the fuel lines or carburetor jets, a few hours of strong head winds, fog or storm—these things, remotely beyond our control, could destroy our carefully laid plans and nullify our most determined efforts.

Still, it was not these things that entered our minds. Rather it was the thought of the "Hump," and how we should fare with it.

Soon after passing the crevasses we picked up again the vast escarpment to the right. More clearly than before we saw the white-blue streams of many glaciers discharging into the Barrier, and several of the inner and higher snow-clad peaks glistened so brightly in the sun as to seem like volcanoes in eruption.

Our altitude was then about 1500 feet.

Now the Queen Maud Range loomed ahead. I searched again for the "appearance of land" to the east. Still the rolling Barrier—nothing else.

The quartering wind from the southeast blew with fluctuating direction and velocity, imparting an angle of drift as high as 20° at times.

At 8:15 o'clock we had the Geological Party in sight—a cluster of little beetles about two dark topped tents. Balchen dropped to an altitude of about 750 feet, and McKinley put overboard the photographs of the Queen Maud Range and the other things we had promised to bring. The parachute canopy to which they were attached fluttered open and fell in gentle oscillations, and we saw two or three figures rush out to catch it. We waved to them, and then prepared for a settlement of the issue at the "Hump."

Up to this time the engines had operated continuously at cruising revolutions—1580 R.P.M.'s for the big center engine, 1600 for the smaller engines outboard. Now Balchen opened them full throttle—1750 R.P.M.'s for the center engine, 1700 for the two outboard—and the Ford girded its loins for the long, hard, fighting pull over the "Hump." We rose steadily. We were then about 60 miles north of the western portal of Axel Heiberg, and holding our course steadily on meridian 163° 45′ W. with the sun compass.

I watched the altimeters, of which there were two in the navigation compartment. The fingers marched with little jumps across the face of the dial—3000 feet, 3500, 4000, 4500. The Ford had her toes in, and was climbing fast.

Drawing nearer, we had edged 30° to the west of South, to bring not only Axel Heiberg but also Liv's into view. This was a critical period. I was by no means certain which I should choose. I went forward and took a position behind Balchen. We would figure this thing out together.

The schemes and hopes of the next few minutes were beset by many probabilities. Which would it be—Axel Heiberg or Liv's Glacier?

There was this significant difference between flying and sledging: we could not pause long for decision or investigation. Minutes stood for gasoline, and gasoline was precious. The waste of so little as half an hour of fuel in a fruitless experiment might well overturn the mathematical balance on which the success of the flight depended. The execution of the plan hung on the proper judgment of the route over the "Hump."

True, we had a 40 percent safety factor over fuel needs to the Pole and back. This, of course, was a theoretical margin. It was a precaution against depletion resulting from head winds, and its value could not be weakened by a mistake in judgment. In fact, head winds had already exhausted some of this reserve.

Yet how well, after all, could judgment forecast the ultimate result? There were few facts on which we might base a wise decision. We knew, for example, that the highest point of the pass of Axel Heiberg Glacier which Amundsen reported was 10,500 feet. We would know, in a very few minutes, after June had calculated the gasoline consumption, the weight of the plane. From that we could determine, according to the tables which we had worked out and were then before me, the approximate ceiling we would have. We would know, too, whether or not we should be able to complete the flight, other conditions being favorable.

These were the known elements. The unknown were burdened with equally important consequences. The structural nature of the head of the pass was of prime importance. We knew from Amundsen's descriptions and from what we could see with our own eyes, that the pass was surrounded by towering peaks on each side, extending much higher than the maximum altitude of the heavily loaded plane. But whether the pass was wide or narrow; whether it would allow us room to maneuver in case we could not rise above it; whether it would be narrow and running with a torrent of down-pressing wind which would dash a plane, already hovering at its peak of maximum efficiency, to the glacier floor—these were things, naturally, we could not possibly know until the issue was directly at hand.

I stood beside Balchen, carefully studying the looming fortress, still wondering by what means we should attempt to carry it. With a gesture of the hand Balchen pointed to fog vapor rising from the black rock of the foothills which were Nansen's high priests—caused no doubt by the condensation of warm currents of air radiated from the sun-heated rocks. A thin layer of cloud seemed to cap Axel Heiberg's pass, and extended almost to Liv's Glacier. But of this we were not certain. Perhaps it was the surface of the snow. If cloud, then our difficulties were at hand. Even high clouds would be resting on the floor of the uplifted plateau.

There was, then, a gamble in the decision. Doubtless a flip of the coin would have served as well. In the end, we decided to choose Liv's Glacier, the unknown pass to the right, which Amundsen had seen far in the distance and named after Dr. Nansen's daughter. It seemed to be wider than Axel Heiberg, and the pass not quite as high.

A few minutes after nine o'clock we passed near the intermediate base, which of course we could not see. Our altitude was then about 9000 feet. At 9:15 o'clock we had the eastern portal on our left, and were ready to tackle the "Hump." We had discussed the "Hump" so often, had anticipated and maligned it so much, that now that it was in front of us and waiting in the flesh—in rock-ribbed glaciated reality—we felt that we were meeting an old acquaintance. But we approached it warily, respectfully, climbing steadily all the while with our maximum power, to get a better view of its none too friendly visage.

June, wholly unaffected by the immediate perplexities, went about his job of getting the plane in fighting trim. He ripped open the last of the fuel cans, and poured the contents into the main tank. The empty tins he dropped overboard, through the trap door. Every tin weighed two pounds; and every pound dropped was to our advantage. The fumes filled the cabin, offending one's stomach and eyes. June examined the gauges of the five wing tanks, then measured with a graduated stick the amount of fuel in the main tank. He jotted the figures on a pad, made a few calculations and handed me the results. Consumption had thus far averaged between 55 and 60 gallons per hour. It had taken us longer to reach the mountains than we had expected, owing to head winds. However, the extra fuel taken aboard just before we left had absorbed this loss and we actually had a credit balance. We had, then, enough gasoline to take us to the Pole and back.

With that doubt disposed of, we went at the "Hump" confidently.

We were still rising, and the engines were pulling wonderfully well. The wind was about abeam, and, according to my calculations, not materially affecting the speed.

Liv's Glacier was before us almost in its full sweeping entirety—a Niagric torrent doomed to rigidity, with frozen whirlpools and waterfalls. Far ahead it bent in a wide curve to the west of south. About thirty-five miles away it disappeared into a vague white surface—could it be the plateau? We then had nearly the whole of Nansen's foothills on the left. One of these formed the eastern portal of Liv's Glacier. When we first saw them on the base-laying flight, they had seemed to be high and imposing mountains; but now they were obscure and small. Nansen was on the left, to the southeast, and filled the horizon. The marbled walls of Fisher Mountain, with its company of stalwart foothills, was on the right, crowding into the horizon on the southwest. The ice line of the glacier, where it met the Barrier, was quite distinct; but the immense crevasses which we had seen before were softened and subdued by the difference in altitude, and now resembled the fluted surface of a washing board.

The floor of the glacier rose sharply, in a series of ice falls and terraces, some of which were well above the (then) altitude of the plane. These glacial waterfalls, some of which were from 200 to 400 feet high, seemed more beautiful than any precipitous stream I have ever seen. Beautiful yes, but how rudely and with what finality they would deal with steel and duralumin that was fated to collide with them at 100 miles per hour.

About ten miles up, the glacier was given over to terrific crevasses, where the weight of the flow carried it against solid rock.

At this point the stream of air pouring down the pass roughened perceptibly. The great wing shivered and teetered as it balanced it-

293

self against the changing pressures. The wind from the left flowed against Fisher's steep flanks, and the constant, hammering bumps made footing uncertain. But McKinley steadily trained his 50-pound camera on the mountains to the left. The uncertainties of load and ceiling were not his concern. His only concern was photographs— photographs over which students and geographers might pore in the calm quiet of their studies. Had we gone down in a tailspin, I am sure that McKinley would have operated his camera all the way down.

The altimeters showed a height of 9600 feet, but the figure was not necessarily exact. More likely than not, the barometric principle on which it operated was influenced by local changes in pressure. Nevertheless there were indications we were near the service ceiling of the plane.

The roughness of the air increased and became so violent that we were forced to swing slightly to the left, in search of calmer air. This brought us over a frightfully crevassed slope which ran up and toward Mount Nansen. We thus escaped the turbulent swirl about Fisher, but the down-surging currents here damped our climb. To the left we had the "blind" mountain glacier of Nansen in full view; and when we looked ahead we saw the plateau—a smooth, level plain of snow between Nansen and Fisher. The pass rose up to meet it.

In the center of the pass was a massive outcropping of snow-covered rock, resembling an island, which protruded above and separated the descending stream of ice. Perhaps it was a peak or the highest eminence of a ridge connecting Fisher and Nansen which had managed through the ages to hold its head above the glacial torrent pouring down from the plateau. But its particular structure or relationship was of small moment then. I watched it only with reference to the climb of the plane; and realized, with some disgust and more consternation, that the nose of the plane, in spite of the fact that Balchen had steepened the angle of attack, did not rise materially above the outcropping. We were still climbing, but at a rapidly diminishing rate of speed. In the rarefied air the heavy plane responded to the controls with marked sluggishness.

It was an awesome thing, creeping (so it seemed) through the narrow pass, with the black walls of Nansen and Fisher on either side, higher than the level of the wings, watching the nose of the ship bob up and down across the face of that lone chunk of rock. It would move up, then slide down. Then move up, and fall off again. For perhaps a minute or two we deferred the decision; but there was no escaping it. If we were to risk a passage through the pass, we needed greater maneuverability than we had at that moment. The pass was uncomfortably narrow. Once we entered it there would be no retreat. It offered no room for turn. If power was lost momentarily or if the air became excessively rough, we could only go ahead, or down. We needed power, and there was only one way in which to get it.

June, anticipating the command, left the radio and put his hand on the dump valve of the main tank. A pressure of the fingers—that was all that was necessary—and in two minutes 600 gallons of gasoline would gush out. I signalled to wait.

Balchen held to the climb to the last degree of safety. But it was clear to both of us that he could not hold it long enough. Balchen began to yell and gesticulate, and it was hard to catch the words in the roar of the engines echoing from the cliffs on either side. But the meaning was manifest. "Overboard—overboard—200 pounds!"

Which would it be—gasoline or food?

If gasoline, I thought, we might as well stop there and turn back. We could never get back to the base from the Pole. If food, the lives of all of us would be jeopardized in the event of a forced landing. Was that fair to McKinley, Balchen and June? It really took only a moment to reach the decision. The Pole, after all, was our objective. I knew the character of the three men. They were not so lightly to be turned aside. McKinley, in fact, had already hauled one of the food bags to the trap door. It weighed 125 pounds.

"Harold, a bag of food overboard," I said to June. He signalled to McKinley. The brown bag was pushed out and fell, spinning, to the glacier. The improvement in the flying qualities of the plane was noticeable. The Floyd Bennett took another breath and renewed the climb.

Now the down-currents over Nansen became stronger. The plane trembled and rose and fell, as if struck bodily. We veered a trifle to the right, searching for helpful rising eddies. The issue was still in doubt and Balchen's irritation with the inexorable laws which limited our altitude waxed and grew profane. The head of the pass was still on a level with the plane's line of flight. Balchen was flying shrewdly. He maintained flight at a sufficient distance below the absolute ceiling of the plane to retain at all times enough maneuverability to make him master of the ship. But he was hard pressed by circumstances; and I realized that unless the plane was further lightened, the final thrust might bring us perilously close to the end of our reserve.

"More," Bernt shouted. "Another bag."

McKinley shoved a second bag through the trap door, and this time we saw it hit the glacier, and scatter in a soundless explosion. Two hundred and fifty pounds of food—enough to feed four men for a month—lay on that lifeless waste.

The sacrifice was the saving factor. The plane, literally, rose with a jump; the engines dug in and we soon showed a gain in altitude of from 300 to 400 feet. It was what we wanted. We would clear the pass with about 500 feet to spare. Balchen gave a shout of joy. It was just as well. We could dump no more food. There was nothing left to dump except McKinley's camera. I am sure that had he been asked to put it overboard, he would have done so instantly; and I am equally sure he would have followed the precious instrument with his own body.

The next few minutes dragged. We moved at a speed of 77 nautical miles per hour through the pass, with the black walls of Nansen on our left. The wing gradually lifted above them. The floor of the plateau stretched in a white immensity to the south. We were over the dreaded "Hump" at last. The Pole lay dead ahead over the horizon, less than 300 miles away. It was then about 9:45 o'clock (I did not note the exact time. There were other things to think about).

Gaining the plateau, we studied the situation a moment and then shifted course to the southward. Nansen's enormous towering ridge, lipped by the plateau, shoved its heavily broken sides into the sky. To the right of it Ruth Gade's tented arch gradually became, as we watched, a white inverted porcelain bowl. A whole chain of mountains began to parade across the eastern horizon. How high they are I cannot say, but surely many of them must be in excess of 15,000 feet, to stand so boldly above the rim of the 10,000 foot plateau. Peak on peak, ridge on ridge, draped in snow garments which brilliantly reflected the sun, they extended in a solid array to the southeast. But can one really say they run in that direction? The lines of direction are so bent in this region that 150 miles farther on, even were they to continue in the same general straight line, they must run north of east. This is what happens near the Pole.

However, such preoccupations did not bother us then. We were on a flight of discovery, and wanted to see things and record them. To bring them nearer, we had soon edged the course slightly to the east of the southern course we had taken. McKinley's camera, which had never ceased to operate, trained on them, taking a succession of oblique, overlapping mapping photographs. Far to the left I made out what appeared to be the largest glacier we had yet seen, discharging into the new range we had first observed on the base-laying flight.

We laid our line of flight on the 171st meridian.

On the right was a range, which appeared to trend to the south nearly to 87° and more or less parallel to and perhaps a little beyond the 180th meridian—a line of low-hung peaks standing above the swelling folds of the plateau. Now, with the full panorama before us, in all its appalling ruggedness and gothic massiveness, we had a conception of the ice age in its flood tide. Here was the core, the center point of the Antarctic ice sheet. How deep it lay under us, whether 1,000 feet or 8,000 feet, we could not tell. But deep it must be, thus to dominate nearly all but the highest peaks which rimmed it, like the walls of a dam. Seeking an outlet to relieve its incalculable pressures, it presses through the passes which become glacial spillways, and makes for the sea. The parade of the mountains, the contrast of black and white, the upreaching peaks and the trisulcated troughs of the glaciers, the plateau spreading to an illusory horizon—it was something never to be forgotten.

The plateau seemed to be falling in a slope to the south. Our altitude was then between 10,500 and 11,000 feet. We were "riding" the engines, conscious of the fact that if one should fail we must come down. Once the starboard engine did sputter a bit, and Balchen nosed down while June rushed to the fuel valves. But it was nothing; to conserve fuel, Balchen had "leaned" the mixture too much. A quick adjustment corrected the fault, and in a moment the engine took up its steady rhythm. Moments like this one make a pioneering flight anything but dull; one moment everything is lovely, and the next is full of forebodings.

The drift indicator showed a variable wind from the east. To compensate for it, we had to point the nose of the plane an average of about 12° to the east, in order to steer a straight course for the Pole. The influence of the drift on the course was always a bothersome element. It had to be watched carefully, and any change in the angle of drift detected at once, so as to make good a straight course south. Fitted in the floor of the plane was a drift indicator which McKinley used in connection with his photographic work, and during the flight he constantly checked the drift with me. Whenever I noted any change in the direction or strength of the wind, I would steady Balchen on his course with the sun compass, first shaking the trolley line to attract his attention, then waving him on to the new course.

The basis of these calculations was the ground speed; and owing to the impossibility of determining the height of the plane above the snow, this value was not easily accessible. The altimeters register altitudes, only in reference to sea level. There is a way, however. By timing with a stop watch how long it takes a crevasse, sastrugi or smoke bomb to run the length of the drift indicator wire in the floor of the plane, and then turning north and passing over the object again, timing it a second time, it is possible by mathematics to get the speed.

Consequently, I spent a great deal of time kneeling on the floor of the plane, sighting sastrugi whenever I detected any change in drift. It was by no means a comfortable position. The temperature had dropped steadily since we reached the plateau, and when I opened the trap door a torrent of sub-zero atmosphere swirled in, numbing my face and hands.

These readings showed that while the engines were cruising at about 100 miles per hour, the plane was actually moving over the snow at the rate of 90 statute miles per hour.

The character of the plateau surface varied from time to time. There were stretches of smooth, soft snow, colonies of domed hay-cocks and arrow-headed sastrugi. To have been forced down in these latter areas would have been as dangerous as being forced down in a rock-strewn field. From the time we reached the plateau its level appeared to fall gently toward the Pole; the altimeter showed that the Ford was maintaining a fairly steady ceiling at approximately 11,000 feet, and the plateau fell farther below.

While the mountains on the left were still in view, I attempted to shoot the sun with the sextant to get its altitude. This would give us a sun line which would cut our line of flight and at the point of intersection tell us what the sun had to say about our progress. The air, however, was slightly rough; the powerful center engine, laboring to keep the heavy load at an altitude of two miles, produced a weaving in the plane; and the most patient efforts failed to bring the sun and the bubble together long enough for a dependable sight. This was bothersome, but relatively unimportant at the time. We were quite confident as to the accuracy of the dead reckoning, and hoped that conditions would improve in the vicinity of the Pole.

From time to time June "spelled" Balchen at the controls; and Balchen would walk back to the cabin, flexing his cramped muscles. There was little thought of food in any of us—a beef sandwich, stiff as a board, and tea and coffee from a thermos bottle. It was difficult to believe that in recent history the most resolute men who had ever attempted to carry a remote objective, Scott and Shackleton, had plodded over this same plateau, a few miles each day, with hunger— fierce, unrelenting hunger stalking them every step of the way.

Between 11:30 and 12:30 o'clock the mountains to the eastward began to disappear, gradually of course, dropping imperceptibly out of view, one after another. Not long after 12:30 o'clock the whole range had retreated from vision, and the plateau met the horizon in an indefinite line. The mountains to the right had long since disappeared.

At 12:38 o'clock I finally shot the sun. It hung, a ball of fire, just beyond *south* to the east, 21° above the horizon. So it was quite low, and we stared it in the eye. The sight gave me an approximate line of latitude, which placed us very near our position as calculated by dead reckoning. That dead reckoning and astronomy should check so closely was very encouraging. The position line placed us at Lat. 89° 4½' S., or 55½ miles from the Pole. A short time later we reached an altitude of 11,000 feet. According to Amundsen's records, the plateau, which had risen to 10,300 feet, descended here to 9,600 feet. We were, therefore, about 1400 feet above the plateau.

So the Pole, the mysterious objective, was actually in sight. But I could not yet spare it so much as a glance. Chronometers, drift indicators and compasses are hard task-masters.

Relieved by June, Balchen came aft and reported that visibility was not as good as it had been. Clouds were gathering on the horizon off the port bow and a storm, Balchen thought, was in the air. A storm was the last thing we wanted to meet on the plateau on the way back. It would be difficult enough to pass the Queen Maud Range in bright sunlight; in thick weather it would be suicidal. Conditions, however, were merely unpromising: not really bad, simply not good. If worse came to worse, we decided we could out-race the clouds to the mountains.

At six minutes after one o'clock, a sight of the sun put us a few miles ahead of our dead reckoning position. We were very close now. The sight was a check, but I depended more on the previous sight. At 1:14 o'clock, Greenwich Civil Time, our calculations showed that we were at the Pole.

We turned right and flew three or four miles. Had we turned right just before reaching the Pole, one could say that we had turned westward; but having reached the Pole we really turned northward, because all directions at the South Pole are north. We now reversed our direction, which had been northward, and flew toward the Pole again. Our direction then was southward, although at right angles to our previous line of course, which was also southward. It is difficult, therefore, to speak of directions during these maneuvers. For example, the moment we crossed the Pole again after this second change of course our direction, which had been southward, instantly became northward, although we were still on the same straight line.

We continued on the same straight line of flight for about six miles, and this took the plane about three miles beyond the original line of flight we had followed from the mountains. Then we cut diagonally across an extension of our line of flight, which we hit five miles beyond the Pole. At 1:25 o'clock we turned back—toward the Pole and Little America.

It is a confusing place, this imaginary point, the South Pole. All the time meridians converge there. A person unfortunate enough to be living in the vicinity would have difficulty in telling just what time to keep. Time is reckoned by the interval between two successive crossings of the sun over the meridian at the place at which the time is reckoned. As all meridians intersect at the South Pole, there is no particular meridian. The sun circles the sky at the same height above the snow horizon, and this height changes only an imperceptible amount every twenty-four hours. Directions, as we reckon them, would likewise mean nothing to this unfortunate creature. For unless he were travelling either north or south, it would be impossible for him to walk in a straight line and still retain the same direction. His direction would change noticeably every few minutes; and to keep his original direction he would be forced to follow a spiral course.

A few minutes after the turn I opened the trap door and dropped over the calculated position of the Pole the small flag which was weighted with the stone from Bennett's grave. Stone and flag plunged down together. The flag had been advanced 1,500 miles farther south than it had ever been before our expedition reached the Antarctic. June radioed the following message to Little America: "My calculations indicate that we have reached the vicinity of the South Pole. Flying high for a survey. Byrd."

The altimeters indicated our altitude as 11,000 feet.

For a few seconds we stood over the spot where Amundsen had stood, December 14, 1911; and where Scott had also stood, 34 days later, reading the note which Amundsen had left for him. In their honor, the flags of their countries were again carried over the Pole. There was nothing now to mark that scene; only a white desolation and solitude disturbed by the sound of our engines. The Pole lay in the center of a limitless plain. No mountains were visible. In the direction of Little America visibility was good, and so it was on the left. But to the right, which is to say to the eastward, the horizon was covered with clouds. If mountains lay there, as some geologists believe, they were concealed and we had no hint of them.

And that, in brief, is all there is to tell about the South Pole. One gets there, and that is about all there is for the telling. It is the effort to get there that counts.

We put the Pole behind us and raced for home.

□ *Byrd's accomplishments on his first expedition left him conscious of the magnitude of the work yet to be done. The economic exuberance of 1928, though, had given way to bleak depression by* the time Byrd began raising funds in 1933 for a second Antarctic venture. Private subscriptions brought in only $150,000. Byrd was able to borrow much of the needed equipment in return for commercial sponsorship, a necessary resort that gave the new expedition an oddly corporate flavor. In January, 1934, Byrd's vessels moored at the Ross Ice Shelf. Little America was clogged with four years' deposits of drift snow; the base was dug out, and a new one, Little America II, superimposed on the original buildings. Once again, there were aircraft (including a helicopter), radio transmitters, and many of the comforts of home. The Little America dairy even boasted three cows and a bull.

The achievements of Byrd's second expedition were impressive. A sledging team entered Marie Byrd Land and discovered an oasis of warmth, with flowing streams and ice stained by the presence of algae. Other groups penetrated unknown territory in westerly directions, while Byrd himself made flying trips to the still unexplored interior of the continent.

The most dramatic exploit of all was Byrd's winter-long vigil of solitude in a cabin 123 miles south of Little America. Originally, Byrd had intended to have two companions in this lonely outpost, where weather observations would be taken through the long night of winter. It proved impossible to get supplies for three men to the cabin before winter arrived; and, on the theory that two men sharing the cabin for the winter would grate intolerably on each other's nerves, he chose to perform the tour of duty alone. It meant seven months of the most absolute isolation possible.

Byrd settled in for the winter on March 28, 1934. His tasks were routine, and he withstood the solitude and silence well. But in May his health began to fail. He found that a faulty stove burner was letting carbon-monoxide fumes into the cabin. He repaired the stove and patched the cracks in the hut walls. But at the end of May, he suffered an attack of gas poisoning caused by a malfunction in his gasoline-powered radio generator, and just barely managed to shut the generator down before the fumes took his life. That episode is described in the account reprinted here. Never in sound health after his gas poisoning, Byrd did his best to conceal his predicament from the men at Little America, fearing that they would attempt a dangerous midwinter rescue mission if they knew his troubles. As his mes-

*sages grew more erratic, it became apparent that something was amiss, and in July Byrd's second-in-command, Dr. Thomas Poulter, set out to reach the winter outpost. Not until August 10, after several abortive starts, did the rescue party succeed in getting to Byrd; he was so weak that the rescuers had to remain with him at the base for two months before he could be taken back to Little America.*

*Byrd's own description of his ordeal appeared as* Alone, *by Richard E. Byrd (New York, G. P. Putnam's Sons, 1938). The section that follows is reprinted from that book by permission of the publishers.*  □

# BYRD'S SECOND EXPEDITION

[May, 1934]. Out of the cold and out of the east came the wind. It came on gradually, as if the sheer weight of the cold were almost too much to be moved. On the night of the 21st the barometer started down. The night was black as a thunderhead when I made my first trip topside; and a tension in the wind, a bulking of shadows in the night indicated that a new storm center was forming. Next morning, glad of an excuse to stay underground, I worked a long time on the Escape Tunnel by the light of a red candle standing in a snow recess. That day I pushed the emergency exit to a distance of twenty-two feet, the farthest it was ever to go. My stint done, I sat down on a box, thinking how beautiful was the red of the candle, how white the rough-hewn snow. Soon I became aware of an increasing clatter of the anemometer cups. Realizing that the wind was picking up, I went topside to make sure that everything was secured. It is a queer experience to watch a blizzard rise. First there is the wind, rising out of nowhere. Then the Barrier unwrenches itself from quietude; and the surface, which just before had seemed as hard and polished as metal, begins to run like a making sea. Sometimes, if the wind strikes hard, the drift comes across the Barrier like a hurrying white cloud, tossed hundreds of feet in the air. Other times the growth is gradual. You become conscious of a general slithering movement on all sides. The air fills with tiny scraping and sliding and rustling sounds as the first loose crystals stir. In a little while they are moving as solidly as an incoming tide, which creams over the ankles, then surges to the waist, and finally is at the throat. I have walked in drift so thick as not to be able to see a foot ahead of me; yet, when I glanced up, I could see the stars shining through the thin layer just overhead.

Smoking tendrils were creeping up the anemometer pole when I finished my inspection. I hurriedly made the trapdoor fast, as a sailor might batten down a hatch; and knowing that my ship was well secured, I retired to the cabin to ride out the storm. It could not reach me, hidden deep in the Barrier crust; nevertheless the sounds came down. The gale sobbed in the ventilators, shook the stovepipe until I thought it would be jerked out by the roots, pounded the roof with sledge-hammer blows. I could actually feel the suction effect through the pervious snow. A breeze flickered in the room and the tunnels. The candles wavered and went out. My only light was the feeble storm lantern.

Even so, I didn't have any idea how really bad it was until I went aloft for an observation. As I pushed back the trapdoor, the drift met me like a moving wall. It was only a few steps from the ladder to the instrument shelter, but it seemed more like a mile. The air came at me in snowy rushes; I breasted it as I might a heavy surf. No night had ever seemed so dark. The beam from the flashlight was choked in its throat; I could not see my hand before my face.

My windproofs were caked with drift by the time I got below. I had a vague feeling that something had changed while I was gone, but what, I couldn't tell. Presently I noticed that the shack was appreciably colder. Raising the stove lid, I was surprised to find that the fire was out, though the tank was half full. I decided that I must have turned off the valve unconsciously before going aloft; but, when I put a match to the burner, the draught down the pipe blew out the flame. The wind, then, must have killed the fire. I got it going again, and watched it carefully.

The blizzard vaulted to gale force. Above the roar the deep, taut thrumming note of the radio antenna and the anemometer guy wires reminded me of wind in a ship's rigging. The wind direction trace turned scratchy on the sheet; no doubt drift had short-circuited the electric contacts, I decided. Realizing that it was hopeless to attempt to try to keep them clear, I let the instrument be. There were other ways of getting the wind direction. I tied a handkerchief to a bamboo pole and ran it through the outlet ventilator; with a flashlight I could tell which way the cloth was whipped. I did this at hourly intervals, noting any change of direction on the sheet. But by 2 o'clock in the morning I had had enough of this periscope sighting. If I expected to sleep and at the same time maintain the continuity of the records, I had no choice but to clean the contact points.

The wind was blowing hard then. The Barrier shook from the concussions overhead; and the noise was as if the entire physical world were tearing itself to pieces. I could scarcely heave the trap-door open. The instant it came clear I was plunged into a blinding smother. I came out crawling, clinging to the handle of the door until I made sure of my bearings. Then I let the door fall shut, not wanting the tunnel filled with drift. To see was impossible. Millions of tiny pellets exploded in my eyes, stinging like BB shot. It was even hard to breathe, because snow instantly clogged the mouth and nostrils. I made my way toward the anemometer pole on hands and knees, scared that I might be bowled off my feet if I stood erect; one false step and I should be lost forever.

I found the pole all right; but not until my head collided with a cleat. I managed to climb it, too, though ten million ghosts were tearing at me, ramming their thumbs into my eyes. But the errand was useless. Drift as thick as this would mess up the contact points as quickly as they were cleared; besides, the wind cups were spinning so fast that I stood a good chance of losing a couple of fingers in the process. Coming down the pole, I had a sense of being whirled violently through the air, with no control over my movements. The trapdoor was completely buried when I found it again, after scraping around for some time with my mittens. I pulled at the handle, first with one hand, then with both. It did not give. It's a tight fit, anyway, I mumbled to myself. The drift has probably wedged the corners. Standing astride the hatch, I braced myself and heaved with all my strength. I might just as well have tried hoisting the Barrier.

Panic took me then, I must confess. Reason fled. I clawed at the three-foot square of timber like a madman. I beat on it with my fists, trying to shake the snow loose; and, when that did no good, I lay flat on my belly and pulled until my hands went weak from cold and weariness. Then I crooked my elbow, put my face down, and said over and over again, You damn fool, you damn fool. Here for weeks

I had been defending myself against the danger of being penned inside the shack; instead, I was now locked out; and nothing could be worse, especially since I had only a wool parka and pants under my windproofs. Just two feet below was sanctuary—warmth, food, tools, all the means of survival. All these things were an arm's length away, but I was powerless to reach them.

There is something extravagantly insensate about an Antarctic blizzard at night. Its vindictiveness cannot be measured on an anemometer sheet. It is more than just wind: it is a solid wall of snow moving at gale force, pounding like surf.[1] The whole malevolent rush is concentrated upon you as upon a personal enemy. In the senseless explosion of sound you are reduced to a crawling thing on the margin of a disintegrating world; you can't see, you can't hear, you can hardly move. The lungs gasp after the air sucked out of them, and the brain is shaken. Nothing in the world will so quickly isolate a man.

Half-frozen, I stabbed toward one of the ventilators, a few feet away. My mittens touched something round and cold. Cupping it in my hands, I pulled myself up. This was the outlet ventilator. Just why, I don't know—but instinct made me kneel and press my face against the opening. Nothing in the room was visible, but a dim patch of light illuminated the floor, and warmth rose up to my face. That steadied me.

Still kneeling, I turned my back to the blizzard and considered what might be done. I thought of breaking in the windows in the roof, but they lay two feet down in hard crust, and were reinforced with wire besides. If I only had something to dig with, I could break the crust and stamp the windows in with my feet. The pipe cupped between my hands supplied the first inspiration; maybe I could use that to dig with. It, too, was wedged tight; I pulled until my arms ached, without budging it; I had lost all track of time, and the despairing thought came to me that I was lost in a task without an end. Then I remembered the shovel. A week before, after leveling drift from the last light blow, I had stabbed a shovel handle up in the crust

[1] Because of this blinding, suffocating drift, in the Antarctic winds of only moderate velocity have the punishing force of full-fledged hurricanes elsewhere. [Byrd's note.]

306

somewhere to leeward. That shovel would save me. But how to find it in the avalanche of the blizzard?

I lay down and stretched out full length. Still holding the pipe, I thrashed around with my feet, but pummeled only empty air. Then I worked back to the hatch. The hard edges at the opening provided another grip, and again I stretched out and kicked. Again no luck. I dared not let go until I had something else familiar to cling to. My foot came up against the other ventilator pipe. I edged back to that, and from the new anchorage repeated the maneuver. This time my ankle struck something hard. When I felt it and recognized the handle, I wanted to caress it.

Embracing this thrice-blessed tool, I inched back to the trapdoor. The handle of the shovel was just small enough to pass under the little wooden bridge which served as a grip. I got both hands on the shovel and tried to wrench the door up; my strength was not enough, however. So I lay down flat on my belly and worked my shoulders under the shovel. Then I heaved, the door sprang open, and I rolled down the shaft. When I tumbled into the light and warmth of the room, I kept thinking, How wonderful, how perfectly wonderful.

My wrist watch had stopped; the chronometers showed that I had been gone just under an hour. The stove had blown out again, but I did not bother to light it. Enough warmth remained for me to undress. I was exhausted; it was all I could do to hoist myself into the bunk. But I did not sleep at first. The blizzard scuffled and pounded gigantically overhead; and my mind refused to drop the thought of what I might still be doing if the shovel hadn't been there. Still struggling, probably. Or maybe not. There are harder ways to die than freezing to death. The lush numbness and the peace that lulls the mind when the ears cease listening to the blizzard's ridiculous noise, could make death seem easy.

The wind was still blowing, but not so violently, when I awakened at 7 o'clock the next morning. Dressing in the yellow light of the storm lantern, I shivered in every bone. My clothes, rigid with frost, lay in a grotesque heap on the floor, exactly as they had fallen a few hours before; they crackled like paper when I put them on. Starting up the ladder, I thought glumly, It will be stuck again for sure.

Therefore, I had no misgivings at finding the door jammed. Armed with a saw, a shovel, alpine rope, and a lantern, I walked to the far end of the Escape Tunnel. It didn't take long to breach a hole in the roof, which was less than two feet thick at this point.

Before leaving the tunnel, I drove a stout stick into the roof, to which I made fast one end of the line. With the other end secured to my belt, I clambered to the surface over a ladder made of boxes. The drift was still heavy, but with a flashlight it was possible to see a yard or two. After a couple of false stabs I finally fetched the anemometer pole. The drift packed in the cups was almost as compact as cement; I cleaned them out and scraped the contact points. It was an abominable task; but it had to be done, because the fouling slowed down the cups and hence the wind-speed reading. Yet, after what I had been through the night before, there was little reason to complain.

For once "daily promenade" was missed. Every moment that could be spared from the instruments and my own personal needs was devoted to leveling drift around the shack. Luckily the new snow wasn't packed hard. I just shoveled it into the air and let the wind dissipate it to leeward. That done, I sealed off the breach in the Escape Tunnel with the sides of a couple of food boxes and reopened the hatch. The faint lightening in the gloom that came with midday was draining away; heavy shadows were pressing down through the ghostly billowing of drift. But the wind was spent; and so was the cold, temporarily. The temperature kited to 10° below. Safe in the bunk, I slept the sleep of a man who had been working a hundred years.

Thursday the 24th was unbelievably warm. At the 8 A.M. "ob" the maximum thermometer read 2° above zero. The wind still haunted the east; and puffs of drift came erratically from that quarter, thickening the steady fall of snow from the sky. I was nearly an hour late meeting the radio schedule, because the antenna had been blown down and I didn't find it out until after I had checked the transmitter and receiver. I made a hurried splice at a break and re-rigged the antenna temporarily on two poles. Dyer was still calling patiently when I made contact. My signals, he said, were weak but intelligible. Beyond discussing arrangements for me to participate in a special broadcast, we had little to talk about. At Little America the tempera-

308

ture was 25° above zero, and Bill Haines officially announced a "heat wave."

I was informed that on Saturday Little America was broadcasting a special program to the Chicago World Fair; would I mind adding my greetings? Certainly not. It was agreed that I should spell out in code, "Greetings from the bottom of the world," which message was to be picked up and relayed by Little America's more powerful transmitter. I reduced the message to dots and dashes and practiced religiously. When Saturday came, Charlie Murphy broke the news, just before the broadcast, that New York now wanted me to spell, "Antarctic greetings," instead. "I'm given to understand," he said sententiously, "they intend to translate the damn thing into fireworks."

"Let it be on their own heads, then," I said.

Charlie chuckled. "If the fireworks are supposed to spell out what you send, then Chicago is in for the wildest display since the Fire."

As excited as an actor making his debut, I sat at Advance Base listening to the broadcast from Little America; and, when somebody said, "We shall now attempt to make contact with Admiral Byrd," I reached for the key and worked it furiously. But it went for naught. Dyer reported a few minutes after that he had heard it clearly, but Chicago hadn't heard anything. "No doubt the fireworks went off anyway," he observed dryly.

Bill Haines's forecast of a "heat wave" was no jest. That afternoon the thermometer rose to 18° above zero—the second highest point it ever reached. The wind, dallying in the east, flooded the Barrier with warm air from the distant ocean. From then until the end of the month the coldest temperature recorded was 23° below zero; and most of the time it was above zero or close to it.[2] Snow fell in a relentless flutter; the Barrier became a concentrated gloom, except when the moon, fetched back on its fortnightly errand, was able to break through the cloud rack and bathe it briefly in an astringent light.

*May 25*—This is my sixty-fourth day at Advance Base, and it just

[2] Studied as a whole, the records show that May was not exactly a hot month. The cold passed 40° below zero 20 days out of the 31, crossed 50° below, 12 days; crossed 60° below, 3 days; and 70° below, 2 days. [Byrd's note.]

so happened that I had some leisure time. I have been taking advantage of this to think back over my stay here and take stock of my situation.

There are three things for which I am particularly thankful. The first is that my records so far are complete (though blotted and splotched a bit). The second is that my defenses are perfected, and the third is that I have become well adjusted to conditions—especially psychologically. I feel able now to withstand any assaults the beleaguering night may launch. Indeed, I look forward to the rest of my sojourn with pleasure.

Though I am not quite as heavy as when I came out here, I feel all right. I was probably a bit overweight, anyway. Perhaps the fumes have had something to do with the lost pounds, though because of my precautions I think I am getting less fumes than at first.

I am finding that life here has become largely a life of the mind. Unhurried reflection is a sort of companion. Yes, solitude is greater than I anticipated. My sense of values is changing, and many things which before were in solution in my mind now seem to be crystallizing. I am better able to tell what in the world is wheat for me and what is chaff. In fact, my definition of success itself is changing. Just lately my views about man and his place in the cosmic scheme have begun to run something like this:

If I had never seen a watch and should see one for the first time, I should be sure its hands were moving according to some plan and not at random. Nor does it seem any more reasonable for me to conceive that the precision and order of the universe is the product of blind chance. This whole concept is summed up in the word harmony. For those who seek it, there is inexhaustible evidence of an all-pervading intelligence.

The human race, my intuition tells me, is not outside the cosmic process and is not an accident. It is as much a part of the universe as the trees, the mountains, the aurora, and the stars. My reason approves this; and the findings of science, as I see them, point in the same direction. And, since man is a part of the cosmos and subject to its laws, I see no reason to doubt that these same natural laws operate in the psychological as well as in the physical sphere and that their operation is manifest in the workings of the consciousness.

Therefore, it seems to me that convictions of right and wrong, being, as they are, products of the consciousness, must also be formed in accordance with these laws. I look upon the conscience as the mechanism which makes us directly aware of them and their significance and serves as a link with the universal intelligence which gives them form and harmoniousness.

I believe further that the age-tested convictions of right and wrong, in which individual aberrations must have been largely canceled out, are as much a manifestation of cosmic law and intelligence as are all other phenomena.

Therefore, the things that mankind has tested and found right make for harmony and progress—or peace; and the things it has found wrong hinder progress and make for discord. The right things lead to rational behavior—such as the substitution of reason for force—and so to freedom. The wrong things lead to brute force and slavery.

But the peace I describe is not passive. It must be won. Real peace comes from struggle that involves such things as effort, discipline, enthusiasm. This is also the way to strength. An inactive peace may lead to sensuality and flabbiness, which are discordant. It is often necessary to fight to lessen discord. This is the paradox.

When a man achieves a fair measure of harmony within himself and his family circle, he achieves peace; and a nation made up of such individuals and groups is a happy nation. As the harmony of a star in its course is expressed by rhythm and grace, so the harmony of a man's life-course is expressed by happiness; this, I believe, is the prime desire of mankind.

"The universe is an almost untouched reservoir of significance and value," and man need not be discouraged because he cannot fathom it. His view of life is no more than a flash in time. The details and distractions are infinite. It is only natural, therefore, that we should never see the picture whole. But the universal goal—the attainment of harmony—is apparent. The very act of perceiving this goal and striving constantly toward it does much in itself to bring us closer and, therefore, becomes an end in itself.

Snow was still falling on Thursday the 31st. The morning was dreary and stagnant; the temperature about 5° above. The calendar warned: "Radio schedule." I went about the preparations methodi-

311

cally. Before me now are the messages which I dispatched to Little America that day. One was to Chief Pilot June and Navigator Rawson, reminding them to swing the planes for compass deviations. Another was to my wife, suggesting that she take up with my secretary, Miss McKercher, and my representatives in the United States ways and means of reducing the expedition's expenses.

Dyer took these messages down, then read them back. Poulter, he said, had already arrived in the radio shack in response to my summons. I had a long talk with him and Charlie Murphy over the proposed operations, and was particularly emphatic about the dangers from crevasses confronting the tractors. Poulter finished his business with me; and Charlie Murphy stayed to finish a few matters, one having to do with the engagement of an ice pilot for the *Jacob Ruppert* on her return voyage to Little America in December. We talked back and forth nearly an hour and a half. From my desk in the shack I could hear the engine in the tunnel; for some reason it started skipping. "Wait," I spelled out to Dyer. Unhooking the lantern, I went into the tunnel. The air was thick with exhaust gases. Thinking the mixture was at fault, I bent over the carburetor and tinkered with the needle valve. This had little effect. I remember straightening up. And that was the last conscious act of mine that I do remember. The next thing I recall, I was down on my hands and knees; and through the drowsiness, like an echo from far away, came an insistent notion that something terribly important ought to be done. What it was exactly my mind couldn't tell; and I felt helpless to do anything about it. I don't know how long I remained in that position. It may be that the cold aroused me. Anyhow, after a little while I crawled into the shack. The radio desk emerged from the blur, and then I remembered what I was supposed to do. I fumbled for the key and signed off, thinking how hard it was to spell out what I had to say. If any acknowledgment came, I did not hear it; for I couldn't get the earphones on.[3]

My actions thereafter are uncertain; I don't really know which were nightmare and which were fact. I remember lying on the bunk, fully dressed, and hearing, as if with surprise, the irregular beat of

[3] The radio log at Little America shows that twenty minutes or so elapsed between the time I said, "Wait" and the time I signed off, saying, "See you Sunday." This fixes approximately the interval I was in the tunnel. [Byrd's note.]

the engine in the tunnel and realizing that I must shut it off to escape asphyxiation. I rolled off the bunk and staggered to the door. Dizziness seized me, and my heart turned fantastic somersaults; but, as from a great distance, I could see the gray fumes of the exhaust smoke curling under the top sill; and the upper half of the tunnel, when I entered, was so foggy that I could not see as far as the alcove where the engine lay.

Very probably I dropped to my hands and knees, as I must have appreciated the necessity for keeping my head under the fumes and in the uncontaminated air near the floor. Anyhow, I was on my knees when I reached into the recess and threw the ignition switch. When I turned around, the light was gone in the doorway; this was puzzling until I recalled that the only light in the shack was the electric bulb over the radio desk, which burned only while the engine supplied current. Luckily the lantern was still burning on a box, where I had set it down before adjusting the engine. Pushing the lantern ahead of me, I crawled back to the shack and to the bunk.

Whatever did, in fact, occur during the rest of this last day in May, this I do know: that much of it was probably fantasy—a slow and wearying fantasy. Perhaps I did in truth roll off the bunk and try to replace the sheets on the register drum; else how to account for the vague recollection of seeing the glass frame on the floor some time in the afternoon. But the rest of it—the skyrocketing pain in my forehead and eyes, the nausea, the violent beating of my heart, the illusion of being a thin flame drawn between two voids—they could not have been real. Only the cold was real: the numbness in the hands and feet, creeping like a slow paralysis through my body. At least, I could cope with cold. I grasped for the throat of the sleeping bag, and eased in.

□   *Byrd returned to the Antarctic in 1940 for a brief third expedition, motivated as much by political considerations as by scientific ones. Many nations were claiming sections of Antarctica—France,*

New Zealand, Great Britain, Chile, Argentina, Norway, and others. Germany had made three landings in what was considered the Norwegian sector. With world tensions rising, Antarctica might prove to be of strategic importance in the coming war. The United States, while not recognizing any other national claims, and continuing to regard Antarctica as international territory, wished to establish semipermanent occupation of one zone which could be declared American if necessary. President Roosevelt set up a continuing U.S. Antarctic Service, and placed Byrd in command of an expedition to Marie Byrd Land, with joint government and private sponsorship.

The involvement of the United States in the war ended these activities for a while; from 1942 to 1945, Byrd served on active duty, but at the close of the war he began to organize his fourth expedition, under the Navy tag of Operation Highjump. It brought 4,000 men to the Antarctic—more than six times as many as had set foot there in the whole previous history of Antarctic exploration. This massive attack on the Antarctic marked the opening of a postwar era of discovery that would see the continent thronging with men of many nations and dotted with permanent bases.

On this expedition, Byrd made a second flight to the South Pole. No man had seen it since his flight in 1929. Aided by JATO—Jet-Assisted Take-Off—there were no problems of gaining altitude, and the flight was notable mainly for its ease of accomplishment.

During the International Geophysical Year of 1957-58, the United States was deeply committed to Antarctic research. A large-scale enterprise called Operation Deep Freeze had been organized in 1955, under Admiral Byrd's direction, and Byrd himself made a fifth Antarctic trip to see Deep Freeze through its early stages. He remained in Antarctica from late 1955 to early 1956; his participation in the expedition was vicarious from then until his death the following year.

During this final Antarctic visit, Byrd made a third flight to the South Pole. His brief description of it forms an interesting counterpart to his account of the first flight in 1929. It appeared in the article, "All-Out Assault on Antarctica," by Rear Admiral Richard E. Byrd, published in The National Geographic Magazine, August, 1956, and is reprinted here by kind permission of The National Geographic Society.  □

# BYRD'S LAST FLIGHT TO THE SOUTH POLE

To me, of course, my own flight to the Pole—my third—stands out with special vividness.

We took off from McMurdo Sound, and our first goal was the so-called "area of inaccessibility," the heart of the United States-size section of "East Antarctica" that, until this year's survey flights [1956], never had been seen by man. I also wanted to go to the South Pole to inspect the surface of the snow and névé there to get an idea of what conditions may be found by the plane, or planes, that will have to land the Pole Station construction personnel this fall.

With me rode Paul Siple, who has been asked to take charge of the U.S. base to be built at the Pole.

During the long flight we kept checking the navigator's headings with the same Bumstead sun compass we used in 1929. This simple but ingenious device was invented by Albert H. Bumstead, first Chief Cartographer of the National Geographic Society.

At a point 20 minutes beyond 85° S. and 90° E. we began to ice up and flew into a thickening whiteout. So we headed for the Pole, the visibility improving en route. Each time I've approached the Pole from a different direction. This time we came in along the 90th meridian, east.

It's quite easy to find the Pole when the sun is visible. Using the periscopic sextant, we took a true south heading. From tables we knew the angle of declination of the sun south of the Equator at the Pole for the day, January 8. When the sextant showed the sun's altitude above the horizon equal to its declination, we would be over the Pole.

The trouble was that broken clouds interfered with our sun fixes, and we overshot the Pole by 17 minutes. But we promptly back-tracked and soon hit our almost featureless target, hub of the vast flat snow field of the polar plateau.

Our altimeter reading, plus radar, confirmed the Pole's elevation at about 10,000 feet.

We circled the Pole three times, the first time any of us had made three round-the-world trips in 10 minutes. Naturally we kept crossing the international date line (180° east and west from Greenwich).

"How should we count this on per diem?" quipped Commander Ebbe, squadron CO along for the ride.

We dropped an American flag and a brown paper bag signed by all of us and stuffed into a piece of pipe. The crew chief threw out four pennies.

Pilots of other expedition aircraft had reported the Pole blanketed with snow so soft as to preclude a plane landing either on skis or on wheels. Our findings differed. We flew very low and concluded that the snow surface looked firm enough to land on. This was indicated by the crisscrossing and fan-tailed form of the sastrugi, or snowdrift pattern.

Our homeward flight track shadowed the route by which Captain Scott trekked back from the South Pole in 1912 and perished with his four companions.

What changes two generations had wrought! Where Scott and his ill-fated trail mates man-hauled heavy sleds, we rode past at three and a half miles a minute with the security of four engines and magical new electronic navigating equipment. Tea was served at intervals.

At the head of the majestic Beardmore glacier, route of both Scott and Shackleton to the polar plateau, we found the mountains bare over broad areas. And from the upper Beardmore, blue ponds, completely ice-free, winked up at us. Many of the bowl-like mountain cirques were empty of ice.

Paul Siple agreed with me that these features gave evidence of slight glacial withdrawal—or at least snow starvation—in this area. Certainly glaciers here once had greater extent.

At 10:30 on the evening of January 8 we landed smoothly at the Hut Point airstrip. In 11 hours and 10 minutes we had flown 2,310 miles. I had never before made a polar flight under such comfortable conditions.

□ *Among the many Antarctic expeditions of the postwar world was the first truly international one, a joint Norwegian-Swedish-British effort, directed by Captain John Giaever of the Norwegian Air Force. Captain Giaever, head of the Norwegian Polar Institute, had taken part in many Arctic explorations before becoming leader of this venture.*

*From January, 1950, to February, 1952, the members of this expedition studied conditions in the Norwegian sector of Antarctica, Queen Maud Land, on the continent's Atlantic side. One of the most interesting results of the work was the discovery of one of the "oases" of life scattered across Antarctica. This was found by a glaciological party that set out on December 18, 1950, under the leadership of Valter Schytt, the Swedish-born scientist who was the expedition's second-in-command.*

*The official account of the expedition was published as* The White Desert, *by John Giaever (London, Chatto & Windus, 1954). Included in the book are chapters by other members of the team, and the following extract, by Valter Schytt, describes the discovery of the "oasis." It is reprinted by permission of the publishers.* □

# THE NORWEGIAN-BRITISH-SWEDISH EXPEDITION

On the night of December 29 [1950] we drove on over a difficult surface. The fresh snow was lying loose and in some depth, with drifts of irregular size. Wilson went in front on skis all night, in order to find the best route. From time to time we saw the little cone-shaped hill that was our lodestar, but then it would disappear again from the horizon. At about two in the morning visibility became worse in the west, and soon we were in a snow-storm.

The blizzard went on into the New Year. Now that we were not tired out, had no torn stockings to mend and no notes to classify, time began to hang heavy on our hands. All New Year's Eve the wind was blowing at a speed of about forty miles per hour, but just after midnight the force of the storm began to lessen.

New Year's Eve, 1951, was not specially exciting or eventful for us. And yet I think that we had no regrets for our absence from celebrations at home in London, Oslo, Lund or Stockholm—for we had come to look upon this tent existence in the Antarctic as our normal way of life.

With the dawn came brilliant sunshine, and the next night we drove thirteen miles eastwards in heavy slush. But bad weather once more forced us to lie up for four days and nights, till on January 6 we set out again about midnight. There was something of a gale blowing still, and the snow flurries were rather a nuisance; but by this time we were heartily sick of inaction. Towards morning the wind dropped and the sky cleared. To the right of the hill which we were using as our guide we could see a clearly defined spur projecting from the Førstefjell ridge, and beyond it there was a broad depression that looked as if it might provide an excellent route southwards to the Advanced Base. More mountains now began to show along the horizon. A series of sharp peaks rose in the southeast, and, as we went on eastward, mountains and still more mountains came into view behind the spur.

It soon became apparent that the snow cover on this spur was not so massive as to prevent the emergence of seven rock outcrops over the ice-level. We decided to camp near one of these and collect some specimens of rock for the geologists, who would probably never reach these parts.

At a distance of a mile from the spur Wilson went ahead. The terrain looked smooth and even, but there was a good deal of fresh snow, so there might well be hidden crevasses in our path. At about five in the morning, for no obvious reason, I began to feel rather uneasy—perhaps because the long parallel drifts of fresh snow reminded one of crevasses. Or maybe it was that seventh sense—presentiment.

Suddenly the right runner on my sledge cut down into the snow and the sledge tumbled over on that side. With the help of the vertical handles on the sledge I managed to get the weight pushed over to the left runner, and in a few seconds the sledge was on firm ground. Wilson and I went back to look and the first thing we saw was a hole, between ten and fifteen inches wide, where the runner had cut through the snow. Looking down, we could see only a dark blue chasm. Evidently we had been driving parallel to a wide snow-covered crevasse. It was overlaid with drift snow, but on the right (farther) edge the bridge was weak; and here the runner had cut through. It was lucky that the other end of the bridge had been firm. The crevasse was at least seventy feet deep.

There was no reason to believe that this crevasse was an isolated instance, it was pretty sure to be on the fringe of an extensively crevassed area. So we drove back on to the ice shelf.

We now made straight for the little cone-shaped hill which for nearly a fortnight had been our landmark. About half a mile from the hill we entered a new crevasse area but came safely through it, and at about eight in the morning we made our camp within a few hundred yards of the hill. At one to two miles east of our hill there was another small nunatak, and it soon became clear that this must be what the Germans had called Boreas. The Boreas we had found was about 750 feet high, whereas the Germans' version was 2,500 feet. Theirs was situated at 70° 59' south, and our sun observations gave us an approximate latitude of 71° 18' south—i.e. 20 miles farther southward. In spite of those great discrepancies, we had no doubt at all that these hills were Boreas and Passat.

Swithinbank and Wilson went over to Passat to scan its surroundings from the summit. And now something strange occurred. They had hardly set foot on solid ground before they discovered that in places the hill was bright with lichens of various colours—black and white, yellow and grey, orange and red—an absolute jungle for people who had seen no plant life whatsoever throughout the year 1950. As well as the lichens, there was a green moss, almost luxuriant in growth and sometimes nearly an inch high.

With all this vegetation to be inspected, they took some time to reach the top, though the climb is an easy one. Once up there, Swithinbank began to take compass bearings, while Wilson sat on a rock to write down the figures. He whiled away the intervals by looking at some beautiful and curious small stones that lay around. Suddenly something moved across the stone he held in his hand. He took out the magnifying-glass, and the next moment was introduced to two species of settled inhabitants that spent their winters in Queen Maud Land. Wilson collected some and carried them to the tent and the microscope.

319

Meanwhile Melleby and I, tired out yet unable to sleep, could not understand why the other two were so long away. We grew more and more anxious, and rather annoyed when we thought of the night drive before us. But if we had felt any irritation, it vanished like mist before the sun when the others arrived back in the dusk of evening. Out came the microscope, and we sat for a long time studying the real inhabitants of this land. There were two kinds of mites or arachnids: the one red and swift in motion, the other moving only slowly or not at all. The red one was 0.11 millimetre wide and 0.24 millimetre long; while the brown one measured 0.25 × 0.5 millimetre.

Just after midnight three of us went across to Boreas again. With the binoculars we were able to see bright-hued lichens growing all the way up the slopes; but down at the foot of the hill, too, where Melleby and I now had our first sight of the Antarctic vegetation, there was a great deal of lichen. The rock faces were heavily scratched by ice, and we saw many fine examples of such striations. All this was important to glaciologists. There was no doubt, then, that the inland ice had been more massive at an earlier period, and certainly Boreas had once been entirely covered in ice. But it was equally certain that this had been the case only in a very remote past, and that the ice had not subsided in recent decades. For here were lichens growing all the way down to the ice edge, and we knew by experience of mountain areas in Scandinavia that the establishment of lichens on areas where the ice has disappeared is a relatively slow process. There is obviously no reason to believe that lichen would spread more rapidly in a severe Antarctic climate than in a temperate climate like that of Scandinavia.

On that morning, in other words, we established the fact that the general recession of the glaciers in the north has no direct counterpart in the inland ice of Queen Maud Land. Not until much later were we able to state that the inland ice itself is not increasing.

The radiation was now intense, and the dark rock ridges felt quite hot. We could hear, and occasionally see, water trickling down towards the small partially frozen puddles at the foot of the hill. This was an absolute oasis in the desert of ice, but in such an oasis neither we nor our dogs could eke out an existence.

□   *Nothing is more indicative of the revolution in Antarctic explo-*
*ration than the presence of a permanent base at the South Pole.*
*Until 1956, only one group of men had ever stood at the Pole and*
*returned to tell the tale—Amundsen and his companions in 1912.*
*On October 31, 1956, during Operation Deep Freeze, a Navy R4D*
*plane commanded by Rear Admiral George J. Dufek flew to the Pole*
*and landed there for forty-nine minutes. Three weeks later, the Pole*
*became a center of unaccustomed human activity when two dozen*
*Navy men arrived to set up the seven buildings of the permanent*
*polar outpost, named Amundsen-Scott Station.*

*In the Antarctic winter of 1957, eighteen Americans occupied*
*Amundsen-Scott Station. They were led by Dr. Paul A. Siple, a*
*geographer who has probably spent more time in Antarctica than*
*any other human being. In 1928, as a nineteen-year-old Eagle Scout,*
*he was chosen to accompany Byrd on his first expedition. Since then,*
*Dr. Siple has returned many times to Antarctica. His account of life*
*at Amundsen-Scott Station was published under the title of 90°*
*South (New York, G. P. Putnam's Sons, 1959). The excerpt from*
*that book which follows is reprinted by permission of the pub-*
*lishers.*   □

# DR. PAUL SIPLE

Then there was still another radio report. Moose Remington came
to me about three P.M. on March 12 [1957]. His face was clouded
and his eyes avoided mine. "What is it?" I asked him.

"I just heard the news over the Armed Forces Radio," he said
softly, "that Admiral Byrd died today in Boston."

A wave of sorrow swept over me though I tried to remain composed. "Of all the people in the United States," I told Moose, "Admiral Byrd was undoubtedly the most interested in what we were
doing here at the Pole." I felt numb.

321

Remington offered to lower the flag to half-mast on the barber-pole South Pole atop the garage, but I wanted to do this myself. When he left I wrote a message for Mrs. Byrd, Marie, Dick's loving helpmate:

> *My grief is as one of the family. I am here at the Pole largely because Dick wished it so. I will do my best to continue my job as he would want it to be done. Please accept my deepest sympathy for the loss of a loving husband, father, loyal comrade and one of our greatest American citizens.*
>
> *Affectionately,*<br>*PAUL*

The men one and all came around when they heard the news. But outside of a press on my shoulder and a "We understand how you feel," I was left to my own thoughts.

I finally went out and put the flag at half-mast. We would keep it flying thus until the sunset on March 22. And as the cold struck me and the wind rattled the flag, the full meaning of Dick's death slowly overtook me. This day I had lost my best friend.

I recalled the day I last spent with him and how he had given me the watch I was wearing. He had seemed to realize more than I that this was our last meeting. His eyes and voice on that occasion had revealed more sentiment than I had ever before witnessed. My mind flitted to Mrs. Byrd. How sad for Marie. She had spent many difficult hours worrying about him during his many flirtations with death, but she had been his strength—and he had known it and had never forgotten it.

A kaleidoscope of random episodes in our experiences together flashed before my eye: how he had wanted to take one last look at the Antarctic sky before leaving the continent during Operation Highjump; his fiery temper, which he rarely displayed; his graceful mastery of the art of living which was distinguishable even in the confines of Little America; his remarkable leadership abilities and his optimism; his willingness to withstand insults when he believed that the honor of the nation or the Navy was at stake; and his many kindnesses.

322

Nor was my sorrow alleviated the following day when I was handed a message Byrd had sent me shortly before his death.

*Delighted to learn all men safely at Pole and nearly all supplies in. Please convey my wholehearted congratulations to all hands at Station on their part in this splendid achievement. Am sending separate messages to Seabees and USAF. Confident that under your leadership scientific achievements will be significant contribution to over-all IGY Program. Regret I cannot be with your history-making sojourn. But at least the U.S. Antarctic Program will be represented in the person of my deputy. My best wishes to you and all the men. Please continue to keep me informed. Warmest regards.*

Hard work was the best way to keep from thinking about Byrd and I plunged back into our multitudinous physical activities. Before the new personnel had arrived, our small IGY contingent and Doc Taylor had completed 400 feet of the 1,000-foot geomagnetic and seismology tunnel. Now with a ten-man working party we went ahead at the rate of 100 feet a day. But even so this was not as swift as I had hoped, for I had not taken into consideration the fact that the air and snow temperatures were now almost identical, and compaction of the mixture of undersurface and surface snow did not result as easily as before when the temperatures had varied considerably.

By the close of Saturday, March 16, with the temperature at —76°, our tunnel diggers were within 150 feet of the tunnel end. Some of the men welcomed the opportunity to dig in the trench instead of standing in the raw wind to put up the abovesurface two feet of snow wall and then cover the three-foot-wide tunnel top with wood rafters and burlap.

On March 19 we finally completed the tunnel, but when I tried to take pictures to record this happy event I found my camera was frozen. We also dug two necessary pits, one about 20 feet off the tunnel at the 500-foot mark for the geomagnetic instrument, an oscillation-deflection type magnetometer which measured the changes in the declination and intensity of the magnetic field in all directions. This geomagnetic pit was ten feet deep, four feet wide and six feet long and was aligned along the magnetic meridian. The seismic pit at the end of the 1,000-foot tunnel was also ten feet deep, but was six feet wide and six feet long. Here we would later install a Benioff Vertical Seismometer to record seismic vibrations, or earthquake waves. About 25 feet from the seismic pit, we dug access stairs up and out to the south. As a last step Mel Havener drove the D-2 out and pushed a 1,200-pound platform to the top of the snow mound circling the seismic pit. Then with cable and winch, we gingerly moved the platform over the ten-foot pit to form a roof. It was a tricky operation and I sighed thankfully when it was over. Then Mel bulldozed eight feet of snow over the lid and we congratulated each other.

March 22 arrived, the day for the sun to set. The temperature reached a minimum of $-81°$ and the wind hit 18 miles an hour. All morning my crew worked hard covering the cache in front of the mess hall with parachutes. Then in the afternoon we covered the tunnel along the east side of the science building, and hauled nearly all the loose material remaining in the "front yard" under cover.

True to schedule the sun was actually below the horizon this day, but because of refraction and an ice-crystal phenomenon a column of light shone directly up into the sky above the sun. I could see in the faces of some of the men growing concern about what life would be like in a dark world.

We held our official sunset ceremony at five P.M. Dickey and Moose took pictures of the ceremony as Dr. Taylor and John Guerrero first raised the flag, which had remained at half-mast in honor of Admiral Byrd, and then they lowered it for the winter night.

I took a last close look at the Pole area that day. Here, where Amundsen and Scott had once stood for a few fleeting moments, the IGY and the American Navy and Air Force had accomplished a miracle. And we who had finished the construction job Dick Bowers and his remarkable Seabees had begun would work and live here through the winter night. I glanced out toward our South Pole marker, then I looked at our Station village—above the snow now but in time to be brought level with the surface by the heavy cold katabatic winds blowing snowdrifts downhill against our shelter.

Then I thought of my family and my departed friend Dick Byrd, and walked indoors.

"Will it be pitch dark?" one of Tuck's Navy men had asked me when he first arrived at the Pole.

"Not very often," I had assured him, though he was far from convinced.

All my previous experience in Antarctica's winter night had been centered at Little America off the Bay of Whales on the Ross Ice Shelf. What would happen at the geographic South Pole some 800 miles inland was something we would experience for the first time in man's long history on earth.

Three times I had spent winter nights at Little America. There the sun disappeared for four months beginning in late April, and during the first and last months of the winter night there was enough light to permit work outdoors several hours a day. During May, even though the sun dropped deeper below the horizon each day, we had a twilight around noon. And even during the two real months of total darkness at Little America there was a flush of pale reddish light to the north over the Ross Sea, for at most the noon sun lay only about 12° below the horizon.

The dark we faced at the South Pole, however, would be deeper and would last far longer. For our night would last six months instead of the four at Little America, and the sun at its farthest point from us on June 22 would lie a full 23½° below our horizon instead of 12°.

Our neighboring Antarctic IGY stations would fare better than we with respect to the amount of light they would have. The British, Argentine and Chilean stations on the Graham-Palmer Peninsula north of the Antarctic Circle would, of course, have sunrises and sunsets every day in the year. The sun would not rise very high nor would their day be very long on midwinter day (June 22), but nevertheless they would have several hours of light each day. The U.S. Wilkes Station, France's D'Urville Station, Russia's Mirny and Oasis stations, Australia's Mawson and Davis stations, Japan's Showa Station, Belgium's Baudoin Station and Norway's Maudheim Station were all so close to the Antarctic Circle that they would celebrate midwinter season with gaudy brilliant sunsets with the sun barely, if at all, below the horizon at noon.

Other stations, like Little America, McMurdo, Ellsworth, Byrd, Hallett, New Zealand's Scott Station, Argentina's Belgrano Station, and British Halley Bay, Shackleton and South Ice would have respectable polar nights but they would be nowhere near as long or dark as ours would be at the Pole Station.

Inside the polar areas the four seasons of the year take on a meaning of their own. Summer and winter are of course the periods of 24-hour sun and sunlessness respectively. Fall and spring apply to the periods when there are true sunrises and sunsets. How long these periods last depends on one's latitude. At Little America halfway between the Antarctic Circle and the Pole fall and spring last for two months each. The length of the sunup and sundown periods during these two months ranges from one minute to 23 hours and 59 minutes.

The twilight season at the South Pole lingers from sunset on March 22 until May 4 when the sun's angle, from its position below our horizon, was 18°. This latter date represented the real beginning of the dark period. Just how dark it is when the sun is 18° below the horizon can be garnered from the fact that a smaller 6° to 8° angle represents twilight back in civilization, or the time for turning on streetlights. Twilight lasts much longer in the polar regions than anywhere else because of the relatively flat trajectory of the sun's rays. It is longest at the Poles themselves, where twilight lasts for a whole month.

During this prolonged twilight from March 22 until May 4, when we walked outdoors we could distinguish an ominous and ever-increasing gray arc rising farther from the horizon opposite the sun each day. It was the earth shadow, a phenomenon rarely noticed in temperate latitudes where the sun sets in a matter of minutes rather than weeks as at the Pole. This earth shadow is actually the portion of the atmosphere completely shaded from the setting sun by the earth, and here at the Pole was separated from the sunlit portion of the atmosphere by a distinct gray line which rose higher in the sky each day. As it advanced across the sky, the oranges, yellows and pinks of the sunset seemed actually to increase in brilliance and intensity. It was my observation on such days that the beauty of the sunset at the Pole surpassed that at any other point on the globe. For with the occasional red of the sky and the white surface, we were living in a pink world. And then before my eyes, our pink world would turn green or purple or a host of other pastel shades.

The ending of the astronomical twilight was another matter, however. Now not even the faintest glimmer of twilight loomed over our horizon. Yet oddly, only 300 miles above our cone of darkness the sun shone brightly into space all the while. But this offered little compensation to us on the ground, for there is no side emanation from a beam of light, and there were not enough atmospheric particles of moisture or dust that high up to reflect back any light to us. The sun's rays went by us invisibly, as they do in the sky until the moon or a planet reflects them to let us know they are there. Sunlight, or even the indirect light the sun sheds, is one of the accepted blessings of life. Without it, apprehension crept into the hearts of the uninitiated.

This was so even though the South Pole winter night frequently has periods of light from other sources. For two winter weeks each month, the black sky would be punctured by the light of the moon as it swung around the sky from right to left. During the first week the moon would spiral its way upward and ride higher in the sky each day. The second week it would creep down toward the horizon and then disappear. In addition the Pole sky, except on cloudy days, would be dotted with starlight and occasional auroral light. It would only be on these cloudy days that the blackness would be all-encompassing.

The men's reaction to the winter night varied from individual to individual. A few of the men expressed their apprehension about the unknown perils ahead in blustering aggressiveness or in elaborate practical jokes as some men do when depressed. Others turned to the hamset for reassurance that there still was an outside world. Oz, our builder, sawed wood and pounded nails as nonchalantly as if he were back home in Pennsylvania. Some of the other men grew quieter while others grew noisier.

I realized what was running through most minds. We were like men who had been fired off in rockets to take up life on another planet. We were in a lifeless, and almost featureless, world. However snug and comfortable we might make ourselves, we could not escape from our isolation. We were now face to face with raw nature so grim and stark that our lives could be snuffed out in a matter of minutes. Every day would bring us new problems to solve and our ingenuity would be taxed over and over again. And all this to carry out a somewhat difficult fragment of the world-wide scientific program of the International Geophysical Year.

An occasional overheard conversation gave me good evidence of the concern the men felt at living in a dark, womanless wasteland. The blink of an eye revealed the wonder that crossed a mind. There was no escape now from the truly lethal wall that separated us from the rest of mankind.

The perils of polar life were many. A fire could toss us to the bitter mercies of a savage, unknown land. If a man were lost outdoors he could not hope to survive more than a few hours. After that he would run out of energy and his body would cool down to the danger point. There was danger also from the restricted vision possible in the darkness, cold and wind-drifting snow. A man wandering only a hundred yards from camp under such conditions might lose his way and never be found. Vapor from a man's breath could freeze his eyelashes shut in an instant and make him believe he had gone blind. His breath would come in gasps and his joints would ache. The intense pain of the cold on fingers and toes could easily distract him, and even destroy his ability to reason clearly.

The dark presented its own danger, for there were no landmarks to help a man find his way. It was like walking out on the ocean where every wave was like every other. If the stars were out, it was possible to fathom your direction—if you knew your stars. But even then it was possible to walk right past the station. Jack and I found this out one time when we walked out 200 yards to collect snow samples. We thought we were walking parallel to the thousand-foot seismic tunnel when suddenly we crossed it and almost fell in. Had this fortuitous accident not occurred and given us our bearings, we might have gotten well lost.

The wind also presented a danger. If it was strong (and it often blew in excess of 30 miles an hour), it was natural to turn your face away when traveling downwind. But returning to camp a man would also tend to avert his face and might easily wander off course. With the surface rough, walking was often a matter of stumbling along and this, too, would tend to turn a man off his path. Then again, the winds blew up snow and drift and made the horizon indistinct. Herb Hansen, one of our Met men, got religion polarwise as the result of a wind on one occasion. Out to check meteorological observations, he became befuddled due to the wind and drifts. For safety we had placed flags along the route to the meteorological station, but Herb could not find them. He changed his direction several times when he saw he was lost, though he managed to keep himself from growing panicky. Then by sheer accident he found himself at camp. "Guess where I've been?" he whispered when he got indoors.

There was danger also in the very temperature outdoors. My early observations led me to believe that the winter night temperature might easily reach a low of $-120°$ F. If such cold was combined with even a modest wind, a man had little chance for lengthy survival, for almost any wind would triple the body's rate of cooling. I had spent years developing tables to show the effect of wind chill on humans, and the prospects of outdoor movement at this temperature were nil.

The wind-chill factor is an index expressing the relative loss of heat from a heated body. It is determined from the formula which I developed: $K_0 = (\sqrt{V \times 100} + 10.45 - V) \times (33 - Ta)$. Here $K_0$ equals the total cooling power of the atmosphere in complete shade without regard to evaporation expressed in terms of kilogram calories per square meter per hour; V the wind velocity in meters per second, and Ta the temperature of ambient air in degrees Centigrade. With a temperature of $-40°$ (the point at which the Fahrenheit and Centigrade temperature scales coincide) and a wind of 2 mph ($1°$ meter per second) or more, the wind-chill factor is 1,400, at which exposed flesh freezes! There was every indication now that on the coldest and windiest days of the winter night, the wind-chill factor would surpass 3,000!

Still another danger to be faced was the possibility that an ice fog would roll over you outdoors. An ice fog is a mass of crystals of ice that float and form a fog. An ice fog could render the camp invisible from a very short way off. Our camp formed its own ice fogs as a result of the clouds of steam which poured from exhaust pipes and condensed on contact with the frigid air, erasing most outside markers from sight.

So in a physical sense we at the Pole were 18 men in a box. Only with the aid of our "box" could we survive, yet it bound us in. There was no way we could make our way to the outside world. Nor was there any possibility that we could be rescued should tragedy strike. We would have to remain put until the next summer—in October or November—come what might.

There was also the very large problem of how the men would stand each other's company in the daily rub and grind that would be their steady routine for months without respite. Friction was bound to arise from a variety of minor details, from the way a man chewed to how he closed a door or talked. There would be the monotony of constantly seeing the same faces when one rose, ate, worked and relaxed. Whatever a man was inherently would be intensified during the close-quarters winter night. A mean man would grow meaner; a kind man would grow kinder.

Men in a box; that was what we were.

□   *It had been Ernest Shackleton's dream, as far back as 1912, to lead a transantarctic trek, crossing the continent overland from the Weddell Sea to the Ross Sea. His attempt to make such a trip, several years later, ended in glorious failure. For a generation it remained only a dream.*

*In 1950, Dr. Vivian Fuchs, an English geologist, revived the project, and the British Government agreed to support it as part of Great Britain's participation in the International Geophysical Year. The plan called for Fuchs to lead one party from the Weddell Sea to the Pole, while a supporting party, starting from the Ross Sea, would lay a line of depots along the route. The leader of the Ross Sea party was Sir Edmund Hillary, the explorer who in 1953 had been the first to climb Mount Everest. Late in 1955, Fuchs entered the Weddell Sea with his advance party, but it was not until January 30, 1956, that they made their way through the pack ice to land on the shelf that fringed the shore. A base was established one mile inland, and named for Shackleton. The following spring, a second base was set up 300 air miles south of Shackleton Base, called South Ice. On November 24, 1957, after almost two years of preparation, Fuchs set out for the Pole, leading a convoy of snow tractors. The departure and journey are described here. Hillary, meanwhile, arrived at the Pole on January 4, 1958, and awaited Fuchs. After their much-publicized meeting, Fuchs continued on to Scott Base on the Ross Ice Shelf, completing the transantarctic crossing of 2,158 miles on March 2, 1958. Fuchs had made the unprecedented journey in ninety-eight days. It formed a climax to some sixty years of overland exploration in Antarctica.*

*The story of the trek is told in* The Crossing of Antarctica, *by Sir Vivian Fuchs and Sir Edmund Hillary (Boston, Little, Brown, 1958), from which our selection is reprinted, by courtesy of the publishers.*  ▫

# FUCHS: SOUTH ICE TO THE SOUTH POLE

At twenty minutes to eight on Christmas Evening [1957] we finally left South Ice and set out for the Pole just 555 statute miles distant. There were many last-minute tasks to perform: David Stratton leveled a line of pegs over the snow for 3½ kilometers for Geoffrey Pratt's seismic refraction shots, and then a further line of 50 stakes, extending over a mile, for Hal Lister's glaciological work. While this was going on, Ralph Lenton removed the transmitter from the hut and installed it in the *County of Kent*, replacing it by less powerful equipment which would meet the needs of the RAF party during their brief stage at South Ice, before they flew across to Scott Base. Another major task was undertaken by Hannes, Geoffrey and Ralph: this was to scrub out and tidy the hut itself, so that everything should be in good order for the new occupants. The rest of us were working outside, tidying up the whole area, digging out from the snow the aviation fuel which would be needed for the Otter, and last of all lashing down on top of the sledge loads the tents, skis, crevasse flags, probes and other items required immediately to hand when traveling.

Overriding them all was our determination to listen to the Queen's Christmas Day Broadcast before we left. The radio at South Ice was the only type capable of receiving the particular frequency, and at five minutes to three we were all congregated in the tiny living room. Bulky forms filled every chair, sat on bunks and table, or leaned against the walls, then in silence we listened to that faraway voice speaking across the world. To us, who were, perhaps, the most isolated listeners, there seemed to be special encouragement, not only because we were proud that Her Majesty was the expedition's Patron, but because we were engaged upon a Commonwealth enterprise.

Outside once more, we still found many last-minute things to do and as each vehicle and its sledges was completed, the drivers decorated them in Christmas spirit. Besides Union Jacks and flags of the Commonwealth, a white ensign and the ensign of the RAF appeared, the gay scene being enhanced by the fluttering of dozens of red and black trail pennants, together with the larger red and white checkered crevasse flags. Here and there colored streamers trailed in the wind, while Ralph Lenton's low-slung Muskeg *Hopalong* looked more like a carnival with its motif of tiny Chinese lanterns. As we moved off, the long column was a gay, colorful sight, the vehicles winding their way round the mound that hid the deserted hut, and turning south to follow the trail pioneered by the dog teams.

Blaiklock and Stephenson had already reported that they had found no trouble over the first 32 miles, although the surface consisted of patches of iron-hard sastrugi, with areas of very soft snow lying between. That first evening progress was slow as the vehicles and sledges bumped and banged over the ridges, but we pushed on for three hours to camp at the second of the 6-foot snow cairns built by the dog party. These were constructed of sawed snow blocks placed one on top of the other, and stood up like shining white pillars at a distance of two or three miles.

In the morning, whiteout prevented us from seeing the surface, so that it was impossible to move without the probability of damage to the vehicles. We therefore took the opportunity to make a seismic sounding of the ice and to do some glaciological work. Radio conditions were very bad, and we could hear nothing from either Shackleton, Halley Bay or the Pole Station. This was a pity, as on this day we had planned our first attempt at direct contact with Hillary's field party and Depot 480. Nothing was heard.

By a quarter to six the sky was beginning to clear, and we could see something of the surface, so we moved off over the terribly hard and extensive sastrugi. The course led due south over a series of undulations extending across our path. These appeared to have an amplitude varying from 80 to 280 feet, and a wave length of approximately four miles. We discovered that the worst sastrugi always occurred on the north-facing slopes, while the tops of the ridges were relatively smooth, and the south-facing slopes were only cut to a minor degree. That night we stopped at the dog party's 35-mile cairn, after traveling 25 miles. During the day there had been periodical trouble with coolant leaks on the Weasel driven by Hal Lister, and David Pratt in *Able* was keeping him company. When the time came to camp there was no sign of either of them. When next morning they had still failed to appear, Roy Homard and Allan Rogers went back in the Muskeg, which could travel more quickly and easily over the sastrugi. At half past three I sent Geoffrey Pratt and Hannes La Grange ahead in *Haywire*, telling them to complete the next seismic station 30 miles on, so that we should not be held up by that particular task when we got on the move again.

During this long wait Ralph Lenton made radio contact with Scott Base, and conditions were so good that I was able to speak with John Claydon and to discuss the flying conditions as they would affect John Lewis when he attempted his transpolar flight. This direct voice contact with Scott Base was most gratifying at this long range, but we still could not get in touch with Hillary, who was reported to be 290 miles from the Pole, nor with Depot 480, where a static radio transmitter had been set up.

At last, just before nine o'clock, the breakdown party pulled into camp, having cured the trouble by fitting a new Weasel radiator. Setting off at twenty past ten that night, we were in trouble again when George's *Wrack and Ruin* lost power and was only able to crawl. Roy Homard soon cured this, and we were able to make 15 miles by a quarter to four in the morning, when we stopped at the 55-mile cairn. So developed the picture of travel which was to be our lot throughout almost the entire journey—long hours slowly grinding over hard sastrugi, or through deep soft snow, frequent minor troubles with one or other of the vehicles, time spent every three hours in taking meteorological and gravity observations, and the periodic boring of holes for seismic shooting. Camping, eating, vehicle maintenance and sleeping had all to be fitted into what hours remained. As a result there was generally very little time for sleeping, and at the end of the journey I am sure that we all considered the outstanding hardship to have been lack of rest.

On December 29 we reached the cairn marking 100 miles from South Ice, where we found Ken and Jon with the dog teams, and Geoffrey and Hannes with *Haywire*. The cairn stood in a hollow running east-west to join another deep curious-looking depression which appeared to extend almost north-south. Unfortunately we had no time to investigate, but Geoffrey's gravimeter indicated a sudden shallowing of the ice, and we thought that the surface disturbances were probably due to this. Our position at this time, as observed by David Stratton, was 83°33′S, 29°02′W, and the approximate altitude 5800 feet.

General vehicle maintenance, carried out every 200 miles, was now due, and in addition a number of sledge towbars which had been broken by the heavy going had to be electric-welded. We therefore knew that our stop was bound to be longer than usual, and this had the advantage of allowing the dogs to get well ahead again. Our increasing altitude was making the Sno-cats overheat as they hauled their 6-ton payloads in second and third gears. I therefore took the opportunity of replacing the four-bladed fan on *Rock n' Roll* with another having six blades.

December 31 was a day of beautiful clear weather, but not a good day for us. Troubles came one after another: first the welding of the towbars proved to be a much longer job than we had expected, then there were difficulties with two of the Weasels, and when we were finally about to start, at seven in the evening, Hal's rammsonde became stuck three meters down, and we had to dig a pit to that depth before we could recover it. By half past eight we had moved off, but we did not get very far, for first George Lowe broke a sledge runner, and then Allan's Weasel *Rumble* broke a track and had to be abandoned as no replacement was being carried. Fortunately we had left the Muskeg tractor at the last camp only six miles back, for it was the first of the vehicles to be dropped, according to plan, when the consumption of fuel had sufficiently lightened our loads. Now, it was possible to go back and pick it up to replace *Rumble*.

As the result of these troubles we camped where we were, but I again sent Hannes and Geoffrey on with *Haywire* to get into position for another seismic shot. At midnight I made the rounds, giving everyone a tot of brandy with which to see in the New Year.

On New Year's Day conditions were so good that we hoped to cover 50 miles, but the surface was too soft for the Muskeg, which was towing two heavy sledges, and it could not travel faster than 2 to 3 mph. Everyone had a soft spot for *Hopalong* because it had gone so far and so well with a heavy load, and had given no trouble. When first we had left it, we had all been sad, then delighted when it had joined us again, but there was no place for sentiment where the efficiency of the party was concerned, and having no Muskeg spares, it must be the next to go. In the circumstances we worked it as hard as possible, saving extra load on the Weasels which would have to travel farther.

To speed our progress the second sledge was taken from *Hopalong* and put as a third behind the *County of Kent*, which seemed to take it easily. *Hopalong* could now keep up 5 mph in third gear, which was reasonable, for it had never been in top gear for the entire 530 miles from Shackleton. In all we covered 39 miles that day, the last nine over increasingly severe sastrugi, which in the end so separated the vehicles that we were forced to camp. This worsening surface was the beginning of our most continuously bad area, and next day, January 2, I wrote:

*Another 30 miles today, but what a labour! All vehicles in first and second gear all the way over the most corrugated fields of continuous sastrugi. The strain on vehicles and sledges is prodigious; particularly I worry about the gear-boxes, for these constant hours of heavy work in low gear is bound to tell on them. Already "Rock 'n Roll's" lay-shaft is very much noisier than it was. One bright spot is that the six-bladed fan now maintains the engines at 160°F. even with the radiator doors half shut.*

With the dog tracks still extending ahead of us, there was no need for navigation, and Geoffrey and Hannes again went on ahead, followed by the two Weasels and the Muskeg, which were slower than the cats over the murderous sastrugi. It was impossible to go round the high ice-hard ridges, for they formed a great field that extended out of sight in all directions. The best that could be done was for each driver to judge the course for his own particular type of vehicle, and often we found ourselves scattered a mile or two apart, working and weaving our way among the ridges four and five feet high. Sometimes, when there was no easier way, vehicles and sledges had very deliberately to be driven at a speed of half a mile an hour or less over vertical drops. Wending our way, twisting and turning, sometimes at right angles to the course, we tried to keep within reasonable distance of the dog sledge tracks which preserved a fairly steady line and prevented us from making too much extra mileage. When the snow cairns were visible (usually at a distance of about two miles) they were an excellent guide, for we could work steadily toward them. Even the trail of the dog teams wandered considerably and here and there the tracks in the snow revealed the upsetting of a sledge, or where two ski tracks ended abruptly against a ridge we knew that someone had come to grief.

Over this terrain the Sno-cats handled much better than the Weasels, for their articulated tracks conformed more easily to the surface and their great power, and five forward gears, gave easier control. Yet the drivers had their own problems, because the second or third sledges tended to swing more freely and, linked with a wire tow, would catch up and ram the cat on the sledge ahead. The Weasels, on the other hand, did not roll but pitched heavily. Climbing to the top of a sharp-topped ridge, they would tilt up and up, then suddenly dip violently forward, followed by the plunging 2½-ton sledge. Some drivers had the added irritation of towing a dog sledge behind the main load and this, being narrow, would yaw from side to side, often turning over and having to be righted by a fuming passenger. And yet we had good reason for taking these additional dog sledges. Should the vehicles break down, making it necessary for us to walk the remainder of the distance, we had to have sledges that we could manhaul.

Mile after mile this trial of tempers and equipment continued—

would it ever stop, we wondered? By now we had expected to be well up on the polar plateau, experiencing relatively easy going instead of these endless sastrugi stretching at right angles to our path. The winds, it seemed, must blow perpetually from the east, scouring and grooving the surface year after year.

As the day progressed, David Stratton and I first found Allan Rogers with a steel towbar that had caught in a snow ridge and been bent right back beneath the sledge. This was unscrewed and replaced with a wire tow. Then, farther on, we found Geoffrey and Hannes together with Hal and George. The seismic spread was ready, but it was essential to wait until the last of the vehicles had ceased to roll, for the extremely delicate instruments would record their vibrations even at a distance of a mile or two. While they were waiting, Hal had decided to drive his rammsonde into the bottom of the pit that had been prepared for the explosive charge. There it had again become jammed in a hard layer of ice several meters down, and a new pit had to be dug before the seismic shot could be fired. When this had been done, we pushed on again to catch up the dog teams, and found them encamped after we covered 30 miles in the day.

That night I was able to speak to Hillary, who said that he was expecting to arrive at the Pole the following day, which for him would be January 4, as he was on the other side of the date line.

All day on the 3rd we traveled over the most vicious sastrugi, the vehicles making very heavy weather and the sledges suffering severely. More and more towbars were getting damaged, so that most of the towing was by steel wire rope which was very hard on the transmissions. We had hoped to make 25 miles in the day, to give us an average of 20 miles per day from South Ice, but all that we could do was 18. By then the blue skies had clouded over, and visibility became too bad to travel over such terrain.

We had taken to traveling by sun compass, for the magnetic compass was already showing some sluggishness. We had therefore mounted a pair of these instruments, one on either side of *Rock n' Roll,* and when the driver's side was obscured by the shadow of the vehicle, the co-driver would call out the heading at frequent intervals.

As the altitude at which we were traveling increased, it was necessary, for the sake of efficiency and economy, to change the carburetor jets on all the vehicles. This we did every 2000 feet above 4000 feet—not, of course, to increase the power of the engines in any way, but only as an economy measure. Indeed, as we gained altitude, our unsupercharged engines were continually losing power, though such was their reserve that no loss was yet apparent, and the Sno-cats continued to haul their maximum loads without trouble. Furthermore, for the last 57 miles we had been running in first and second gears, yet the average for the whole distance that we had traveled was still 1.25 miles per gallon, certainly better than we had expected.

That evening I received a message from Hillary suggesting that, as we were delayed, I should consider stopping at the South Pole and flying the party out with the assistance of the Americans. To this I was unable to agree, and replied explaining the situation. The messages exchanged were as follows:

*Dear Bunny:*

*I am very concerned about the serious delay in your plans. It's about 1,250 miles from the Pole to Scott Base, much of the travelling north from D700 being somewhat slow and laborious, with rough hard sastrugi. Leaving the Pole late in January, you will head into increasing bad weather and winter temperatures, plus vehicles that are showing signs of strain. Both of my mechanics regard such a late journey as an unjustifiable risk and are not prepared to wait and travel with your party. I agree with their view and think you should seriously consider splitting your journey over two years. You still probably have a major journey in front of you to reach the Pole. Why not winter your vehicles at the Pole, fly out to Scott Base with American aircraft, return to civilization for the winter, and then fly back into the Pole station next November and complete your journey? This plan would allow you to do a far more satisfactory job of your seismic work, and I feel fairly confident that Admiral Dufek would assist with such a flying programme. Personally I feel the need for a break from the plateau after nearly four months of tractor travel, and there's a lot to do. I prefer not to wait at the Pole station, but will get evacuated*

*to Scott Base as soon as possible. If you decide to continue on from the Pole, I'll join you at D700. Sorry to strike such a sombre note, but it would be unfortunate if the sterling work you've put into making your route through to South Ice and the Pole should all be wasted by the party foundering somewhere on the 1250 miles to Scott Base. I will go ahead with the stocking of D700, and I will leave at the Pole station full details plus maps of the route from Scott to the Pole.*

HILLARY

*Hillary Pole Station:*

*Appreciate your concern, but there can be no question of abandoning journey at this stage. Innumerable reasons make it impracticable to remount the expedition after wintering outside Antarctica. Our vehicles can be, and have been operated at minus 60 but I do not expect such temperatures by March. Whiteout and drift will be our chief concern. I understand your mechanics' reluctance to undertake further travel, and in view of your opinion that late season travel is an unjustifiable risk I do not feel able to ask you to join us at D700, in spite of your valuable local knowledge. We will therefore have to wend our way, using the traverse you leave at the Pole. The present field of giant sastrugi has extended 57 miles so far, and continues with ridges up to 4 ft. Are we to expect similar fields north of D700, and approx how many miles in toto? Main damage is to sledge tow bars, which have to be electrically welded causing delay. Am shortly abandoning second vehicle as planned, leaving us 4 cats 2 weasels. Max interval seismic stations 30 miles, gravity stations 15 miles, rammsonde once or twice daily, meteorology includes fluxplate and radiation measurements. Present position 84° 43' S altitude 7,000 ft.*

BUNNY

Unfortunately this exchange became known publicly, and although we were quietly getting on with our own work, it gradually became apparent that the press had turned the matter into a *cause célèbre*. It was not until we reached the Pole Station that I began to realize the amount of publicity which the expedition had now acquired. For the next fortnight it was argued and debated in newspapers and journals throughout the world, and much well-meant advice was given to members of the Committee at home, where our small office staff took the brunt of a press onslaught none of us had ever visualized.

Meanwhile I had received encouraging support from the Committee, who told me to take any decisions that might be necessary in the light of the situation in the field. As I, and all my party, had complete confidence in our ability to carry the journey through, and were considerably surprised at the turn of events, there was virtually no decision to make. We continued with our work, and traveled at our normal rate of about 30 miles per day whenever possible, intending to increase that speed by spreading the seismic shots more widely beyond the Pole.

On January 4 Hillary had arrived at the Pole, stayed a few days, and then flown back to Scott Base where he set about building up the supplies of fuel at Depot 700, as I had requested. This seemed a wise precaution, for we had no means of estimating our fuel consumption in the soft snow which, he had reported, lay before us.

At last, on January 5, Blaiklock and Stephenson reported that they were passing out of the bad sastrugi, and it seemed that we should be able to make better progress. This proved to be true and that day we thankfully completed 32 miles. It was with a tremendous sense of relief that we were at last able to drive two or three consecutive miles in top gear. Up to now, the vehicles had ground along in a lower gear nearly the whole distance from Shackleton. We estimated that from Shackleton, 575 miles away, we had traveled, perhaps, 45 miles in "top."

As the time had come to abandon our second vehicle, we again regretfully prepared to leave the Muskeg behind. This also entailed leaving one of the large sledges which could no longer be towed. Together with fourteen empty fuel drums this formed a memorial pile to *Hopalong*, a hard-working and still active friend, whose life ended in latitude 85° 15′ S.

From January 6 onward the dog teams ran with the vehicles. That day they kept up well, covering a total of 30 miles, and loving the novelty of following a track and the company of the strange-looking tractors.

The days' route took us over almost continuous low, hard sastrugi which, although not so damaging as the really high ridges we had encountered before, was none the less very hard on the vehicles and sledges. The general surface was still undulating, the long rises and falls being steeper toward the north. Here and there during the course of the journey there appeared to be arcuate snow forms, of considerable size, rising perhaps thirty feet or more above the surface. Because of the general nature of the terrain it was difficult to decide whether or not these were a part of the normal, rolling snow ridges, but there were occasions when one gained the impression that we might be seeing "snow dunes" formed in the same way as sand dunes. Having completed another 30 miles on the 8th, we found a broken U bolt on Hal's Weasel, but George Lowe's *Wrack and Ruin* was burning a pint of oil every five miles, with a petrol consumption of 1½ miles per gallon, and soon we should have to decide which of the two should be the next vehicle to be abandoned. The 9th was a maintenance day. Various repairs were carried out and the fan on *Haywire* was changed to a six-bladed type. A seismic shot, fired in a hole 36 feet deep, showed the thickness of the ice to be about 6500 feet. As our altitude at this time was about 7850 feet, the rock below the camp site must have been at 1350 feet above sea level. Although these figures have yet to be worked out in detail, they indicate that where we then were (86° 31′ S), at 240 miles from the Pole, the rock surface was lower than in the vicinity of South Ice, which was so much nearer to the coast.

When all our work was completed, we made a short run of 20 miles to maintain the daily average which we had at last raised to just above that distance. This brought us up with the dog teams, which had gone on ahead while the maintenance work was in progress. We found the men asleep in their tent, which was pitched not far from the beginning of an extremely bad belt of giant sastrugi. It proved to be 10 miles wide, and was probably "Gordon's Bank," a name given to it because, when flying across the continent, Gordon had reported that around 87° S there was a steep slope with an extremely badly cut up surface which might cause us a lot of trouble. We found that, for a short distance near the bottom of the slope, which was after all only about 200 feet high, there were very high ridges, but after that it was no worse than many other areas. When the day's run of 30 miles was complete we were 192 miles from the Pole, and if the air report was correct we could expect better conditions over the remaining distance. In this we were disappointed, for the next two days provided more and more sastrugi, together with constant whiteout which reduced our movement to 15 and 16 miles. On the 13th the sastrugi continued but it was another misadventure that halted our movement. Both the dog drivers, Ken Blaiklock and Jon Stephenson, had to halt with severe stomach disorders, sickness and temperatures around 101°F. We quickly pitched their tent, and made them as comfortable as possible in their sleeping bags. This was not the first time this curious sickness had hit us, though on this occasion the attack seemed to be much more severe than others had experienced. During the past days Roy Homard, Hal Lister, George Lowe and David Pratt had all suffered the same trouble in varying degrees, and it seemed that some infection was running through the whole party. Our difficulty was to trace the source, for apart from speaking to each other in the open air, there was no other direct association of all the people who were involved. In any event, infections of any kind are rare in the Antarctic, and practically unknown when people have been long isolated from outside communities. Later all the rest of the party, except Ralph Lenton and myself, fell ill with the same complaint.

For the next two days David Stratton and George Lowe drove the two dog teams to give Ken and Jon time to recover from their sickness and subsequent rather weak state. It was here that we abandoned Hal Lister's Weasel in latitude 88° 03′ S. By now it had four broken U bolts, and for some time had leaked oil in ever-increasing quantities. The leak could not be cured without removing the engine—a three-day task—and we were not altogether surprised when it finally broke down with a "run big-end." Uncertain as to which of the two remaining Weasels would last the longer, we had brought both forward for 100 miles beyond the point where it had been planned that we should drop one on the grounds of fuel economy. Now we were glad that we had done so, and all Hal's glaciological equipment was stripped from his Weasel and transferred to *Rock 'n Roll*, in which he was to travel in the future. We had also to abandon another large sledge, sharing its remaining load among the others. When we moved on, the five surviving vehicles were still transporting 22 tons between them.

By this time we were moving fairly steadily over a surface which was still undulating, with very rough sastrugi on the northern slopes, and were wondering when we should finally reach the smooth level surface which we had expected the polar plateau to present. The maximum day's run was limited to 30 miles, but this was as much on account of the dog teams as it was for the seismic work. On the 13th I had already radioed to Hillary at Scott Base asking him to inquire from the Americans whether there was any possibility that our dogs could be flown out, for they would be too tired to accomplish the increased daily mileage we intended beyond the Pole. Next day I heard from him that Admiral Dufek had most kindly agreed to do so, and this relieved my mind of a considerable weight, because it was certainly impossible to take them with us over the next 1250 miles.

All this time our communications with Scott Base were either direct or through Peter Mulgrew, who had been left by Hillary at the Pole Station. There he was able to use radio equipment in the traveling caboose, which had been left with the three tractors and all the party's sledges and other equipment. This relieved the Pole Station of considerable traffic at a time when they were extremely busy with their own final problems before the supply planes left the Antarctic.

On the morning of January 17 we were camped at 88° 45' S when two American planes flew over the camp while we were still in our sleeping bags, but Ralph scrambled outside to speak to them from the *County of Kent*. He heard that they were carrying Admiral Dufek, Ed Hillary, John Lewis and, to our considerable surprise, a posse of nine reporters. It also transpired that it was the evening of their day. Again we traveled 30 miles over sastrugi and undulating country, and it was not until the morning of the 18th, when we began the day's run only 55 miles from the Pole, that the surface at last became smooth and soft. That night our position was 89° 37' S, or just over 26 miles from the Pole, and Geoffrey Pratt's seismic shot told us that the rock surface had risen steeply to lie only about 2000 feet below the ice.

When on Sunday, January 19, we began our last run before reaching the South Pole, we found that the surface continued soft and smooth as it had been throughout the previous day, but after a few miles more undulations became apparent.

And then we saw it. At the top of a snow ridge, from which the surface fell away in a long gentle sweep, we had halted to climb on top of our vehicles and scan the horizon for the markers we had been told to expect. Then, suddenly, into the field of vision sprang what seemed to be a small cluster of huts and radio masts. Although it could only just be discerned with the naked eye, it seemed so short a distance from us that our first instinct was to drive straight to the beckoning black spot in the white expanse. But remembering a radio request from Major Mogesson, scientific commander at the station, who had asked us to avoid the snow areas which they were studying and proceed along the 24° meridian, we turned to the southeast and drove along the top of the ridge until we found the line of flags which showed the correct route. At the end of the day I described our arrival in my journal.

*Today we have run in to the Pole, the distance being 32 miles instead of only 26 as we expected, because when we sighted the Pole Station we were too far west in longitude and they had asked us to come in on meridian 24° W to avoid the snow areas being studied. It took us some time and seven miles to find the barrel and line of flags which marked the route in. When the Pole Station came into view it was about seven miles distant and though apparently on a ridge there was a hollow between us and it.*

*By the time we had turned south along the line of flags, the dogs were tiring and the convoy moved slowly so that they could keep up and arrive together with the vehicles. The day was a brilliant one, without a cloud and only a light wind from about 80° meridian. As the party moved towards the Pole, I looked back and thought our convoy a brave sight: the orange "cats" and Weasel, together with the loaded sledges, bearing many fluttering flags of different colours. Besides the national Commonwealth flags, there was that of the city of Bristol, a T A E flag embroidered by Ralph, chequered crevasse flags, trail pennants, and a special green one embroidered by Hannes with a springbok on one side, and a protea on the other. Above all this the great exhaust plumes streamed away from the high, open exhausts of the Sno-cats.*

*Ahead of us we could see two Weasels moving out towards us from the station, but they stopped two miles before meeting us. As we approached nearer we could see quite a crowd, in fact over 30 people all armed with cameras. These included Admiral Dufek, Ed Hillary, Griff Pugh, Peter Mulgrew, the reporters and all the base personnel. Among the latter were Lieutenant Verne Houk, United States Navy Medical Service, in administrative control of the base, and Major Mogesson ("Moggy") in charge of the scientific work.*

*On jumping out of the "cat," I first shook hands with Ed, then George Dufek and the base leaders. There was such a press of photographers and recorders that it was quite difficult to move about. After the first "milling" had subsided, Houk and Dufek climbed into my "cat" and I drove them on to the base where Houk directed me to the parking site.*

*The next move was to wash and have a meal, followed by a press conference and a radio recording for the BBC through McMurdo Sound.*

*Our reception has been a most warm one and we have been invited to sleep and eat in the base instead of our tents. This makes our stay here pleasant, informal and a complete rest.*

*As we had not crossed the "date line," our day was still the 19th, but we find the Americans are keeping NZ time which makes it 20th January. Their actual time is GMT plus 12 hours. We therefore arrived in our night and their midday. I decided we should change over to their time at once by treating our night as day, and going to bed early if individuals wished. In fact I think most of us have missed a complete night's sleep.*

That night Admiral Dufek had to return to McMurdo Sound and flew away in a Neptune aircraft, taking with him Sir Edmund Hillary, John Lewis and all the reporters. We then realized the difficulties with which the Americans had been faced in establishing the station by air, for at that altitude the loaded aircraft, using two jet engines, two piston engines and 16 JATO bottles, failed to get off in the still air. After several attempts the flight had to be postponed until more JATO bottles could be brought in by another plane. Then, when some of the load had been removed, the pilot got away in great billowing clouds of snow driven by the blast from the soft surface.

Our days at the Pole Station were very crowded, for there was much to do. First of all the loads had to be unlashed and restowed, which relieved us of nineteen empty fuel drums. At the same time our electric welder was set up on *Haywire*, which had been taken into the station workshop. There work went ahead on repairing our broken towbars and battery heating equipment. Outside, Geoffrey Pratt fired a number of seismic shots, but the first of these were unsuccessful, as the records were upset by the high winds and the drift blowing across the station causing static electrical interference.

At a party on the evening of the 22nd each of us was presented with a fine colored testimonial, after the fashion of "Crossing the Line" certificates, stating that we had been around the world on our feet. This was possible because one had only to walk a few yards round the flags marking the site of the Pole itself. These flags were those of the United Nations and the United States, flying side by side on two tall masts surrounded by a great ring of empty fuel drums. At the party, we in our turn presented the station with the expedition pennant in memory of our visit, and were proud to display Her Majesty's signed portrait which we had carried with us all the way from Shackleton. We also unfurled the flag of the Scottish National Antarctic Expedition 1901-1903, which had been taken by William Spears Bruce on his voyage in the *Scotia*, when he discovered Coats Land on the east side of the Weddell Sea. This had been handed to me in Edinburgh by the President of the Royal Scottish Geographic Society with the request that we carry it with us to Coats and on across the continent. Another item of interest was Captain Scott's watch which I had worn on a leather thong round my neck since starting the journey. This had been taken from their museum by Smiths of Cricklewood and entrusted to me to take back to the South Pole and on to Scott Base.

We had hoped to leave on the 23rd, but strong winds and high drift still prevented the completion of the seismic work, and this was very necessary. The Americans had flown equipment in and made a sounding at the Pole, and this was the one opportunity of checking the instruments against one another. I therefore decided at six o'clock that we would stay one more night and complete the work in the morning.

□   *Today Antarctica is populated in a way that Scott or Shackleton would find difficult to believe. More than a dozen nations maintain permanent or semipermanent bases there. At any time, several large-scale expeditions into the still not yet fully explored interior are under way. Planes crisscross the continent. A wealth of scientific information is constantly being gathered.*

*Such intense Antarctic exploration would be infinitely more difficult if there were political obstacles as well as those of nature to hurdle. For many years, bitter national feuds threatened to disrupt the program of Antarctic research. In 1959, though, an international treaty was signed by the nations involved in Antarctica, removing that continent from the frictions and tensions that seem so eternal a feature of modern civilization. It seems fitting to end this anthology with the text of that treaty, one of the few glowing instances of international cooperation in a century marred by dispute and rancor.*   □

# THE ANTARCTIC TREATY

The Governments of Argentina, Australia, Belgium, Chile, the French Republic, Japan, New Zealand, Norway, the Union of South Africa, the Union of Soviet Socialist Republics, the United Kingdom of Great Britain and Northern Ireland, and the United States of America,

Recognizing that it is in the interest of all of mankind that Antarctica shall continue forever to be used exclusively for peaceful

347

purposes and shall not become the scene or object of international discord;

Acknowledging the substantial contributions to scientific knowledge resulting from international cooperation in scientific investigation in Antarctica;

Convinced that the establishment of a firm foundation for the continuation and development of such cooperation on the basis of freedom of scientific investigation in Antarctica as applied during the International Geophysical Year accords with the interests of science and the progress of all mankind;

Convinced also that a treaty ensuring the use of Antarctica for peaceful purposes only and the continuance of international harmony in Antarctica will further the purposes and principles embodied in the Charter of the United Nations;

Have agreed as follows:

## ARTICLE I

1. Antarctica shall be used for peaceful purposes only. There shall be prohibited, *inter alia,* any measures of a military nature, such as the establishment of military bases and fortifications, the carrying out of military maneuvers, as well as the testing of any type of weapons.

2. The present Treaty shall not prevent the use of military personnel or equipment for scientific research or for any other peaceful purpose.

## ARTICLE II

Freedom of scientific investigation in Antarctica and cooperation toward that end, as applied during the International Geophysical Year, shall continue, subject to the provisions of the present Treaty.

## ARTICLE III

1. In order to promote international cooperation in scientific investigation in Antarctica, as provided for in Article II of the present Treaty, the Contracting Parties agree that, to the greatest extent feasible and practicable:

(a) information regarding plans for scientific programs in Antarctica shall be exchanged to permit maximum economy and efficiency of operations;

348

(b) scientific personnel shall be exchanged in Antarctica between expeditions and stations:

(c) scientific observations and results from Antarctica shall be exchanged and made freely available.

2. In implementing this Article, every encouragement shall be given to the establishment of cooperative working relations with those Specialized Agencies of the United Nations and other international organizations having a scientific or technical interest in Antarctica.

## ARTICLE IV

1. Nothing contained in the present Treaty shall be interpreted as:

(a) a renunciation by any Contracting Party of previously asserted rights of or claims to territorial sovereignty in Antarctica;

(b) a renunciation or diminution by any Contracting Party of any basis of claim to territorial sovereignty in Antarctica which it may have whether as a result of its activities or those of its nationals in Antarctica, or otherwise;

(c) prejudicing the position of any Contracting Party as regards its recognition or non-recognition of any other State's right of or claim or basis of claim to territorial sovereignty in Antarctica.

2. No acts or activities taking place while the present Treaty is in force shall constitute a basis for asserting, supporting or denying a claim to territorial sovereignty in Antarctica or create any rights of sovereignty in Antarctica. No new claim, or enlargement of an existing claim, to territorial sovereignty in Antarctica shall be asserted while the present Treaty is in force.

## ARTICLE V

1. Any nuclear explosions in Antarctica and the disposal there of radioactive waste material shall be prohibited.

2. In the event of the conclusion of international agreements concerning the use of nuclear energy, including nuclear explosions and the disposal of radioactive waste material, to which all of the Contracting Parties whose representatives are entitled to participate in the meetings provided for under Article IX are parties, the rules established under such agreements shall apply in Antarctica.

## ARTICLE VI

The provisions of the present Treaty shall apply to the area south of 60° South Latitude, including all ice shelves, but nothing in the present Treaty shall prejudice or in any way affect the rights, or the exercise of the rights, of any State under international law with regard to the high seas within that area.

## ARTICLE VII

1. In order to promote the objectives and ensure the observance of the provisions of the present Treaty, each Contracting Party whose representatives are entitled to participate in the meetings referred to in Article IX of the Treaty shall have the right to designate observers to carry out any inspection provided for by the present Article. Observers shall be nationals of the Contracting Parties which designate them. The names of observers shall be communicated to every other Contracting Party having the right to designate observers, and like notice shall be given to the termination of their appointment.

2. Each observer designated in accordance with the provisions of paragraph 1 of this Article shall have complete freedom of access at any time to any or all areas of Antarctica.

3. All areas of Antarctica, including all stations, installations and equipment within those areas, and all ships and aircraft at points of discharging or embarking cargoes or personnel in Antarctica, shall be open at all times to inspection by any observers designated in accordance with paragraph 1 of this Article.

4. Aerial observation may be carried out at any time over any or all areas of Antarctica by any of the Contracting Parties having the right to designate observers.

5. Each Contracting Party shall, at the time when the present Treaty enters into force for it, inform the other Contracting Parties, and thereafter shall give them notice in advance, of

(a) all expeditions to and within Antarctica, on the part of its ships or nationals, and all expeditions to Antarctica organized in or proceeding from its territory;

(b) all stations in Antarctica occupied by its nationals; and

(c) any military personnel or equipment intended to be introduced by it into Antarctica subject to the conditions prescribed in paragraph 2 of Article I of the present Treaty.

## ARTICLE VIII

1. In order to facilitate the exercise of their functions under the present Treaty, and without prejudice to the respective positions of the Contracting Parties relating to jurisdiction over all other persons in Antarctica, observers designated under paragraph 1 of Article VII and scientific personnel exchanged under subparagraph 1(b) of Article III of the Treaty, and members of the staffs accompanying any such persons, shall be subject only to the jurisdiction of the Contracting Party of which they are nationals in respect of all acts or omissions occurring while they are in Antarctica for the purpose of exercising their functions.

2. Without prejudice to the provisions of paragraph 1 of this Article, and pending the adoption of measures in pursuance of subparagraph 1(e) of Article IX, the Contracting Parties concerned in any case of dispute with regard to the exercise of jurisdiction in Antarctica shall immediately consult together with a view to reaching a mutually acceptable solution.

## ARTICLE IX

1. Representatives of the Contracting Parties named in the preamble to the present Treaty shall meet at the City of Canberra within two months after the date of entry into force of the Treaty, and thereafter at suitable intervals and places, for the purpose of exchanging information, consulting together on matters of common interest pertaining to Antarctica, and formulating and considering, and recommending to their Governments, measures in furtherance of the principles and objectives of the Treaty, including measures regarding:

(a) use of Antarctica for peaceful purposes only;

(b) facilitation of scientific research in Antarctica;

(c) facilitation of international scientific cooperation in Antarctica;

(d) facilitation of the exercise of the rights of inspection provided for in Article VII of the Treaty;

(e)  questions relating to the exercise of jurisdiction in Antarctica;

(f)  preservation and conservation of living resources in Antarctica.

2.  Each Contracting Party which has become a party to the present Treaty by accession under Article XIII shall be entitled to appoint representatives to participate in the meetings referred to in paragraph 1 of the present Article, during such time as that Contracting Party demonstrates its interest in Antarctica by conducting substantial scientific research activity there, such as the establishment of a scientific station or the despatch of a scientific expedition.

3.  Reports from the observers referred to in Article VII of the present Treaty shall be transmitted to the representatives of the Contracting Parties participating in the meetings referred to in paragraph 1 of the present Article.

4.  The measures referred to in paragraph 1 of this Article shall become effective when approved by all the Contracting Parties whose representatives were entitled to participate in the meetings held to consider those measures.

5.  Any or all of the rights established in the present Treaty may be exercised as from the date of entry into force of the Treaty whether or not any measures facilitating the exercise of such rights have been proposed, considered or approved as provided in this Article.

## ARTICLE X

Each of the Contracting Parties undertakes to exert appropriate efforts, consistent with the Charter of the United Nations, to the end that no one engages in any activity in Antarctica contrary to the principles or purposes of the present Treaty.

## ARTICLE XI

1.  If any dispute arises between two or more of the Contracting Parties concerning the interpretation or application of the present Treaty, those Contracting Parties shall consult among themselves with a view to having the dispute resolved by negotiation, inquiry, mediation, conciliation, arbitration, judicial settlement or other peaceful means of their own choice.

2. Any dispute of this character not so resolved shall, with the consent, in each case, of all parties to the dispute, be referred to the International Court of Justice for settlement; but failure to reach agreement on reference to the International Court shall not absolve parties to the dispute from the responsibility of continuing to seek to resolve it by any of the various peaceful means referred to in paragraph 1 of this Article.

## ARTICLE XII

1. (a) The present Treaty may be modified or amended at any time by unanimous agreement of the Contracting Parties whose representatives are entitled to participate in the meetings provided for under Article IX. Any such modification or amendment shall enter into force when the depositary Government has received notice from all such Contracting Parties that they have ratified it.

(b) Such modification or amendment shall thereafter enter into force as to any other Contracting Party when notice of ratification by it has been received by the depositary Government. Any such Contracting Party from which no notice of ratification is received within a period of two years from the date of entry into force of the modification or amendment in accordance with the provisions of subparagraph 1(a) of this Article shall be deemed to have withdrawn from the present Treaty on the date of the expiration of such period.

2. (a) If after the expiration of thirty years from the date of entry into force of the present Treaty, any of the Contracting Parties whose representatives are entitled to participate in the meetings provided for under Article IX so requests by a communication addressed to the depositary Government, a Conference of all the Contracting Parties shall be held as soon as practicable to review the operation of the Treaty.

(b) Any modification or amendment to the present Treaty which is approved at such a Conference by a majority of the Contracting Parties there represented, including a majority of those whose representatives are entitled to participate in the meetings provided for under Article IX, shall be communicated by the depositary Government to all the Contracting Parties immediately after the termination of the Conference and shall enter into force in accordance with the provisions of paragraph 1 of the present Article.

(c) If any such modification or amendment has not entered into force in accordance with the provisions of subparagraph 1(a) of this Article within a period of two years after the date of its communication to all the Contracting Parties, any Contracting Party may at any time after the expiration of that period give notice to the depositary Government of its withdrawal from the present Treaty; and such withdrawal shall take effect two years after the receipt of the notice by the depositary Government.

## ARTICLE XIII

1. The present Treaty shall be subject to ratification by the signatory States. It shall be open for accession by any State which is a Member of the United Nations, or by any other State which may be invited to accede to the Treaty with the consent of all the Contracting Parties whose representatives are entitled to participate in the meetings provided for under Article IX of the Treaty.

2. Ratification of or accession to the present Treaty shall be effected by each State in accordance with its constitutional processes.

3. Instruments of ratification and instruments of accession shall be deposited with the Government of the United States of America, hereby designated as the depositary Government.

4. The depositary Government shall inform all signatory and acceding States of the date of each deposit of an instrument of ratification or accession, and the date of entry into force of the Treaty and of any modification or amendment thereto.

5. Upon the deposit of instruments of ratification by all the signatory States, the present Treaty shall enter into force for those States and for States which have deposited instruments of accession. Thereafter the Treaty shall enter into force for any acceding State upon the deposit of its instrument of accession.

6. The present Treaty shall be registered by the depositary Government pursuant to Article 102 of the Charter of the United Nations.

## ARTICLE XIV

The present Treaty, done in the English, French, Russian, and Spanish languages, each version being equally authentic, shall be deposited in the archives of the Government of the United States of

America, which shall transmit duly certified copies thereof to the Governments of the signatory and acceding States.

*In witness whereof,* the undersigned Plenipotentiaries, duly authorized, have signed the present Treaty.

*Done* at Washington this first day of December, one thousand nine hundred and fifty-nine.

For Argentina:
 *Adolfo Scilingo*
 *F. Bello*
For Australia:
 *Howard Beale*
For Belgium:
 *Obert de Thieusies*
For Chile:
 *Marcial Mora M.*
 *E. Gajardo V.*
 *Julio Escudero*
For the French Republic:
 *Pierre Charpentier*
For Japan:
 *Koichiro Asakai*
 *T. Shimoda*

For New Zealand:
 *G. D. L. White*
For Norway:
 *Paul Koht*
For the Union of South Africa:
 *Wentzel C. du Plessis*
For the Union of Soviet
  Socialist Republics:
 *V. Kuznetsov* [Romaniza-
  tion]
For the United Kingdom of
  Great Britain and North-
  ern Ireland:
 *Harold Caccia*
For the United States of Amer-
  ica:
 *Herman Phleger*
 *Paul C. Daniels*

# INDEX

Adams, John Quincy, 73
Adams, Mr., 196, 202, 208
Adélie Land, 95, 103, 266
Admiralty Range, 155
*Adventure*, the, 25
Africa, 4, 7-8
Aladdin's Cave, 263, 264
Albatross, 19, 21, 55, 58, 188
Alexander I, Czar of Russia, 49, 51
Alexander I Land, 51, 57
*All-Out Assault on Antarctica*, 314
*Alone*, 303

Amundsen, Roald, 141, 148, 209, 210, 235-252
Amundsen-Scott Station, 321
Andersson, Gunnar, 186
Andersson, Karl Andreas, 172, 173, 179, 180, 186
*Andromache*, the, 42
*Annawan*, the, 73
Annewkow Island, 281
Anson, Lord, 44
*Antarctic*, the, 137, 172
Antarctic Circle, 26, 119, 129, 187
*Antarctic Manual, The*, 79, 93

Antarctic Ocean, 51, 53
Antarctic Peninsula, 42, 63, 78, 142, 172
Antarctic Treaty, 347-357
Antarctica, 16, 107, 114, 117, 129
*Antarctica,* the, 173
Antarktikos, 3
   *See also* Antarctica
Arabia, 4
Archimedes, 12
Arctowski, 144
Arias, Juan Luis, 11-13
Arktikos, 3
*Astrolabe,* the, 92, 95, 101, 105
*Aurora,* the, 252, 253, 265, 266
Aurora Australis, 70, 82
Aurora Peak, 256
Australia, 11, 15, 25
   *See also* Terra Australis Incognita
Australia del Espiritu Santo, 11
*Australische Navigatien,* 13
Axel Heiberg Glacier, 288, 290, 291
Azores, 7


Bage, 265
Bahia de Todo Santos, 17
Balchen, Bernt, 286, 289, 290, 292, 295, 297, 298, 299
Balleny, John, 85-87, 92
Barlow, Mr., 70
Barnevelt, Islands of, 15
Bartholomew Island, 4
Barton, Ethel S., 93
Baudoin Station, 325
Bay of All Saints, 17
Bay of Whales, 235, 325
*Beagle,* the, 86, 88
Beaglehole, J. C., 26
Beaufort, Francis, 125
Beaufort Island, 125

*Beaufoy,* the, 62
*Belgica,* the, 142
Belgica Expedition, 142-148, 235
Belgrano Station, 326
Bellingshausen Sea, 142
Bennett, Floyd, 285, 287
Bering Straits, 71
   *See also* Bhering's Straits
Bernacchi, Louis, 153, 155, 156-59, 160
Bhering's Straits, 71
Bickerton, Mr., 265
Biscoe, John, 78-84, 87, 88
Bjaaland, 239, 241, 242, 243, 247, 249, 250
Blaiklock, Ken, 332, 334, 340, 342
Bodman, Mr., 187
Bone, Thomas, 42
Borchgrevink, Carstens, 138, 149-56, 172
Boreas, 319, 320
Borneo, 4
Borodino Island, 59
Bourbon Island, 24
Bouvet Island, 26
Bowers, Dick, 324
Bowers, H. R. "Birdie," 210, 212, 216, 217, 218, 219, 220, 222, 223, 227, 228, 229, 232, 234
Bransfield, Edward, 42, 43-46
Brisbane, Matthew, 62, 65
*Brisk,* the, 128
Brooks, seaman, 112
Brouwer, Hendrik, 15
Brower's Strait, 16
Bruce, W. S., 187, 191
Buchanan, Mr., 134
Bull, H. J., 137-141, 172
Bullough, Edward, 51
Burdick, Christopher, 61-62
Butter Point, 171

Byrd, Richard Evelyn, 285-301, 302-313, 314-316, 321, 322-324
Byrd Station, 326

Caird, Sir James, 267
Cambodia, 4
Camell, William, 21
Camp Ridley, 150, 152, 153
Canberra, 351
Cape Adare, 138, 141, 156, 158, 172
Cape Ann, 84
Cape Bird, 126, 127, 171
Cape Circumcision, 24
Cape Crozier, 127, 220, 221, 222, 224
Cape Découverte, 104
Cape Evans, 210
Cape of Good Hope, 24
Cape Hoorn, 13, 15
    See also Cape Horn
Cape Horn, 9, 15, 18, 25, 42, 43
Cape of the Southern Continent, 23
Cape Phillips, 158
Cape Royds, 171, 195
Cathay, 4
Cathedral Rocks, 171
Challenger, the, 129, 143
Cherry-Garrard, Apsley, 219-234
Chiloe Island, 16
Churchill, Winston, 267
Claydon, John, 333
Coats, Andrew, 191
Coats, James, 191
Coats' Land, 191
Colbeck, Lt., 150, 155, 156, 157, 159
Coleridge, Samuel Taylor, 19, 188
Collection of Voyages Chiefly in the Southern Atlantick Ocean, A, 16

Commonwealth Bay, 252, 262, 265
Conway, the, 70
Cook, Frederick A., M.D., 142
Cook, James, 25-37, 41, 64, 70, 71, 87
Coulman Island, 118
County of Kent, the, 331, 335, 343
Cowley, Ambrose, 17
Crean, Thomas, 267, 277
Crescent Bay, 151
Crossing of Antarctica, The, 331
Crozier, Comm. F. R. M., 123, 126, 127, 128
Cruise of the 'Antarctic,' The, 137

Da Gama, Vasco, 22
Dalrymple, Alexander, 16, 25, 26
Darwin, Charles, 86-88
David, Edgworth, 195
Davis, Capt., 264, 265, 266
Davis, Edward, 17
Davis, John, 61, 138
Davis Station, 325
Davis's Straits, 24
De Gerlache, Adrien, 141-142
"De Insidentibus Aquae," 12
De Villiers, J. A. J., 13
Debenham, Frank, 51
Deception Island, 46
Demidov, Mr., 55
Depot 480, 333
Depot Nunatak, 163, 166-67
"Description of a New Crustaceous Animal Found on the Shores of the South Shetlands, with Remarks on their Natural History, A," 74
Desolation Camp, 163, 167
Diaz, Bartholomew, 7
Dickey, 324

Disappointment Bay, 108
"Discoveries in the Antarctic Ocean in February, 1839," 85
*Discovery*, the, 160, 171, 220
Douglas, John, 26
Drake, Sir Francis, 8
Drake Passage, 9
Dubouzet, Monsieur, 100-103
Dufek, George J., 321, 343, 345
Dugdale Glacier, 153, 155, 156
Duke of York Island, 151, 153, 154
Dumoulin, Monsieur, 94, 95, 100, 104
Dumoutier, Monsieur, 95
Dunbar, F:, 48
D'Urville, Jules Sebastien Cesar Dumont, 92-105, 106, 114, 116, 117
D'Urville Station, 325
Duse, Mr., 172, 173, 186, 187
Duus, Mr., 185
Dyer, 308, 309, 312

*Early Voyages to Terra Australis*, 11
*East and West Indian Mirror, The*, 13
East Antarctica, 315
*Edinburgh Philosophical Journal*, 43
Egypt, 4
Eights, James, 73-78
Elephant Island, 267
Elizabeth Island, 9
*Eliza Scott*, the, 85-88
Ellefsen, Mr., 153
Ellsworth Station, 326
Enderby Brothers, 78-79, 87, 128
Enderby Land, 191
*Endurance*, the, 267

*Erebus*, the, 117, 123, 124, 128
Evans, Edgar, 210
Evans, Mr., 149-50, 159 (Borchgrevink)
Evans, Mr., 162, 164-165, 169 (Scott)
*Express*, the, 48

Falkland Islands, 42, 117
Fanning, Edmund, 42, 46, 48-50, 73, 77
Fernand Noronha Island, 25
Ferrar Glacier, 168
Ferrar group, 167
Fiji, 106
Finger Mountain, 167
*First on the Antarctic Continent*, 149
Fisher Mountain, 293, 294, 296
Fletcher, Francis, 8-10
*Floyd Bennett*, the, 287, 295
*Flying Fish*, the, 106
Foster, Mr., 70
Fougner, Mr., 150, 159
Foyn, Svend, 137
*Fram*, the, 192, 235
Franklin, Sir John, 123
Franklin Island, 123-124, 158
*Frederick*, the, 48
*Free Gift*, the, 48
Frezier, Monsieur, 20
Fuchs, Vivian, 330-347
Furneaux, Capt., 64
Fur-seals, 45

Geikie, Sir Archibald, 155
Geikie Land, 155
Gervaize, Monsieur, 94
Giaever, John, 317

Giava, 5
Gonneville, Binot Paulmier de, 22, 24
Gordon's Bank, 341
Graham-Palmer Peninsula, 325
Gravelius, H., 51
Great Ice Barrier, 158, 190, 193, 194, 219, 220, 221
Grunden, Mr., 172, 173
*Gull*, the, 106

Haines, William, 286, 287, 288, 309
Hakluyt Society, The, 4, 6, 11, 13, 18, 26, 51
Hall, Capt. Basil, 70
Hallett Station, 326
Halley Bay Station, 326, 332
Hannam, Mr., 265
Hansen, Herb, 329
Hansen, Nicolai, 149
Hanssen, Mr., 236, 238, 239, 241, 243, 245, 248, 249, 250
Haslum, Mr., 182
Hassel, Mr., 238, 247, 249, 250
Havener, Mel, 324
*Haywire*, 334, 335, 341, 346
*Heart of the Antarctic, The*, 196
Henry the Navigator, Prince, 7
Herd Island, 134
*Hero*, the, 46, 48
*Hersilia*, the, 46, 48
High Island, 125
Hillary, Sir Edmund, 330, 331, 333, 337, 338-39, 340, 343, 345
Hodgeman, Mr., 265, 266
Homard, Roy, 333, 342
*Home of the Blizzard, The*, 253
Hooker, J. D., 119, 133
*Hopalong*, 332, 335, 341
Hudson's Bay, 24

*Huntress*, the, 61
*Huron*, the, 61
Hut, the, 254, 257, 263-265
Hut Point, 160, 209, 316

India, 4
Indonesia, 4
International Geophysical Year, 321, 328, 330, 348
*Itinerary*, 4

Jackson, President Andrew, 106
*Jacob Ruppert*, the, 312
Jacquinot, Commander, 101
*James Caird*, the, 267, 268, 273, 274, 275, 276, 280, 282
*James Monroe*, the, 49
*Jane*, the, 62
Java, 4, 5
Jeffryes, Mr., 265, 266
Johansen, Mr., 159
Jones, John Winter, 4
"Journal of a Voyage Toward the South Pole on board the brig Tula with the cutter Lively in company," 79
"Journals of Captain James Cook, The," 26
Juan Fernandez, 45
June, Harold, 286, 287, 289, 292, 295, 297, 299, 312

Kerr, piper, 194
King Haakon Bay, 281
Klövstad, Dr., 153
Knob Head Moraine, 167
Kristensen, Leonard, 137
Kublai Khan, 4

La Grange, Hannes, 331, 333-337
La Roché, Anthony de, 16-17
Larsen, C. A., 172, 173, 177
Lashly, 162, 164, 165, 167, 169
Laurie Island, 188
Lazarev, Mr., 57
Le Maire, Jacob, 13-15
Lenton, Ralph, 331, 333, 343
Lewis, John, 333, 343
Lister, Hal, 331, 334, 337, 341, 342
*Literary Gazette, The*, 42
*Little America*, 286
Little America, 286, 289
Little America II, 302, 308, 309, 312, 322, 325, 326
Little Yaroslavetz, 59
*Lively*, the, 78, 79
Liv's Glacier, 291, 292, 293
Louis Philippe, King of France, 92
Lowe, George, 334, 337, 341, 342
Lozier, Bouvet de, 22-25
Lyeskov, Mr., 55

McKinley, Ashley, 286 287, 289, 290, 294, 296, 297, 298
McLean, Mr., 265
McMurdo Bay, 158
McMurdo Sound, 117, 160, 209, 315
McMurdo Station, 326
Macnab, Mr., 87-88
Madagascar, 22
Madigan, Mr., 265
Madigan Nunatak, 262
Magellan, 8
Magellan's Strait, *see* Strait of Magellan
Major, R. H., 11
Malay Peninsula, 4
Marie Byrd Land, 286, 302, 314
Markham, Clements R., 6, 141, 160

Marshall, Mr., 196, 200, 203
Martin, Mr., 182, 184
Maudheim Station, 325
Mauritius de Nassauw, 14
Mawson, Douglas, 195, 252-66
Mawson Station, 325
Meares, Mr., 215
Medici, Lorenzo Piero Francesco de, 5
Melleby, Mr., 320
"Memorial Addressed to His Catholic Majesty, Philip the Third, King of Spain, by Dr. Juan Luis Arias, Respecting the Exploration, Colonization, and Conversion of the Southern Land, A," 11
Mendanius, Alvarus, 10
Mertz, Dr. Xavier, 252-255
Mertz Glacier, 256, 257, 261
Midwinter Camp, 151-52
Mill, Hugh R., 128
Mirny Station, 325
Mirnyi, The, 51, 57, 59
Mogesson, Major, 344, 345
Monroe Bay, 50
Moseley, H. N., 129-34
Mossman, Mr., 188
Mount Erebus, 125, 126, 163, 195, 252
Mount Hooper, 214, 215
Mount Melbourne, 121, 122
Mount Monteagle, 121
Mount Nansen, 294, 295
Mount Sabine, 153, 155
Mount Terror, 125-127, 220, 230
Mulgrew, Peter, 343, 345
Murphy, Charlie, 312
Murray, George, 93
Murray, Sir John, 129, 192
Murray Glacier, Sir John, 155

Nares, George, 129
*Narrative of the United States Exploring Expedition During the Years 1838, 1839, 1840, 1841, 1842,* 107
Newfoundland, 25
New Guinea, 10, 11
New Hebrides, 10
New Shetland, 58, 60
New South Britain, 42
New South Shetland, 42
*New Voyage & Description of the Isthmus of America, A,* 18
New Zealand, 25, 26
*Nimrod,* the, 195
*90° South,* 321
Ninnis, Lt. B. E. S., 252
Nordenskjöld, Otto, 172, 173, 267
Northern Plateau, 199
North Magnetic Pole, 91, 285
Norwegian-British-Swedish Expedition, 317-320
*Notes by a Naturalist on H.M.S. Challenger,* 129

Oasis Station, 325
Oates, Lawrence, "Titus" or "Soldier," 210-216
One Ton Camp, 210, 214, 215
Operation Deep Freeze, 314, 321
Operation Highjump, 314, 322
*Otter,* the, 331

*Pagoda,* the, 128
Palmer, Nathaniel, 46, 47, 49, 60, 61, 73
Palmer's Harbor, 50
Palmer's Land, 48, 49, 77
Paris Geographical Society, 92

Parry, Sir William Edward, 117, 125-26
Parry Mountains, 126
Passat, 319
Patagonia, 6
Paulet Cottage, 182
Paulet Island, 172, 173, 174, 177, 179-87, 267
*Peacock,* the, 106, 115
Peary, Robert, 235
Pendleton, Benjamin, 46, 48, 73
Penguins, 9, 14, 44, 222, 224-227
Persia, 4
Peter I Island, 51, 55, 57
Philip III, 11
Point Geology, 104
Pole Station, 326, 332, 344, 346
Polheim, 251-252
Polo, Marco, 4
*Porpoise,* the, 93, 106, 109, 110, 115
Poulter, Thomas, 303, 312
Powel Islands, 93
Pratt, David, 342
Pratt, Geoffrey, 331, 334-337, 343, 346
Ptolemy, Claudius, 3, 8, 10
Pugh, Griff, 345

Queen Maud Land, 317, 319, 320
Queen Maud Range, 290, 300
Quiros, Pedro Fernandez de, 11

Racovitza, M., 189
*Relief,* the, 106
Remington, Moose, 321, 324
*Resolution,* the, 25
Reynolds, Jeremiah N., 73, 106
Ringgold, Lt., 105-106, 114-15, 116
Robertson Bay, 149, 152, 153

*Rock n' Roll*, 334, 335, 337, 342
Rogers, Allen, 333, 337
Roosevelt, President F. D., 314
Ross, James Clark, 19, 85, 106, 115, 116-28, 129, 157, 159
Ross, Admiral Sir John, 117
Ross Ice Shelf, 117, 157, 158, 160, 235, 267, 286, 325, 331
Ross Island, 219
Ross Sea, 117, 118, 138, 158, 195, 220, 227, 325, 330
*Rumble*, 334

*Sabrina*, the, 85
Sabrina Land, 85
Saint George's Island, 10
Saint Pierre, 71
Samarkand, 4
Samoa, 106
Sandwich Land, 34, 63, 65
*San Jacinto*, the, 107
Schouten, Willem, 13, 15
Schytt, Valter, 317
*Scotia*, the, 187, 189, 192, 194
Scotia Expedition, 188-195
Scott, Robert Falcon, 160-172, 199, 209-218
Scott Base, 331, 333, 343
Scott Station, 326
*Scott's Last Expedition*, 210
Sea-lions, 44, 45
Seals, 44
Seixas y Lovera, Francisco de, 16
*Seraph*, the, 73
Serra Liona, La, 7
Shackleton, Ernest Henry, 160, 195, 196-209, 266-282
Shackleton Base, 331, 335
Shackleton Station, 326, 332

Sharpe, Bartholomew, 17, 18
Sheffield, James, 48
Shelvocke, George, 19-22
Shireff, Capt., 42
Showa Station, 325
Siple, Paul, 315, 316, 321-330
Skelton Group, 167, 171
Skottsberg, C. J., 173-87
*Slaney*, the, 46
Smith, William, 42
Snow Hill Island, 172, 173
Solitary Rocks, 167
Solomon Islands, 10
Sorrell, Mr., 88
*South: The Story of Shackleton's Last Expedition*, 267
South Geographical Pole, 196, 205, 286, 297, 300, 321
South Georgia, 6, 16, 41, 55, 60, 267, 269
South Ice Station, 326, 331, 332, 334
South Magnetic Pole, 91, 134, 196
South Orkney Islands, 187
*South Pole*, 235
South Shetlands, 42, 46, 58, 71-74, 79
South Victoria Land, 139
*Southern Cross*, the, 149
Southern Gateway, 198
Southern India, 22
Stackpole, Edouard A., 62
*Stancomb Wills*, the, 268
Staten Island, 13-16, 19
Stephenson, Jon, 332, 334, 340, 342
Strait le Maire, 14, 16, 19, 21
Strait of Magellan, 8, 9, 13, 15, 16, 19-20
Stratton, David, 331, 337, 342
Swithinbank, 319
Symmes, John Cleves, 73, 106

Tasman, Abel, 15
Tasmania, 117
Taylor, Dr., 323, 324
Teille Island, 60
*Terra Australis Cognita: or Voyages to the Terra Australis, or Southern Hemisphere, during the Sixteenth, Seventeenth, and Eighteenth Centuries,* 22
Terra Australis Incognita, 3-37, 71
Terra del Visto, 23
*Terra Nova,* the, 209
*Terror,* the, 117, 123, 127, 128
*Through the First Antarctic Night,* 142-148
Tierra del Fuego, 13, 18, 19, 142
Torres, Luis Vaez de, 11, 15
*To the South Polar Regions,* 156
*Tula,* the, 78, 79
*Two Voyages of exploration in the Antarctic Ocean and a circumnavigation of the world in the years 1819, 1820, 1821,* 51

Underwood, Lt., 108

Varthema, Ludovico di, 4, 5, 10
Vespucci, Amerigo, 5-7, 8
Victoria Land, 117, 138, 154
*Vincennes,* the, 106, 107, 108, 115
Von Bellingshausen, Fabian Gottlieb, 47, 50, 51-60, 61, 87
Von Seraskerken, Baron de Teille, 58
*Vostok,* the, 51, 58
*Voyage of Captain Bellingshausen to the Antarctic Seas, 1819-1821, The,* 51

*Voyage of Discovery and Research in the Southern and Antarctic Regions During the Year 1839-43, A,* 118
*Voyage of the 'Discovery,'* 161
*Voyage of the Huron and the Huntress,* 62
*Voyage au Pole Sud et dans l'Oceanie sur les corvettes l'Astrolabe et la Zélée execute par ordre du Roi pendant 1837-40,* 93
*Voyage Round the World, A,* 19, 188
*Voyage of the 'Scotia,' The,* 187
*Voyage Towards the South Pole, and Round the World, A,* 26
*Voyage Towards the South Pole, Performed in the Years 1822-24, A,* 63
*Voyages & Discoveries in the South Seas, 1792-1832,* 47
*Voyages Round the World; with Selected Sketches of Voyages to the South Seas, North and South Pacific Oceans, China, etc., Performed under the Command and Agency of the Author,* 47
*Voyages to the South Seas, Indian and Pacific Oceans, China Sea, North-West Coast, Feejee Islands, South Shetlands, etc.,* 74

Wafer, Lionel, 17-18
Washington Strait, 50
Weasel, 333
Weddell, James, 62, 77-79, 92, 120

Weddell Sea, 63, 92, 106, 118, 172, 187, 192, 267, 330
Wennersgaard, Mr., 184-85
*White Desert, The,* 317
Wild, Frank, 196, 197, 266, 268
Wilkes, Charles, 104, 105, 106-16, 118, 132, 134
Wilkes Expedition, 106
Wilkes Station, 325
Wilkes' Termination Land, 134, 252
*Williams,* the, 42, 60
Williams, Capt. E., 48
Wilson, Edward "Bill", 160, 210, 212-224, 227, 229-233
Wilson, Mr., 319

Wisting, Mr., 238, 239, 241, 243-247, 249, 250
Wordsworth, William, 19
*World Encompassed by Sir Francis Drake, The,* 8
Worsley, Frank, 267, 270, 275-277
*Worst Journey in the World, The,* 219
*Wrack and Ruin,* 333, 341
Wytfliet, Cornelius, 10

Yankee Harbor, 48
Young, Dr., 42
Zavodovski, Mr., 55, 60
*Zélée,* the, 92, 97, 98, 100

## DATE DUE

| JUL 3 | | | |
|-------|-----|-----|-----|
| DEC 18 1989 | | | |
| | | | |
| | | | |
| | | | |
| | | | |
| | | | |
| | | | |
| | | | |
| | | | |
| | | | |
| | | | |
| | | | |
| | | | |
| | | | |
| | | | |
| GAYLORD | | | PRINTED IN U.S A. |